WEE WILLIE
Sherdel
THE CARDINALS' WINNINGEST LEFT-HANDER

Written by John G. Coulson
with John T. Sherdel

FriesenPress

Suite 300 - 990 Fort St
Victoria, BC, V8V 3K2
Canada

www.friesenpress.com

Copyright © 2018 by John G. Coulson
First Edition — 2018

With John T. Sherdel

All rights reserved.

No part of this publication may be reproduced in any form, or by any means, electronic or mechanical, including photocopying, recording, or any information browsing, storage, or retrieval system, without permission in writing from FriesenPress.

ISBN
978-1-5255-1743-3 (Hardcover)
978-1-5255-1744-0 (Paperback)
978-1-5255-1745-7 (eBook)

1. SPORTS & RECREATION, BASEBALL

Distributed to the trade by The Ingram Book Company

"Some are born great, some achieve greatness, and some have greatness thrust upon them."

—William Shakespeare

Red Land Community Library
70 Newberry Commons
Etters, PA 17319

This book is dedicated to the Sherdel family
and to the people of Midway, Hanover, and McSherrystown.

TABLE OF CONTENTS

Beginnings 1

The Big Show 65

Post Seasons 315

Acknowledgments........... 349

Notes 351

Index..................... 380

INTRODUCTION

This is a story about a life devoted to baseball at a time when baseball was truly the national pastime. William Henry Sherdel loved the game and accomplished much in a lengthy career. And his legacy endures. Sherdel is ranked fourth in career wins for the St. Louis Cardinals, a fact that most people don't know. He is also celebrated to this day for having the most wins for a left-hander. But his story is bigger than baseball. Sherdel was a very humble hero, a man devoted to his family and with the heart of a lion.

Bill attracted many nicknames over his baseball career. When he began to play in his teens, he was called "the Kid." Later, his teammates referred to him as "Sherry" or "Slow Ball Bill." In the early 1920s, the national sportswriters started to call him "Wee Willie," a nickname that seemed to stick. That it was in fact a misnomer because Bill was five feet ten inches tall and weighed about 160 pounds never seemed to bother anyone. At that time, many players had colorful nicknames—"Babe" Ruth, "Dizzy" Dean, "Hack" Wilson, etc. Syd Keener, former sportswriter for the *St. Louis Star,* said, "The Wee Willie was hung on Sherdel because he was just about the smallest man on the team."[1]

This book is really about Sherdel's life and times because there was so much happening in the history of baseball and the world while he was playing ball. I have tried to tie many of these stories in with the story of Bill Sherdel. For example, Sherdel joined the St. Louis Cardinals at a time when Branch Rickey was just starting to develop the concept of a farm system. Throughout his career, Sherdel interacted with more than ninety of baseball's greatest players and managers—Hall of Famers. Babe Ruth and Sherdel began as rivals, but became great friends through later life.

I was also struck through my research by the many tragedies that teammates and family members suffered, tragedies that must have deeply affected

Sherdel. Kidney disease plagued his wife's family, and it would provide a tragic storyline throughout the baseball player's life.

Now is also an opportune time to explain that there are, in fact, three different William Sherdels in this story, and it behooves me to distinguish among them to avoid confusion. William Martin Scherdel is Bill's father. William Henry Sherdel is the main subject of this book. William James Sherdel, also known as Junior, is Bill's son, and the third generation to bear that name. Where there might be confusion, I will use the names William M., William H., and William J., or Junior, to clarify. Bill Sherdel is the main subject. Also, you will note that the name Sherdel begins as Scherdel. At the time of the First World War, many Americans of German descent changed the spelling of their last names to disassociate themselves from Germany, America's enemy. While William Henry removed the "c" from the family surname, his father William Martin never did. I am going to use the more familiar spelling Sherdel throughout this story to provide consistency and clarity. The only exception will be cartoons and newspaper articles in which different spelling may appear; I will use [sic] to mark these.

I expect that many of my readers will initially ask, "Why a book about Wee Willie Sherdel?" But it is my hope that, after reading this account of a true and humble sports hero, they will change the question to: "Why did it take so long to write it?" Better late than never. Please enjoy!

—John G. Coulson

BEGINNINGS

CHAPTER ONE

On October 10, 1926, the St. Louis Cardinals baseball team defeated Babe Ruth, Lou Gehrig, and the powerful New York Yankees to end an exciting seven-game World Series. It had been the St. Louis Cardinals' first world championship in forty-four years.

St. Louis came to life with celebration. The *St. Louis Post-Dispatch* described what took place in its column the next day.

> From game's end at 3:20 o'clock yesterday afternoon to an early hour this morning, St. Louis abandoned itself to tumultuous celebration of the Cardinals' baseball championship of the world.
>
> The downtown thundered with unceasing din for more than nine hours. Thousands of automobiles wormed and twisted in a never-ending circle of the business district. Machines chalked with exultant jibes at the Yankees, extravagant praises of the Cards—windows painted with slogans of victory—cars draped with Cardinal red, their horns sounding ceaselessly, filled with costumed, shouting men, women, and children.
>
> The sidewalks overflowing into the streets with milling thousands—a mob with cowbells, horns, rattlers, musical instruments, tin pans, gongs, bells, and lusty voices that seemed never to hoarsen. A crowd garbing itself grotesquely snake-danced in the street, elbowing its way, throwing paper, slapping backs, shoving ticklers into one another's faces—a grinning, laughing, happy crowd.
>
> The celebration spread itself throughout the city, beyond the city into the suburbs, beyond the suburbs into the state, beyond the state

into the Southwest and Southeast. Telephones and telegraph brought word that hundreds of loyal Cardinal towns were celebrating.

It all began on a quiet Sunday afternoon. However, it was only a surface quiet, for the entire city was waiting and eager to shatter the calm if the right sort of news came from Yankee Stadium in New York. Groups were gathered about radios in the downtown. Throughout the city, in private homes, there were radio parties. Each block had several. The whole city had its ear to one voice—the voice of the announcer on KSD from the scene of the decisive contest.

Twice before the city had given itself up to celebration of the Cardinals—on their winning of the National League pennant and when they came home—but here was a world's pennant in the weaving.

The eighth inning. The city held its breath through three outs. Now the ninth. One out, two out, but no outburst is safe yet. The mighty Ruth at bat. One strike, two strikes. Now a ball—two-three. Was ever torture more acute? The flash. The Cardinals win.

It was like a city-wide detonation. It was as if dynamite had been planted in a hundred scattered spots and all touched off at the same instant. The downtown exploded in noise. Two minutes after the victory the din was deafening. Automobile horns and sirens, back-firing of motors, tin horns, bells that had been muffled in silence for the one moment all turned loose.

Shouts of men and women at their radios in their homes, telegraphed the victory to their neighbors. Men, women, and children poured into the streets, shouting and laughing.

They rushed for their automobiles and headed them into the downtown. From all directions they came, north, south, and west—even east. Because within half an hour the Municipal Bridge was jammed with a one-way traffic—everyone coming, no one going. In twenty minutes, all the east and west streets east of Twelfth Boulevard were a solid mass of cars from curb to curb. The noise now was almost entirely from automobiles. The sidewalks were virtually deserted.

Now the busses and street cars begin to be loaded. The sidewalks fill. On every corner, street hawkers of noise-makers, of pennants, of buttons are mobbed. The crowd outfits itself for a deafening night.[1]

After midnight, the crowd began to disperse and return home. They needed to rest before the next celebration when the team reached St. Louis.

The Cardinals team, traveling by train, arrived home in the late afternoon. A thousand fans gathered at the railroad station to welcome them. Most of the players used a police escort to slip away to their homes or hotels. They hoped for a little rest before a formal celebration with 40,000 fans planned that night at the home ballpark, Sportsman's Park.[2]

Cardinals' star pitcher Bill "Wee Willie" Sherdel did not accompany his teammates on their return. Oh, he had participated in earlier celebrations that fall. On September 25, he had relieved in the second inning against the Giants in New York and held on to win, 6–4, and clinch the Cards' first National League pennant in forty-four years. That day Sherdel smiled silently and slipped across the field to the clubhouse where the team celebrated privately, shaking hands and slapping each other on the back.[3]

On October 4, Sherdel and the Cardinals returned to St. Louis after the first two Series games in New York with the Series tied. The team rode the rails for 1,158 miles in twenty-four hours. Word had spread and over 100,000 fans jammed the railroad station and streets to await the club. There was a symphony of whistles, horns, bells, and yelling. The fans swept away the police lines. They choked the downtown streets. The crowd was so dense that it took more than one hour for twenty cars carrying the players to travel fifteen blocks from the train station to the Jefferson Hotel. As the Cardinal players slowly moved up the street, the police and firemen attempted to clear a path for the autos. Showers of paper floated down from the office buildings. As the parade reached the hotel, players were smuggled to their homes to get rest before the third Series game. It was the largest celebration in St. Louis since the Armistice was declared to end the First World War.[4]

With those earlier celebrations, Sherdel had felt obligated to join in the festivities. He had considered it part of his trade. This time, the humble hero sought to avoid the excitement in St. Louis and was quietly traveling with his wife and two small children on a Pennsylvania Railroad train from Union Station in New York City to the York, Pennsylvania, depot.

It had been a bittersweet Series for Sherdel. He had drawn the opening assignment against Yankee ace Herb Pennock and suffered a tough loss, 2–1. Sherdel accepted his defeat gracefully. His second Series start was in the fifth game. Again, he was matched against future Hall-of-Famer Pennock. The Series was now tied at two wins apiece. Sherdel pitched a great game. He lost a heartbreaker in ten innings, 3–2. Earlier in the game, star outfielder Chick Hafey slipped and muffed an easy fly ball. It cost the Cardinals dearly. Despite Sherdel's second loss, he had masterfully handled the great Babe Ruth. The Babe had hit three home runs in the previous day's game to grab national attention. This time, Sherdel was on the mound. Ruth hit a weak grounder in the first inning, struck out with two men on base in the sixth and walked in two other inconsequential at-bats. Sherdel also struck out Lou Gehrig during the contest. Still, his personal victory over Ruth and Gehrig offered small consolation. After this loss, Sherdel sat in the clubhouse and wept. His teammates surrounded him and tried to comfort him.[5]

The train moved along through Pennsylvania. Sherdel's hand was still hurting from a painful injury he'd suffered in the fifth inning of that last Series' start against the Yankees. His hand was struck by a ball thrown back from the catcher. The return pitch severely bruised the index finger of his pitching hand. Sherdel had concealed the seriousness of the injury until the game ended five innings later. Three-quarters of his nail was black and blue and his finger was badly swollen.[6]

At 8:30 p.m., the train finally pulled up at the York station. The Sherdel family noticed fans and friends from Sherdel's adopted home of McSherrystown, Pennsylvania, waiting in their automobiles to welcome them. Their supporters loaded the Sherdels into a car and transported them to McSherrystown. As the car caravan reached the outskirts of the town, some 600 or 700 residents (more than three-quarters of the entire town) met their hero, and the men, women, and children paraded joyfully down Main Street. A brass band led the way. It was followed by citizens engaging every conceivable noisemaker, from battered tin pans to exploding firecrackers. Many had hastily prepared signs. There were frequent outbursts of applause and cheers throughout the night. Finally, Sherdel received the peace and quiet he sought. At 3:00 a.m., the Sherdel family went to bed in their Ridge Avenue home.[7]

Sherdel's role in the Cardinals' championship season and World Series was not overlooked. After the Series was over, Babe Ruth was interviewed about his friend Sherdel's efforts. The Great Bambino stated, "Sherdel had two of the toughest breaks that ever came to a pitcher. He pitched two great games against us. In many ways, I think he was even better than [Grover Cleveland] Alexander. But he lost both games simply because he happened to hook up with Pennock at a time when Pennock was simply unbeatable."[8]

There was a testimonial banquet held at the Richard McAllister Hotel in Hanover a week after Sherdel's return home. William Duncan, a sportswriter for the *Philadelphia Inquirer* and a close friend of Sherdel's, announced at the latter's banquet that "Sherdel deserves to be crowned the king of McSherrystown and that no one would be worthy to replace him."[9]

There were many newspaper columns and letters crediting Bill Sherdel for his accomplishments. They softened his disappointment.

Cullen Cain, publicity director of the National League and future Hollywood screenwriter, addressed a letter to noted columnist Grantland Rice in hopes that Rice would include these sentiments in his weekly sports column. On October 26 of that year, the columnist did. He included the following letter, titled "Glory of Sherdel," in his piece:

> Dear Sir: Everybody seems to be agreed that [Grover Cleveland] Alexander, [Tommy] Thevenow, [Babe] Ruth, and [Herb] Pennock were the stars of the late series. For my part, I think more often of Bill Sherdel than of anyone else when I think of that struggle. To me, Sherdel was the outstanding figure of the contention.
>
> His mates made one run behind him in the first game and he lost it, 2–1, after a hard struggle. He pitched to Ruth and held him to a single. In his next game, he opposed Pennock once again and outpitched him, and yet he lost, 3–2, in ten innings. He fanned Ruth with two on in that game, and that was at a time immediately following the Babe's home-run outbreak of three in a row.
>
> Pop flies fell safe to beat Sherdel. He smiled after the first defeat and said not a word. He was grim after the second loss, but he said not a word. His courage was unabated up to the last ball he pitched of that game.
>
> His work will go in the records as two defeats. That is all. Ten years hence the scroll will show him as just a loser and a beaten man. But to me he will always stand as one of the greatest pitchers the Series ever knew. He yielded one earned run in two games. But the records will not dwell upon this. Cold figures will stand against him. But your column

is human, and deals in heartbeats rather than figures, and I thought maybe you would want to set something down about Sherdel.[10]

Perhaps Sherdel's greatest compliment was delivered on September 22, 1926, when Mr. and Mrs. James Lauck, of 649 Edmond Avenue in St. Louis, welcomed a new baby boy into the world. The couple chose to name their son William Henry Sherdel Lauck. They had agreed that if the Cardinals won the pennant, they would name their child after the pitcher who would start the first World Series game.[11] Years later, a grandson would be named Keith Sherdel Lauck, and the honor and memory would continue.

In 1926, Bill Sherdel achieved his greatest goal—a world's championship. This was a man who had always loved baseball. It had consumed him from a young age, and dreams of future success had filled his juvenile brain for years. Now Sherdel had just pitched in front of 64,000 fans in Yankee Stadium. He had been idolized by crowds of 100,000 people in St. Louis. Over ten million people had followed the Series,[12] and his name was even known in Alaska, since the Series' play-by-play was relayed there within seconds of its unfolding.[13] But despite his celebrity, Bill Sherdel still preferred going home to a quiet, humble life in McSherrystown.

His incredible story follows.

CHAPTER TWO

On December 31, 1862, Wilhelm Martin Scherdel was born in Germany. Little is known of his life there, but at age nineteen in 1882, he arrived in America and settled in New York City. In 1890 in that city, he met and married Margaretha Stertzer. Margaretha was born in the community of Pettstadt, by the city of Schweinfurt, Germany. The couple Americanized their first names and became William and Margaret Sherdel. Margaret gave birth to two children, Frederick and Theresa, while in New York.

Three years later, William M. and his family traveled to Pennsylvania and settled in the tiny village of Midway,[1] so named because it was between the towns of Hanover to the east and McSherrystown to the west. Today, it's difficult to distinguish where one borough ends and another begins. Located on the county line, Midway is considered part of Adams County, in south-central Pennsylvania.

There, William M. opened a blacksmith shop where he shod horses, fixed wagons and farm implements, and performed other smithing jobs.[2] Margaret gave birth to two additional children in that little village, William and Ruth. William Henry, the third child, was born on August 15, 1896.

When young Bill was about two years old, his family moved to 454 High Street in Hanover, next to the Hanover Heel Manufacturing Company. And while it might appear a big change, it's conceivable that the distance between the two homes was only a few blocks. Hanover, Pennsylvania, was a shoe factory town in the late 1890s, a reputation it maintained until the 1970s or 1980s. The place was probably best known for the June 30, 1863, Battle of Hanover that delayed Jeb Stuart's arrival at Gettysburg and influenced the outcome of the pivotal Civil War battle there. Today, Hanover is considered the snack food capital of the world thanks to the many well-known pretzel and potato chip brands that are manufactured there. It is also the home of the Hanover Shoe Farms, world-famous harness racing horse breeders.

Bill Sherdel started school in Hanover at age seven. He later stated, "I had a dollar watch, and that watch is responsible for my being so dumb, for all I did in school was to look at it and count the minutes until the various recesses when I could play baseball." Bill finished Bunker Hill Grade School, where he had a record of excellent attendance, and began high school at Hanover.[3]

On June 22, 1908, Sherdel was eleven when he experienced the first of many tragedies in his life. Bill, his older brother Fred, and two other boys, Arnold Hiltebridle and David Staub, spent the day playing ball, as usual. In the evening, the foursome decided to go swimming at a quarry on the farm of Andrew Rebert, about a half mile north of Hanover. Eighteen-year-old David Staub climbed upon a rock and, after exclaiming, "Here goes, boys," jumped into the deepest part of the quarry. Staub returned to the surface twice and made no sound. The second time he disappeared and remained underwater. The younger boys, Fred, Bill, and Arnold, ran to their homes to tell family members and get help. An hour later, David Staub's body was located by divers. It was generally believed that he had taken a chill as he plunged into the very cold spring water and drowned.[4]

Fred and Bill spent much of their early days playing baseball. Fred, the older brother by five years, was the pitcher. Although a natural left-hander, Bill was Fred's catcher. It's not clear if Bill wanted to be the catcher or if he was forced to by his older sibling. Either way, the Sherdel boys developed a strong reputation as a battery that was hard to beat. The brothers' first team was the West End Sluggers, which claimed High Street, Hanover, as their home base.[5]

At age fourteen, Bill learned that he might earn a living by playing baseball. He was paid twenty-five cents to play for Midway in an away game against neighboring New Oxford. The Midway club traveled by a two-horse wagon to the nearby town. The wagon driver charged Bill the same twenty-five cents for the ride.[6] That trip may have been the last time young Bill paid to play baseball.

The earliest newspaper account of the boys playing baseball was printed in 1912. Both Fred and Bill played for the Hanover Wagon Makers.[7] Twenty-year-old Fred was the pitcher and fifteen-year-old Bill handled the catching. The Wagon Makers were sponsored by Hopkins Wagon Works, a business located near the boys' High Street home. By that time, William M. was employed by Hopkins.

Two stories float about to explain Sherdel's switch from catcher to pitcher. Both are probably true. At a 1925 testimonial banquet for Sherdel, his childhood friend Robert "Rube" Smith provided his recollection of when Rube was the pitcher and Bill was the catcher. The *Gettysburg Times* reported it this way:

> Bill . . . and 'Rube' grew up together from boyhood, and as 'kids' could be found on the sandlots in and about McSherrystown and Midway [and Hanover] playing baseball. Bill yearned to be a catcher, according to friends of both him and 'Rube,' who vouch for the story, and as a youngster was eager to stand behind the batter, taking care of the 'hot ones,' which Rube served.
>
> But one day, the story goes, Bill believed that 'Rube' was not doing his best, and with an aggrieved air of disgust for the latter's pitching, Bill Sherdel threw off his glove and said:
>
> "Holy smoke, 'Rube,' you can't pitch; let me pitch."
>
> Bill did pitch; it was his first appearance on the mound, according to his friends.[8]

Bill told another story to the *St. Louis Star* of how his baseball future changed dramatically when he switched from the catcher post to the one on the mound:

> My brother, Fred, was a pitcher and I was a catcher. We had quite a reputation as a battery that was hard to beat. I found I could make more money playing baseball than in the factory, so I set out to rent my services as a catcher and caught games in all the little towns near Hanover. I could throw a hard, fast ball, and one day the manager of a team in the industrial league in which Fred and I were playing said he wanted me to pitch. I told Fred, and he laughed at me.

"Don't be a fool, Willie," Fred told me. "You are going to make good in the big league someday as a catcher. There is a great demand for small, left-handed catchers."

Now every baseball fan understands that small men do not make good behind the plate and that left-handed catchers are a rarity, but I believed Fred and refused to pitch.

Some weeks later a team in a nearby town invited me to come over and catch a game. I reported, found the pitcher was sick and that the club had an extra catcher, so I volunteered to pitch. We won the ball game and from then on I was a pitcher.[9]

Sherdel began to develop his control by throwing balls into a bucket. In no time, he was earning $1 for each game he pitched for local town and company teams.[10] He lost his older brother and baseball teammate in 1913 when Fred married Eleanor Delgado of New York City. The couple eventually moved to Valley Stream, Long Island, New York, where they would remain for the rest of their lives.

Bill said that he didn't last long in high school, but he did pitch for the Hanover High team, and became a local phenomenon. His senior team finished 8–2 and his record was 5–1. He averaged more than nine strikeouts per game. Sherdel told a story that he was among nine students who put a calf in a teacher's office and were expelled for their troubles. Five were members of the baseball team. They formed their own outlaw team, the Hanover High Federals, and continued to play. By this time, Sherdel was five feet ten inches tall, but only weighed 160 pounds. Despite his slight build, the young man was considered an excellent prospect as a left-handed pitcher.

Bill Sherdel's high school photo
—Sherdel Family

The summer of 1914 was a busy baseball season for Bill Sherdel. Throughout May and early June, he was pitching for both the renegade Hanover High team and the Hanover Athletic Club. The latter team represented Hanover in games against other towns' teams, with the local squad playing their games at McAllister Field on High Street, a third of a mile from Sherdel's home. Sherdel was developing his pitching skills as the team's second pitcher while also playing other games as an outfielder. The opposing players were more talented than Sherdel's high school opponents. Some had minor and major-league experience. Hanover ended the season as the official champions of York County and the unofficial best of Adams and Franklin counties. Bill had performed impressively throughout. He finished with a 9–4 record and batted over .300. Twice, Bill fanned eleven batters.

Hanover's *Record Herald* newspaper marked Sherdel's development. The May 1, 1914, edition stated, "Bill Scherdel [sic] of High School fame, is a promising 'comer.' He shows remarkable pitching ability for his short experience. It is reported that several colleges are after him to sign up for next season."[11] Bill was also earning a reputation for being "cool as an iceberg on the mound."

In the fall of 1914, Sherdel entered the Gettysburg College Preparatory Department, but did not remain long. He continued to play ball wherever possible. He also enjoyed fishing and swimming. Now without school to attend, he went to work with his father at the Hopkins wagon factory. It was there one day that a wrench slipped from his hand and tore the skin on his knuckles. Realizing his future might be baseball and that he couldn't risk permanently injuring his hand, Sherdel quit. He also thought he could make more money playing ball than working in a factory.[12]

Sherdel always sought to improve his pitching skills by emulating others and learning from their knowledge. If the young athlete had a hero or pitching idol, it had to be Eddie Plank. By 1914, Plank was one of the best left-handers in major-league baseball, and Sherdel was very fortunate that he lived nearby, in Gettysburg. Twenty-one years older than Sherdel, Plank was a star pitcher for Connie Mack and the Philadelphia Athletics. Plank could be seen at local town games, and he pitched in many after his major-league season ended each September.

Born in 1875, Plank played baseball as a boy on the fields in and about the Gettysburg area, including Hanover. He attended Gettysburg Academy and Gettysburg College. He was big and strong. He was a thrower, but not yet a pitcher. He had a fast ball in his early years, for sure, but there was so much more to learn to become a major-league pitcher. He improved while pitching in college for two years and then signed a professional contract with Connie Mack and the Athletics organization in 1901.

Immediately to follow, Plank jumped to the American League A's with Mack as his manager. Connie Mack had been a catcher, and was instrumental in developing many great pitchers. Plank won seventeen games in his first professional year. In his second, 1902, he helped the Athletics win their first American League pennant. He was now a legitimate star. By the time he reached his fourteenth season in 1914, "Gettysburg" Eddie had already won 269 major-league games. More than that, he had achieved the magical twenty wins on seven occasions. And by the end of his baseball career after the 1917 season, Plank had amassed an incredible 326 wins with only 194 losses. Eventually, Eddie Plank would be considered one of the greatest left-handed pitchers of all time.

In 1914, Bill Sherdel was just beginning his baseball journey, and had so much more to learn. What a blessing it was for him to have his idol, this great left-hander, living only fourteen miles away. In an interview with the *Philadelphia Record,* Plank offered some insight about how he approached pitching and how he had been so successful for so many years. Sherdel, who was Plank's disciple, would no doubt have lapped it up with enthusiasm.

> "I never had a sore arm and when I quit the game, it will be because I'm tired of it. I'm forty now, but I'm going to stick in the big leagues for five years more. At forty-five, then I think I'll be prepared to stay at home.
>
> "Pitching is a job. It must be studied by the pitcher. He must study the other fellow—the batter—and then give him what he knows he cannot hit. That is the way I have pitched for fifteen years.
>
> "The fellow [pitcher] with the fast ball will last longer than the ones with the curve. I'll pitch five fast ones to a single curve or slow ball. But the winning pitcher must have the combination. He must mix 'em to the batter. Control is the biggest point. If you can put it where you want it, then you'll win more games than you'll lose.
>
> "In spring training, I take my time. Never a curve until after the first week, and then I start my speed gradually. I believe this system has kept my arm in shape for fifteen years.
>
> "I never try for a strikeout record. You won't last long if you attempt to fan every batter."[13]

In another article about Eddie Plank that would also apply to his pupil Bill Sherdel, manager Fielder Jones of the St. Louis Browns had this to say:

> "I'll tell you why Eddie Plank today, at forty-one, is a wonderful pitcher and why he may be still a great hillman at fifty. Plank has a golden asset—he has always had it—control. That has kept him up there. He wastes nothing. He cuts the corners with his strikes and gives the batter the minimum. His pitches that are 'balls' are the ones that look good a couple of feet before they reach the batter. Plank can give

any batter two balls and then hold his own. Few pitchers ever had the wonderful control that Plank possesses.

"The old boy knows every batter in the league. If he has a lead on the opposing team and a new batter faces him, watch his experiment with that newcomer. While it's safe, Plank will test the batter and ascertain what he will hit at, what he ignores, and so on. Then when the time comes and the game is close, that batter is not a gamble to Plank—he knows him."[14]

It is amazing how, in later years, Bill Sherdel would be similarly described. Sherdel certainly learned a lot from his mentor, and he applied it to his own career.

One more article discussed Eddie Plank's frustrating delivery. That annoying form may also explain his successful career, although that is one way in which Plank and Sherdel differed.

"I have been pitching this way for sixteen years," said Eddie Plank when called to task the other day for stepping off the rubber before delivering the ball. Eddie's way is unique, however, as well as tiresome, in that he usually drags a game over two hours.

His endless delays fret the batters, but amuse the fans. The former Mackman's routine in delivery is approximately as follows:

Hitches belt, adjusts cap, walks back to the box in half circles, faces batter and stretches arms, steps on rubber with left foot and taps right foot to ground eight times when ball is delivered to batter, tucks in shirt with every third ball pitched, gazes into sky over third base on every called ball, dislodges imaginary pebble in pitcher's box every time batter has three balls and one strike or three and two.[15]

Eddie Plank's older brother Ira, who also had a strong influence on Sherdel, was an excellent baseball player and coach in his own right. Although Ira was not quite as talented as his famous brother, he did pitch right-handed for Gettysburg College for three years. Ira then tried the minor leagues with a Norwich, Connecticut, team. He had two twenty-win seasons there, and won a 1906 pennant. After, he was drafted by the New York Highlanders. The *Norwich Bulletin* remembered Ira as "one of the greatest pitchers who ever stepped on a diamond in Connecticut." He spent several more seasons in the minors until he was offered the baseball coaching position at Gettysburg College in 1913. Ira accepted, and was in that post in 1914 when he aided in Bill Sherdel's pitching development.[16]

Sherdel would take another huge step in his baseball journey of development in 1915.

CHAPTER THREE

At this time, when baseball was exploding in popularity across America, an earth-shifting development was taking place in another part of the world. War had begun in Europe in 1914 after the assassination of Archduke Ferdinand of Austria. Germany, Russia, Serbia, France, Belgium, Great Britain, and Italy had chosen sides quickly based on their alliances. The United States, meanwhile, was working on maintaining its neutrality, a task that was becoming increasingly less tenable with the passage of time. President Woodrow Wilson was dragging his heels in the hopes that some dramatic change might save the United States from the conflict. Then, on May 7, 1915, a German submarine sank the RMS Lusitania and 128 dead Americans were among the 1,198 casualties. From there, it became apparent that young men across the country would lose their innocence. They would learn how to pronounce French and German names. They would receive first-hand geography lessons on European towns and cities. The whole baseball world would be affected over the next few years. Even young Bill Sherdel in Hanover would become involved, eventually.

Charles H. Boyer of Hagerstown, Maryland, wanted to start a new baseball minor league in 1915. He had previously served as president of the South Atlantic and the Southern leagues. Boyer knew that any new league must have a minimum of six teams to be accepted by the National Commission, the ruling body for all professional leagues. Years later, the National Commission would become the National Association of Professional Baseball Leagues (NAPBL).

Boyer discovered baseball groups in Frederick, Maryland, and Martinsburg, West Virginia, to join his Hagerstown, Maryland, club in a new venture. Next, he added groups from Chambersburg and Gettysburg, Pennsylvania. He still needed one more franchise. Boyer thought about Hanover, Pennsylvania, where he had once leased an opera house. Hanover had always had a town baseball team and had won several county championships in recent years. It would also be a natural rivalry for nearby Gettysburg. The league was to be called the Blue Ridge League, since it encompassed teams along the Blue Ridge Mountains of West Virginia, Maryland, and Pennsylvania. Boyer found the perfect partner in Ira Plank, Eddie's brother, to approach the Hanover leadership. Ira was going to be the manager of the Gettysburg franchise. Hanover agreed to join, and the new Blue Ridge League was formed.

Having secured his teams, Boyer then applied to the National Commission for acceptance. The commission approved the Blue Ridge League as a class D minor league, the lowest minor-league level within professional baseball.[1]

The six teams determined their nicknames. In Hanover, they chose Hornets because, the fans reasoned, the team would sting the ball. The other inaugural 1915 clubs were the Hagerstown Blues, Frederick Hustlers, Martinsburg Champs, Chambersburg Maroons, and Gettysburg Braves.[2]

The Hanover Baseball Association chose Billy Starr, a well-known and experienced player from Littlestown, Pennsylvania, as its first manager.[3] Starr needed to work quickly to secure players for the inaugural Hanover squad. He didn't need to look very far. Young Bill Sherdel of local high school and town ball fame was the first to sign a contract. The Hornets would pay Sherdel $40 per month to live his dream and play minor-league baseball.[4]

The timing of the formation of the Blue Ridge League and the Hanover Hornets in 1915 was fortuitous for the nineteen-year-old pitching prospect. He now had the opportunity to learn from more experienced players. Sherdel would also gain a chance to test his skills against future and past major leaguers. The Blue Ridge League would later develop Hall-of-Famers Hack Wilson and Lefty Grove and many future major-league stars. Young Sherdel would also develop friendships with teammates and foes that would continue later into the major leagues and throughout the rest of his life.

That first Hornets team included many players from the Hanover squad that had been so successful from 1912 to 1914 in the independent sandlot league. They would play their home games at McAllister Field. The *Martinsburg Journal* labeled the High Street diamond "the best in the circuit."

Bill Sherdel was recognized as the youngest pitcher in the 1915 Blue Ridge League. Consequently, local sportswriters gave him the nickname "the Kid." On May 31, Hanover hosted a double-header against Chambersburg. The Hornets lost the second game, 3–2, but the match was not without excitement. Sherdel was introduced to the 1,400 local fans in the ninth inning. "Billy the Kid" struck out the side to the roaring applause of the crowd. The Hanover *Record Herald* reported, "Kid Scherdel [sic] made the visitors look 'silly' in the ninth inning when he went in and fanned three in a row. Those who were fortunate enough to be behind the plate say that the 'Kid' has 'some stuff.'"[5]

By June 5, Hanover was in second place, and Bill Sherdel earned his first minor-league win in a game against Martinsburg. He relieved in the fourth inning with one out and runners on second and third. Hanover was behind, 3–0, at the time. Sherdel shut down the visitors for the balance of the game and the Hornets prevailed, 4–3. In an exciting ninth inning, the first Martinsburg batter tripled. Sherdel then coolly struck out the next two batters and forced the third batter to fly out to centerfield to end the game. It was in this game that Sherdel earned his first hit, a single in two at-bats.

The Kid earns his first win
—*Record Herald,* June 7, 1915

"The Kid" Sherdel delivered a strong performance during his first start on June 11 against Hagerstown. Hanover was experiencing a four-game losing streak that had bumped the team down to third place. Sherdel pitched a complete game victory that allowed five scattered hits. *The Evening Sun* wrote, "Billy Scherdel [sic] the local 'wonder' came through with the right stuff and made the strong Hagerstown team look like a bunch of boys. Scherdel [sic] held them powerless throughout the game; and would have scored a shut out [sic], had it not been for the sun preventing one of the local outfielders from catching an easy fly, which was responsible for the only run scored by Hagerstown."[6]

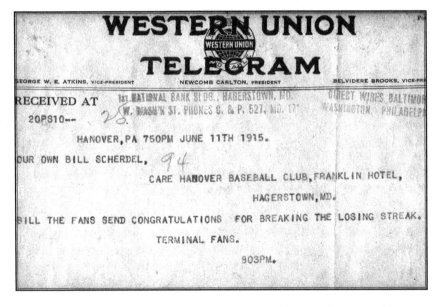

Fans' telegram congratulating Bill on ending the team's losing streak
—Sherdel family

Manager Starr gave Sherdel his next start five days later. Once again, he rose to the call, and pitched a second complete game with a 4–0 shutout of Hagerstown. He scattered five hits with excellent control and allowed no free passes. He also collected another hit at bat. In his first twenty-five innings pitched, "the Kid" had given up only one run.

Sherdel's third start was even better. On June 19, he defeated Gettysburg and Ira Plank, and set a league record with fifteen strikeouts. He scattered eleven hits that time, but was never in danger, though his own hitting did suffer (he struck out five times). Hanover remained in second place behind Frederick.

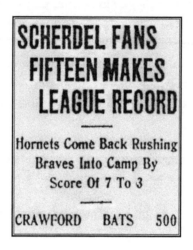

Sherdel sets BRL record with fifteen strikeouts
—*The Evening Sun*, June 21, 1915

Two days later, a player transaction took place that would help young Sherdel's pitching development meaningfully. Catcher George Stroh had begun the season as Chambersburg's manager, but his actions in recent weeks had caused much trouble. He had argued with the umpires and been ejected from games. The Chambersburg board of directors released him as a result. Hanover gambled and quickly signed him to a contract.

Stroh was an experienced catcher and leader. His baseball biography included many years in the New York State, International, and Tri-State leagues. The scouting report identified Stroh as a good hitter with an excellent build for a catcher. His throws to second base were steady and he was very quick. He would play excellent ball for the Hornets and, more importantly, he would mentor young Sherdel. "The Kid" had two pitches—a good fastball and an excellent curve. Stroh would call the pitches from behind the plate and teach Sherdel when to throw each of them.

In 1917, *The Evening Sun* discussed Stroh thus: "'Uncle' George Stroh is still there with the big mitt and pad. George is a wizard at handling young pitchers and his head and steadiness contribute fifty per cent of the effectiveness of the youngsters whom he handles . . . 'Kid' Scherdel [sic] developed under George's careful tutelage."⁷

Young Sherdel excelled through the remainder of June with two more complete-game victories. The *Hagerstown Herald* noted, "It appears that nothing can stop Kid Scherdel [sic] of the Hornets. The High School lad won again yesterday, shutting the [Martinsburg] Champions out, 7 to 0."⁸

Kid Sherdel on the 1915 Hornets
—Sherdel family

After the first full month of the season, Sherdel had shown that he belonged. His pitching record was six wins and only one defeat. In eight games, he was also batting .304 with a perfect fielding record. The Hanover club remained second in the standings. League-leader Frederick had won their first fourteen of sixteen games and would remain very difficult to catch.

Every pitcher builds his reputation upon his body of work. How does he do in pressure situations? Can he overpower hitters? Can he last nine innings?

Does he have a strike-out pitch? Does he have excellent control? These questions were starting to be answered about Bill Sherdel. At only age nineteen, he was cool under pressure. He seemed to pitch better when the game was on the line and the odds were against him. And "the Kid" was accumulating strikeouts with very few walks. He was always learning. Later in his career, Sherdel would be described as possessing the heart of a lion. He was developing that heart and strength of mind and body in the Blue Ridge League. Those traits would carry him far in the baseball profession.

The month of July proved to be a difficult one for young Sherdel. Oh, he continued to excel on the mound, but there were less pleasant happenings outside the white lines. Before a game on July 1, he was struck on the nose by a pitched ball from the visiting team and knocked unconscious. The players suspected that Sherdel's nose was broken, but a local doctor determined it was just a very bad bruise. For the following week, he sported two very ugly black eyes.[9]

Then something happened on July 14 after a ballgame in Gettysburg, an event that must be examined with an appreciation for the fact that Sherdel was still a teenager and that local rivalries can often become heated. In the game that day, Gettysburg defeated Hanover, 4–1. Gettysburg was in the cellar while Hanover was holding onto second. During the game, some Hanover fans and players ridiculed the Gettysburg chief of police Wallace Emmons in a spirit of "fun." As the crowd was exiting the field, Chief Emmons was directing traffic. Sherdel was riding on the running board of an automobile as it was leaving the parking lot. Apparently, some disparaging remarks were exchanged between him and the chief, and the officer struck Sherdel in the face with a hard blow.

Gettysburg burgess (mayor) J. W. Eicholtz suspended Chief Emmons for ten days without pay for the assault. Eicholtz also issued strict orders that, in the future, Gettysburg police officers should not tolerate any ridiculing of them, and should take all offenders into custody and bring them before the burgess for a hearing.[10]

William M. Sherdel, Bill's father, placed the information before squire V. H. Lilly of McSherrystown on oath of young Bill and a warrant for assault and battery was issued for Chief Emmons. Emmons produced bail and waived a hearing. He agreed to pay a fine and all costs, and Mr. Sherdel withdrew the warrant. The point had been made.[11]

Fortunately, Sherdel's encounter with Chief Emmons did not affect his ability to pitch. By the end of July, the young lefty was 9–1 on the mound and hitting .289 at the plate. Hanover ended the month in third place behind Frederick and Martinsburg. While other teams were improving their rosters for a run at the championship, Hanover was making few changes.

Throughout August, Sherdel continued to carry the workload like an experienced professional and not a nineteen-year-old youth. He won six more complete games with little trouble, and lost only two. All told, it was a very good first season for the Hanover team, which represented the next-to-smallest town of the league's six. Only Gettysburg was smaller. The Hanover Hornets finished the 1915 Blue Ridge League season in third place. During the final month—August—they were the best team in the league. Frederick led from start to finish and Martinsburg held on to the runner-up spot. It was also a very good first season for the Blue Ridge League. The league netted a profit, including a $1,000 profit in Hanover.[12]

The final statistics were released by the league office. Young Sherdel had had a fantastic season for a nineteen-year-old. He was second among league pitchers in winning percentage: .833 with a 15-3 mark. He led the league in hitting with a .368 batting average, but did not have enough plate appearances to qualify for the official title. "The Kid" also finished the season with a perfect fielding percentage of 1.000. *The Evening Sun* stated rather boldly that "Scherdel's [sic] remarkable performance during the 1915 season is said by old baseball men to be unsurpassed in the history of minor league baseball."[13]

Headline summarizes 1915 season
—*The Evening Sun,* January 24, 1916

If there were ever any doubters that the youngster was ready for minor-league competition, he had produced the statistics to silence them. He had proven he belonged. He was also making significant strides in his personal life. On August 18, young Bill Sherdel attended a surprise birthday party for

Miss Sarah Small. The party was given by Mr. and Mrs. John A. Small of 124 Main Street, McSherrystown. Many young people attended the celebration, including young Marguerite Strausbaugh, a girl who would later become Mrs. Marguerite Sherdel.[14]

After the Blue Ridge season ended, Sherdel continued to look for more practice. He hurled several games in York, including a victory for the York Moose that won the York Amateur City Championship. There was no question that all his pitching strengthened his arm. As a result, he would be known as a nine-inning, complete-game workhorse on the mound.

Over the winter in Hanover, nineteen-year-old Bill continued to enjoy hunting and fishing with his local friends. He also competed on a Hanover Independents bowling team.

CHAPTER FOUR

In 1916, Coca-Cola brought its current formula for Coke to market, *The Saturday Evening Post* published its first Norman Rockwell cover, Henry Ford manufactured his one millionth Model T, and the first Rose Bowl football game was held with Washington State versus Brown University. Overseas, the major war in Europe was escalating. The Battle of Verdun would last most of the year and result in over a million casualties before the French defeated the Germans. The Germans launched their first air attack on London in this year, too. In America, President Wilson ran for re-election on a platform of United States neutrality and a campaign slogan of "He kept us out of war." In November, the American people voted him in for a second term. This time, Wilson would not be able to meet his promise. The winds of war were now blowing much more strongly, and they were making their way across the Atlantic Ocean. Even twenty-year-old William H. Sherdel would feel that tempest in Milwaukee in 1917.

Bill Sherdel's baseball contract included a reserve clause. The Hanover Baseball Association exercised that clause for the 1916 season and Sherdel signed for the new campaign. The club retained the nucleus from its third-place team, but not the team nickname, which they ditched (perhaps because the team had not stung the ball enough in the previous year) in favor of the Raiders. Indeed, all the clubs but Chambersburg changed their names that year.

After a winter in Fort Lauderdale on his forty-acre vegetable farm, Hanover manager Billy Starr returned for another Blue Ridge campaign. He brought Raider prospects from scouting trips throughout Florida, northern Pennsylvania, and southern New York.

The Raiders played four exhibition games and won all of them, allowing only one run. "The Kid" Sherdel continued to impress, with nine strikeouts and four hits allowed in his seven innings. He was ready for the opener. Sherdel was happy to see that his catcher George Stroh had returned for the new season. The *Record Herald* stated, "'Kid' Stroh is working in great form and is most valuable as an assistant to Scherdel[sic]."[1]

The Hanover board and fans were very optimistic about the second season. Hanover had had the best team in the league during the final month of the 1915 season, and now the nucleus was returning for the new campaign.

Bill Sherdel on the 1916 Raiders
—Sherdel family

One event on May 10 added to the town's optimism. While manager Starr was standing on the Hanover Square talking about the team's chances with a representative of the *Record Herald*, a young sparrow landed on his right arm.

The bird chirped happily and remained there for a full minute before flying away. Everyone considered that a good omen for the baseball season.[2]

Starr selected Bill Sherdel to start the 1916 opener at home against Gettysburg. He did not disappoint. Sherdel pitched a fantastic game in front of a record home crowd of several thousand baseball-starved fans. "The Kid" scattered two singles, struck out seven, and walked none in a 3–0 shutout. He also contributed two of the team's six hits. Sherdel began the 1916 season precisely where he had ended in 1915.

"The Kid" ended the first month with a 4–1 record. The Hanover team was in first place. All was good. The *Hagerstown Mail* stated, "If Kid Scherdel [sic] does not go higher by the end of the present season it will be a wonder. For a nineteen-year-old boy he is a marvel. Since last summer much of the youthfulness has vanished from his face."[3]

Sherdel continued to take the mound on a regular basis during June. His hitting was good enough to earn him some pinch-hitting assignments and off-the-mound starts in right field. His club had dropped into second. Sherdel's chance to save the Raiders' season came in the first game of a June 17 double-header against Martinsburg. Hanover won both games to retake first place in the standings. In the first game, Sherdel hurled a nifty three-hit shutout for a 3–0 victory. He faced only twenty-nine batters with six strike-outs. No Mountaineer reached second base. *The Evening Sun* writer said, "If 'Bill' keeps up the great work he's been handing out, the Blue Ridge will see him no more."[4] Sherdel's teammate George Holbig pitched a two-hit shutout in the second game. In the two games that day, the Hanover pitchers surrendered only five hits in sixteen innings. The Raiders' hitters bunched sixteen hits into just five innings for the two wins.

Young Sherdel continued to dominate the Blue Ridge League with three more complete game victories to end June. On June 29, he defeated Gettysburg, 8–1. Sherdel held a shutout until the ninth inning. *The Evening Sun* described Sherdel's pitching thus: "Have you ever noticed Scherdel's [sic] perfect control? This, to a great extent, is the secret to Bill's success, as unlike most left-handers, his passes are very few."[5]

There was a close rivalry between the towns of Hanover and Gettysburg, and baseball games only increased the bitterness when they weren't tightly controlled by the umpire and the police. Gettysburg's *Star and Sentinel* felt compelled to write an editorial about their own fans' behavior during a Hanover game at Gettysburg:

> A regrettable feature of yesterday's game was the display of poor sportsmanship on the part of the local fans. It bordered on rowdyism at times, so careless were the rooters in evidencing their protests at some of umpire Hanks' decisions. Twice they surged on the field when close plays were decided against the home team and at least a half hour was lost in the two games by this wrangling.
>
> One fan even went so far as to throw a large rock into the playing field, barely missing catcher Stroh. In any well-regulated ballpark, he would have been ejected from the field, no matter how excusable his act might seem. But not a move of this sort was made by the baseball authorities. It can be said for the directors that they were helpless to handle the crowd any better, for a sufficient force of policemen had not been secured and proper roping off of the field had not been done before the game. Knowing of the intense rivalry that exists between the two towns, it would be well for the directors to make an effort to handle fans, who are wont to show rowdyism of the sort, when an apparently bad decision is made.[6]

The *Star and Sentinel* editorial provided some insight into what Bill Sherdel's baseball world was like in the Blue Ridge League. It wasn't difficult to imagine how some fan would steal his glove. Nineteen-year-old Bill experienced crowd rowdyism not only in Gettysburg, but also in other Blue Ridge towns. Safety was quite often an issue for the teams.

Sherdel launched July with a record of 9–3; only one pitcher had a higher winning percentage. The Hanover youngster was also batting .300 in seventeen games. Many big-league scouts were attending Blue Ridge League games over this month, looking for the next year's prospects. The scouts were pleasantly surprised by the quality of play in the class D league. Scouts Charles "Heinie" Wagner for the Red Sox and Charles "Pop" Kelchner for the Browns were in the Hanover grandstands to watch young Bill Sherdel.

"The Kid" was now well known throughout the league, and all the league's newspapers were following his exploits. A Chambersburg sportswriter selected his mid-season all-star team and included Bill Sherdel on his four-man pitching staff.[7]

Young Sherdel was piling up more complete game victories. In mid-July, he picked up two wins over Hagerstown, allowing only one run with fourteen strikeouts over the two games. In the second Hagerstown game, he was matched against one of the best pitchers in the league, "Wick" Winslow. Earlier in the season, "Wick" had pitched a no-hitter against Chambersburg. In this game, Winslow allowed only four hits while Sherdel surrendered five scattered hits and no walks. The Raiders prevailed, 1–0.

"Wick" Winslow was an interesting player. He and some other players in the Blue Ridge League used aliases to play class D professional ball. It was a practice adopted by college players to maintain their amateur status. Other players did it to avoid binding contracts or to play in a lower-class league. Winslow was not a college player. The spitball pitcher, whose supposed real name was Walter P. Warwick, probably used an alias because it was later determined that he was still under contract to a Massachusetts team.[8]

Hagerstown manager Bert Weeden came from Brockton, Massachusetts, and brought Warwick with him. As the story goes, Weeden and Warwick were standing in a post office when Weeden spotted a sign advertising Mrs. Winslow's Soothing Cough Syrup. Weeden gave the last name Winslow to his pitcher and added the first name Warwick or "Wick" for short.[9] Winslow would become a star pitcher in the league, winning twenty-one games for Frederick in 1917. Eventually, Weeden would manage and Winslow would pitch for the Hanover Raiders. Winslow would prove to be nomadic, and would hurl for four of the six Blue Ridge clubs.

Before Sherdel's next mound assignment, Detroit scout and former major-league catcher Joe Sugden asked Bill to pitch to him. Sugden wanted to judge the youngster's "stuff" for himself. After displaying his skill to the scout, Sherdel threw another complete game win, this time over Gettysburg. The Raiders' star allowed only two base hits and added two singles of his own. Despite Sherdel's best efforts, Hanover was trailing Chambersburg by a half game in the standings.

The Evening Sun wrote about Sherdel's efforts. "'Billy' Sherdel has faced Gettysburg many times and just as many times has he been returned victor. Never was he in better form, after the opening session, than Saturday. . . . Surely scout Joe Sugden has watched few better prospects than this boy."[10]

In another article the following day, *The Evening Sun* added this comment:

> The name of Scherdel [sic] is already reaching beyond the bounds of the Blue Ridge and into the ranks of the biggest figures in the diamond world. In the column "Just Bunts" of the *Philadelphia North American*, right among the names of Plank, [Christy] Mathewson . . . is the following. Before quoting it might be said that 'Just Bunts' is a very appropriate title after yesterday's game. The N. A. says: "Pitcher Scherdel [sic], of the Hanover club of the Blue Ridge league, looks like a comer. Although this is only his second year in professional ball, he is piling up a string of victories, just the same as he did last season."[11]

Another report came from the *Hagerstown Globe*. "Hagerstown without a doubt considers the Hanover youngster a jinx, 'or something unbeatable.' And the same way with about all the rest of the teams. Scherdel [sic] is simply working hard and taking care of himself to make a try for higher circles in baseball."[12]

Players often develop friendships with teammates and opponents that last way beyond their competitive years. Sometimes, an opponent can later become a teammate. That was true for Bill Sherdel during his time in the Blue Ridge League. One of his friends was Marvin Goodwin, an outstanding pitcher on the Martinsburg team. Bill and Marvin would become teammates on several teams in their future baseball careers.

Marvin "Nat" Goodwin was born in Gordonsville, Virginia, in 1891—five years before Bill Sherdel. Goodwin was an established local semi-pro star at age twenty-five when he was offered a contract by Clark Griffith of the Washington Nationals. At the time, the pitcher was also working for the Chesapeake and Ohio Railroad as a telegraph operator. He had a great fastball, impressive control, and an outstanding spitball.

Goodwin signed his contract with Washington in early 1916, and owner Griffith sent him to Martinsburg for some experience with the understanding that Washington still owned his rights and could recall him later. Goodwin became a star at Martinsburg. He became known as "the Iron Man," because he pitched whenever needed. He even pitched a double-header against Chambersburg on July 18. He won the first game, 7–2, and lost the second contest, 2–0.

By the end of July, Bill Sherdel's record was 13–5, with a winning percentage of .722—second best in the league. Marv Goodwin's record, meanwhile, was 12–8, with a .600 percentage—the fourth best. The two outstanding hurlers met in an August 2 game at McAllister Field. Goodwin won, 4–0. Sherdel was unusually ineffective and very wild at times. Local scribes were concerned that he was either ill or that his arm was tired. Martinsburg was now in second place and Hanover was in third.

There did indeed seem to be something wrong with Sherdel at this point in his fledgling career. In his next two outings, he surrendered eleven and ten hits, respectively. He seemed wild and missing his usual pinpoint control, although he only surrendered three total walks in the two games. Young Sherdel split the decisions: he lost, 8–3, to Martinsburg and then defeated Gettysburg, 4–3. Even a local sportswriter commented in the first game recap that the superstar pitcher had not been well for some time and was not in his usual form.[13]

On August 16, the entire town of Hanover was excited by the following news article in the *Record Herald*. "William Scherdel [sic] of this place, better known as 'Kid,' the star pitcher on the Raiders staff, has been sold to the Milwaukee Club of the American Association. He will report to this club on August 21. Scherdel [sic] was the leading pitcher of the Blue Ridge League last season. He is the youngest twirler in the league. He is also a good hitter."[14] *The Evening Sun* added, "Best wishes of all true fans that nothing may befall him but good fortune and success."[15] Hanover's board of directors also celebrated—the Sherdel sale added $700 to its treasury.

The Milwaukee Brewers competed in the American Association minor league. The American Association, just one class below the major leagues, was considered the "major minor" league. Milwaukee scout Billy Doyle had been following Sherdel's success for two years, and had beaten all other scouts to the young prospect. At the same time, St. Louis Browns' scout "Pop" Kelchner had forwarded information to the Browns' front office and was awaiting word to sign the Hanover idol. But Kelchner was too late.

Sherdel was with the Raiders in Frederick when the news broke. He would pitch one more game for his club on August 18. In that final contest, he allowed ten hits, but only one walk. He also fanned Frederick's three best hitters consecutively in the fifth inning. Sherdel surrendered an untimely eighth-inning home run to Clyde Barnhart, future Pittsburg Pirate star, and lost the pitchers' duel, 2–1, to end his Blue Ridge experience. He returned to Hanover the next day to say goodbye to his family and many friends.

His final 1916 Hanover Raiders statistics included fourteen wins, nine losses, and one tie with a .609 winning percentage. As a hitter in thirty-five games, Sherdel batted .265—not bad for the so-called deadball era. This stretch in baseball history, generally considered to have extended from the founding of the American League in 1901 to the elimination of the spitball in 1920, was characterized by low scoring and an emphasis on pitching and defense. The baseball was heavier and harder to hit by design. The same ball would be used throughout the game and pitchers would benefit from the scuffing.

Other league newspapers commented on the sale. Perhaps they were happy to see him leave. The *Hagerstown Globe* wrote, "The sale of Kid Scherdel [sic] into higher circles brings to fans of this city considerable gratification. The Kid has put it over on Hagerstown about every time and has always pitched a clean-cut game and won it by clever twirling. His rise in the game is certain."[16] The *Chambersburg Public Opinion* stated, "He [Sherdel] goes to Milwaukee on Monday and leaves his old circuit with the sting of a defeat in his last go. For our own sake as well as his, we hope we don't see him again around here."[17] Gettysburg's *Star & Sentinel* added, "Scherdel [sic] has been nearly as effective against other teams in the league as he has against Gettysburg and it is the hope of Blue Ridge League fans that he will stick in faster company for he is a hard-working and promising youngster."[18]

As a final compliment, the *Frederick Post* announced its 1916 all-star team. Bill Sherdel was chosen. So, too, was Marv Goodwin of Martinsburg and two other pitchers.

After Bill Sherdel left the Raiders, the Hanover club dropped to fourth place in the standings. They would end the 1916 Blue Ridge League season behind Chambersburg, Martinsburg, and Hagerstown. The season had been very competitive. No team had held first place for more than fifteen consecutive days.

In the later 1920s, the Blue Ridge clubs would affiliate with major-league organizations: Chambersburg with the Yankees, Frederick with the Indians, Martinsburg with the Athletics, Hanover with the Tigers, and Waynesboro, a replacement for Gettysburg, with the Cardinals. Hagerstown would remain independent. The league would fold in 1931 due to economics and, ironically, its established associations with the majors. Major-league teams would have little extra money and so would stop supporting many of their minor-league affiliates when the Great Depression hit.

CHAPTER FIVE

On Sunday, August 20, 1916, William Henry Sherdel boarded a train to take him to Milwaukee, Wisconsin. That would be his first trip west. His family and most of his friends knew that he would be a success. Although he was only now twenty years old, he was following his lifelong dream to earn a living playing baseball. And while the young man may have been suffering some anxiety, he was always very confident in his baseball skills. He knew that he would need more than an adequate fast ball and an outstanding curve to be successful in a higher-class league. The American Association was a class AA league, only one step below the major leagues. In it, Sherdel would find many old veteran pitchers and catchers who would help him develop another pitch—a change-up—that would add to his success.

Not everyone in Hanover was optimistic about Sherdel's future. Ned Crowder, the Hanover Raiders' veteran shortstop, and Bill Duncan, a Hanover sportswriter, were sitting on a bench in the Hanover Square when young Sherdel told them he had been sold to Milwaukee. Afterward, Duncan relayed this story about their response to the news:

"Ned shook his head as Bill walked away from us.

"'A great kid and a smart pitcher, but he's too small to stay long up there,' said the veteran shortstop. 'I'll give him a year.'

"'I agree with you, Ned,' I said. 'My hope is that he can last three seasons.'"[1]

Crowder and Duncan had not accurately measured Sherdel's heart, confidence, or desire. He would prove them wrong.

The American Association was the great minor league in the middle of the country. Along with the Pacific Coast League in the west and the

International League in the east, these three leagues comprised class AA baseball. (Years later, the minor-league classifications would change—the old AA class would become today's AAA class.) These leagues were just one step below major-league baseball. Of this trio, the American Association was considered the "major minor," and the best. The Milwaukee Brewers competed along with the Kansas City Blues, the Louisville Colonels, the Indianapolis Indians, Toledo Ironmen, the Minneapolis Millers, the St. Paul Saints, and the Columbus Senators for the league honors.

Unfortunately, Sherdel was joining a team that was in the league's cellar. The manager had recently resigned because of the team's poor play. The Brewers' roster was undergoing many changes. Pitchers were especially needed. That would mean opportunity for Sherdel.[2]

Young Sherdel was a country boy headed to the city—a whole new world to conquer. He was not knowledgeable in the ways of big-time baseball. Harry Brundidge of the *St. Louis Star* wrote this story about his arrival in Milwaukee.

> On a hot day in the summer of 1916, a diminutive blond youth with a huge straw suitcase arrived at the office of the secretary of the Milwaukee American Association Baseball Club. He had walked out from the depot, and was perspiring freely.
>
> "I'm the pitcher you bought from the Blue Ridge League," he told the secretary.
>
> "Glad to see you. Come in. You paid your own expenses here, didn't you? Well, suppose I start by refunding the money you spent. How much was your railroad fare?"
>
> "Thirty dollars and forty-two cents."
>
> "And your Pullman berth?"
>
> "I didn't want to ride in one of those cars; I never even been in one of them."
>
> "How much did you spend for meals?"
>
> "Nothin'. Ma fixed me a basket of sandwiches when I left home."
>
> "And you've been living in day coaches and eating sandwiches all the way from Hanover, Pa?"
>
> "Yes, sir."
>
> "By the way, what's your full name?"

"William Henry Sherdel, and I'm left-handed, sir."

The Milwaukee club secretary gave Bill some money and told him to go get a good meal. Later, Sherdel admitted that he was very green when he arrived. He thought a batting cage was where they confined hitters who were in a slump.[3]

If young Sherdel was anxious, it was understandable. Hanover had a population of around 8,000 while Milwaukee's population swelled closer to 400,000. Milwaukee was the largest city in Wisconsin and the fifth largest city in the Midwestern United States. It was located on Lake Michigan's western shore at the confluence of three rivers—the Menomonee, the Kinnickinnic, and the Milwaukee.

Milwaukee's major industry was brewing, a natural fit for a city whose population included a large group of Germans. With his last name, Sherdel would be welcomed by the Brewers' many fans. Milwaukee was once home to four of the world's largest breweries and, for many years, it was the number one beer-producing city in the world. It seemed appropriate that the baseball club chose the nickname Brewers.

Sherdel would find the Milwaukee baseball season temperatures cooler than in Hanover. The average July temperature in Milwaukee was seventy-one degrees. He would also discover that the American Association teams played a longer season—168 games from April 18 until October 1—and had a larger, twenty-player team roster.

The Milwaukee Brewers played their home games in Athletic Park on a city block bordered by North 7th, 8th, Chambers, and Burleigh Streets. The ballpark had a seating capacity of 13,000 in 1916, although large crowds were unusual when Sherdel played there. The park's design was described as a bathtub, like the Polo Grounds in New York City. The field dimensions were listed as left field (267 feet), centerfield (392 feet), and right field (268 feet), with very deep power alleys in left and right center. Later in 1928, Athletic Park would be renamed Borchert Field in honor of the owner Otto Borchert.

That was the city and the ballpark that twenty-year-old William H. Sherdel would call home from April to October.

As mentioned, Sherdel was joining a last-place team that had just changed managers. The previous manager had also been the team's third baseman, and he had directed the Brewers to league titles in 1913 and 1914. In 1915, however, the team's fortunes started to decline. And by 1916, the Milwaukee Brewers were not a competitive team. They would spend the 1916 season in the American Association cellar. The manager's frustration reached a peak when he resigned for the good of the team on August 15,[4] the same day Bill Sherdel signed his contract.

By the time Sherdel's train arrived at the Milwaukee station on August 21, the Brewers had named twenty-nine-year-old shortstop Jack Martin as temporary manager. Martin had been obtained in a trade with the Philadelphia Phillies near the end of the 1915 campaign.[5] Through the remainder of the 1916 season, there would be many roster changes. The club would become younger and, hopefully, better.

The most notable player on the Brewers' roster when Sherdel arrived was twenty-nine-year-old Jim Thorpe. Thorpe would be recognized in 1950 by the nation's press as the most outstanding athlete of the first half of the twentieth century. Later, ABC's "Wide World of Sports" would call him the athlete of the century.

James Thorpe was born in Oklahoma in 1887, but gained sports prominence while attending the Carlisle Industrial Indian School in Carlisle, Pennsylvania. There, Thorpe became an All-American football player for the legendary coach Glenn "Pop" Warner. He also ran track for the school. At age twenty-four, Thorpe represented the United States in the 1912 Olympic Games in Stockholm. He won gold medals and set records in both the pentathlon and decathlon. King Gustav V of Sweden told Thorpe, "Sir, you are the greatest athlete in the world."[6] In 1913, it was determined that Thorpe had played two semi-professional seasons of baseball and was considered a professional athlete. Since the Olympics were restricted to amateurs, he was forced to surrender his gold medals.

Thorpe soon signed a professional baseball contract with the New York Giants and legendary manager John McGraw. Between 1913 and 1915, he played infrequently in the Giants' outfield. He appeared in only sixty-six games with an anemic .195 batting average. Given that, it's not surprising that John McGraw decided to farm Thorpe to Milwaukee for the 1916 season. Thorpe signed a contract with the Brewers on April 1. The Giants maintained an option to recall Thorpe and agreed to pay most of his Brewers' salary, so it was an attractive deal for Milwaukee ownership. And McGraw wanted Thorpe to gain some additional "seasoning" and to experiment with batting left-handed instead of his normal right. He felt that, by batting left-handed, Thorpe could benefit from hitting against the many right-handed pitchers and would be one step closer to first base when exiting the batter's box. Secretly, McGraw stated that he didn't think Jim Thorpe would ever be a major-league player, but why not try? By June 10, Thorpe had given up on becoming a switch hitter and was focusing on batting right-handed. He was benefitting from his experience in class AA ball and was improving.

Jim Thorpe was an outstanding athlete. While he continued his development as a baseball player, Thorpe played professional football with the Canton Bulldogs.

Jim Thorpe, Sherdel's teammate in Milwaukee
—Coulson collection

Prior to Bill Sherdel's arrival in Milwaukee, two other young players had been added to the Brewers' roster. Both arrived from Portsmouth, where they'd been part of the recently disbanded Ohio State League. William "Pickles" Dillhoefer was a twenty-two-year-old catcher who had played for Portsmouth since 1914. "Pickles" would become Sherdel's catcher. Twenty-year-old outfielder Austin McHenry had arrived in Portsmouth for the 1915 season. McHenry hit .297 in ninety-seven games there. Eventually, both Dillhoefer and McHenry would follow Bill Sherdel to St. Louis. They would become good friends as well as teammates in the Cardinals' youth movement.

Bill Sherdel saw his first American Association action the day after he arrived in Milwaukee. It did not go well. The newcomer entered the first game of a double-header in relief. The starter had been hit hard. Sherdel entered in the second inning and immediately surrendered six hits and seven runs. The Brewers lost, 14–6. Sherdel did look good at bat. He collected two hits and a walk in four plate appearances.

The Hanover *Record Herald* received this summary from Milwaukee. "Lefty Scherdel [sic], formerly of the Hanover team, in the Blue Ridge league, pitched his first game for Milwaukee today and though he was slaughtered by the Indianapolis batsmen, he made a good impression upon the fans, who realized he was sent in hurriedly without a chance to warm up when the game was already lost. He allowed six hits and seven runs. He hit three batsmen, but gave no bases on balls."[7]

The Evening Sun from Hanover printed these comments from the *Indianapolis Star:* "Bill was, no doubt, hit hard but he was rushed in the breech with the bases full . . . making the 'Kid's' first appearance a very trying one. If given a rest and fair chance Hanover fans are certain their favorite will remain in fast company. . . . It is certain that the Brewers will give him a thorough trial under more favorable circumstances and his work is bound to improve as he acquires more knowledge of the great Association."[8]

The Brewers headed out on a late August road trip. Manager Martin gave Sherdel the ball to start the second game of a double-header against Minneapolis on August 26. He pitched great for eight innings, but he lost the game in the ninth, 2–1. After a walk, a ball hit over Jim Thorpe's head in centerfield scored the tying run and advanced the batter to third on the throw to home. Sherdel left the mound. His replacement got an easy first out, and then gave up the winning run on a single.[9]

Four days later, Sherdel came back to start a game against the St. Paul Saints. He pitched respectable ball, but lost again, 4–1, and he surrendered eight hits. The St. Paul crowd numbered only about 1,000 fans—a good crowd at McAllister Field in Hanover. An article by B. O. Kirkham stated:

On the whole, Scherdel [sic] made a fairly respectable showing, but he was nicked for hits at opportune times.[10]

"Kid" Sherdel sent a letter home to his family and many friends. Everyone was excited to read how he'd been doing in *The Evening Sun*.

A letter from "Billy" Scherdel [sic] states that he is in fine condition, likes the American Association greatly, and is confident of remaining in this fast company. "Bill" says that he had no trouble whatever in becoming acquainted with the "Big guns" of the Milwaukee club and was chosen to do relief duty the day after arriving. The "Brewers" were very well pleased with his work not only as a pitcher but as a .667 hitter, putting the pride of Hanover at the top of the American Association batting list—temporarily. . . . He closes with best wishes to all Hanover fans and every player in the Blue Ridge, hoping that his hometown may land high in the race for the Blue Ridge bunting.[11]

Bill Sherdel with the Milwaukee Brewers
—*St. Louis Star*, January 28, 1918

Young Sherdel got his first September start in Kansas City. There, he pitched a complete game, but lost thanks to walks and errors, 6–3. The *Record Herald* remarked that "Bill now has a change of pace and his stuff is baffling. Right now, manager Martin thinks that he has the best southpaw in the league and with a little more seasoning Scherdel [sic] will cut a name for himself in Association ball."[12]

Four days later, on September 7, Sherdel gave it another try. This time, he beat Toledo, 5–4, in ten innings for his first American Association victory. In his next start, Sherdel was chosen to face first-place Louisville. He lost his fourth game, 8–1. It could have been discouraging, but he maintained confidence in his ability. He knew that by developing his change of pace pitch and learning more about the hitters, he would be successful. Sherdel never doubted his ability.

The Milwaukee Brewers returned home for a final home stand on September 21. A thirteen-game losing streak meant the mood was low. Sherdel drew the starting assignment against St. Paul, and he pitched a complete game shutout win, 3–0. Sherdel scattered only five hits and allowed no free passes. The Saints threatened in only two innings, but in each case, Sherdel tightened and held them scoreless. It was a great game to end the streak.

Sherdel's pitching at this point could still be considered a "work in progress." He lost his next start to Minneapolis and did not pitch well, allowing four runs with two outs in the first inning. He left for an early shower. Sherdel took the hill for his last 1916 Milwaukee start on September 29. He came to the rescue once more in this game against Kansas City, throwing another complete shutout, with a 6–0 win. A two-hit masterpiece with five strikeouts and he didn't allow a hit until the sixth inning. It was a great way to end his first season in class AA ball.

The Evening Sun included these comments in its article: "With great control, and his ball breaking sharply, Kid Scherdel [sic], the Brewer southpaw recruit, established himself in the hearts of Milwaukee fans, yesterday, when he downed the Kansas City Blues in the first game of the series. Scherdel [sic] pitched the best game of his young career and it is freely predicted that the youngster will be one of the best bets in the Association next year."[13]

In the end, temporary manager Jack Martin fared little better than his predecessor. Martin's Brewers finished last in the standings, last in hitting, last in runs scored, and next to last in fielding. Jim Thorpe hit .274, Austin McHenry settled for a .240 average, and Bill Dillhoefer's average was a very respectable .292. Bill Sherdel's final pitching record was two wins and five losses in nine games.

Sherdel's teammate Jim Thorpe would return to the National League in 1917. The Giants sold him to Cincinnati in April. It was a surprise, because Thorpe had shown promise at Milwaukee and was looking good in the New York spring training camp. Reporter Paul Purman visited the Giants' camp and wrote these comments on the player:

> He has developed into a dangerous hitter and his fielding has improved wonderfully. . . . Thorpe should develop into a great ballplayer, under [Christy] Mathewson's tutelage and his extra base clout should be of great value to the Cincinnati club.
>
> If Thorpe can make himself of enough value to the Reds to earn a regular berth on the team he will have realized his greatest ambition. . . .
>
> "I want to play big league ball," Thorpe told me. "I want to be a regular on a big-league club. It means more to me than my Olympic medals or my football letter."[14]

Thorpe would fulfill his greatest dream and play regularly for most of the 1917 season with the Reds. Later in that year, he would return to the New York Giants and remain into 1919. Thorpe would finish his professional baseball career that year with the Boston Braves and a career .252 major-league batting average.

With baseball on hiatus until next year, Bill Sherdel headed home to High Street in Hanover to spend the winter with his parents. Still, the inveterate ball player was not prepared to rest his arm. On October 15, Sherdel pitched one more game, an exhibition match that saw him take the mound for a makeshift Blue Ridge club against fellow Raider hurler Pat Kunkle and the St. Mary's of McSherrystown team. Kunkle had become the Raiders' ace after Sherdel left for Milwaukee. Spectators enjoyed a great game. Sherdel and Kunkle battled for eleven innings to a 1–1 tie. With this, Sherdel took a breather from baseball playing and turned his attention to winter hunting and fishing.

Milwaukee Brewers' owner A. F. Timme knew that he needed to find a better manager for the Brewers. Turning around from the last-place finish called for a strong, knowledgeable leader. Timme began his search in earnest as soon as the 1916 campaign ended. The press leaked many candidates' names to the public. On October 27, Timme selected Danny Shay, former Kansas City skipper, to be his new manager. Unfortunately, that would eventually prove to be a regrettable choice—but not initially.

Forty-year-old Danny Shay was a career baseball man with very strong credentials. Shay had spent five years in the minors before reaching the majors in 1901 with the Cleveland team. The middle infielder played only nineteen games before being released. Shay returned to the minors and stayed there until he was given another shot at the big leagues in 1904. He played two years with the Cardinals and then briefly experienced the big time once more with John McGraw's 1907 Giants.

At a certain point, Danny Shay began to realize that his best future in baseball might be in managing. He started with the Stockton club of the California League, where he won a first-half title before jumping to Kansas City in the American Association. Shay remained there for 1910 and 1911, bringing the team a second-place finish in his last year. He steered clear of baseball until July 1915, when he returned to Kansas City. In 1916, Shay had Kansas City in the pennant race until something happened, and he resigned. Various stories existed, but the club announced that the manager had left because of poor health. Shay seemed to have a different story but was reluctant to share it. He commented cryptically at one point that, "Later on, I'll say plenty. It looks like they're trying to make me the fall guy."

Either way, Shay was headed to the Brewers. The Milwaukee fans liked the selection. The *Milwaukee Sentinel* reported that Shay "is a fiery, fighting leader, knows the game from all angles, knows a player when he sees one and knows how to develop youngsters." Timme gave Shay complete control and promised to get him whatever he needed to place a winning team on the field again.[15] Danny Shay would be young Sherdel's new skipper. Everyone was optimistic.

New Brewers' manager Danny Shay
—Coulson collection

In November, the Milwaukee club announced its reserve list for 1917. Bill Sherdel and Austin McHenry were on it. Dillhoefer was missing; "Pickles" had been drafted by the Chicago Cubs. Another exciting name on the list was Marvin Goodwin, Sherdel's friend from the Blue Ridge League days. Goodwin had been drafted by Milwaukee from the Martinsburg club in baseball's fall draft. But there were problems. The National Association returned Milwaukee's check for Goodwin, stating that Clark Griffith of Washington had claimed the ball player. As the story goes, Griffith had sent Goodwin to Martinsburg for a $100 consideration. Martinsburg's owners had never paid the bill, so Griffith recalled Goodwin to Washington on August 29 with the consent of Martinsburg. However, Goodwin was still pitching for Martinsburg up to September 1.

The National Commission ruled that, according to the National Baseball Agreement, no player could be sold within twenty days of the minor-league club's season end. The Blue Ridge League season ended on September 4. Washington had waited too long to recall Goodwin. Clark Griffith's recall of Goodwin was ruled invalid, even though he had pitched several games for Washington. Through the baseball agreement's draft clause, Marvin Goodwin was awarded to the Milwaukee club, and Martinsburg was ordered to pay the original $100 consideration to Washington. Both Martinsburg and Milwaukee were winners, while Washington suffered a big loss. Unfortunately, that whole story would be clouded in confusion that remains to this day. In any event, Marv Goodwin and Bill Sherdel would be teammates on Danny Shay's pitching staff.[16]

Over the winter, the American Association decided it needed to sign younger players for the following year. If teams carried young players on their rosters, they could reduce their payroll expense. More than that, the teams would enjoy the benefit of developing young players and then selling them to major-league clubs for more income.

CHAPTER SIX

On January 31, 1917, Germany announced a new submarine offensive, and President Wilson broke diplomatic ties with it in response. Almost a month later, the British government intercepted a telegram sent by the German foreign secretary Arthur Zimmerman that was intended for the Mexican government. In it, Zimmerman was proposing an alliance between Germany and Mexico. If war did break out with the United States and Mexico supported Germany, Germany would help Mexico reclaim the southwestern part of the United States. The British government showed this telegram to Wilson, who realized he could no longer support neutrality. On April 6, 1917, the United States cleverly declared war on the German government but not on the German people. With this gesture, Wilson was expressing his concern for all the German-Americans, like the Sherdels, living in the US. By the end of 1917, the United States would also declare war against Austria-Hungary.

President Wilson sent an American Expeditionary Force under General John "Black Jack" Pershing to the European Western Front. Congress would pass the Selective Service Act, which gave the president the right to raise a volunteer infantry force—all males between twenty-one and thirty were required to register for military service. Over the course of the balance of the war, four million men would be drafted into the armed services and half would be sent overseas.

That was the backdrop for Bill Sherdel's next baseball season—1917—in Milwaukee, a city that many German-Americans called home. It would be an interesting season, to say the least. Young Sherdel from the little town of Hanover, Pennsylvania, who wouldn't turn twenty-one until August 15, would experience four managers, a murder, and his part in preparations for what would initially be called "The Great War."

In February, Bill Sherdel returned his signed 1917 contract to the Brewers. Marv Goodwin was not ready to sign his. Goodwin had been offered a salary that was $25 less per month than the amount he had been guaranteed by Washington for 1916. By early March, Goodwin's contract problems were resolved and he joined Bill Sherdel on the Brewers' staff.

In one interview, Danny Shay talked about his staff with a *Sporting Life* writer. "Manager Shay is insistent on having a strong pitching staff," the article explained. "Red Shackleford, Cyril Slapnicka, Allie Reeb, Kid Scherdel [sic], Lefty Moran, Cuban [Pedro] Dibut, and Goodwin compose the hurling staff. Great things are expected of Scherdel [sic] and Reeb this season. The pair showed flashy stuff last season for recruits, and they are expected to win many games."[1]

As spring training approached, the *Milwaukee Sentinel* wrote this appraisal of the new team: "On paper the club looks pretty fair, though the pitching staff is not one of great promise. There are a lot of likely youngsters on the hurling corps, and any one of them may come through with flying color. If such is the case, manager Shay will not have to worry, but should all the colts fall by the wayside it will probably be tough sledding for the club.... If the youngsters come through the team should finish among the first four at least."[2]

On March 10, young Sherdel packed his bags, said goodbye to his family and friends, and boarded a train for Wichita Falls, Texas. Sherdel would experience his first spring training camp in a warmer climate. And, for the first time, he'd start practice without returning home for his meals and sleeping in his own bed. This would be the first of many more springs like this one.

Spring training camp opened on March 10. The players were expected to report two days later. Sherdel arrived right on time.

Wichita Falls, Texas, was located about fifteen miles south of the Oklahoma border. The Milwaukee Brewers' spring camp took place at Lake Wichita, a large man-made lake area located several miles southwest of Wichita Falls. The lake itself measured three-and-a-half miles by one mile. There was a big baseball diamond and a grandstand. The Milwaukee players stayed at a large summer resort there—during the three weeks of training camp, the players were the only guests. There was a two-story pavilion used for dancing and for the team's indoor practices if the weather was bad. The team also enjoyed a boardwalk along the lake. The year after Sherdel's camp, the hotel burned.

As required, the players could also travel into Wichita Falls, where all the usual amenities existed. There were picture shows, vaudeville acts, and an opera house, as well as many saloons.

Unfortunately, reality must not have been as good as the brochures. A *Milwaukee Journal* reporter named "Brownie" described the environment this way:

> But I was going to tell you about the lake where the boys are camping. It's a regular place; that is, there is plenty of room for the water, but at this time of the year most of it is missing. What is left is so muddy-looking that [Bill] Jap Barbeau says if he had skis he would be able to walk on it. According to the best of information, there is one fish in the lake, and this one the entire team has been trying to catch ever since the squad landed here. Barbeau had a line out, with fifty hooks on it, while it is said [Cy] Slapnicka had 150 hooks out from his line. But so far there has been nothing stirring.
>
> Manager Shay brought a gun with him and with this the boys have had a little more luck, as jack rabbits are more plentiful than fish. Hardly a day has passed but what one or more jacks have been bagged.[3]

Training camp conditions did not impress Danny Shay. There were too many sandstorms and strong winds. The baseball diamond had a dirt infield, which made it difficult for the players when the winds were blowing. The team could only get in one daily practice, usually in the afternoon. In the mornings, Shay didn't want to take any chances with his players, so he ordered them to take long walks. By noon, the temperature would rise and the conditions would improve. As far as the team meals went, one individual remarked, "The boys knew just what they were going to eat at every meal. Ham and eggs, or bacon for breakfast; roast beef at noon; steak for supper. This was the unvarying menu. It got monotonous after a time."[4]

There was one other unique thing about Bill Sherdel's first spring training camp. Owner Al Timme knew that a war was approaching and that it would involve many young baseball players. He wanted his players to set a good example and to be prepared for military service. Timme contacted the United States War Department and secured the services of a drillmaster, Sergeant John Waidley, US Army of Chicago. Waidley arrived at camp with the players. His job was to drill the team in military preparedness.

Timme told the *Milwaukee Sentinel*, "While I am strong for peace, I believe in preparedness, and the club intends to do its bit in case of trouble. The players will be given military drill every day, so that if any of them are called they will be able to tell their right foot from their left and know which end of a rifle the bullets come out. Even if there is no trouble the drill will help condition the athletes and loosen the winter kinks in their systems. In the event of trouble the club will endeavor as far as it can to help the families who are called. I hope there will be no necessity of any of the boys going, but if they do we will go the limit to help those they leave behind."[5]

Sgt. Waidley drilled the Brewer players throughout training camp. No one was excused. Even super scout Billy Doyle participated in the drills. Surprisingly, the players took the drills very seriously. By the second week of camp, the Brewers were practicing the manual of arms using baseball bats instead of rifles. Sometimes, the team drilled in front of fans.[6]

One unusual camp note was written by Manning Vaughan of the *Milwaukee Sentinel.* Vaughan wrote, "Some of the Brewers had possum dinner a few days after playing in Oklahoma. It happened that Jap Barbeau killed the animal by hitting it with an automobile returning from Lawton. The fat creature was squatting in the middle of the road when it met its fate."[7]

Camp finished with the Brewers winning two games in Dallas. The weather had been outstanding. The Brewers had not lost a single game to rain. The club then began its trip north, playing exhibition games throughout Oklahoma, Kansas, and Nebraska as they proceeded to Milwaukee.[8] Bill Sherdel pitched the last two innings in a 2–1 victory over a Lincoln, Nebraska team. The *Nebraska State Journal* stated, "'Lefty' Scherdel [sic], who pitched the last pair of innings, had so much stuff that we couldn't even see the ball."[9]

As opening day approached, manager Shay was very confident about his team's chances. The sportswriters in the other American Association cities, however, were not as optimistic. One picked Milwaukee for next to last place and the rest guessed that the Brewers would not escape the league basement.[10]

When the Brewers arrived in Milwaukee, three team representatives reported for duty to the ranking officer of the United States Army in

Milwaukee. In a brief ceremony, the team's three leaders were introduced as non-commissioned officers of the team to Captain T. T. Cathro, in charge of army recruiting for the Wisconsin district. With their reporting for duty, the team now came under the direct jurisdiction of Captain Cathro, as Sgt. Waidley returned to the army. Outfielder John Beall became the team's drillmaster and drilling continued in the early afternoons throughout the season. Owner Timme believed that his players would be qualified for non-commissioned officers' duties if they joined the army.[11] In an additional act of patriotism, Timme created a military look to the new Brewers' uniforms. He placed a military collar and an American flag on the 1917 shirts.[12]

Opening day for the 1917 Brewers was Wednesday, April 11, at their home, Athletic Park. The opponents were the St. Paul Saints from Minnesota. A pleasant day brought close to 7,000 baseball-ready fans to the park. Before the game, the Brewers players formed a line at home plate and marched to the flag pole in left field. Once there, they conducted an impressive military drill using their bats instead of rifles. The men stood at attention while the band played "The Star-Spangled Banner." Milwaukee mayor Daniel Hoan threw out the first pitch and the umpire yelled, "Play ball!"[13]

Danny Shay gave John "Red" Shackelford the ball to start the game. Shackelford did not disappoint the home crowd. He allowed seven hits but no runs and the Brewers won, 4–0. The Brewers and Saints played again the next afternoon in very miserable conditions. Manager Shay stated, "In all my years of baseball I doubt whether I saw a colder game than this one."[14] Marv Goodwin did the job this time, with relief help from Bill Sherdel. They surrendered a combined eight hits and fashioned a 6–4 victory. The final game of the series was cancelled due to the frigid weather. The Milwaukee Brewers were undefeated and in first place on April 13.

During the cold-weather delay, Shay improved his pitching staff. He purchased Dickie Kerr from the St. Louis Browns organization. Kerr was twenty-three years old and a southpaw like Sherdel. Kerr had pitched well during spring training but the Browns already had three excellent left-handers. Like Sherdel, he had begun in the minors at age nineteen. He had an outstanding career. In the previous four seasons, he had won nineteen, twenty-two, twenty-one, and twenty-four games at different class levels.[15] This year in

Milwaukee, Kerr, along with Marvin Goodwin and Bill Sherdel, would become the Brewers' "Big Three."

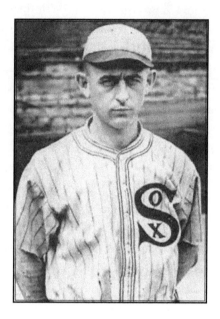

Brewers pitcher Dickie Kerr
—Coulson collection

By the end of April, Milwaukee had dropped to fourth place and was headed to play the first-place Indians in Indianapolis. Shay's club won the first game, but could not gain any momentum, and lost the final two games of the series. The Wisconsin club had now slumped down into fifth.

Sherdel, Goodwin, Kerr, McHenry, and the other Milwaukee Brewers spent the evening in Indianapolis licking their wounds and preparing for the trip to Louisville the next morning. They had no idea how their world would change in a few hours. Events would occur at the Hotel English Café in downtown Indianapolis that would affect several people's lives forever, including Brewers' manager Danny Shay.

Normally, the team would travel immediately after the last game in a series and arrive at the next city that same evening. This time, Brewers' secretary Louis Nahin asked manager Shay when he wanted to travel and Shay said he would spend the night in Indianapolis and take the morning train to Louisville. Nahin would feel partially responsible for that decision's outcome.[16] To understand what happened next, it is important to learn more about manager Shay. Danny Shay was a widower with two small children. His wife had died in an auto accident about three years before. He was known for his fiery temper. He was also known for his hard drinking. Owner Timme had even added a non-drinking clause to Shay's contract, although it was never exercised. There were two different stories about what happened. This much was known for sure. On the evening of May 3, Danny Shay stopped for a manicure with Mrs. Gertrude Anderson. Mrs. Anderson was already divorced twice and lived with her mother. Shay invited the manicurist to have dinner with him at the Hotel English Café. Mrs. Anderson accepted and arrived at the restaurant before Mr. Shay. Shay joined her at the table several minutes later. A thirty-year-old African-American waiter named Clarence Euel waited on the couple. During the meal, Shay and Euel argued about the amount of sugar that was in the bowl at their table. Shay became angry when Euel brought two more sugar bowls and placed them on the table. Euel walked away and Shay called him back to serve him and place three lumps of sugar in Shay's drink. Euel did this, and a heated conversation ensued. Shay arose and shot Euel in the abdomen. Later in the evening, Euel died. The police arrested Danny Shay and placed him in the county jail. Shay's friends, including managers Jack Hendricks of Indianapolis and Mike Kelley of St. Paul, tried unsuccessfully to secure Shay's release. Shay was charged with second-degree murder. He would remain in jail without bail for over seven months until his trial could be held in November.[17]

Though their thoughts were with their manager, the Milwaukee players needed to continue with their baseball schedule. Unlike many other owners, A. F. Timme was not having attendance problems. The Brewers were averaging 1,200 fans for weekday games, 2,000 fans for Saturday contests, and 7,000–8,000 fans for Sunday games.[18] More pressing was the need to pay attention to management. Timme named Billy Doyle interim manager until the team could return from its road trip. Doyle was the scout who had signed Bill Sherdel to a Brewers' contract. The thirty-five-year-old had played ball in the Texas League and had managed in the Texas and Ohio State leagues. Since 1910, Doyle had worked as a scout for several clubs.[19] He was very good at his job and was considered one of the best scouts in the country.

The Brewers won Billy Doyle's first game over Louisville, with Dickie Kerr knocking in the winning runs in the eighth. They evened the team's record, and the Brewers jumped back to fourth place. The next day was a doubleheader. Milwaukee lost both games. In the first encounter, Marv Goodwin pitched a great game only to lose, 2–0. He allowed only five hits, but the Brewers provided no run support. In the second contest, Bill Sherdel was hit hard. They lost, 6–0, again with no support.

Sherdel's next outing went better, and he allowed only two Columbus runs in eight innings. But the Brewers still lost, 3–2. At this point, none of the Brewers' "Big Three" were doing very well. Billy Doyle's managerial record—1–4—was no better, and the team batting average was a horrendous .207.

Owner Timme knew it was time for a new manager. He announced that William "Bill" Friel would fill the post and that Doyle would return to scouting. Friel was a forty-one-year-old Pennsylvanian. Like many of his contemporaries, his baseball career had been nomadic. He had bounced around the minors from 1895 to 1900. His big-league career had spanned three seasons and 283 games. Friel returned to the minors and played nine seasons with Columbus. He began managing the last three years there and then continued by leading St. Paul for two campaigns. Friel was well liked in Milwaukee. He had also served the past two years as an American Association umpire.[20] With his varied baseball career, he seemed an ideal choice to lead Bill Sherdel and the Brewers.

In Friel's first managerial appearance, the Brewers lost 5–1 to Hall-of-Fame pitcher Mordecai "Three Finger" Brown and the Columbus Senators. The next game was rained out, and Friel took the opportunity to give his boys a lengthy batting practice. He also announced changes to the batting order to improve the hitting and make the team his own.[21]

The Brewers played an unusual game with Indianapolis on May 16. Milwaukee came up in the bottom of the seventh inning behind, 4–0. Suddenly the Brewers' bats exploded: four, five, six, seven, eight, nine, ten runs. Friel's club won, 10–7. Interestingly, the Brewers only had six hits for the entire game and four of them were in the ten-run seventh.[22] As for Sherdel, his early 1917 record was misleading. He was continuing to study the batters and was working on his pitch selection and location. The results would improve as the season continued.

"It looks as though the club needed a couple of experienced boxmen [pitchers]," Manning Vaughan offered, of the Brewers' current team. "The youngsters on the club are promising kids, but two high-class flingers of major-league experience would help a lot and also assist the youngsters over the rough spots. Barring the pitching staff, Bill Friel has a fine-looking ball club, and if two more experienced boxmen are landed, the team will stack up with the best in the league."[23] Vaughan's analysis was probably very accurate. The youngsters—Goodwin, Sherdel, and Kerr—could have benefitted from working with an experienced staff.

Young Austin McHenry was hitting very well. After one powerhouse game where he hit a triple and a home run, Vaughan wrote, "McHenry looks better every time he goes to bat, and if he keeps pulling many more of his [Happy] Felsch-like drives the scouts will be giving him the O. O. [once over] before the season is much older."[24]

On June 10, Sherdel lost a twelve-inning heartbreaker to Indianapolis, 2–1. He surrendered ten hits but only two runs. George Kiick from Hanover attended the game and visited with him. Kiick was a member of the 45th US Infantry stationed at Fort Benjamin Harrison, Indiana. The local paper remarked, "Incidentally, the Indians had a lot of trouble with 'Lefty' Scherdel [sic]. The kid kept them from getting around until the ninth." Sherdel did get his customary hit at bat.[25] St. Louis Cardinals' president Branch Rickey was also watching that game, in town to see Marv Goodwin. Sherdel had started poorly that season and had just lost his tenth straight game. Unbeknownst to him, this was to have been his last day with the Brewers. Owner Timme intended to sell Sherdel to the Little Rock club. But Rickey saw something in the pitcher's mound work that impressed him. He offered Timme the same amount of money that Little Rock would pay, provided that Timme allow Sherdel to remain with the Brewers. Luckily, Timme agreed.[26]

Rickey said, "Sherdel is only nineteen years old [actually twenty] and is serving his first season in class AA baseball. He has a great cross-fire delivery, and while I do not think he is ready for the majors, I am going to watch his work for the remainder of the season very closely as I think he is going to develop into a great pitcher."[27] How right Mr. Rickey would prove to be.

Most people are not familiar with the term "cross-fire delivery." Using left-handed Bill Sherdel as an example, he would place his foot on the far-left part of the pitching rubber. Instead of stepping toward home plate in his delivery, Bill would step toward the first-base dugout and then deliver the pitch across his body to the batter, like a current submarine delivery. The cross-fire delivery was very uncomfortable for the batter. Bill Sherdel had added it to his pitching arsenal of a fast ball and curve.

Sherdel next pitched a complete-game four-hit win over St. Paul. Major-league scouts from the Cubs, Cardinals, Browns, and Giants were watching Marv Goodwin at that June 16 game. Luckily for Sherdel, the scouts also had their eyes on him. By late June, he had improved his record to 5–7. The Brewers ended June in sixth place. Despite a few hitting outbursts, the team was only batting a composite .238, the second worst in the league.[28]

Sherdel's good friend Marv Goodwin
—*Milwaukee Sentinel*, June 28, 1917

Still, there was some good news for the club. Timme announced that Marvin Goodwin had been traded to the St. Louis Cardinals for three players worth approximately $14,000. Goodwin would remain with the club for two more weeks and would leave with a record of eight wins and nine losses.

That was probably a good move for the Milwaukee owner. Timme thought there were risks with Goodwin. The national draft of soldiers was going to happen, and since Goodwin had no dependents, he would surely leave the club anyway. Timme could have taken cash for Marvin, but he preferred to improve the team with better players. The Cardinals sent catcher Patrick "Paddy" Livingston and two other players to the Brewers for Goodwin.[29]

Milwaukee continued to play horribly through the first twenty days of July. Manning Vaughan remarked sarcastically, "The team is evidently awaiting the draft or a German invasion. It is absolutely without pep and shows as much fight as a flock of mummies. Furthermore, it lacks class. Outside of that and a hundred other shortcomings, the team is a fairly good one."[30]

Owner Timme knew he needed to make another managerial change before the 1917 season was lost. He hated to remove Bill Friel, whom he considered one of the finest fellows he had ever known, but he felt Friel had "lost the old pep." At last, he announced that newly arrived "Paddy" Livingston would become the skipper. "Paddy" had major-league experience with four clubs, although he had played in only 206 games. His biggest strength was probably his experience with Connie Mack and the Philadelphia A's system. The Milwaukee fans remembered Livingston from the four years he spent with Indianapolis. In 1917, Cardinals' manager Miller Huggins had signed "Paddy" more as a coach than as a catcher, and he was behind the mask for only seven games prior to the trade.[31] Livingston would now get a chance to show what he could do.

Bill Sherdel, meanwhile, was using his difficult experiences to learn and evolve into a successful American Association hurler. On July 21, Sherdel beat the Columbus Senators, 4–3. He would later say that his initial poor showing was due to the lack of a good catching partner. When "Paddy" arrived and took charge of his handling, Sherdel's performance greatly improved.

Marv Goodwin was ready for the majors. *The Record Herald* praised Goodwin: "Slabman Marvin Goodwin reported to the St. Louis Nationals Sunday, July 15. Goodwin holds several records. While with the Mountaineers he went thirty-eight innings scoreless. He has been with the Milwaukee Brewers and reading the scores of the games he pitched, his great work stands out. He is in the habit of allowing but three or near that number of hits a game."[32]

On July 23, Marvin Goodwin took the mound for the Cardinals for the first time. He pitched six innings, allowed eight hits, and gained no decision against Brooklyn. The next day, St. Louis purchased Goodwin's old mound mate, Bill Sherdel. Rickey sent scout "Pop" Kelchner to make the deal. Young Sherdel would finally fulfill his dream to become a major leaguer—but first he needed to finish the American Association season and prove that the Cardinals had not made a mistake.

The *Milwaukee Dispatch* wrote this about the sale:

> The St. Louis Cardinals like the looks of Milwaukee youngsters. They took another pitcher on Monday, this time for cash. Lefty Scherdel [sic], the pride of Hanover, Pa., will wear a Mound City [St. Louis] uniform next spring, providing he is able to hold his own against the American Association batters for the remainder of the season. He will remain here until the A. A. schedule is played out.
>
> Al Timme sold the twirler to the Cards for cash, with a string attached. Scherdel [sic] must deliver the goods for Milwaukee if he is to go up.
>
> Timme did not state the amount and did not say anything on which to hitch an estimate. However, it is a pretty good bundle of kale [money]. Branch Rickey looked over Scherdel [sic] while he was lamping Goodwin, and is sweet on the southpaw youngster.[33]

Sherdel took the ball on July 27 and tossed a six-hit victory over Indianapolis. He also added two hits to his own cause. On July 31, he added another win. This time, he bested Minneapolis. He led the Brewers' pitching staff with an 8–12 record, while Dickie Kerr's record was 7–13. Sherdel won again on August 2. He hurled an eight-hit victory over Kansas City and didn't allow a run after the fifth inning. However, that was not the source of his pride that day. All pitchers loved to brag about their hitting. It had been that way ever since the first pitcher batted a ball into a cow pasture. On this day, "Kid" Sherdel had something to brag about. He belted two home runs. The *Kansas City Star* said, "Lefty Scherdel [sic], aside from pitching good ball, kept his mates in the running with his hitting, by driving two over the right field barrier for home runs. It is the first time that a pitcher has hit two circuit clouts in one game at Association Park. The hurler's clouts, however, came both times with the bases bare."[34]

The Brewers were hitting much better. Sherdel and the other Milwaukee twirlers were benefitting. Bob Bescher's .324 average was fifth best in the league. Austin McHenry was sent down to Peoria for more seasoning. The club felt he was one of their most promising prospects, but that he needed some more experience. His stay in Peoria would last only a few weeks. Timme would soon recall McHenry to replace an ailing Bescher.

Marv Goodwin continued to improve against National League hitting. He defeated John McGraw and the New York Giants, allowing only three scattered hits.

Bill Sherdel was adding win after win to his American Association totals. By the end of August, he had racked up ten straight victories in the games he had started. The Brewers team was also doing much better under the tutelage of manager Livingston. Milwaukee had won fourteen of their last twenty games and was fighting Kansas City for fifth place. Sherdel's record was 15–12 and he was batting .236. The team batting average had jumped to .252, fourth best in the league.[35]

At the beginning of September, Sherdel sustained a loss to St. Paul, 7–2, and his winning streak came to an end. He came right back the next day, though, with a 10–1 victory over the Saints. His teammates helped with fourteen hits. And Sherdel added another win with a five-hit victory over Minneapolis. The Brewers team was also red hot. In the last thirty-two games, Milwaukee was 21–11 and solidly in fifth place.

The Brewers' 1917 home season ended with a double-header against Minneapolis. Between the games, the players did their last military drill of the season. The fans applauded. In the stands, there were about 200 local young men scheduled to leave for the armed forces in a few days. A small band entertained the crowd with military songs. The team completed the happy day by winning the season's final two games at Athletic Park. The *Milwaukee Sentinel* added that the Brewers could go on the road "knowing that they displayed the best brand of baseball in the past month that a Milwaukee team has ever shown."[36]

When the American Association season ended in mid-September, the Milwaukee Brewers were in fifth place in the eight-team league. After "Paddy"

Livingston arrived, the team greatly improved.[37] Twenty-one-year-old Austin McHenry batted .233 with four home runs in 102 games. McHenry would also arrive with the Cardinals in 1918.

For his part, Sherdel compiled nineteen wins with sixteen losses in 262 innings. More importantly, he learned and improved as the season progressed. Over the final seven weeks of the season with a second-division club, Sherdel gained fourteen victories, lost only five games, and had one no-decision. In those last twenty games, he was removed only twice, and one of those he went in to stall until another hurler could warm up. His control was outstanding. In two games, he walked no one and in six others he gave only one free pass. A *St. Louis Star* writer previewed Sherdel for the Cardinals' fans:

> Sherdell [sic] has a fast ball that 'hops' and a nice change of pace. He does not trifle with spitters, shine balls, mud balls, nor any other form of delivery that is likely to be taboo in the near future.
>
> Sherdell's [sic] only handicap is his lack of size, but [it] . . . will not prevent . . . Rickey from giving him a fair trial, especially as he is said to be a modest, energetic, intelligent young man of good habits, and being only twenty years of age will not be eligible for the draft until the 1918 season is over.[38]

After the Brewers' season ended, the *Cleveland Press* added this thought about Bill Sherdel: "Rickey is satisfied that he picked up a coming star."[39]

Dickie Kerr, the only Brewers' pitcher to throw more innings than Sherdel, finished with fourteen wins and nineteen losses in 277 innings. He would eventually reach the majors with the notorious 1919 Chicago White Sox, the team accused of throwing the World Series. Kerr was a rookie that year, and would not be involved in any wrongdoing. He would pitch four seasons for the Sox and win twenty-one games in 1920 and nineteen games in 1921.

Sherdel's old Blue Ridge partner Marv Goodwin continued to pitch well for the Cardinals. In fourteen games and eighty-five innings, he finished with a 6–4 record for the Cards. Sherdel, Goodwin, and McHenry would be teammates again on the 1918 St. Louis club.

After the National League season ended, Cardinals' manager Miller Huggins left to lead the New York Yankees. "Paddy" Livingston was among the rumored replacements for Huggins, but he didn't get the job. Instead, he returned to his home in Cleveland and worked for a ship-building firm. "Paddy" did not want to manage again. His baseball days had ended.[40]

The Danny Shay murder trial finally took place in November. The defense attorney claimed that Clarence Euel was the antagonist and that Shay had feared for his life. Shay pleaded not guilty because, he said, he had shot Euel in self-defense. The prosecutor, meanwhile, tried to prove that Shay had been drinking too much, that he took unprovoked offense to Euel and, while in a fit of rage, had shot the innocent waiter. Unfortunately, the witnesses told different stories about what had happened that night. The trial was also complicated by racial issues. Three ballots were needed before the jury could determine a verdict. In the end, the jury found Danny Shay not guilty of second-degree murder and released him. Shay quickly headed south for a hunting trip before announcing any future baseball plans. Was justice blind? Probably.

Shay would never manage again. He would spend some time scouting, but would end his relationship with baseball after several years. Eventually, he would suffer a paralyzing stroke that would leave his right arm and side useless. Sadly, fifty-one-year-old Danny Shay would shoot himself and die in a Kansas City hotel room in 1927.[41]

THE BIG SHOW

CHAPTER SEVEN

The city of St. Louis, Missouri, was founded in 1764 by French fur traders. It became part of the United States in 1803, when President James Madison acquired the land from France in the Louisiana Purchase. With that, St. Louis became the capital and gateway to this new US territory. It was called the "Mound City" because it was built on bluffs or embankments several hundred feet above the Mississippi River. The city's population would reach almost three-quarters of a million people by 1920. St. Louis was and would remain to this day a major United States port city built on the western bank of the Mississippi River.

Professional baseball began in St. Louis in 1875, when the St. Louis Brown Stockings joined the National Association League. People wondered if the stockings were colored brown originally or were brown from all the tobacco juice spit on them.[1] The National Association ended after 1875 and its successor, the National League, began. The Brown Stockings lasted two years and then folded. St. Louis baseball fans supported independent ball for several years until 1881, when local entrepreneur Chris von der Ahe paid $1,800 for the team and made it professional, again. Von der Ahe named the team the Browns, and leased a ballpark on Grand Avenue for their home games.[2]

The new Browns' owner was an interesting character. "Von der Ahe was an egoist who saw himself as the leader of any enterprise in which he was involved. He dressed like a European nobleman, sporting a flamboyant vest, gleaming top hat, and brilliant shoes. He had a broad-beamed face, in the middle of which protruded a 'broad, purpling, mottled, and bulbous' nose. On his lower lip he wore tiny whiskers, 'like something he had missed while shaving.'"[3]

Von der Ahe, who owned a bar and a meat market, gradually acquired more property and built a rooming house, a grocery store, and a saloon. The beer baron noticed that patrons would fill his saloon and then disappear, only to return several hours later. He realized his patrons were going to the Browns' games. If he could sell his beer in the park during the game, he reasoned, he could make more money. Von der Ahe envisioned his team as an extension of his flourishing business empire. He wanted to use the ballpark and the fans to increase his beer sales.[4] His idea created a problem. The selling of beer in National League ballparks was prohibited by Albert Spalding, the owner of the Chicago White Stockings and the league's unquestioned leader. So, von der Ahe joined several other owners expelled from the league because of beer sales and formed a new professional league they named the American Association. Beer could be sold in that league.[5] It is important to note that von der Ahe's American Association was a different league from the 1917 American Association class AA league that included Bill Sherdel and the Milwaukee Brewers.

Meanwhile, the city of St. Louis continued to grow. Besides beer, the municipality became the world's greatest manufacturer of chewing tobacco by 1885. It also ranked second to Chicago as a railway center.[6]

In December 1891, the American Association and the National League merged. The team owners in both leagues realized that their survival depended upon eliminating the outrageous practice of raiding players. The Browns joined the surviving National League. Von der Ahe thought that, because he was a successful businessman, he could also manage his baseball team. Unfortunately, he became the laughing stock of the league. The National League owners stripped him of his franchise because of unpaid debts in 1899, and the team was sold to Frank and Stanley Robison, owners of the Cleveland streetcar line. The Robisons changed the St. Louis uniforms, including the brown stockings. The new stockings would be red. A *St. Louis Republic* reporter would give the team a new nickname: the Cardinals.[7]

Twenty-one-year-old Bill Sherdel had fulfilled his baseball dream. He was now the property of the St. Louis Cardinals of the National League. Sherdel had left one brewery capital—Milwaukee—for another. He had also traded in one large German population for another. Due to the immigration of hundreds of thousands of Germans, the beer industry had started to flourish in St. Louis in 1849. In fact, some of the largest breweries got their start there. The most well-known beer-maker began in 1859 when German immigrants Eberhard Anheuser and Adolphus Busch started Anheuser-Busch. By the end of the 1870s, the maker of Budweiser had become one of the largest breweries in the Midwest and, a few years later, Anheuser-Busch was recognized as one of the largest breweries in the world. By the 1890s, St. Louis was second to only New York in beer sales.[8]

Bill Sherdel would become a St. Louis Cardinal at the beginning of a great baseball dynasty and, importantly, would participate in perpetuating that development. He would be closely associated with one of the greatest innovators baseball had ever known, Wesley Branch Rickey. One writer described Rickey as "the most brilliant strategist in the history of baseball."[9] Rickey was celebrated for being a great judge of talent. The famous sportswriter Jim Murray wrote, "He could recognize a great player from the window of a moving train."[10] Later, Rickey would be known as the man who integrated baseball.

Branch Rickey was born the second child to Frank and Emily Rickey on December 20, 1881. His parents were originally Baptists, but had gravitated to Methodism. Their son was given the first name Wesley in honor of John Wesley, the founder of the Methodist religion. As a child, Rickey played baseball. He was a left-handed hitter with average ability, but he excelled in his love and enthusiasm for the game. After graduating as an average student, he became a grammar-school teacher. He rode his bicycle eighteen miles from home to school and then back again at the end of each school day. His early adult life could be compared to Abe Lincoln's. After teaching all day, he would study all night by kerosene light. In the spring of 1901, Rickey took the entrance exam for Ohio Wesleyan Preparatory School and passed. Outside of school, he waited on tables in a local restaurant and tried out for the Ohio Wesleyan baseball team. He became the team's top catcher. Rickey also loved football and became an above-average halfback on the school's team.

Branch became a professional baseball player in 1905. He spent two years with the Browns as a catcher. In 1907, manager of the New York Highlanders Clark Griffith acquired Rickey to catch his star knuckleballer Jack Chesbro. When Rickey arrived in New York, he discovered he had a sore arm. In a June

28 game, the Senators stole a record thirteen bases against catcher Rickey. He caught one more game and then left to study law at the Ohio State University and the University of Michigan.

Rickey contracted tuberculosis in April 1909, and remained at a New York sanitarium until August. While in law school, he coached baseball at the University of Michigan and one of his outstanding players was George Sisler. After passing the bar exam, Rickey practiced law in Boise, Idaho. His law office failed and he joined owner Robert Hedges of the St. Louis Browns as executive assistant in 1913. Later that year, Rickey became the Browns' manager, and remained there through the 1914 and 1915 seasons. His teams finished under .500. He signed his Michigan college star George Sisler to a contract. Sisler would become one of the greatest first basemen and hitters in the history of the game.[11]

While with the Browns, the innovative Rickey began to take the team to a milder climate for spring training and established the first all-purpose training-camp facility. One of his truly unique ideas was the use of pitching strings. Rickey used two poles and placed one on each side of home plate. He connected them with two horizontal cords across the front edge of the plate, at average knee and shoulder height. Next, he connected additional vertical cords from the lower to upper cords. These vertical cords were placed seventeen inches apart to match the edges of the plate. With this innovation, Rickey had essentially created a stringed strike zone. The pitcher would then pitch from the rubber to the catcher located behind the strings. It was the pitcher's objective to throw the ball within the strings and, if possible, to hit the strings (the corners of the plate). This pitching aid would be used for years.[12]

Unfortunately for the Browns, Robert Hedges sold the franchise to abrasive and aggressive Philip Ball in 1916. The new owner inherited Rickey's contract, but Ball and Rickey could not tolerate each other. Their personalities were opposite. In addition, Ball was a heavy drinker and Rickey abhorred alcohol. The new owner removed Rickey as manager but retained him as business manager.[13]

Meanwhile, the Cardinals' owners, the Robison brothers, passed away, and their niece Mrs. Helene Britton inherited the Cardinals. By 1916, Mrs. Britton was in the midst of a divorce and needed to sell the team. World War I was raging in Europe, the Cardinals were in last place, and the ballpark seats were empty. The asking price was $375,000 with a $75,000 down payment. It was a reasonable price—but no buyers were found. There was a real concern that the team would be sold to someone who would move it from St. Louis. James Jones, the attorney for Mrs. Britton, found a local civic group of fans to buy the team and keep it in St. Louis.[14] The group sold shares for $25 each. A local insurance executive came up with a novel idea. If someone bought $50 in shares, the investor would get one free Knot-Hole season ticket. The Knot-Hole ticket would allow a deserving underprivileged child to attend the games for free and sit in a special section of the bleachers reserved for children. This new group of young bleacher fans would become known as the Knot-Hole Gang. The name originated with the children that would stand outside the ballpark, remove the knot holes in the surrounding wooden fences, and watch the games for free. Unfortunately, the wealthy patrons purchased the shares and gave the Knot-Hole tickets to their own children. The Knot-Hole campaign netted $50,000—less than the $75,000 down payment. Mrs. Britton accepted the amount and the St. Louis Cardinals now belonged to the fans as stockholders.[15]

Now Jones needed to find a club president. At the time, he had a qualified manager in Miller Huggins, but he needed someone to run the organization. Lawyer Jones assembled seven St. Louis sportswriters and editors in his office and asked each one to recommend a qualified candidate to run the club. All seven picked Branch Rickey, the business manager of the Browns. Jones offered Rickey the job and he accepted without hesitation. In turn, Rickey approached Phil Ball, who was very happy to be rid of Rickey and wished him well. Later, after discussing the loss of Rickey with his advisors, Ball changed his tune on his old colleague. But Rickey had already accepted the Cardinals' top job. Ball sued.[16] The courts decided in the Cardinals' favor, and Wesley Branch Rickey began his long, fruitful relationship with the St. Louis Cardinals in 1917—one year before Bill Sherdel's arrival. Branch Rickey was named club president and general manager.

By age thirty-six, Rickey had been a grammar-school teacher, a college baseball and football player, a college baseball and football coach, an athletic director, a professional baseball player and manager, a lawyer, and a business manager. Throughout his life, he had one strict rule: he would not participate in baseball activities on Sundays. He had made that promise to his very religious parents.

One of the first items Rickey addressed was the Knot-Hole Gang. Author Peter Golenbock described what happened. "Rickey convinced the stockholders to sign over their rights to the free tickets to the club. Rickey then contacted nine or ten large organizations serving St. Louis youth and had them appoint adult Knothole [sic] Gang committee members to select and invite boys between the ages of ten and sixteen to attend Cardinals games for free. The committee agreed on two rules for attendance: (1) No boy could attend without his parents' consent; (2) No boy could skip school to attend."[17] Rickey's ingenious plan involving the St. Louis youth created many new lifelong Cardinals fans.

The Cardinals finished 1917 in third place—a big improvement from seventh in 1916. Unfortunately, Miller Huggins left St. Louis to become the new manager of the Yankees, and Rickey needed to find a Cardinals' skipper. He focused on Jack Hendricks, the manager of the Indianapolis Indians team in the American Association. Hendricks was under contract to Indians' owner James McGill. He and Rickey met at a minor-league meeting in Louisville, and McGill asked for $15,000 to release Hendricks from his contract. Rickey, offended by this demand, refused to negotiate, even as McGill's price dropped to $10,000 and then $5,000. In an early example of Rickey's negotiating skills, he walked away and dismissed Hendricks as a viable option for the Cardinals. Somehow, however, Hendricks secured his release from McGill and approached Rickey, stating that he was now free to sign a contract. Rickey met with Hendricks and a deal was swiftly struck. Details were not released, but it was thought that the deal may have been like Miller Huggins's contract. Huggins had been offered $10,000 plus a share of the profits over $25,000.

John "Jack" Hendricks was the most coveted minor-league manager in professional baseball. Owners had tried for several years to lure him to the majors. Only Branch Rickey could make it happen. After signing his contract, Hendricks said, "I have achieved a life-long ambition. That is, to become a major-league manager. I cannot say yet what my prospects are for next year, but I do say that the Cardinals will give every team in the league a fight. I'm not the sort of a manager that wins pennants in December and finishes in the second division in October."[18]

Hendricks was born in Joliet, Illinois, on April 9, 1875, but spent most of his childhood in his adopted hometown of Chicago. After graduating from high school, he attended law school at Northwestern. Like Branch Rickey, he earned a law degree and became a lawyer. He enjoyed playing semi-pro baseball and attended a tryout with the New York Giants. The Giants signed him as an outfielder and sent him to Columbus for more seasoning in 1902. The following year, he played for Spokane, until he received a tryout with Washington. Washington kept him through the next season, but he was just not good enough to remain a major-league player.

Hendricks began a successful career as a minor-league manager. His specialty seemed to be inheriting a last-place team, improving it, and finishing in the top division. In twelve years of minor-league managing, he had never finished below third place. He had won five pennants, and finished second three times and third four more. Hendricks had also proven he could win at various minor-league levels from class B to AA. He had won the recent 1917 American Association title with Indianapolis.[19]

Manager Jack Hendricks
—*St. Louis Post-Dispatch*, April 6, 1918

Bill Sherdel had one advantage. His new manager Hendricks was very familiar with him from the 1917 American Association. Clarence Lloyd, a *St. Louis Star* writer, asked Hendricks about the young pitcher. "Sherdell [sic] was the most improved pitcher in the league at the end of the season. He was just a 'green' youngster when he joined the Brewers in the spring. But on each appearance against us you could see he was grasping the real idea of pitching."[20] Several days later, Lloyd spoke with Hendricks about Sherdel again. "He has the necessary qualifications and I will be surprised if he fails to make the grade. . . . He came with a rush during the one year he was in that [American Association] league."[21]

Young Sherdel sent in his 1918 contract and attached a note. He wrote Mr. Rickey that he was "glad for the opportunity of affiliating himself with the firm of Rickey and Hendricks," and he expressed the belief that he would make good in the big leagues. Rickey admired Sherdel's confidence.[22]

One pitcher that would not be in the Cardinals' plans for 1918 was Sherdel's old friend Marvin Goodwin. The "Ironman" enlisted in the Army Aviation Corps. But Sherdel would see two other familiar faces when camp started. Pitcher Earl Howard of Everett, Pennsylvania, had hurled for three years in the Blue Ridge League, and outfielder Cliff Heathcote was signed off the Penn State campus.

Like Goodwin and Sherdel, Howard had been an early star in the Blue Ridge League. He'd spent his first Blue Ridge season in Gettysburg, where he won ten games and lost fourteen with a next-to-last-place team. He then moved on to Hagerstown for the 1916 and 1917 campaigns. His performance in 1916 paralleled Goodwin's in Martinsburg. Both pitchers threw no-hitters and hurled double-headers and won. Howard finished 1916 with eighteen victories, and his 1917 season was even better. He won twelve straight, and finished with twenty-five wins and 163 strikeouts to lead all Blue Ridge pitchers. He gained the notice of Branch Rickey and became the third ex-Blue Ridge Leaguer to sign with the Cardinals.

Heathcote grew up near Hanover in Glen Rock, Pennsylvania. Of him, a *St. Louis Star* reporter wrote glowingly:

> Clifton E. Heathcote, Glen Rock, Pa., considered the greatest college outfielder in the East, has been signed by the St. Louis Cardinals. . . . Heathcote is a natural hitter and has a 'follow up' that shoots the ball on a straight line. Those who have seen him work say

Heathcote seldom hits a fly ball and possesses so sure and accurate an eye that he seldom strikes out. His hits have not been long and he is by no means a slugger. Low and on a line are most of his drives.

Pegging is one of Heathcote's best tricks. His arm is true and his aim accurate. At York, he picked runners down with an ease that attracted lots of attention.

It is understood that practically every major-league club had scouts after the Penn State phenom. The fact that Branch Rickey has developed many college stars, it is said, led Heathcote to sign with the St. Louis club.[23]

The Cardinals had two veteran catchers in "Pancho" Snyder and Mike Gonzales. Sherdel was really looking forward to working with these two backstops. He had improved greatly over the previous year when the Brewers brought veteran catcher Livingston on board. Hendricks also added old veteran catcher and scout Joe Sugden to his staff to work with his many young hurlers. Sugden had given Sherdel a tryout in Hanover. When people met him, they were drawn to his hands. His fingers had been broken so many times that they stuck out in all directions like the spokes of a wheel.

Once again, twenty-one-year-old William Sherdel said goodbye to his family and many friends and boarded a train—this time for St. Louis—on March 12. When he arrived, he joined Heathcote, Howard, and eleven others, plus manager Hendricks, and boarded another train for San Antonio, Texas, home of the Cardinals' 1918 spring training camp. The train would arrive on the evening of March 15, so that the players could get a good night's sleep in their new temporary home, the Hot Wells Hotel. Other players would meet them in Texas. Approximately forty candidates would compete for the Cardinals' roster. Practice was scheduled to begin the next morning. The National League had a rule that no team could begin practice before March 15 and that no team could practice more than thirty days at a training site. Players and managers were not happy with this restriction. Because the Cardinals always played an exhibition series with the Browns in St. Louis before the season started, it meant that the Cardinals only had twenty days to train and work out in the warm Texas sunshine.

Jack Hendricks announced his training camp regimen. There would be two workouts daily. Players would be required to report to the ballpark at 9:30 a.m. They would practice until noon, then break for lunch. The team would begin again at 2:00, and finish about 5:30. Rickey also scheduled over twenty exhibition games throughout Texas.[24]

The camp that year included more rookies than veterans, but there were already four experienced starting pitchers—Bill Doak, Leon "Red" Ames, Gene Packard, and Lee Meadows. Packard was the only left-hander. That meant Sherdel would probably need to start the season as a reliever or a spot starter.

The St. Louis Cardinals had one legitimate superstar in Texan Rogers Hornsby. Hornsby was the same age as Sherdel, but was starting his fourth year with the Cards. He had joined the team before Rickey arrived. Hornsby was already a great hitter and would be considered one of the greatest ever by the time he retired. He was also deemed a "different" character. In his wonderful book *The Spirit of St. Louis,* Peter Golenbock described young Hornsby thus: "He was brash, outspoken, sure of his ability, and something of a loner. The veterans considered him strange in that he didn't drink, didn't smoke, and refused to go to the movies, insisting that movie going was injurious to a player's eyesight."[25] Rogers Hornsby and Bill Sherdel would become good friends based upon a shared respect for each other's abilities.

Rogers Hornsby in 1918 training camp
—Coulson collection

As training camp progressed, three young hurlers distinguished themselves with manager Hendricks. He liked Sherdel, Earl Howard, and Frank "Jakie" May, and felt that all three might make the club. Clarence Lloyd wrote, "Hendricks' claims that these three juveniles possess the stuff of which major league pitchers are made is borne out by catchers Joe Sugden, Frank Snyder, and Johnny Brock, who have been handling their shoots in the practice tilts in Texas."[26]

The Cardinals played exhibition games all across Texas, from Fort Worth to Houston, including several on army bases against camp teams. The players were impressed by one game at Kelly Aviation Field when the commanding officer sent a huge army truck to the hotel to pick up the entire team. Over 5,000 soldiers lined the ball field and, later, the players' necks hurt from watching all the airplanes flying overhead. Sherdel started, followed by Howard and Doak. The Cards beat the camp team, 19–2.

Henry J. Smith of New Oxford, Pennsylvania, was a flying cadet stationed in Houston. He sent the following letter home to his father, the editor of the local paper. It provided some insight into young Bill Sherdel.

> Well, "Dad," I saw and spoke with someone from dear, old "Pennsy," yesterday. And you can just bet your boots I was glad to be with someone from up thar! It all happened this way: I was taking it easy on my bunk, yesterday morning, reading the Houston paper when I noticed Scherdel's [sic] name in the St. Louis lineup playing Houston. Quicker than you could say "Jack Robinson," I called up the Rice Hotel in Houston, got Scherdel [sic] on the wire, and planned to meet him at one o'clock—which I did. We were certainly very glad to greet each other, so far away from home. Scherdel [sic] gave me the glad hand; introduced me to the St. Louis players; took me to the game; gave me a ball as a souvenir, and all in all showed some of that old-time "Pennsy" spirit, for which I was heartily glad. After the game, I had the Hanover boy take dinner with me at the Rice; then we went to a movie, and at 8 o'clock I bade him farewell to San Antonio. Scherdel [sic] seems to be a mighty good sort of chap. I have it from some of the St. Louisians that he is showing up well in spring training and seems destined for a successful season in the big league. Of course, we all wish him heaps o' success.[27]

The players liked manager Hendricks. Clarence Lloyd wrote, "Hendricks has won the loyalty and affection of every man in camp and without any apparent effort. It's just natural for him to be nice. His pleasing personality has instilled but one thought into the hearts of all the players and that thought is to produce a winning ball club." Certainly, Hendricks's personality and management style was very different than his predecessor, Miller Huggins. Hendricks was a "pal" to his players while Huggins was aloof and distant. Hendricks only had a few rules for the players: no smoking cigarettes while in uniform and be in your hotel rooms by midnight.[28]

Throughout spring training, Sherdel pitched very well when given the opportunity. Usually, he pitched three innings or relieved a starter in trouble. He showed great control, and allowed very few free passes. The Cardinals completed their spring training with a trip through Kansas, then traveled on to St. Louis for the annual spring series with the Browns in early April.

The series was a huge event in St. Louis. The city was split between Browns and Cardinals fans. It was the first opportunity for all of them to see their teams in action. The Cards' manager was very optimistic. "The Cardinals are fit and ready to make the fight. We are going into the series determined to win. . . . Two clubs in the National League may beat us to the wire, but I am positive I have a first division aggregation. The Giants and Cubs are the clubs we have to beat, the Giants because of their remarkable reserve strength and the Cubs because of their great pitching staff. Barring unforeseen accidents, we will finish ahead of the other clubs and we'll make the Giants know they've been in a battle."[29]

Leading baseball statistician Irvin Howe was not as optimistic about the Cardinals' chances in 1918. Howe picked the Cards to finish fourth. His top three included the Reds, Giants, and Pirates. He wrote, "It is said that Jack Hendricks has never managed a team that finished outside the first four, and if he gets into the top division this season, he will deserve a world of credit.

"With only a mediocre infield—from a fielding standpoint—and only two good outfielders, it is hard to believe that he can wedge his way in among the elect this year. His twirlers are not good enough. It will require more runs than the Cards can furnish to enable Ames, Doak, May, Meadows, Packard, and Sherdel to win much over half the time."[30]

Howe's assessment of the Cards had been accurate. Branch Rickey knew it, too. He picked up an experienced second baseman in a trade with the Phillies. He continued to search unsuccessfully for better players to improve his team. With players entering the service, there were not many quality replacements available. This lack of experienced bench depth would haunt the team all year.

The first test for the Cardinals came in their four-game series with the Browns. The Cards lost every game. In the second game, Sherdel pitched the sixth inning, giving up one run. It could have been worse, but Sherdel was saved by two sensational catches and a double play by Cliff Heathcote in right field. Heathcote had a great game. Offensively, he hit a triple and single, added a walk, and stole a base. Clarence Lloyd lamented, "The Cards have looked anything but the champions of last spring and last fall."[31] Browns fans rejoiced as the American League club swept their National League rivals.

Despite the losses to the hometown rivals, Cardinal fans remained optimistic about the April 16 season opener against the Chicago Cubs at Cardinal Field. Grover Cleveland Alexander was scheduled to start for the visitors. Many people thought this might be the last game for Alexander, since he had already signed to join the army at Camp Funston in Kansas.

With the country now at war, the opening-day celebration was more important than ever. The activities began with John Philip Sousa's Great Lakes Navy Band, whose performance was to aid the selling of liberty war bonds. The players paraded around the field and unfurled the new Cardinal flag, which included stars for each of the Cardinals now serving in the armed forces. The commandant of the local army post threw out the first pitch. All the well-known local singers joined the Knot-Hole Gang in singing patriotic songs. The official 1918 major-league season had begun.[32]

If one game could determine the outcome of a season, then the St. Louis Cardinals would win the pennant with this opening show. The locals pounded Alexander all over the field. Cardinal batters collected nine hits and only four were singles. The final score was 4–2, and the St. Louis club was now tied for first place, with only 130 more games to play. The weekday crowd numbered 8,000 and the patriotic fans subscribed to over $22,000 worth of liberty bonds to support the war effort.[33] Everyone was happy—except Cliff Heathcote, who was released to the minors. Despite his great game against the Browns, Heathcote just wasn't ready for major-league pitching, yet.

Bill Sherdel's first official major-league appearance occurred on April 22. He entered a game against the Pirates in the eighth inning. He surrendered two hits but no runs. The Cardinals lost, 5–1. Four days later, Sherdel again entered a game in relief. This time, Alexander was on the mound for the Cubs. This would truly be his last game. Private Alexander was scheduled to leave for Camp Funston after the game ended. In his final 1918 performance, he was pitching very well, allowing only two Hornsby hits into the ninth. The Cardinals tied the game and Sherdel took the mound. He surrendered a double and was quickly replaced. The Cards lost, 3–2. After the game, the club announced that Earl Howard was being sent to Milwaukee for more seasoning.

On April 28, manager Hendricks gave Sherdel his first starting assignment. He responded to the opportunity. He pitched a complete game victory over the Reds, and helped his own cause with a single through the infield to tie the game. He also connected for a double in the ninth, but rain began and the game was called. The contest reverted to the end of the eighth inning and Sherdel's double was erased. He gave up twelve hits including four doubles, but did not walk a batter. Tom Swope of the *St. Louis Star* wrote, "Sherdel pitched a masterful game. He was hit hard and often by the Reds, but not in the pinch."[34] A *St. Louis Post-Dispatch* reporter added, "He always managed to tighten up when hits meant runs. He had good control, not passing a batter. Sherdel showed plenty of stuff."[35]

Bill Sherdel with the 1918 Cardinals
—Sherdel family

The Cardinals ended the first month of the season in sixth place. The team was getting discouraged. Its bench was too weak to help in late inning pinch-hitting situations and this weakness was obvious. The fielding was also atrocious.

Sherdel continued to get plenty of opportunities to pitch in May. He worked mostly in relief, but did get three starts. He pitched well in them, winning the first and losing the second. In his final start of the month, he hurled a great game, but was outdueled by future Hall-of-Famer Burleigh Grimes of Brooklyn. Sherdel allowed just four hits, but Grimes gave up only two. In fact, Grimes faced only twenty-eight batters in the 1–0 contest. The only run scored in the eighth inning. Sherdel hit the first batter. The next Brooklyn batter sacrificed him to second. He then stole third on a very close call and scored on a sharp single to right. That was Sherdel's only mistake. Many fans thought the umpire missed the call at third, which could have kept the game tied. The Cardinals had already won the first three games of the series, but their short winning streak came to an end. That was only

Grimes's second win in two years. In 1917, the Brooklyn spit-baller had a horrible record of no wins and seventeen losses.

In mid-May, Provost Marshal General Enoch Crowder issued an order that would impact the major leagues. It stated that all men of draft age (twenty-one to thirty-one) who were employed in non-essential work must either fight or work by July 1. In this case, "work" meant work that was essential to the war effort. That edict hit the major leagues like a hammer. Of all professional sports, baseball would be the most impacted. Approximately 237 big league players—or 85% of the roster—would be affected. Only a few youngsters and old veterans would be excluded. That order would mean the end of the baseball season. The National League president tried to get a specific ruling for baseball, but no further definition was forthcoming. The league needed a test case brought before a draft board after July 1. Branch Rickey supported the war effort, no matter what the cost. He stated, "The provost marshal general says he will establish the status of baseball players when a specific case is presented to him. His ruling will ipso facto set a precedent that will determine the future of the game. I will await, abide, and heartily approve his ruling."[36]

William Henry Sherdel registered for the draft at the beginning of June. When he wasn't pitching for the Cardinals, the government listed him as having the "essential position" of farmer.

The Cardinals ended the month of May in seventh place. If they had won half of the games they lost by one run, the St. Louis club would be fighting for a first-division spot. The team was batting an anemic .215. The team's young star Rogers Hornsby had been in a terrible slump. Hendricks had benched Hornsby for playing miserably in the middle of May. Hornsby contended that he had an injury, saying, "For more than a week, I have been bothered by a strained ligament in my right leg. I can walk on it and run on it, too, but every now and then when I make a quick start or sudden move, it pains. I should have been on the bench several days. I realized though that the club was going poorly and that we are shy—far too shy—of substitute players. So I got in and tried my best of it. I have made a poor job of it." Asked about the team's poor performance, Hornsby said they hadn't been getting the breaks and that they needed some new players.[37]

Branch Rickey continued to search the country for exactly that. But the new government edict made his job much harder. He recalled Cliff Heathcote from Houston of the Texas League, but Rickey still needed another outfielder.

Sherdel, meanwhile, struggled at times as he learned about all the new batters. Of course, he would be doing better if he had a better team behind him. In a June 9 double-header, he faced the Giants in front of 20,000 screaming New York fans—his largest audience yet. He lost, 8–1, but scores can be deceptive. The *St. Louis Post-Dispatch* said: "Young Bill Sherdel faced the 20,000 crowd with all his usual confidence in the first game, and though beaten, he was not disgraced. A combination of hard-luck errors and poor judgment gave the Giants six runs in the fifth inning off the young southpaw, where clean fielding would have cut off all of them."[38]

Branch Rickey was doing all that he could to improve the club. Unfortunately, it was like trying to plug the dyke while other holes were opening. As he was signing new players, current players were being drafted. A total of six players had already disappeared. Rickey announced in mid-June that he had signed ten minor-league players for the club. The most notable name was outfielder Austin McHenry from Milwaukee. The other future teammates came from Little Rock, Indianapolis, and Houston. In the case of McHenry, Branch had to send three players to compensate the Brewers.

Sherdel's former teammate at Milwaukee and new teammate at St. Louis, Austin McHenry, was born on September 22, 1895, in Wrightsville, Ohio. He played baseball in high school, but it wasn't until he went to Billy Doyle's baseball school in 1914 that he really began to develop. The next year, nineteen-year-old McHenry signed a professional contract with Portsmouth in the class D Ohio State League. The *Portsmouth Daily Times* wrote, "It seemed that no one could hit it over his head and he was a genius on coming in for short line-drives over the infield. He had the uncanny intuition of playing for this and that batter and it was not long until manager Gableman made him a regular. From that day on, McHenry by his consistent playing began to make baseball history for himself." He was "gifted but raw." What he lacked in knowledge he made up for with hustle, eagerness, enthusiasm, and a determination to succeed.[39]

Manager Hendricks plugged these new players into his lineup, but they could not consistently compete with the well-financed clubs in New

York and Chicago. His frustration reached a peak in a game that Sherdel was pitching against the Chicago Cubs on June 25. Sherdel was handed the ball to begin the game. Everything proceeded well until the horrible fourth inning. In what seemed to be good strategy, Hendricks ordered Sherdel to walk Bill Killefer—a decent hitter—to load the bases and get to the pitcher. The Cubs then flashed a triple steal sign. The runner on third stole home during Sherdel's windup and the play so unnerved Bill that he walked the pitcher and the next batter hit a home run. A total of seven Cubs crossed the plate in that inning—all after two were out. It was apparent that Sherdel could not hold the Cubs and he asked to be removed from the game. Because Hendricks was carrying only eighteen players, he had no other pitcher to use and, sadly, Sherdel had to continue taking a beating. The final score was 14–0.

The St. Louis newspapers commented the next day. The *St. Louis Star* wrote, "Sherdel was the victim of the plan of carrying only a small number of players in the Tuesday engagement. It was apparent in the fourth that he [Sherdel] could not hold the Cubs, and the moment that [Max] Flack landed on him for four bases he should have been relieved. But Hendricks could do nothing. He didn't want to waste either Ames or Packard on a game that was lost, preferring to save them for the final game. . . . So there was nothing to do save permit Sherdel to stand out there and take a beating, and he did. The Cubs landed upon him with all the freedom and abandon that a club does in the hitting practice."[40] The *St. Louis Post-Dispatch* stated, "The St. Louis Cardinals were suffering from a malady similar to shell shock when they arose this morning. . . . Bill Sherdel was the most affected and he was an angry athlete. He asked Hendricks to remove him from the box in the horrible fourth inning, but Jack smiled grimly and kept him under fire. He sent another request in the sixth frame, when the locals scored five runs, and again he was refused.

"If Hendricks thought the experience would do his young hurler any good, none of the local experts agreed with him. It convinced everyone the St. Louis hurler can take punishment. There wasn't anything else to do but stand on the hill and dodge."[41]

Financing was the next major problem that Branch Rickey had to solve. Kindly, Mrs. Britton had granted the Cardinals' stockholders an extension to provide the necessary payment to her, as they were having great difficulty raising money. They needed $60,000 to provide her next payment and to finance the club through 1918. At that point, they had raised only $2,000. The situation looked bleak. It appeared that the club would need to find a new owner with "deep pockets."[42] Mrs. Britton agreed to grant the stockholders a second extension. The board felt that they could find the funds given enough time.

By the end of June, manager Hendricks and his club were mired in last place with little hope for improvement. They remained one-and-a-half games behind the seventh-place Reds. Their outlook worsened as outfielder Walton Cruise was called home by his draft board. Club president Rickey lamented that he knew of no way to strengthen or better the team.

A *St. Louis Post-Dispatch* reporter innocently asked Hendricks why the Cardinals were in eighth place. Hendricks responded:

> "The combined batting average of Cruise, Hornsby, and Jack Smith for the first month of the season was just a little bit above the figure each of them should have had.
>
> "We failed to find a capable second baseman, although I think Bob Fisher (new player) will fill the bill. The same can be said for right field.
>
> "Just as Jack Smith looked like he might begin hitting, he was called for the army.
>
> "Cruise rapped out doubles, triples and home runs on the last eastern trip, then wrenched his knee. He may be out of the game for the duration of the war now.
>
> "Lee Meadows' sore arm prevented him from pitching a game between May 6 and June 6.
>
> "Rogers Hornsby was spiked when it appeared he had regained his batting eye. He's playing on nerve alone right now.
>
> "Gene Paulette played yesterday's game with a broken finger in splints. He also has water on the knee and should be out of the lineup.
>
> "Frank Snyder has joined the army, ditto Oscar Horstman, who couldn't and didn't show his 1917 form because of a sore arm.
>
> "Charlie Grimm is sick in bed with a cold.
>
> "Clifton Heathcote has a sore ankle and should be resting."

The manager then paused and asked, "Have I answered everything?"[43] Hard to believe, but manager Hendricks was still optimistic about the second half of the season. He felt hopeful the Cardinals could reach the first division.

But July provided more of the same for the Cards. On July 9, Sherdel entered a game with the Robins. The tying runs were on base with two outs. Sherdel got the third out to preserve the rare victory.

Money became a primary focus again for Branch Rickey in mid-July. Mrs. Britton's loan extension was ending, and $40,000 was still required to pay her. The team also needed an additional $20,000 to pay its current debts. Another solicitation of the general stockholders yielded only $14,000 more. Saving the club would require a miracle. Rickey provided just that. A group of major stockholders, including Rickey, contributed the necessary funds so that he could hand Mrs. Britton a $40,000 check and pay the other bills.[44] The St. Louis stockholders were just protecting their own interests, but they saved the Cardinals. Everyone was relieved—albeit temporarily. The stockholders still owed $125,000 on the club sale.

Finally, on July 13, the expected happened. Young Sherdel was ordered to report to the draft board in Hanover for a physical examination the following Monday. The club got the location changed to St. Louis. Unlike many other players, Sherdel was ready to serve his country. Other players were deserting their contracts and accepting jobs in steel mills and shipyards in hopes of avoiding the draft. Not William Henry Sherdel. He passed his physical with no problem, although that didn't mean he would be drafted immediately. When completing the service questionnaire, Sherdel wrote that he wanted to serve in the artillery. In an interview, he said, "If I am called, I want to get into the thick of this scrap. I don't know a whole lot about the army, but I want some excitement if I go. Where will I get it?" A friend told him that the artillery was usually in the thick of the fighting, so he wrote "artillery" on his questionnaire.[45] Later, General Enoch Crowder threatened to investigate the players who jumped contracts to take safe jobs.

Sherdel continued to pitch while awaiting his call to service. On July 21, he pitched an excellent game against the Giants for ten innings with no offensive support. He tired in the eleventh, and gave up six runs. They lost, 6–2. Then, six days later, a most bizarre thing happened. Sherdel pitched the second game of a double-header and, unbelievably, the Cardinals scored twenty-two runs on forty-five hits. Sherdel even helped his own cause with a home run. That game set a season record for runs scored.

In late July, Secretary of War Newton Baker made a long-awaited ruling that exempted major-league baseball players from the work or fight edict until September 1. Major-league owners were relieved.

As August began, the Cardinals remained in the National League cellar. Sherdel was scheduled to pitch perhaps his last game before reporting for duty. He took the mound in Philadelphia on August 2. If Sherdel wanted to be remembered, he did his best to see that through in front of his many fans on this day. He fired a five-hitter with five strikeouts. The Cards won, 2–1, and Sherdel even added a single. He was to report to the Hanover Draft Board the following Monday, August 5. The *St. Louis Post-Dispatch* wrote a very nice article for his admirers in which it said:

> It is doubtful whether a more finished bit of pitching will be witnessed this year than the one offered by the youthful Sherdel.
>
> It wasn't the small number of hits that he allowed the Phillies. As a matter of fact, five blows per game, while it is creditable, is hardly noteworthy in itself. Furthermore, Sherdel did not register a shutout, and it is the fact that they scored one run and threatened to ruin Hendricks's entire afternoon in the ninth inning that makes Sherdel's work remarkable.
>
> Few veterans could have maintained their equilibrium under the circumstances that confronted Sherdel in the ninth. Working on a lead of only two runs, he found himself suddenly growing wild and ineffective. The first two men up smote singles and this put the Phillies in a fighting mood. It also put Sherdel in the same sort of humor and he went out and won the old ball game because he declined to quit.[46]

Sherdel returned to Hanover on Monday. The local draft board placed him on the eligible list, but he would not be called until later in the year. He returned to the Cardinals and, to the delight of manager Hendricks, he was able to pitch several more games for the 1918 team. In fact, he tossed some of his best games in August, including one on August 13, when he held the Reds scoreless until the seventh inning. Four days later, he relieved in the ninth and retired the side. The next day, Sherdel pitched a 4–0 shutout of the Phillies. On August 22, he defeated Brooklyn and Hall-of-Famer Rube Marquard, adding a single and scoring a run. Finally, Sherdel beat the Pirates a week later, allowing only four hits, and winning his own game with two singles and a triple in four at-bats.

The St. Louis Cardinals ended the 1918 season in last place, finishing thirty-three games behind first-place Chicago. Bill Sherdel's pitching record was six wins, twelve losses, with a 2.71 earned run average in thirty-five games and 182 innings thrown. He added a perfect fielding record of 1.000 and a decent .242 batting average. In summary, the 1918 club was short of quality players, had too many injuries, and suffered losses from the war effort.

The Cardinal players sent a card to manager Hendricks in which each wrote a personal note of appreciation. Many said that Hendricks was the best manager they had ever had. Bill Sherdel wrote, "Jack Hendricks impressed me as a great manager. Working against him—now working for him—he impressed me as a great manager."[47] Branch Rickey also complimented Hendricks. No one blamed the manager for the team's poor showing.

After the 1918 season ended, the St. Louis board of directors was uncertain when baseball games would be played again. The league had determined that the gates would not open until the war ended. Some directors thought the war might last several years. The club leaders decided to dismiss Jack Hendricks as manager and hire Branch Rickey as both president and manager. The decision was made for two reasons. First, they believed that Rickey was a capable manager. Second, they wanted to save money by giving one person both responsibilities.

Jack Hendricks's record of first-division finishes had been broken, but so much had gone wrong that no one believed he was a poor manager—especially not the players. He would return to Indianapolis in 1919, and get another major league job with the Cincinnati Reds starting in 1924. He would direct that club for six years and accumulate 469 wins and 450 losses. His Reds teams would finish second, third, fourth, fifth, fifth, and seventh.

In October, William Henry Sherdel was sent to the University of Pennsylvania to serve not in the artillery but as an army blacksmith. He joined the 58th US Army Infantry, Company A. The patriotic Cardinals sent sixteen players plus Branch Rickey and Jack Hendricks into the service during the war. Major Rickey was placed in the chemical warfare department along with baseball stars Captain Ty Cobb, Captain Christy Mathewson, and Lieutenant George Sisler. Rickey reported to Washington, DC, and boarded a ship headed to France. While on the voyage, he contracted pneumonia. When the ship reached land, he was so weak he had to be carried from the boat. Rickey recovered and trained twenty men in chemical weapons. Unfortunately, during a training exercise, Mathewson inhaled the deadly mustard gas. He would die prematurely, in 1925. Luckily, the war with Germany ended in November with the signing of the Armistice.[48] Sherdel was discharged from the army in December and was ready for another baseball season in 1919. He returned to his parents' home in Hanover to hunt, fish, and await spring with his girlfriend, Marguerite Strausbaugh.

Bill Sherdel in his army uniform
—Sherdel family

CHAPTER EIGHT

The conclusion of the First World War, with the signing of the Armistice on November 11, 1918, is by far the biggest event of 1919. It would take until June to sign the Treaty of Versailles and officially end the war. As 1919 got started, the armed forces began to slowly release major-league baseball players from their service commitments.

Congress would enact the Eighteenth Amendment to the Constitution that year, prohibiting alcoholic beverages in the United States and creating an illegal cottage industry supplying "booze." The amendment would not be effective until the beginning of the next year.

On January 15, a bizarre event took place in northern Boston. In what would become known as the Great Boston Molasses Flood, a large, fifty-foot-tall storage tank filled with more than two million gallons of molasses burst, and sent a twenty-five-foot high wall of sticky goo rushing thirty-five miles per hour down the city streets. The flood would claim twenty-one lives and injure 150. Decades later, residents would still claim to smell molasses on hot summer days.

In boxing this year, Jack Dempsey would defeat Jess Willard and become the world heavyweight champion. Dempsey, who would go on to become one of the greatest boxers of all time, would be one of several huge sports personalities that defined the 1920s as one of sports' greatest decades. Bill Sherdel would be a part of that memorable period.

In 1919, Branch Rickey continued looking for an improved lineup. Now it was even more important, since he was also the manager. To the delight of the local fans, Rickey made a January trade with the Phillies. He acquired catcher Bill "Pickles" Dillhoefer, the same player who had been Sherdel's catcher in Milwaukee and spent time with the Cubs and Phils. He was still considered young and inexperienced, but was also thought to be talented. Another welcome surprise was catcher Verne Clemons, returning after a stint in the war. Clemons had gained weight in the navy and appeared to be in great shape. Rickey now had a very strong group of backstops that included Frank Snyder, Mike Gonzales, "Pickles" Dillhoefer, and Verne Clemons.

Rickey made the decision not to travel south for spring training that year. Instead, he wanted to hold his workouts at nearby Washington University's Francis Field. He was keen on this for several reasons. First, the National League, unlike the junior American League, restricted the start of spring training to one month before the season began; the American League clubs could begin whenever they wished. Because of the late start and the time committed to the annual spring series with the Browns, the Cardinals would only have roughly two weeks in the south. Second, the Cardinals were experiencing financial difficulties. Rickey planned to house the team at the Hamilton Hotel to save money, and he recycled the 1918 uniforms for another season, asking a seamstress to make repairs where necessary. Rickey also found a local sporting goods store to make the rest and extend credit terms for the payment.[1] Third, if the Cards encountered inclement weather, they could always practice indoors in the school's gymnasium.

Bill Sherdel was excited to start his sophomore year with the Cardinals. He'd sent Mr. Rickey a letter over the winter that was filled with hope for a great season and personal success. When his contract arrived in March, Sherdel signed and returned it quickly. Rickey was impressed with his young southpaw.

When spring training started, twenty-eight of the thirty candidates on the roster were expected to report. Two others were still in France awaiting their release. Of the total, only twelve had been added to the club. Those new players needed to elevate the team from the previous year's cellar. Rickey's biggest concern was the pitching staff. The return of Marvin Goodwin and the improved health of Lee Meadows could make a difference. A *St. Louis Post-Dispatch* reporter wrote:

> Rickey has devoted himself to the task of remodeling an eighth-place club with recruits of doubtful caliber. Given a pitcher of dependable worth—two would be especially welcome—he may elevate the

Cardinals to the first division. But he admitted in an interview, yesterday, that his task was not a simple one.

The best thing Cardinal followers have to hope for is the improvement to morale. There is not a man on the club against Rickey. He has the united support of his players and also has their confidence, which condition did not exist last year.[2]

Practices were planned for Monday through Friday with away exhibition games on weekends. The Cardinals had an agreement with the Browns that neither team could play an exhibition game in St. Louis before their spring series.

James Gould of the *St. Louis Star* provided this look at manager Rickey's first practice:

As usual the squad had not been on the field more than one minute and thirty seconds before half of them had grabbed bats and looked casually around for willing "shaggers." These being forthcoming, the fusillade became fast and furious. Here, in one corner, would be Meadows, Jakie May and Ames, Leon the Red batting them out to the younger pitchers and keeping them busy. There, in another part of the field, was "Pepper Joe" Sugden receiving the best early shoots of Horstman, Marvin Goodwin, and Sherdell [sic]. There were no idlers: everyone was busy and Manager Rickey circled around his protégés, ever watchful and seeming to be looking twenty places at once.

Regular batting practice was started, and the youngsters . . . served 'em up. Rog Hornsby inserted himself into the first batting order and walloped several on a line to right, center, and left. . . . Everywhere was Rickey, now calling a man into the play, now sending a man back to the gym when he considered a day's work had been done. Every player was in earnest, but, withal, was sprightly and in high spirits. . . .

Bill Sherdell [sic] was frisky and had to be cautioned for cutting loose in the box. He looks like July 1. . . .

Austin McHenry's general condition and play evoked praise from Rickey. The former Milwaukeean roamed the gardens and pulled down screaming liners and high flies alike with accuracy and dispatch."[3]

As training camp progressed, manager Rickey was very happy with his team. James Gould wrote:

> Veterans and rookies seem to be imbued with real ambition to cram the most effective work into the hours allowed for training. No one has to be told to get busy: the trouble is to keep the boys from trying to do too much. . . .
>
> Under the present methods, the daily grind of work becomes play and it really is a pleasure to watch what might easily become a dull and stifling routine.
>
> To say Rickey is delighted with the spirit shown is putting it too mildly. Himself a hard worker, he plainly shows his enjoyment of the situation made possible by the earnestness of the men.
>
> Yesterday, the training was again reduced to a single session because the weather made outdoor work impossible. However, the indoor battle with physical culture continued for about three hours, and was full of action every minute. Handball courts were busy and two basketball teams struggled on the gym floor. Joe Sugden warmed up the pitchers in one corner and Verne Clemons and Artie Dunn handled the shoots of others in other parts. . . . Burt Shotton called for handball volunteers and was swamped by enlistments. . . . The irrepressible Sherdell [sic] and Marvin Goodwin went from place to place, trying everything several times. . . .
>
> In the afternoon, Rickey worked with several of the men—pitchers mainly—in throws to the bases and in remedying slight defects in hurling motions. The outfielders and infielders were excused after the hard work of the morning.[4]

Manager Rickey continued to innovate in his first Cardinals' camp. In his book *The Gashouse Gang*, writer John Heidenry stated, "Among Rickey's innovations were blackboard talks, pits where players could practice sliding, and plays to catch a runner off base. He was also a master statistician and kept his figures and other data in a large notebook in the dugout. He knew by how many feet each opposing batter had been thrown out at first on a grounder, and how far each pitcher's different kinds of pitches had been hit. He was able to predict, at least theoretically, how any given batter would perform against any given pitcher."[5] Branch remained always the teacher and student of the game.

The Cardinal players seemed to be enjoying the camp, especially the half-day holidays, as reported by this St. Louis writer:

> There's a deep, dark, dank mystery in the club. On the half-day holiday Wednesday, Paulette, Meadows, Sherdell [sic], and Bob Larmore clutched their golf paraphernalia and hit out for the links. The mystery is just who won and what were the individual [score] cards. Sherdell [sic] admits he played better than the rest, though this is loudly disputed by the other three. Meadows, when asked about his card, throws up both hands and is suddenly stricken dumb.
>
> A "glance" at the actual scores made in this foursome might make interesting reading. . . .
>
> In the clubhouse yesterday, Bill Sherdell [sic] was carelessly caroling a ditty about "his love was a mule that worked in a mine," or words to that effect, when one of the other boys remarked, "Gee, that's funny, Sherry [Sherdel] couldn't sing a bit last year." Just why emphasis was laid on "last year" is a puzzle.[6]

Spring training was approaching the end. Manager Rickey was convinced that the new club could finish in the first division if his pitching staff could do well. As a finale to the pre-season, the Cards and Browns began their St. Louis spring series. The Browns won the first two games. Bill Sherdel was tagged with the loss in the first game. He hurled the first three innings, allowed five hits and three runs. The Cardinals gained bragging rights in the third encounter. Sherdel got the win, 4–3, in relief of starter Bill Doak. Doak was good for the first three innings. Manager Rickey's concerns about his pitching were starting to disappear. And then it happened.

At nine o'clock on the morning of April 16, Lee Meadows picked up fellow pitchers Bill Doak, Leon Ames, Oscar Horstman, and Bill Sherdel and headed to practice in his new Chevrolet. It was raining that morning as Meadows was driving east on Ashland Avenue. As Meadows attempted to turn north onto Union Avenue, the car skidded on the wet pavement. His new Chevy overturned and hit a streetcar. All the passengers were thrown from the vehicle. Meadows was hurled through the car's windshield. Nearby vehicles transported the players back to the Hamilton Hotel where they were placed under the care of Dr. H. G. Nicks, the team's physician.[7]

Branch Rickey was in his office giving an interview when the phone rang. He grabbed the receiver. After a short pause, he shouted, "Judas Priest! What's that? You're not playing a joke on me? Is this April First? Where . . . how . . . badly hurt, you say? Five of my pitchers? Wait'll I get a pencil and write the names." Rickey was now frantic. He walked the floor, mumbling, "What'll I do, what'll I do? The season opens in a week and five of my pitchers have been badly injured." He then rushed to the hotel to check on his pitchers.[8]

The players' injuries were extensive but not deadly. Meadows suffered a bruised knee, strained back, injured leg, and various cuts and other bruises. Doak, initially in shock, remained unconscious for a half hour. He sustained various bruises, including one to his valuable right shoulder. Young Sherdel lost several teeth, suffered a strained back, and sustained cuts on his face and one leg. Ames received a bad cut over one eye, plus injuries to his right knee, left arm, and back. Horstman had various cuts about his face and a badly wrenched shoulder.[9] The players were very lucky to be alive and they knew it. In an instant, Branch Rickey's high hopes for the 1919 Cardinals' season seemed to fade away on a St. Louis street. Thank goodness Marvin Goodwin had returned from duty and Rickey still had promising young Jakie May.

It was hard to measure the crash's impact upon the team's chances. Doak, Sherdel, and Meadows would suffer through the first part of the season. Ames and Horstman would never completely recover. Even young May would be affected. Rickey had been working with the newcomer, who had speed but lacked control, to alter his delivery. He planned to use May sparingly until June when he felt the changes would be mastered. But now he was forced to use him immediately. During the season, general manager Rickey would create a new team that would later be described as "the best young club in the big leagues."[10]

The Cardinals played three more games with their city rivals. Once again, the Browns claimed St. Louis bragging rights by taking the series, four games to two. One ray of hope was the appearance of Doak and Sherdel in the last game. Both crippled hurlers did well and were lauded for their bravery.

The Cardinals opened the 1919 season on the road in Cincinnati. The weather was freezing for the series, but morale was very high. Except for some of the pitchers, the club was in great shape. In the *St. Louis Star,* James Gould wrote, "No team can show a finer set of gentlemen or a cleaner group of athletes and they deserve the support and best wishes of every fan in St. Louis."[11] Some of the players had not yet arrived but were expected within the first week.

The Reds took the opener, 6–2. Bill Sherdel relieved in the seventh inning with the Cards ahead, 2–0. Sherdel gave up a sacrifice fly that scored the Reds' first run. And the eighth inning proved to be the pitcher's undoing. With two outs and the bases loaded, Sherdel had two strikes on the batter. The umpire called the next pitch a ball. The youngster thought it was strike three and became unnerved. He then threw three more wild pitches and walked in a run. Rickey replaced Sherdel on the mound and the Cardinals lost the opener. The umpire was not liked by the Redbird fans and players. Sherdel and the other Cards' hurlers allowed eleven walks.

In the second game of the series, Rickey chose to start Sherdel to improve his confidence. The youngster allowed only six scattered hits, struck out two, and walked an equal number. Unfortunately, however, Sherdel lost the game because of boneheaded base running by young Cliff Heathcote and Rogers Hornsby. In the fourth frame, Heathcote led off with a sharp single to right. The next batter, Hornsby, hit a screaming ball to deep right center. Hornsby's hit should have been an easy triple and Heathcote should have scored. Instead, Heathcote headed to second and incorrectly guessed the ball had been caught. He raced back to first as Hornsby was barreling toward second. Hornsby passed Heathcote and was called out. The next batter singled, which would have scored the second run. The Cards lost, 3–1. So far, Sherdel had pitched in both games and had been charged with both losses.

After another loss in the third game with Marv Goodwin on the mound, Rickey handed the ball to Bill Doak for the final game of the series. Doak only lasted into the second inning. He surrendered three runs in the first and was replaced in the second by—you guessed it—Bill Sherdel again. This time, Sherdel pitched well through the sixth inning, allowing only one run—a homer by football Hall-of-Famer Earle "Greasy" Neale. The final score was 5–1, in favor of the Reds. As Rickey's club headed to Chicago, they were 0–4.

"Iron man" Bill had pitched in three of the four games. In the four contests, the Cards left thirty runners on base. It had not been a good start.

Back in St. Louis after this depressing opening road trip, the Cardinals were in the league basement. The club had poor pitching and feeble batting. The pitching staff was hurting. Doak, Ames, and Horstman were not ready. Sherdel was overworked. Only Goodwin and May were pitching well. Superstar Rogers Hornsby was batting .217.[12] Rickey told a local reporter, "I am worried about the immediate future, not about July and August. My pitching is not ready at this time and, to make matters worse, the club is not hitting. We have averaged one run per game for seven games, which is hopeless. It is possible to get so far behind in the race that it will be hard to get out. I told the boys this: That if they would keep the team in sight of the first division for the next six weeks, I would guarantee them a place in first division by August. That's the way I feel about it."[13]

Troubles continued through the team's brief home stand with Cincinnati and Pittsburgh. Bill Sherdel got plenty of work. He started the first Reds' game and was relieved by Goodwin in the second inning. It would be Sherdel's third loss to the Reds. Rickey also called upon him to relieve Meadows in the first Pirates game. There, Sherdel pitched two good innings, allowing no hits and no runs.

Although the Cardinals were playing terribly, hope persisted. Fans realized how the car accident had affected the team. James Gould wrote:

> It is true that the club is off to a horrible start, but we stand by our statement that the strength is there and will show—and before long, too. It's far too early in the season to give up hope with the roster of hard-working and capable players the Cardinals have.
>
> Stick with them. The fates have been hard-hearted, but the boys deserve better fortune and are going to have it. String along with them a little longer now; then you will be with them when they get going good.[14]

St. Louis won the final game with the Pirates, thanks to Marv Goodwin. Goodwin relieved with one out in the first inning and held the Pirates the rest of the game for a 2–1 victory. Upbeat after their win, the Cardinals headed back on the road.

It was around this time that general manager Rickey purchased veteran shortstop Johnny Lavan from Washington, selling catcher Mike Gonzales to the Giants to finance the purchase. Lavan was Dr. Lavan, a surgeon with the US Navy. The twenty-nine-year-old had played six seasons, mostly with the Browns. Rickey knew him very well. There was one complication. While Lavan's ship was stationed in the Havana (Cuba) harbor, Doc broke his leg playing ball. The leg was almost completely healed and Rickey needed Lavan. The shortstop had planned to retire, but he still wanted to play for Rickey. Lavan joined the team on June 1. An elated Rickey stated, "Lavan is generally conceded to be one of the greatest infielders in the game today. He gives our club a world of additional strength. If our pitching improves, we will give St. Louis some winning baseball."[15] With Lavan in the infield, manager Rickey could move Rogers Hornsby to third.

The Cardinals would be out of St. Louis for almost all of May. Bill would pitch several games in relief and do well. The Cardinals finally won their first series of the year on May 16 against the Boston Braves. They arrived back home on May 30. Their uninspiring road trip had yielded only five wins and nine losses. Manager Rickey was happy to add newly arrived shortstop Johnny Lavan to the lineup.

Sometimes, a team's fortunes can change quickly without notice. Rickey's boys began a seven-game winning streak on June 4 that extended through June 10. The club jumped into sixth place. Leon Ames finally recovered from the car accident and started his first game on June 8. Rickey had predicted the club would get better when the pitchers became healthy. He now had an excellent starting staff of Marv Goodwin, Bill Doak, Oscar Tuero, and Leon Ames. The winning streak came to an end on June 11 when outfielder Cliff Heathcote muffed a fly ball that cost the Redbirds an eighth straight win. But St. Louis came right back to win another three games. Branch Rickey looked like a prophet. The Cardinals had just won fourteen of eighteen games. After Goodwin lost a close game to Brooklyn, the Cards won another two games and jumped into fifth place. The red-hot Redbirds had gone sixteen and five.

Bill Sherdel appeared on the mound again on June 20. He allowed the Giants four hits and no runs over the last five innings. Sherdel also picked two runners off base thanks to Rickey's teachings. It was his first appearance in almost a month, after having injured his arm in a mid-season exhibition game.

Rickey gave Sherdel the ball to start a game three days later. He pitched a complete game against the Pirates, and lost, 7–6. The score is misleading because only one of the Bucs' seven runs was earned. Sherdel had suffered some bad luck.

The Cardinals' hitters continued to improve. In a June 29 game against Cincinnati, Doak and Sherdel defeated the Reds, 14–9, in a slugfest. The Cards pounded six Reds hurlers for twenty-two hits.

At the end of June, the Cardinals were in sixth place. John McGraw and the New York Giants were leading the league. Marv Goodwin (6–3) topped the staff, while Bill Sherdel was pitching mostly in relief.

During the summer in New York, Branch was invited to a meeting with New York Giants' owner Charles Stoneham and manager John McGraw. Stoneham knew of the Cardinals' financial woes and wanted to purchase Rogers Hornsby. He offered $150,000—the amount of the Cardinals' debt—for the infielder. Rickey remembered what had happened to the Philadelphia A's after Connie Mack sold his star players. The Athletics remained in the second division for many years. He was trying to develop a dynasty in St. Louis, so he refused the offer. Stoneham asked what his price was, and Rickey told him $500,000. A frustrated Stoneham raised his offer to $200,000 and Rickey refused again. He then reversed the negotiations and asked to purchase a young, inexperienced infielder named Frank Frisch for $50,000. Stoneham and McGraw were livid because St. Louis had no money to buy their player. They refused. Stoneham made one final offer to Rickey. He would pay $300,000 for Hornsby. The Cardinals could keep him until the end of the season and if the Giants made the World Series, they would pay Rickey an additional $50,000. That was an incredible $350,000 for one player. In today's dollars that would be over $5 million. It took a strong-willed Rickey to turn down all that money when the franchise was in financial trouble. The meeting ended with no deals.

Before the dust could settle, Rickey contacted reporters and announced the Giants' offer for Hornsby. He felt this would make the franchise more valuable in the public's eye. When the Giants later came to St. Louis for a series, manager John McGraw brought another offer to Rickey. McGraw proposed a trade of five Giants players for Hornsby. The offer did not include Frisch. Once again, Rickey turned the Giants down.

Branch Rickey had an idea. He decided that if he ever improved St. Louis's financial situation, he would work to develop a farm system of minor-league clubs. That farm system would develop more players like Hornsby who could improve the Cardinals or be sold for financial gain. Rickey decided to hold tryout camps for young players in the St. Louis area. He found three great prospects—Jim Bottomley, Ray Blades, and "Heinie" Mueller—from his first camp. All three would eventually become Cardinal stars.[16]

The Cardinals' fortunes did not improve in July. In fact, they worsened due to poor pitching. Early in the month, the club hit a seven-game losing streak. In the last three games, Rickey used ten pitchers. The Cards scored twenty-two runs but allowed thirty. The *St. Louis Star* lamented, "The writer has been loyal to the Cards since the season began and is yet, but no loyalty can stand in the way of honest criticism, and the Rickey pitching staff is nothing short of a nightmare. A team with the attack the Cardinals boast and the fielding defense lately shown—to say nothing of reserve strength—should be in the first division easily. Instead, because of the worst pitching it has ever been the misfortune of the writer to see, the team is skating cellarward."[17]

On July 9, Bill Sherdel pitched the final five innings of a wild 12–8 victory over the Giants and was given credit for the victory. The win ended the Cards' losing streak. The Sherdel family celebrated another event that day. Back in Hanover, Bill Sherdel's youngest sister, Ruth, married Ralph Butt of nearby Gettysburg. The Butt family would live in Gettysburg the rest of their lives.

The club reached the half-point of the season on July 11. At that stage, St. Louis was mired in sixth place. Still, the Cards' batting averages were excellent: McHenry (.317), Heathcote (.305), and Hornsby (.303). Bill Sherdel's .300 average was leading the pitchers.

Now on the other side of the mid-season mark, the Cardinals ended another eastern road trip on July 25. Luckily, only four of the ten scheduled games had been played because of rain. The Redbirds lost three of the four, but the Cardinals' staff did get some badly needed rest. McHenry was now hitting

.331 while leading the league in extra base hits and committing only one error in seventy-six chances. The club returned to St. Louis for a long seventeen-day home stand until August 11. Bill Sherdel saw relief action in two of the four contests, with one good and one bad outing.

In the final game of a miserable early August home stand, Sherdel attracted notice when he relieved May against the Braves. James Gould wrote, "Sherdel went in to pitch the ninth. He performed a seldom-seen feat by setting [Rabbit] Maranville down on strikes, whizzing three past [Art] Wilson, and curving a third one over on Ray Keating. He got a big hand for his nifty work. This lad has shown some great stuff in his last trips out and will probably bear a good part of the burden on the trip."[18]

The next day, August 11, Rickey and his boys headed out on a long, difficult eastern road trip. They would not return to friendly St. Louis until September 5. Because the summer rains had postponed so many earlier games, the Cards were forced to play four double-headers in their first week. An already tired pitching staff did not perform well. The club started great, winning six of the first seven against weaker clubs. But as the trip lengthened, the pitchers weakened and the seventh-place Cardinals finished with only one more win and twelve additional losses through the end of August. Bill Sherdel pitched infrequently on the trip, without any noteworthy efforts.

The final month of the long season began with the Cards defeating the Pirates two out of three games. Good news! Marv Goodwin returned to the mound and picked up the second win. A month earlier, he had been badly spiked and his leg had become infected. Doctors were worried the leg might need to be removed. Doctor Lavan, the Cards' shortstop, worked on the leg day and night and saved it from amputation. Goodwin was very happy to be back and so was Rickey to have him.

Rickey was pleased when his boys outplayed the first-place Reds and won a three-game series. In the final contest, Sherdel showed great form again in relief. The Cardinals next won seven of eleven and began an important series with the Boston Braves. If the Cards could take the series, they could advance into sixth place. St. Louis lost and remained in seventh. Sherdel pitched another great game in relief against the Phillies in the final series of the season. The youngster entered in the third inning, scattered eight hits, and surrendered no runs. He was angry when he smashed a ball to deep right field for an apparent triple, only to be robbed by the outfielder's shoestring catch.

And thus, the Cards' dismal 1919 season ended. Despite the poor record, club hitting was excellent. Rogers Hornsby finished with a .318 average—good enough for second best in the league. Bill Sherdel led all pitchers with a .277 batting mark. In pitching, Marv Goodwin (12–8) led the staff, followed by Doak (12–14). Sherdel recorded five wins against nine losses in thirty-six games and 137 innings. He allowed a respectable average of 3.47 runs per nine innings.

Despite the poor record, Branch Rickey and the St. Louis writers were very optimistic about 1920. If September was a hint of what 1920 would bring, then the fans couldn't wait for the next year. James Gould stated enthusiastically, "Of the twenty-five games played, the Cardinals captured fourteen, thereby attaining a percentage of .577 for the month—a percentage that maintained for the year, would have given them third place over the Cubs by a wide margin. . . . Not only did the Cards in September win the majority of their games, they also outscored their opponents . . . and outhit them." Gould also discussed the staff: "In this last month, Bill Doak, working easily, pitched in four games and won every one of them. Marvin Goodwin, recovered from the injury to his leg, pitched six games and won five. . . . Sherdel, with one and one, also got an even split."[19]

After the season ended, John Wray, a reporter for the *St. Louis Post-Dispatch,* interviewed Branch Rickey. Rickey expressed these thoughts:

> I must withdraw one of my complaints against the club, voiced earlier in the season following the auto accident. . . . I said then that weak pitching would cripple our efforts. This club is no longer afflicted with a defective mound department. In fact, I think that as the club now lines up, pitching is one of its strong points. . . . We will no longer fall back on pitching complaints about the team. This weakness is corrected. . . .
>
> I have a great hitting outfield, with McHenry, Heathcote, Schultz, Shotton, and Smith. ALL YOUNG with the exception of Burt Shotton, and certain to reach their prime next year. The infield is, in

my opinion, the best in the league, both defensively and in hitting. Where will you beat Hornsby, Stock, Mollwitz, and Lavan?

Dillhoefer and Clemons, catchers, are going better for us and with more satisfaction to the pitchers than ever Gonzales and Snyder did.

All of this talent is YOUNG—get that? There is now no doddering material nearing the discard on this club. It is the youngest and most virile team in either league today.

John Wray then asked Rickey if there was anything wrong with the team. Rickey responded, "Sure there is . . . inexperience on the part of some of the younger players. Occasionally, games are lost by unthinking players, by the 'crossing' of orders, by throwing to the wrong base, by ill-timed base running, etc. But the point is, there is nothing wrong that cannot be corrected."[20]

For Bill Sherdel, 1919 was another educational year. He continued to learn. The youngster wasn't getting the starting assignments that he hoped for, but he was in Branch Rickey's future plans. It would take time before he fully developed into a great left-handed pitcher, but he was learning from the master. Rickey was slowly building a winning foundation, though it would be years before they earned a title. Rogers Hornsby had been the first building block. Bill Sherdel was now the second. The third would arrive in February.

In the infamous 1919 World Series, the Cincinnati Reds upset the highly touted Chicago White Sox. Although there were immediate suspicions, it would be another year before the public realized that the notorious "Black" Sox threw the Series to benefit gamblers. Gambling was everywhere. Even Branch Rickey was threatened by a gambler who made his way into the clubhouse after a Cardinals' game. Manager Rickey never decided who would pitch a game until he saw the pitchers warming up. That indecision angered the gamblers. They couldn't determine the odds on the games until they knew the pitching matchup, which they usually didn't until the last minute.

When the season ended, Sherdel returned home to 454 High Street in Hanover—his parents' home. His mind on this visit back was occupied with important affairs, affairs that were unrelated to baseball. Many dramatic changes were happening in his life. In October, his parents sold their home to the Hanover Heel and Innersole Company, located next door. Then in November, they sold many of their possessions at a public sale and moved back to New York City to live with their daughter, Theresa, and son-in-law, William Kerwin. Bill's father would continue his blacksmith trade there. Young Bill didn't mind this upheaval, because he was ready to start a new life with his future wife. Sherdel had met and fallen in love with beautiful, dark-haired Marguerite Strausbaugh. She was two years younger than him and lived in nearby McSherrystown, Pennsylvania. On November 24, Bill and Marguerite were married at St. Mary's Rectory in McSherrystown. They left the following day for New York City. They would reside with Bill's older brother Fred and his family in an apartment house at 532 East 85th Street, just around the corner from the rest of the family. The entire Sherdel clan was now gone from Hanover. Only Bill's younger sister Ruth and her husband remained in nearby Gettysburg.

On December 26, Harry Frazee, the owner of the Boston Red Sox, sold George Herman "Babe" Ruth to the New York Yankees for $100,000 and $350,000 in loans to finance his Broadway shows. Ruth had been a top pitcher for the Sox and had begun 1919 on the mound. By late June, his power was so overwhelming that manager Ed Barrow was forced to play him every day in the outfield. Ruth set a major-league record with twenty-nine home runs in 1919—the end of the deadball era. That record would be just the beginning of many for the Babe. After the Red Sox won the World Series in 1918, it would take eighty-six years before they won another. With Ruth, the Yankees would begin a dynasty that would last even to today. Bill Sherdel would cross paths with Babe Ruth many times throughout their careers. They would become good friends and their friendship would continue after baseball.

Over the winter, baseball managers voted to outlaw the spitball. For years, pitchers had put various substances on the baseball to control its movement when it was pitched to the batter. The change was introduced in two parts. First, for 1920, each team could designate a maximum of two pitchers who could still throw the pitch legally. Second, after the 1920 season, the pitch would be illegal except for seventeen pitchers, who would be allowed to continue to throw it until they retired. This change impacted two Cardinal hurlers: Bill Doak and Marvin Goodwin. Both pitchers could throw the spitball until they retired. The spitball had inspired Doak's nickname, "Spittin' Bill." The change would not impact Bill Sherdel, although he would admit later that he did throw the illegal pitch occasionally.

CHAPTER NINE

In 1920, the League of Nations would be established as an outgrowth of the First World War. Its purpose would be to promote world peace. Although President Wilson would support it, the American Senate would not, and so the United States would never officially join. This was the same year Congress would pass the Nineteenth Amendment to the Constitution, allowing women the right to vote.

In other events, US air mail service would begin between New York City and San Francisco. So, too, would construction on the Holland Tunnel, connecting New Jersey to New York City. Warren Harding would be elected the twenty-ninth president and Walt Disney would start his first job as an artist for $40 per week.

In sports, the American Professional Football Association, the precursor to the NFL, got its start this year. Racehorse Man o' War would race for the last time and win. Bill Tilden would become the dominating tennis player in the world, winning the Wimbledon and US men's tennis tournaments.

On November 21 in Donora, Pennsylvania, a small town near Pittsburgh, the greatest Cardinal player of all time would be born. Stan Musial would not reach St. Louis for twenty-one years, but he would dominate the National League for a long time once he did.

On January 13, 1920, the St. Louis Cardinals' board of directors made a move that would positively impact the future of the club. Branch Rickey stepped down as president in favor of Samuel Breadon. Rickey would remain as vice president, business manager, and playing manager.

Sam Breadon was born in Greenwich Village, Manhattan, New York, in 1879. He was the son of a poor truck driver. In 1902, a friend invited him to St. Louis to open a garage and sell cars for him. His timing was perfect. St. Louis hosted the World's Fair in 1904 and automobiles started to become popular. Breadon was a very successful salesman. Eventually, he went out on his own and started the Western Automobile Company, and named himself president and treasurer. When the Cardinals went public, Breadon bought some stock, and continued that practice as opportunities presented themselves. By 1919, he was asked to join the board of directors.

Meanwhile, Branch Rickey knew that he needed to solve the Cardinals' financial problems. If he was going to build a winning team, he needed to have money to develop a farm system where he could assign the players, ensure they were developed properly, and recall or sell them as needed. If he could develop more Hornsbys, the club could make money and win championships. Rickey sold 4,000 shares of stock to Mr. Breadon. That made Breadon the largest stockholder and gave the club enough money to operate.

Breadon and Rickey were perfect partners. The former had no knowledge of baseball and was happy to allow the latter to do whatever he wanted to better the club. Sam Breadon was very smart. He knew that the Cards' ballpark, Cardinal Field, was in bad shape. He approached Browns' owner Phil Ball, and threatened to build a new ballpark close to Ball's Sportsman's Park if he wouldn't allow the Cardinals to rent the field. Reluctantly, Ball agreed to share Sportsman's Park. That now allowed Breadon to sell the old Cardinal Field and other land for $275,000—enough to pay off Mrs. Britton and provide additional money for Rickey to operate.

With Breadon's blessings, Branch Rickey started to buy minor-league teams. Over the next several years, Rickey would buy clubs at various class levels so that he could develop players for the Cardinals. He started with the purchase of Ft. Smith, a class C team in the Western Association. Next, he bought Houston, a class B team in the Texas League. Later, he purchased Syracuse, a class AA team in the International League. Usually, Rickey started with a minority interest and then increased his holdings until the Cards gained control.

Breadon and Rickey became very close and enjoyed a mutual respect. Peter Golenbock described the relationship thus: "They were an odd couple. Breadon was a Democrat, a barbershop quartet singer, and a sharp shooter.

His word was his bond. Rickey was a Republican, a teetotaler, a bible thumper, and slick around the corners of the rules."[1]

In February, vice president Rickey made a big acquisition that would strengthen the team. Toward the end of the previous year, he had scouted a big Kansas City right-handed pitcher named Jesse Haines. Haines had spent several years in the lower minors with limited success. He had begun the previous year with Tulsa of the Western League. On July 1, Tulsa traded twenty-five-year-old Haines to Kansas City. He improved significantly with his new club, and finished the year with a 21–5 mark that led the American Association. Several clubs wanted Haines, but Rickey outplayed them and paid $10,000 for the future Hall of Famer. Braves' manager George Stallings called Haines "the best pitching prospect to come out of the minors this year."[2] Haines became the third building block, joining Hornsby and Sherdel, as Rickey continued his quest to construct a championship team.

Young Bill and Marguerite Sherdel spent the winter in New York City. To strengthen his arm, Bill spent the time working as a blacksmith with his father. By the time spring training arrived, his arm was in great shape. Now that the Cardinals had money, Rickey decided to again take the club south for spring training. He chose Brownsville, Texas, a town of about 12,000 people. Brownsville was located on the southernmost tip of Texas, on the northern bank of the Rio Grande River that separated Texas from Mexico. Connie Mack was bringing his Philadelphia Athletics club to the same region and the two teams planned to play a sixteen-game exhibition schedule throughout Texas.

Bill Sherdel said goodbye to Marguerite and his family and climbed on a train bound from New York to St. Louis. He stopped in Gettysburg to visit his sister while on his way. A *Gettysburg Times* reporter caught up with him and asked who the most dangerous hitter in the National League was. "Zach Wheat" was Sherdel's reply. He also stated that the Cardinals' Bill Doak was the equal of any pitcher in the league.[3] When he reached his destination, he joined twenty-seven others including Rickey and boarded another train for Brownsville. They arrived and prepared for practice to begin on March 1. Other players traveled from across the country to join the team there. Rickey had expected forty-one players to participate in camp.

The Redbirds held morning and afternoon practices. Rickey worked them hard, but he also understood the need to grant the boys some fun time. He accomplished this at meal time. Reporter James Gould provided some insight into the Cardinals' fun.

> In order to make proceedings at meal time lively and productive of real fun, he [Rickey] has concentrated most of the funmakers at one table. This one table belongs to them and they are allowed to do about as they please—which is plenty. Only the innate modesty of the writer forbids his naming the man assigned to head the table of what Rickey terms "crabs." That these "crabs" realize the purpose of the manager is easily seen at any meal. The place is generally in an uproar at that one end of the room and "picking on" some player at another table is considered the best of baseball form. Really, eating is the chief, almost the only, relaxation of the players and they make the most of the time assigned.
>
> A glance at the roster of the "Genial Order of Crabs" will make plain how most of the time—though eating is not neglected—is passed. Bill Sherdel and Bill Dillhoefer sit next to the head of the table and they are flanked by Johnny Lavan and Hal Janvrin [veteran utility infielder picked up late in 1919 season], next to these boys come Jess Haines—Haines, by the way, has made an instantaneous hit with Rickey and the players—and Elmer Jacobs.
>
> The two next to the foot of the table are two of the most prominent in this newly organized order, Verne Clemons and Ferdie Schupp—and what rough-housing these two forget is hardly worthwhile. As is appropriate, the foot of the table is occupied by a recruit . . .
>
> Rickey's psychology is at work again in this. He realizes that the men, after working out twice daily, are apt to become rather tired and lackadaisical unless livened up a bit. Some critics—the biased ones—may consider the Card chieftain a spoilsport, but those who know him know better. The result is that the present St. Louis squad is probably the most contented and best spirited bunch that ever trained for a major-league season. Every one of them works hard, relaxes, and is happy.[4]

Branch Rickey instructs Bill Sherdel in the finer points of pitching
—Sherdel family

By March 5, Rickey was ready for his team to start playing games. The club headed out on a 1,300-mile trip to Dallas and back while playing games along the way. Bill Sherdel seemed to be ahead of the other hurlers; he was already throwing curves by the third practice. He was the only regular pitcher taken along. During the games, he pitched mostly in relief. Rickey was not excited to use him, since he already knew what he could do. The player that most impressed manager Rickey was young Cliff Heathcote. He arrived in great shape and was hitting the ball very well. Rickey came to camp thinking he might try Heathcote at first base, but now he was satisfied that he would be a regular member of the outfield. After two weeks of practice, Rickey was so pleased he decided to give his players a holiday. The local citizens arranged a fishing trip to Point Isabel on the Gulf of Mexico for the squad.

By mid-March, the *Cardinals* started to play exhibition games with the Athletics. Connie Mack's squad traveled from Houston while Rickey's club came from Brownsville. They met at Mercedes, Texas, and rode together from there. The clubs played sixteen games through the end of March. Both teams considered the series a success. Rickey was pleased with the development of his squad.

The Cardinals arrived home for the annual spring series with the Browns. This was always the first opportunity for the St. Louis fans to see both of their new clubs. All St. Louis fans were optimistic. Once again, the Browns proved to be the better team at this point in the spring. Rickey's club won the first game, but the Browns took the series, 4–2. Branch remained optimistic about the Cards' chances in 1920. His biggest concern was the arms of his second baseman Hornsby and his shortstop Lavan. Both men had trouble strengthening their arms during March.

The Redbirds opened at home against the Pirates that year on April 14. Attendance was estimated at 10,000. The Pirates defeated the Cardinals in ten innings to begin the new campaign. After the Redbirds took the second contest, Rickey handed Bill Sherdel the ball for the third encounter. Sherdel pitched a complete game but lost, 5–0, with no offensive support. He added a single and triple to his own cause. Jess Haines lost the fourth game, 3–0, after pitching a shutout for twelve innings. Where was the Cards' offense?

The Chicago Cubs came into St. Louis for the next series. The Cubs took the opener and the Cards grabbed the second game. Rickey's sluggers collected twenty-nine hits and sixteen runs in the two games. Bill Sherdel hit a pinch-hit home run in the second contest. The offense was back. The Cardinals took the third game and headed out on the first road trip.

The Cardinals train headed to Pittsburgh, Cincinnati, and Chicago. Sherdel entered several games in relief. Rickey's clan returned from the short road trip on May 4. The sixth-place Redbirds had played only seven of eleven scheduled games because of rain. Despite more losses than wins, the Cardinals had outhit and outscored the opposition. One local sportswriter now called the Redbirds the "Larrupin Legion" thanks to their potent hitting attack. They had improved since 1919. Vice president Rickey reduced his roster to seven pitchers, including Doak, Haines, Goodwin, and Sherdel; three catchers; five infielders; and five outfielders. A seven-pitcher roster would be unthinkable today, and one must wonder if Rickey really used his pitching staff effectively. It seemed his hitting had greatly improved but his pitching remained the club's weakness.

The Cards played at home for most of May with a quick trip to Chicago and Pittsburgh. By month end, Rickey's team remained in sixth. Chicago held the top spot. Bill Sherdel had worked eight of the last fourteen days with only one start—the final day of the month. In that game, he had pitched great ball for seven-and-a-third innings before he needed help. He ended a Cards' four-game-losing streak. The *St. Louis Post-Dispatch* wrote, "Bill Sherdel, the diminutive southpaw who has been doing heavy duty for the Rickeymen as a reliever, was started and hurled brilliantly until the eighth inning."[5] James Gould of the *St. Louis Star* added, "Sherdel started for Rickey and pitched in his usual, superb style, until the eighth."[6] Rickey was using young Sherdel as his primary reliever and Bill was probably happy for the work. The St. Louis fans were proud of league-leading .404 hitter Rogers Hornsby, despite the team's sixth position in the standings. In early June, the Cardinals finished their home-stand with three victories over the Cubs. In the first contest, Bill Doak stopped Grover Cleveland Alexander's eleven-game-winning streak. In the second game, Sherdel gained the victory in relief. A *St. Louis Post-Dispatch* reporter wrote, "Meantime, William Sherdel, who is constructing a niche in the Hall of Fame as the iron man of the age, relieved Jess Haines in the terrible first inning and thereafter made the Cubs lie down and be dead."[7]

On June 8, the Redbirds headed out on a road trip that would keep them away from St. Louis for the rest of the month. In a game in New York, Branch Rickey and the team received quite a scare. In the Giants' seventh inning, the Cards held a comfortable lead. There were two outs and the bases were loaded. The next batter hit a grounder to shortstop Lavan. Doc Lavan fielded the ball and threw it toward first base. The ball hit second baseman Hornsby in the head just above his left ear and he dropped, unconscious, to the ground. When he revived, Hornsby was led to the bench. His ears were bleeding from the force of the blow. After the game, he complained of a violent headache. A doctor examined Hornsby and suggested he miss a few games, but Hornsby was back in the lineup the next day.[8] Just imagine what Branch Rickey was thinking when he saw his $350,000 star and league-leading hitter lying unconscious on the ground. Luckily, Hornsby returned to the team quickly.

After series in Philadelphia and Boston, the Redbirds headed for a final away series in Cincinnati against the league leaders. The teams split the six games. Jess Haines pitched a three-hitter for the first win. In the second Cards' win, Sherdel relieved Doak in the seventh inning and held the Reds hitless. Sherdel did his job, but not without witnessing some excitement. In the eighth inning, Reds' pitcher Dolf Luque walked up to Hall-of-Fame umpire Bill Klem and struck him in the face, twice. A policeman grabbed Luque quickly and had started to lead him away when Luque broke free and headed for the home plate umpire again. Luckily, another Reds' pitcher grabbed Luque and muscled him to the bench. A near riot developed, as fans threw hundreds of soda bottles onto the field. Both Luque and Klem were fined $100—Luque for fighting and Klem for using abusive language.[9]

At the end of June, the upbeat Cards returned home to St. Louis after a very successful road trip. The fans were excited. The pennant race was very close. Cincinnati remained in first by three games. Rickey's team was tied for second with Brooklyn and Chicago. Boston was right behind them. St. Louis baseball fans were very proud. The Cardinals' Rogers Hornsby (.380) was leading the National League and the Browns' George Sisler (.427) was leading the American League.

The home stand burst the bubble of optimism in the hearts of Cardinal fans. Rickey's team split games with the Cubs, took two of three from the lowly Phillies, and lost all the other series. There were a few highpoints. On July 5, the Cards swept a double-header from the Cubs. Bill Sherdel started and outpitched the great Grover Cleveland Alexander, 2–1. Later in the month, young Sherdel pitched another great game. A *St. Louis Post-Dispatch* reporter started his column the next day, "Brilliant and courageous pitching by Wee William Sherdel inspired the Cardinals yesterday to depart from the paths of batting impotence and fielding mediocrity long enough to defeat the Phillies, 3 to 2, in twelve innings of the highest brand of baseball the most meticulous fan could desire."[10]

This unnamed *St. Louis Post-Dispatch* reporter used "Wee" to describe Bill Sherdel for the first time on July 20. Sherdel pitched a masterful twelve-inning complete-game victory. In the twelfth, he opened with a double to right center. He stretched a single into a double with a great slide. Unfortunately, he was spiked on his right hand during the slide. Sherdel called for time out while the wound was dressed, but he continued. Later, he scored the winning run.

Rogers Hornsby continued to lead the league in hitting during July. Austin McHenry clouted three home runs over three games. As July ended, the Cardinals occupied three of the top five hitting positions, including Hornsby (.367) in first. In the rival American League, Babe Ruth was just destroying pitching. He ended the month with thirty-five home runs and a .393 batting average. There was no question that the deadball era had ended in 1919.

July was a bad month for the St. Louis Cardinals. They dropped back to sixth place and ended the month with six straight losses. June's optimism had disappeared. Brooklyn was in the top spot with superior pitching and the hitting of Zach Wheat. Pitching was the real problem for the Redbirds, although many of the losses were close. During one stretch near the end of the month, eight consecutive games were decided by one run. Jess Haines, who had looked like the new staff ace in June, lost badly in five of his July starts. Sherdel entered most games in the late innings, often pitching three or four contests in a row.

Did Rickey use his pitchers effectively? It's a question that must be asked. In one situation, he had both Haines and Sherdel warming up for a half hour before he picked his reliever. Sherdel entered the game, surrendered two singles and a sacrifice, then Haines gave up the winning hit. Starters were relieving and relievers were starting. There was no question that Rickey saw the durable-armed Sherdel as his primary reliever. Would August be any better?

It didn't look so at the beginning of the month, which produced more of the same, with series losses to Brooklyn and Boston. And then the Cardinals' fortunes suddenly turned around. Rickey's boys outplayed the Phils, Pirates, Braves, Giants, and Robins, and won every series. They remained in sixth place, but now only three games below .500. Cincinnati occupied the top spot. Bill Sherdel did not get many pitching assignments during the month. He was ill and confined to bed for several days.[11] He was also hit by a bat in practice. Sherdel did get a few starts but relieved less often. It was Bill Doak's month. On August 10, he pitched a one-hitter against the Phillies. Only six balls were hit out of the infield. "Spittin' Bill" also contributed a four-hitter, two five-hitters, and a six-hitter.

The "Larrupin' Legion" had awakened. Most of August, Rickey had three of the top five hitters in the league. Hornsby (.363) was still leading the National League. Austin McHenry and Cliff Heathcote were also producing in the lineup. St. Louis fans continued to be proud because the Browns' George Sisler (.398) remained in the American League lead. Meanwhile, Babe Ruth's home run total climbed higher. The ex-pitcher now had forty-four.

On August 16 of 1920, the baseball world came to a standstill. In New York City, Cleveland Indians' shortstop Ray Chapman came to the plate to lead off the fifth inning against sidearm-thrower Carl Mays of the Yankees. Left-handed hitting Chapman took his normal stance. He liked to crowd the plate. In the dimly lit park, Mays threw the first pitch inside and struck Chapman over his right temple. The batter fell unconsciously to the ground. He was bleeding from both ears. A doctor rushed to Chapman and helped him to his feet, but he collapsed again and had to be carried to the Indians' clubhouse. Chapman was admitted to the hospital with a fractured skull and internal hemorrhaging.[12] Sadly, he passed away the next morning. That was the first time a major-league ballplayer had been killed by a thrown ball (though on two previous occasions, minor leaguers had died from beanings).

Chapman was considered one of the best shortstops in the game. The *St. Louis Star* wrote, "Modest at all times and a thorough gentleman, he had won a real place in the hearts of the fans not only of his home town, but wherever he played. He always gave his best."[13] Branch Rickey stated, "It is a terrible thing, a terrible thing. I knew Ray Chapman perhaps better than I knew most players on other teams. He was one of the finest characters in baseball and his place, not only as a player, both as a real man and a gentleman, will be a hard one to fill. His character was of the finest fiber. Always standing for the highest ideals of sport, he never faltered in practicing what he always preached—clean sport for sport's sake. His loss is a heavy one for the game."[14] Chapman had been married for less than a year. The next day, all major- and minor-league ball games stopped at four o'clock for five minutes as a silent tribute to Ray Chapman. Ballparks would fly their flags at half-mast for a week. Players would wear mourning armbands for the rest of the year.

On August 29, Bill and Marguerite Sherdel experienced a very happy event. Marguerite presented hubby Bill with a newborn baby girl. The couple named her Patricia Kathryn Sherdel and she became their pride and joy. Ironically, Bill Doak's wife gave birth to an eleven-pound baby boy two days later. The

Doaks named their son Robert. At sixteen, Bobby Doak would become the 1936 Florida State Amateur Golf Champion.

Bill and Marguerite with young Patricia
—Sherdel family

The Cardinals began the last month of the season on the road, and it didn't start well. The Cards lost series in Cincinnati and Brooklyn but, like the previous month, came back with series wins in New York, Boston, Philadelphia, and Chicago.

Rickey's 1920 Cardinals finished in a tie with Chicago for fifth place. Brooklyn won the title and would face the Cleveland Indians in the World Series. Babe Ruth blasted an incredible fifty-four home runs and hit .375—fourth best. For its part, St. Louis boasted two batting titles: Rogers Hornsby (.370) won the National League championship, while George Sisler (.407) took the American League title. The "Larrupin' Legion" led the league with a .289 team batting average. Rickey's club also led the league in hits, total bases, singles, and doubles—not bad for a fifth-place team.

As far as individual Cardinal players' seasons went, Rogers Hornsby had a fantastic year. He led the league in batting average, hits, doubles, and runs-batted-in. He also finished second in triples and fourth in runs scored. It was no wonder that the Giants had been willing to pay $350,000 for this player. McHenry blasted ten home runs for fourth place and batted .282. Bill Doak (20–12) topped an improved Redbirds' pitching staff. Rookie Jess Haines (13–20) led the league with forty-seven appearances and was fourth in strikeouts. Marv Goodwin (3–8) weakened in 1920. He pitched in thirty-two games.

Bill Sherdel (11–10), meanwhile, led the league with six saves and twenty-eight games finished. His 3.92 strikeouts per game earned him the league's fifth spot. After the season, James Gould wrote a nice article about him in the *St. Louis Star.*

> The Cardinals have a hurler who worked in forty-two games last year—a left-hander, too—who gave but thirty-nine bases on balls all season. This remarkable control record was established in 1920 by Bill Sherdel, relief pitcher extraordinary. While Bill was passing the thirty-nine, he was causing seventy-one of the foe to take three futile swings and begin the long march back from the plate to the water cooler.
>
> Sherdel is now counted as a regular member of the Cards' hurling staff. He has earned his place by his steadiness and his constant applying of himself to the task of perfecting his pitching style. In 1919, Sherdel was a splendid hitter, but he couldn't pitch. In 1920, his hitting fell off badly, but his pitching was of such caliber as to stamp him as one of the future stars of the game. Game after game, Sherdel was called on to relieve a tottering moundsman. Time after time did he make good in holding the opposition. Once or twice, of course, he didn't seem to fit in the rescue role, but none of us . . . are altogether perfect.
>
> How great was Sherdel's mastery of the ball is shown by the fact that in fifteen of the games he appeared in, Bill never issued a pass. In seventeen of his battles, he gave but one free ticket to first and, on only two occasions, did he give as many as three passes . . . Sherdel really is not given credit for his masterly work, for many a game he saved, but could not be credited with the victory. He won nine, lost ten and tied one on the actual figures. . . .

The game that Sherdel was more tickled about winning than any other was that of July 5, when he faced Alexander the Great and trimmed the Chicago star, 2–1. Bill allowed nine hits in the game, but kept them beautifully scattered. He walked but one man. Another game written down in Bill's book was fought out on June 5. Playing against Chicago, the Cubs slammed Haines for six runs in the first inning. Sherdel went in and held the Cubs scoreless for eight innings, while the Cardinals picked up eleven juicy runs and won out.[15]

Even *The Sporting News* headquartered in St. Louis commented about Bill Sherdel, "Scherdel [sic] has a whole lot of ability as he proved on numerous occasions in games that were already lost when he was sent in and it was not treating him fairly or getting the best results out of him to keep him solely for relief roles."[16]

Over the winter, Bill, Marguerite, and baby Patricia traveled from their home in New York City to Gettysburg to visit Bill's sister and brother-in-law. They also spent time in McSherrystown with Marguerite's father, James Strausbaugh, who lived on North Street. While they were in the area, Bill and Marguerite visited with their many friends and fans. Residents had switched their allegiance from the Pennsylvania teams in Philadelphia and Pittsburgh to the St. Louis Cardinals. Bill Sherdel was now a famous baseball pitcher and celebrity.

CHAPTER TEN

In 1921, the first-ever Miss America would be crowned. The Clair Brothers of the Acme Packing Company of Green Bay would be granted an American Professional Football Association franchise. Golfer Walter Hagen would win the PGA Championship and dominate golfing. Paavo Nurmi would set his first world record in the 10,000-meter run in Stockholm. He would own middle- and long-distance running throughout the 1920s. The New York Yankees would purchase twenty acres in the Bronx to build Yankee Stadium.

Major-league baseball received a huge black eye when it was finally acknowledged that eight of the Chicago White Sox had been influenced by gamblers and thrown the 1919 World Series. In response, the leagues established a baseball commissioner and named Judge Kenesaw Mountain Landis to fill the position. Landis would rule with an iron hand. Although the players were not convicted in court, he banished the Black Sox eight—Eddie Cicotte, Lefty Williams, Joe Jackson, Chick Gandil, Happy Felsh, Buck Weaver, Fred McMullin, and Swede Risberg—for life. The gambling purge even touched the Cardinals. Gene Paulette, former Redbird first baseman, was also banned for life, just for fraternizing with St. Louis gamblers.

By 1921, all the other major-league managers knew of Rickey's skill in evaluating talent. It was becoming much harder to acquire good ballplayers. As soon as word traveled that Rickey was interested in a player, some other club would quickly sign him.[1]

Before training camp launched, Bill Sherdel sent his signed 1921 contract to vice president Rickey. James Gould wrote:

Patent-medicinally speaking, Southpaw Bill has become widely and most favorably known in the pitching world as 'Rickey's Ready Relief.' Time after time, when the starting hurler showed signs of faltering, Bill was rushed to the rescue and succeeded in staving off further attacks. Sherdel appeared in forty-two games last season. In May, he relieved three days in a row against the Giants and, during one stretch, pitched parts of six games in nine days. . . . While Bill appreciates that a real relief man is a great asset to a club, he is beginning to think that he has won the right to take his regular turn on the hill. That is his present ambition and it would not be at all surprising were he to realize it this summer. He is a hard worker, a fine clean-living kid, and a great fellow to have on a club. St. Louis fans are strong for him. They saw him save many a game last year and they want him to win a full-sized flock in 1921.[2]

Branch Rickey moved the Cardinals' training camp to Orange, Texas, for 1921. Orange was the easternmost town in the state. It was located along the Sabine River and across from Louisiana. The town had a population of 9,200 at that time and was only about fifty miles from Lake Charles, Louisiana, where Connie Mack held his camp. That proximity allowed Rickey and Mack to plan a series of twelve exhibition games throughout March. Rickey predicted, "The players will be pleased with the arrangements." The players were to live at the Holland Hotel and take their meals at the adjacent Sabine Clubhouse. The ballpark with a new clubhouse was located nine blocks away.[3]

The first trainload of players arrived on February 20, after a twenty-seven-hour trip from St. Louis. This group included mostly rookies. Rickey wanted time to work with the youngsters before the second train of veterans arrived a few days later. Once they did, workouts began in earnest. That year, Rickey reduced the practice time. Instead of twice a day, the players just worked from 1:30 to 5:00. They could arise later in the morning and have free time in the evenings until 11:30. The players were happier with this arrangement, and the results showed it. Rickey added one new idea this year. Out in right field, he constructed three batting cages. They were seventy-five-feet long with netting on either side. Balls hit to the right or left bounced off the net and rolled to the pitcher. Only balls hit straight went to the outfield. Three batters and three pitchers could work at the same time. Rickey restricted his pitchers to straight balls the first week.

One day, writer Robert Maxwell stopped to chat with manager Rickey, and asked for Rickey's thoughts on the coming season. Rickey remarked, "Give me one good pitcher, a pitcher who can go out and win twenty-five ball games in a season, and I will not be afraid of any ball club in the National League. I am not about to explode with enthusiasm, nor can it be said that I am overly optimistic, but if a man like [Grover Cleveland] Alexander . . . stepped into the lineup of the Cards this year, we would be battling for a pennant from the very start. As I see it now, everything depends upon the slab artists."

Rickey looked out over his pitchers and continued, "You can see for yourself. There are six good performers, but Haines is the only husky one in the bunch. Most of our moundsmen are small, weighing from 150 to 165 pounds. They do good work, but seem to lack the endurance of an Alexander . . . and a lot of the other big boys. Judas Priest, but I wish I could find a husky pitcher some time."[4]

The Cardinals split the exhibition series with Connie Mack's Athletics. However, the most exciting exhibition game took place on March 16 at Lake Charles, Louisiana, between the Cards and the powerful New York Yankees. Although it was just an exhibition, the ballpark had been sold out for several weeks and the largest crowd ever in the region was expected. The game was billed as Rogers Hornsby versus Babe Ruth. Branch Rickey picked Bill Sherdel to start against the Bronx Bombers. Before the game, a reporter wrote:

> On the shoulders of Bill Sherdel, kid southpaw, will rest the responsibility of keeping Babe from losing a couple of perfectly good league balls, and Bill is far from worried at the assignment. He hasn't boasted any, but he is anxious to have his best slants working when he faces the American League terror. Yesterday, Bill was so upset that he went fishing. . . .
>
> But Bill insists that Babe will have to hit a bad one if he hits at all, for the reason that he [Bill] isn't going to give the Bambino any good ones to hit, which it must be admitted seems logical enough.[5]

Sherdel struck out Babe Ruth in the first inning and the crowd erupted in applause. In Ruth's next at-bat, he walked him. Unfortunately, the other Yankees did better and young Sherdel left the game after three innings with a 6–0 deficit. Babe did hit a home run later in the contest. The game ended in New York's favor, 14–9. The two teams combined for thirty hits and twenty-three runs. Oddly, the hitting star was not Hornsby or Ruth, but the bespectacled Cards' rookie George Torporcer, who hit a home run and three singles in four plate appearances.[6]

Looking forward to the upcoming season from there, young Sherdel was optimistic. He wrote the following in a letter to a Gettysburg friend:

> My arm is sure feeling fine and I look for a good year. Orange, Texas, was a good training camp and we had fine weather every day. Everybody is in fine shape and I am sure we will finish in the first division if we have any breaks at all. But you know how it is. If a few players get laid up the club will be shot. We have a few good-looking pitchers, but it's a little too early yet to say much about them. . . .
>
> We leave here soon and I'll be glad to get back to God's country and the family. Please remember me to Eddie and Ira Plank and all my old friends in Gettysburg.[7]

The Cardinals completed their exhibition season with the annual spring St. Louis series against the Browns. The Browns took the series again in 1921. The two clubs were evenly matched. The series came down to the seventh game. The Cardinals led until late in the game, but the Browns won the game and the series. That was still an improvement for Rickey's club. Again, he felt the success of the season would depend on the hurlers.

The Cardinals opened the new season in Chicago against the Cubs on April 13. New Baseball Commissioner Landis was in attendance. He greeted each of the players before the game began. The Cards' lineup included rookie Clarence "Heinie" Mueller in right field and Jess Haines on the mound. Mueller, who'd been discovered during Rickey's tryouts, was not lacking in self-confidence. When he arrived for the workout, "Heinie" told the Cardinals' scouts that he "ran like Ty Cobb, hit like Home Run Baker, and fielded like Tris Speaker."[8] Haines lost the opener to Grover Cleveland Alexander—and the 1921 season began.

April was another bad opening month for the Cardinals. Once again, pitching was considered the culprit. Bill Sherdel was unavailable until late in the month. He suffered a fractured little finger on his right hand and was sent home to St. Louis for ten days. Sherdel entered the seventh inning against the Pirates on April 27. He provided two scoreless innings. He relieved one more time two days later against the Reds. In that game, he held the Reds scoreless for three innings, but then surrendered four in the ninth. The Redbirds ended the month in the National League cellar. Writers and fans were asking Rickey to trade a position player for a pitcher.

The month of May went much better. After a rocky start, the Cardinals finished the month in fifth place. Doak was now ready to go. Goodwin was having trouble returning to form after a poor 1920 showing. Sherdel was still recovering from his broken finger. Position players were also recovering. Cliff Heathcote's leg was in a cast. He had torn a ligament in his hip and would be out for perhaps a month. Austin McHenry had also broken a finger and didn't return to the lineup until mid-May. Once again, the Cardinals possessed three of the top five hitters in the league. Hornsby was number one at .434, utility player Joe Schultz was fourth (.412), and outfielder McHenry occupied the fifth spot (.363). McHenry was much more selective at bat. He reduced his strikeouts and his average improved.

The May issue of *Baseball* magazine included a nice article on Bill Sherdel. He was now considered an unrecognized star. The story began:

> A pitcher with a second-division club seldom gets much notice in the write-ups and, although he may be doing yeoman service, some other men of lesser merit, who are fortunate enough to work with a victorious team, bask in the baseball spotlight while he must be content with his knowledge of work well done.
>
> Bill Sherdel, Cardinal left-hander, has been pitching some fine ball for the St. Louis team, good enough to hold a regular place for the past three seasons, and yet seldom does one read an appreciation of his work.[9]

During the month of June, the Cardinals started to move up in the standings. They returned home from a successful road trip on June 7 and would remain home until month end. Goodwin had been having problems since his leg infection the previous year and the outlawing of the spitball. He was still struggling to develop his other pitches. Rickey's squad reeled off ten straight victories to move to third place, then lost five consecutive encounters.

St. Louis ended June in fourth place. In a very productive home-stand, the Cards won seventeen of twenty-eight games. The Pirates were leading the league. Hornsby was still the league's top hitter at .407. In the American League, Babe Ruth continued to amaze fans with his power. He had already blasted twenty-eight home runs by month end. Bill Sherdel remained in the bullpen as the club headed back out on the road in July.

The Cardinals' east-coast road trip was dismal. Bill Sherdel continued to work in relief without fanfare. The disappointing club returned to St. Louis on July 26 to begin another lengthy home-stand. The following day was Tuberculosis Day at Sportsman's Park. This was the seventh annual benefit for the St. Louis Tuberculosis Society. The 15,000 fans in attendance gave three cheers for Hall-of-Fame pitcher Christy Mathewson, who was in a life-and-death struggle with the deadly disease. The Cardinals defeated the Phillies that day.[10]

As Rickey's squad entered August, the club started to win again. Cliff Heathcote returned to the outfield. The excellent hitting of Hornsby and McHenry was prominent in the box scores. The St. Louis crowd nearly rioted during a game with John McGraw and the Giants on August 4. In the eighth inning, the Giant hurler beaned the Cards' Joe Schulz. Schulz dropped, unconscious, to the ground and was carried from the field. Next, "Pickles" Dillhoefer and Giants' catcher Frank Snyder began a fist fight and tumbled across the ground. That must have seemed rather comical since Dillhoefer was 5'7" and 154 pounds while Snyder was 6'2" and 185 pounds. Snyder probably held a grudge since Rickey had traded him away in 1920. The St. Louis fans ridiculed Snyder and the hefty catcher tried to climb into the stands. Police intervened and halted the near riot. The Cardinals got their revenge and won the game, 1–0.[11] Word must have spread. For the next game, 12,000 Cardinal fans arrived looking for more action. That was a record for a weekday game.

Bill Sherdel pitched a great game in relief on August 6 against the Boston Braves. He had entered in the first inning without warming up. He pitched nine innings, allowed no runs, and struck out five. A *St. Louis Post-Dispatch* reporter remarked, "Wee William Sherdel, the tiniest hurler on Rickey's staff, replaced the husky [Jeff] Pfeffer, and he proved an uncharted snag in the course of the good ship Boston. The little left-hander toiled smoothly and with characteristic nonchalance and held the men of Fred Mitchell to four hits during the balance of the game."[12]

The Rickeymen spent the second half of August touring the east-coast parks. The winning continued. Rickey granted Bill Sherdel a rare start on August 27 against the Braves. He did not disappoint the boss. He allowed only six hits and one run for a complete game victory. The St. Louis Cardinals remained in fourth place. The Pirates and Giants still led the league. The Redbirds were playing great defense with a team fielding mark of .967—the best average in many years. The club batting average was an incredible .307. Rogers Hornsby now had twenty home runs and 200 hits for the year. Austin McHenry was having a breakout season. He was becoming a legitimate superstar.

As September began, the Cardinals were in Pittsburgh. Rickey gave Bill Sherdel the ball to start the second game of a double-header. Once again, Sherdel pitched well, as a *St. Louis Star* reporter summarized: "With the way Bill Sherdel was southpawing, the Pirates never had a chance. Bill walked two and fanned the same number, but allowed only four hits and was never in danger. Counting his last game against the Braves in Boston—he won it, 2–1—Sherdel has allowed but one run in eighteen innings and permitted only ten hits off his delivery in the two games. Which, it may be remarked, is pretty nifty pitching."[13] Sherdel hurled the Cards into third place. Several days later, he got another start, this time against the Cubs. He held the Bruins to one hit through the first seven innings before surrendering two runs in the final two frames. He won again.

A week later, Sherdel started another game against Chicago. In this, he allowed one run until the eighth inning when he needed help from Jess Haines. The Cardinals won, 10–5. After that game, the Rickeymen returned home to fight for second place and finish the season. The Cards ran off seven straight victories but remained in third. The Giants had now moved into first place ahead of the Pirates.

Bill Sherdel provided one more quality start at the end of September against the second-place Pirates. He allowed only five hits with three strikeouts and no walks in a 3–1 win that was called in the sixth inning because of darkness. It would prove to be Sherdel's final start of the year. The Cardinals had a great September. They won twenty out of twenty-seven games.

After several games in early October, the 1921 season came to an end. The St. Louis Cardinals finished with an outstanding record. Only the New York Giants and the Pittsburgh Pirates had done better. Rickey's boys had outplayed every other team in baseball during the second half of the campaign. If it hadn't been for the first month of the season, the Cardinals may have won the pennant. There was certainly much optimism for the next year. Oddly, the other St. Louis club, the Browns, also finished in third place—in the American League. The Cardinals' and Browns' players earned $585 each for their third-place finishes. In today's dollars, each player would have received $7,280. The 1921 World Series would be played between two New York teams, the Giants and the Yankees.

Branch Rickey had built an offensive juggernaut. The team batting average of .308 led the league. Nine Redbirds batted over .300 for the season. Once again, Rogers Hornsby led the league in hitting with a .395 average. Rookie "Heinie" Mueller hit .352 while McHenry reached .350. Mueller did not achieve the minimum number of at-bats to qualify for the top hitting spots, but Hornsby and McHenry finished as the top two official hitters in the National League. Hornsby had a Most Valuable Player season. He led the league in batting average, runs, hits, doubles, triples, runs-batted-in, slugging average, and on-base percentage. Hornsby finished second in home runs (21). Of course, these numbers paled when compared to those of the American League's "Sultan of Swat." Babe Ruth bettered his home run record of 1920 with fifty-nine homers in 1921. Finally, Austin McHenry had a breakout year. He proved he had reached superstardom by finishing second in batting average, third in total bases, fourth in home runs and runs-batted-in, and fifth in doubles.

Top Cardinal hurlers were Haines (18–12) and Doak (15–6). Bill Doak led the league in winning percentage and earned run average. Bill Sherdel

(9–8) remained mostly a reliever again in 1921. He appeared in thirty-eight games, but only eight were starts. Bill pitched 144 innings with a 3.18 earned run average. Sherdel's good friend Marv Goodwin spent much of the season in the Texas League and pitched well. He had never recovered totally from an arm he'd injured two years earlier, and an infected leg from the previous season. Marv was also trying to develop another pitch to replace his dominating spitball. Rickey added Goodwin to the Cards' roster at the beginning of October so he could evaluate if Goodwin deserved to be part of the Redbirds' future.

On October 6, Bill Sherdel returned with his wife and daughter Patsy to McSherrystown, where the family would spend the winter at the home of Marguerite's father, James Strausbaugh, on North Street. Local fans were happy to see Sherdel. Everyone hoped that 1922 would be the year the St. Louis Cardinals would finally win the National League pennant.

CHAPTER ELEVEN

In 1922, the first-ever issue of *Reader's Digest* magazine would be published. Many radio stations across the country would begin transmission. The British courts would sentence Mahatma Gandhi to six years in prison for civil disobedience. The American Professional Football Association would change its name to the National Football League. And, in a major decision, the US Supreme Court would rule organized baseball a sport and not a business, and so therefore not subject to antitrust laws.

For Bill Sherdel and his teammates, 1922 would be a challenging year. It was a year of tears and cheers, of great sadness, and of much joy. It began with the wedding of Sherdel's good friend and young, peppery catcher Bill "Pickles" Dillhoefer in Mobile, Alabama, on January 14. Dillhoefer, a Cleveland native, had spent the winter in St. Louis selling automobiles. He traveled to Mobile to wed schoolteacher Miss Massie Slocum and, after a brief honeymoon, the couple returned to St. Louis to live. After several days, "Pickles" became very ill. On January 19, he was admitted to St. John's Hospital with what was diagnosed as a "hard cold, which he may have neglected long enough to make it hard to check."[1] Dillhoefer was hoping to recover quickly and make it to Orange, Texas, to join the Cardinals for their second spring training in that town. Later, it would be determined that Dillhoefer had contracted typhoid fever. Rickey stopped to see his likeable backstop many times before heading to camp.

Bill Sherdel was pleased to learn that Branch Rickey intended to use him as a regular on the mound that year. The pitcher believed that he deserved the chance, and now Rickey agreed. In the previous year, Sherdel had been ranked next to veteran Bill Doak in pitching effectiveness. Branch penciled Doak, Haines, and Sherdel as starters.[2]

Rickey was busy planning for the year's camp in Orange. He scheduled thirteen exhibition games with American League clubs, including the Yankees. The pitchers and catchers were expected to take the first train from St. Louis on February 20, with the regulars traveling a week later. Several position players including Cliff Heathcote had received permission to also arrive early. Heathcoate had had a difficult 1921 due to several leg injuries. He was ready to go and stated as much in a letter to a St. Louis friend, "Anyone who is counting me out of a regular job has several new guesses coming. . . . If I ever was fast, I'm seconds faster now and sometimes I wonder in my Pennsylvania way how a guy can be so speedy without scorching himself. Don't know whether Rickey figures on me for regular work, but if he doesn't, he isn't the smart baseball manager I always have considered him."[3]

The first group of pitchers, including Bill Sherdel, and the catchers, arrived in Orange on February 20 after a thirty-four-hour train ride from St. Louis. That was the earliest a Cardinal team had started camp. The National League had finally removed the restriction on when practice could start. The pitchers began getting into physical shape, although Rickey would not allow them to throw hard. They had a week to prep before the rest of the players arrived.

On February 23, Branch Rickey and the players received word from St. Louis that "Pickles" Dillhoefer had passed away that morning. The twenty-eight-year-old catcher was one of the most popular players on the club. A *St. Louis Post-Dispatch* reporter described him this way:

Although not a catcher of surpassing brilliance, he had such a fighting spirit, boundless enthusiasm, and excellent base line coaching qualities that he was considered one of the club's best assets, on the field and at the box office.

His expressions of hope when on the coaching line brought many laughs from the grand stand. . . . So closely did he follow the game that frequently he got into trouble with the umpires for his over-eagerness. Frequently when catching he would run halfway into the outfield to see that the outfielders did not interfere with each other in the fielding of a fly. Also when on the bench, from which he was not supposed to emerge when the opposing team was batting, he would dart out at critical moments to coach a fielder. After his purpose had been accomplished he would realize his rule infraction and would sheepishly scurry back to cover.⁴

Many of Dillhoefer's teammates seemed stunned when they heard the news. Most had thought that "Pickles" was on the road to recovery. They just couldn't believe the report was true. The players gathered in groups and all the usual horseplay disappeared. Bill Sherdel was greatly affected. "Pickles" had caught Sherdel's pitches many times. They both possessed that fiery spirit and were quite close. Branch Rickey took the news very badly, also. He said, "I can hardly believe Dilly is gone. Of course, I knew he was very sick when I left St. Louis, but it is a shock to learn of his death."⁵ Dillhoefer's body was taken to Mobile for burial. A small contingent of Cardinals' personnel headed to Alabama for the service. The group included Branch Rickey, Milt Stock (Dillhoefer's roommate), fellow catcher Verne Clemons, scout Charley Barrett, and Bill Sherdel. They served as pallbearers for the funeral.

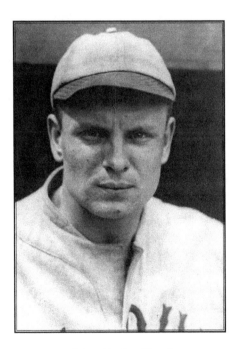

Bill "Pickles" Dillhoefer
—Coulson collection

The veterans arrived in camp by the beginning of March. Hornsby was a holdout. Rickey was starting to regret the return to Orange. The weather was terrible that year. The team was only able to practice three of the first nine days because of constant rain and cold temperatures. Some of the players went duck hunting. Finally, by March 8, the club began playing intra-squad games. Rickey reported that he had only two pitchers in good shape—Sherdel and Haines. That did not last long. Sherdel, Haines, Lavan, and Heathcote contracted the flu and remained weak and in bed for several days. Then, some good news! Hornsby signed his contract and joined the club in time for exhibition games. His new three-year deal was for $22,500 per year—quite a change from 1915 when the Cards purchased him for $600. Managers John McGraw (Giants) and Wilbert Robinson (Robins) stated that they would rather have Hornsby than Ruth on their team. McGraw even called Hornsby the greatest player in baseball.[6]

The Cards started their exhibition season. Bill Sherdel took the mound for the first time against the A's in Galveston. He looked ready for the season to begin. Sherdel pitched a great six innings, allowing only two hits. He also looked ready to hit. He collected two singles and a double in four plate appearances and the Cards belted nineteen hits in a 13–3 win.

Next, the Redbirds split two games with the Browns in New Orleans—not St. Louis. Rickey gave Sherdel the ball for the first encounter and he pitched all nine innings. The Browns scored one run in the ninth to defeat the Cards, 6–5. With the series tied at 1–1, Rickey handed the ball to Sherdel again. Sherdel pitched another complete game, but lost once more in the ninth, 3–2. That game was not without controversy. Harry Pierce of the *St. Louis Star* reported the events to his readers. "A miniature riot was precipitated in the final half of the ninth, when Sherdel slipped a second strike over on [Bill] Jacobson by a quick return delivery. Jimmy Austin rushed up to Umpire [Dick] Nallin and protested vigorously. The entire Brownie team followed the Pepper Pod. Manager [Lee] Fohl pulled Austin away, but Jim flew right back at his royal nibs—the Ump. Nallin then grabbed Austin and pushed him into the hands of other players. A captain of police and three patrolmen appeared on the field at this stage of the argument, and peace was quickly restored."[7] "Baby Doll" Jacobson gained his revenge by knocking a single over second base on the next pitch. That started the Browns' rally, which ended with a 3–2 victory over Sherdel and the Cards. That wouldn't be the last time that Sherdel's quick-pitch delivery would create a controversy.

The 1922 season began on April 12 against the Pirates at Sportsman's Park. Most preseason polls named the Giants, Pirates, and Cardinals as the three best teams in the National League. Branch Rickey was determined to see his club get an improved start this year, and why not get the lead on one of its closest competitors—the Pirates. The club he brought north was perhaps a little better. Normally, you pick your best starter to open the season. Branch selected Bill Sherdel to take the mound, a nice compliment. The Pirates' lineup included Hall-of-Famers "Rabbit" Maranville, Max Carey, and "Pie" Traynor. Sherdel and the Redbirds looked great. The little southpaw pitched a complete game victory, 10–1, allowing only seven scattered hits. His teammates collected eleven safeties. Even Sherdel helped his own cause with two singles. The 18,000 fans went home happy and optimistic about the new season.

Bill Sherdel in his new 1922 uniform
—Sherdel family

After the Pirates series, the Cubs came to town. Once again, Branch handed the ball to young Sherdel. He pitched another complete game victory in front of 25,000 loyal fans. His control was outstanding. He walked only one batter in two starts. From there, the Cards headed to Pittsburgh, where Sherdel received the starting assignment again. This time, he didn't survive the first inning. Sherdel surrendered four straight singles and two runs before leaving. The Redbirds eventually won. Southpaw Bill pitched once more in April, when Rickey handed him the ball against the Cubs on April 28. Sherdel won again, 11–3, with great offensive support. He was never in trouble, scattering six hits while his teammates collected fifteen. Hornsby hit two homers. McHenry had a great day at the plate, picking up a home run and three other hits in five at bats. Rickey's club ended its best April in third place behind the Giants and Cubs. The Cardinals' hitting was outstanding, but their fielding was bad. The club was last in fielding percentage.

The Cardinals spent almost the whole month of May at friendly Sportsman's Park. There, they entertained six of the other seven clubs. When the month ended, the Cards were still in third place—behind the Giants and Pirates. Sherdel was off to a great start. He extended his win streak to six before he suffered his first loss. The Midway native ended May with a 7–2 record. He was now recognized as a star pitcher of the Cardinals. The difference for Sherdel in 1922 was his development of a change-of-pace pitch to fool the batters.

Trader Rickey made a move at the end of May that left many baseball men scratching their heads. The Cardinals were in Chicago playing a doubleheader on May 30 and, between games, Rickey traded promising twenty-four-year-old star outfielder Cliff Heathcote to the Cubs for thirty-two-year-old veteran outfielder Max Flack. The players traded places and uniforms, and played the second game with their new teams. Flack was a good hitter and very fast on the bases. For the Cardinals, he would lead off the batting order and play right field.

June was another good month for the Cardinals. They spent most of it on the road, stopping in every National League city except Cincinnati. Rickey's crew returned home on June 22 in second place, only four-and-a-half games behind the Giants. Sherdel had worked several games again from the bullpen. Rickey seemed to use whichever pitcher was ready at that moment with no thought about establishing a routine for starting pitchers. Sherdel did make several excellent starts during the month, however, including a five-hit win over the tough Pirates. No wonder his rising star had attracted the attention of consumer companies who wanted to trade on his popularity. In 1922, this recognized Cardinals' luminary began earning extra money through advertising.

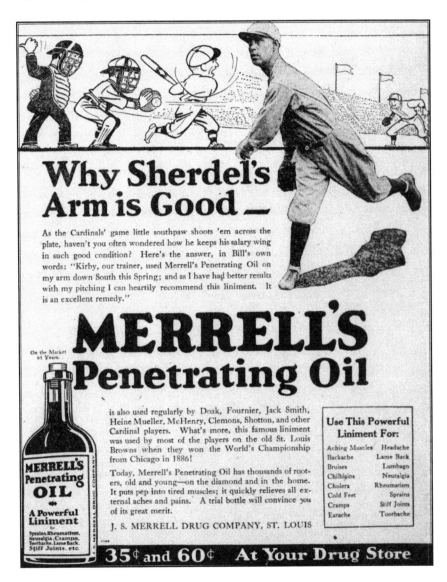

A Bill Sherdel endorsement
—*St. Louis Post-Dispatch*, May 1, 1923

Doak and Sherdel continued to win and now Haines was also pitching better. The Redbirds continued to produce runs. Hornsby was leading the league with a .396 average and sixteen home runs. In the American League, the St. Louis Browns were in first place and George Sisler was leading the league with a .432 average. It was going to be an exciting summer for St. Louis sports fans.

Still, not everything was going well for Branch Rickey's club. In early June, Austin McHenry had gone on a tear with his bat. In the first nine games of the month, he'd batted .485, including ten runs, six doubles, and two homers. On June 10, he clouted two four-baggers to defeat the Phillies. By the middle of the month, McHenry had bumped up his average to an excellent .306 with five home runs.[8] He was now recognized throughout the league as a star. But something strange was happening to him. He was losing his strength and his ability to follow a ball while running. If McHenry could stand still, he could see the ball's path and catch it, but if he had to run after the ball, his vision immediately became blurred.[9] Branch Rickey asked him if he was all right. McHenry responded, "Yes, I feel all right, but I can't see. I don't know what it is. Maybe I'm going blind." Rickey was worried about his star. He sent the twenty-seven-year-old left-fielder home to Ohio to rest and, hopefully, recover.[10]

Even without McHenry, the Cardinals did very well in July. They finished the month in second place, only a half game out of first. Rickey's club even touched first for one day, on July 22. Then the Cards faced the Giants in New York in a big series, and the New York club clobbered them, winning four of five battles. The St. Louis squad did score twenty-eight runs in five games, but their twirlers surrendered forty-two. The Cardinals' pitching was shattered. Sherdel saved the month by defeating the Robins on the final day of July, bringing his club back to within a half game of the lead. Sherdel was 13–6. Hornsby continued to lead all National League hitters with a .391 average and twenty-seven home runs.

Rickey had proved his talent-scouting prowess again when he'd signed catcher Eddie Ainsmith in 1921. Ainsmith was now doing most of the catching. He was fifth in the league with ten homers. Ainsmith had been the battery-mate of Walter Johnson in Washington until he was traded to Ty

Cobb and the Tigers. Cobb decided to rebuild the Detroit club and made Ainsmith available to his friend Branch Rickey. The *St. Louis Star* wrote:

> Eddie is a horse for work, and, apparently, has no sense of fear so far as injuries go. He will block a plate as prettily as you please and has done everything but actually climb the screens to capture foul flies.
>
> Ainsmith's continued stellar work can only be taken as a big boost for manager Rickey's judgment of a player and a player's ability to deliver.[11]

Austin McHenry returned to the club in late July and Rickey inserted him into the lineup for one game against the Giants. McHenry went hitless. Three days later, he pinch-hit and singled before leaving the game for a pinch-runner. Rickey realized there was still something wrong. Sadly, he sent McHenry back home to seek medical advice.

Whether it was the loss of McHenry, the mismanagement of the pitching staff, or something else, August was the month that probably decided the pennant hopes of the Cardinals. The club flirted briefly with first place several times, but just couldn't build a winning streak strong enough to propel them forward. The Redbirds had two critical series—one with the leading Giants and one with the quickly rising Cubs—late in the month. Rickey's squad lost both series. They continued to get run support, but the pitching just couldn't hold leads.

The *Philadelphia Bulletin* did a nice article on Bill Sherdel in August. "He [Sherdel] is the rare case of a pitcher staying around for three or four years, not showing a heap of efficiency, and then buzzing forth in full blast and astonishing the world. . . . Sherdel has breezed through the league this year. How do you do it? 'Slow ball,' he testifies, laconically. Didn't have any change of pace when I started in this league. Now I got one.'"[12]

Branch Rickey was doing his best to improve the squad. He recalled two youngsters—first baseman Jim Bottomley and third baseman Ray Blades—from Syracuse. Bottomley and Blades would be the first rewards from Rickey's new farm system. Both players had been signed from Rickey's inaugural tryout camp in St. Louis several years earlier. These youngsters would become the next building blocks in architect Rickey's creation of a Cardinals' dynasty.

Pete Golenbock described "Sunny Jim" this way: "Bottomley was recommended by the principal of his high school in Nokomis, Illinois. When he arrived for the tryout, the nineteen-year-old wore his father's street shoes with spikes nailed to the front and a tattered uniform."[13] After several successful years in the minors, Rickey brought him to St. Louis. Golenbock goes on: "Jim Bottomley, who lived life with a perpetual smile . . . became the idol of the Knot-Hole Gang youngsters. . . . He was an old-fashioned, old-time player, a guy who played mostly for the love of the game." Many would consider him to be the best first baseman the Cardinals ever had.[14] He would be elected to the Hall of Fame in 1974.

Ray Blades was originally signed as a pitcher, but Rickey played him at third base and in the outfield. He described Blades as a "natural athlete with speed." Blades would become a career .300 hitter with the Cardinals, but his full potential would never be realized because of a leg injury.

Even with those additions, though, it was difficult to measure the loss of McHenry to the team. James Gould wrote in the *St. Louis Star* on August 21.

> Fans have noticed recently some of the famous Cardinal punch has been missing. Runners get on with no one down, and are left because succeeding batters cannot smash them across. It certainly was a blow when McHenry, third in the league last year in batting runs in, was compelled to doff his spangles and hie himself away to the Ohio for recuperation and rest just when his comrades needed him and his bludgeon most. . . .
>
> Mac was a long hitter, a hard hitter, a man who drove out extra base blows almost as often as he did singles. . . . Moreover, McHenry is a sterling fielder and a fighter. His arm is good, and he has cut down many an aspiring base runner trying to take an extra sack on hits to left. Last year, he was fourth in total chances handled by National League outfielders.
>
> Manager Rickey has had a tough time trying to fill the gap left by McHenry. Jack Smith, Mueller, Mann, Shotton, Schultz, and Blades already have tackled the proposition and, while every man-jack of them have done their best, they have not succeeded in filling the shoes of 'Ole Mac.'

Not only for his fielding and hitting ability is McHenry missed. The players miss his spirit, his constant desire to win and his wonderful and cheerful personality. . . . He is a hard man to find a substitute for.[15]

There was another big addition to the Cardinal family in August, and Branch Rickey had nothing to do with this one. Marguerite Sherdel presented Bill with an eight-pound son, William James Sherdel, on August 27, in St. Louis, where the family was living at 3522 Sullivan Avenue. Bill was so excited he sent word to manager Bert Weeden of the Hanover Raiders, writing "his name is Billy, Jr." and asking Bert to "tell all the boys."[16] Unfortunately for Sherdel, the Cardinals' team was heading out of town on September 3 and would be gone the rest of the season. Sherdel wouldn't see his wife, daughter, and new son for a month. Back in Pennsylvania, manager Weeden was busy selling Bill Sherdel cigars. He also hired well-known Frederick Hustlers' manager George Washington "Buck" Ramsey to sell the cigars throughout the Blue Ridge League region.

As the Cardinals entered September, Bill Sherdel (15–9) was leading the starting staff. The pennant race was extremely close. New York was leading (74–47), followed by Chicago (69–55), St. Louis (68–55), Pittsburgh (68–56), and Cincinnati (68–57). In the American League, the Browns (75–53) had now dropped into second behind the Yankees (77–50). It was going to be a very exciting final month of the season. As the Cards headed out on September 3, they were missing Haines, McHenry, and Bottomley. All were injured or ill. There were rumors that McHenry might rejoin the team, but his eyesight continued to be a problem.

The Cardinals traveled to Pittsburgh and Cincinnati, bouncing back and forth from third to fifth place. The race was so close that, every day, the top five clubs switched places. By the middle of the month, the Cards encountered the easier teams in Philadelphia and Boston. Rickey's club won five of six and returned to third place. Next, the club headed to Brooklyn. They split the series with the Robins. The Redbirds headed into New York to do a final battle with John McGraw and his first-place Giants. New York proved to be the better team, winning three of four and clinching the pennant. Sherdel picked up the only Cards' win. St. Louis was now in fourth place and out of the playoff money. Only the top three clubs in each league split the World Series profits. The extra money was on the line for the players. Rickey's club headed to Chicago for a money series. The Cubs took the opener, and it appeared the Cardinals would finish a very disappointing fourth. But Branch Rickey rallied the team and the Redbirds won the next three games. They finished in a tie with the Pirates for third place and post-season winnings. Sherdel hurled the first win.

It had been a successful season for the Cardinals, but the fans expected better. The New York Giants finished first and then swept the New York Yankees in the World Series. The Cincinnati Reds (86–68) ended in second ahead of the Cardinals and Pirates (85–69). The St. Louis Browns finished second in the American League. The Cards, Pirates, and Tigers split $24,731 three ways. Bill Sherdel and his teammates each received an extra $329.75— $4,602 in today's dollars.

Rogers Hornsby led individual honors in 1922. He'd had an incredible triple-crown year, leading the National League in average (.401), home runs (42), and runs-batted-in (152), plus runs, hits, doubles, total bases, on-base percentage, and slugging average. McHenry hit .303 in his shortened season. New players Bottomley (.325) and Blades (.300) showed signs of what was to come. Unfortunately, errors cost the club many games. The Cardinals finished last in fielding. Once again, St. Louis had two batting champs: Hornsby and George Sisler of the Browns with a .420 mark.

Rickey's pitching staff was led by Jeff Pfeffer (19–12), who finished fourth in league wins. Bill Sherdel (17–13) accumulated the second-most mound appearances (47). It was no wonder that Sherdel's arm had seemed to tire by the end of the season, given that he'd appeared in so many games and pitched 242 innings. Sherdel also gained two saves. Other top starters were Haines (11–9) and Doak (11–13). Marv Goodwin did not improve in 1922, and was released to Houston in the Texas League, with hopes of returning.

Sherdel's teammate Bill Doak struggled half the season before he was pitching easily. This didn't help the staff. However, Doak made a major contribution to the Cardinals and all baseball players in another way. Back in 1920, he had approached Rawlings about a new model baseball glove. He'd suggested that they lace a web between the thumb and first finger, creating a natural pocket in the glove. Rawlings started to produce that glove in 1922 and named it the "Bill Doak Model." The new design revolutionized the baseball glove. The Doak Model would be manufactured up until 1953, and would be the ancestor of all modern gloves used today.

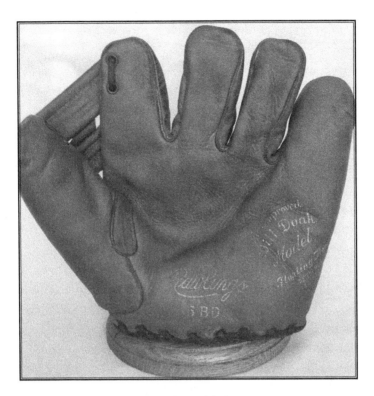

Bill Doak model glove
—Coulson collection

The Sherdel family left after the last game and arrived home by train on October 5. Home for them was McSherrystown, where they would stay with Mrs. Sherdel's father, who was now living on Church Street. The McSherrystown baseball team had already lined up Sherdel to pitch for the local team in an upcoming game against the Harrisburg All-Stars. That must have been like David versus Goliath. Sherdel displayed his major-league ability to the local fans, pitching a 6–0 shutout that allowed the Harrisburg boys only four scattered hits.

While in McSherrystown, Sherdel learned of the severity of Austin McHenry's physical condition. After visiting several physicians, it was discovered that McHenry had a brain tumor. His good friend, the scout Billy Doyle, felt that the brain tumor had developed after McHenry suffered a beaning above his left temple in 1916. On October 19, Dr. George Heuer at the Good Samaritan Hospital in Cincinnati operated on McHenry. His condition was critical. Heuer stated, "We could not remove all of the tumor, but got out the major portion and I think his recovery is assured. He is now resting easily."[17]

Dr. Heuer had been overly optimistic. McHenry suffered a relapse several weeks later and the doctors decided to send him home to spend his final days with his wife and two young children in Blue Creek, Ohio. Twenty-seven-year-old Austin McHenry, promising St. Louis Cardinals' superstar outfielder, passed away on November 27, 1922. His loss affected the City of St. Louis and the Cardinals' team in many ways. He was beloved by the children—the Knot-Hole Gang—that populated the left-field bleachers. The Gang would whoop and holler loudly after McHenry made a clutch hit or hit a home run. And the ball player always had time for the children and fans. The *St. Louis Post-Dispatch* wrote, "McHenry was one of the most popular players in St. Louis. He did not have an enemy in the stands or on the field. The players loved him. They called him 'the Airedale' because of his fleetness of foot, his tenacity, courage, and spirit." Branch Rickey said sadly, "Mack was loved by all the players and every member of the Knot-Hole gang will mourn the loss. The boys in the bleachers worshipped McHenry."[18]

James Gould, reporter for the *St. Louis Star,* wrote about McHenry's last at-bat. "A sick man—how sick not even he realized—McHenry was called upon the afternoon of July 31, in Brooklyn, to act as pinch-hitter. Little did he reckon that it was his last appearance, but what he did on that occasion was indicative of the character of the man. . . . [Milt] Stock was on first when Mac came up. [Sherry] Smith shot over a strike, at which McHenry did not offer. The next was over and McHenry swung as he always did—hard and on a line. The ball screeched its way to right center, Stock scoring all the way from first. Then the pathetic part, McHenry, his speed gone, used all he had in reaching first, turned that bag—and fell down, unable to go further on what, in the old days for him would have been an easy triple. That was the final big-league act in the career of one of the greatest performers who ever wore a St. Louis uniform."[19]

Tragic star Austin McHenry
—Coulson collection

Now that Bill and Marguerite Sherdel had two children, they wanted to build a house and establish a more permanent residence. They chose McSherrystown, where Marguerite's family was located and where Bill had already become an adopted son. They purchased a tract of land on Ridge Avenue and began construction of their dream home. By the end of November, the foundation was in place and the house was under roof.

McSherrystown, Pennsylvania, was founded in 1763 in Adams County, just next door to Hanover in York County and on the way to Gettysburg. The quiet little borough occupied one-half square mile and contained 1,800 residents in 1920. It was home to many small cigar manufacturers. It was easy to understand why Bill Sherdel was a celebrity.

CHAPTER TWELVE

In 1923, the Union of Socialist Soviet Republics (USSR) would be established in Russia, thus ending the years of upheaval since Czar Nicholas II had been overthrown and the Bolsheviks had gained control. The power struggle would include Vladimir Lenin, Leon Trotsky, and Joseph Stalin. Eventually, Stalin would become a dictator.

Adolf Hitler would stage a "Beer Garden Putsch" in Munich, Germany, in an attempt to overthrow the government. He would fail, however, and be arrested for his trouble. In other news, *Time* magazine would debut in 1923, and the Disney Company would be founded, too. Magician Harry Houdini would escape from a straitjacket while suspended upside down forty feet above the ground in New York City, and Colonel Jacob Schick would patent the first electric shaver. After Warren Harding died in office, vice president Calvin Coolidge would become the thirtieth president.

In sports, Bill Tilden would continue to dominate men's tennis while Helen Wills Moody would begin her dominance of women's. In golf, Bobby Jones would win his first major tournament—the US Open. He would become one of the greatest amateur golfers of all time.

Construction on the new Sherdel house at 315 Ridge Avenue continued over the winter. By early February, the heating system was being installed. Bill and Marguerite were excited about living near their many friends in McSherrystown. Sadly, on February 3 while the Sherdels were staying with Marguerite's father, her brother Charles, who'd also been living with his father, passed away at age twenty-seven. Charles had just finished the construction of his own new home and was to be married. Death came from complications of the Bright's disease that had just been diagnosed in

November. Today, that disease would be called acute or chronic nephritis. It was characterized by edema—often called dropsy—a painful swelling of the skin, kidney disease, and high blood pressure. Bright's disease had also been responsible for the death of Marguerite's mother at age forty-six, when Marguerite was just sixteen.

Cardinals' president Sam Breadon had now purchased a controlling interest in the club and was considered the owner. In early February, he announced that he had just signed Branch Rickey to a new five-year contract to lead the club. That deal made Rickey the second-highest-paid manager in the National League, behind only John McGraw of the Giants. The contract was also unusual because most managers were only signed for a single season. This deal illustrated the tremendous respect Breadon had for Rickey's abilities. Only four players—Hornsby, Doak, [Jack] Smith, and Sherdel—remained from the period before Rickey became manager. At age twenty-six, Bill Sherdel was now a senior member of the team.[1] He was also recognized for something else. In 1922, there were only ten National League left-handed pitchers who were considered above the ordinary—fewer than two per team. This unusual paucity of southpaws made Bill Sherdel very important to the club.[2]

James Gould wrote a nice piece for the *St. Louis Star,* entitled, "Bill Sherdel Is Only Small 'Package,' but He Is Always 'There.'"

> Bill Sherdel is a living illustration of the saying "good things come in small packages." Physically, there isn't much to the Pennsylvania youth—he would make just about one-third of Jeff Pfeffer or Fred Toney. But neither Pfeffer nor Toney has, in his big frame, more courage than this mite from McSherrystown, who has achieved stardom in the National League through his great pitching performances. Sherdel's all grit and muscle and his relief feats as a Cardinal, considered with his physique, have been nothing short of remarkable. . . .
>
> Possessed of great control, Sherdel has a change of pace that is a beauty. His slow ball seems almost to stop and linger a while on its way to the batter, and it is said to be the nearest approach to the teaser of Eddie Plank's to be seen in many a season. Plank, by the way, lives near Sherdel in the Keystone State and has given him many pointers. Sherdel is another player who never gives club officials any worry.[3]

Reporters asked manager John McGraw of the Giants where he thought the Cardinals would finish in 1923. McGraw suggested that the Redbirds would not escape the second division. Branch Rickey did not disagree with McGraw. Rickey was not very optimistic about the new season. There were just too many questions to be answered. The Cards' outfield was in shambles, a quality shortstop was needed, and the pitching was a concern. This would be an interesting year.

Breadon and Rickey announced that this year's training camp would be held in Bradenton, Florida. The weather had been so bad in Texas the previous year that the Cardinals' leadership decided to move camp to sunny Florida. Breadon had made all the arrangements. The players would stay at the Manavista Hotel, a ten-minute walk from the baseball complex. The town of Bradenton provided beautiful new facilities for the Cardinals. The first squad of players was scheduled to arrive on February 26, with the veterans about a week later.

Bradenton was a town of about 4,500 inhabitants that was located between Tampa and Sarasota on the Gulf of Mexico side of the state. The town was surrounded by waterways—both fresh- and salt-water. The players could enjoy great fishing during their sojourn there. At this point in the twentieth century, Bradenton was not a major Florida city.

By the time the first squad of players left St. Louis for Bradenton, only two players remained unsigned. One was Bill Sherdel. Normally, Sherdel signed his contract quickly, but he must have been unsatisfied with the terms in this year. Sherdel traveled from McSherrystown to St. Louis to talk with Rickey before signing his 1923 contract for $5,100—the equivalent of $72,858 today. Rickey had had surgery for appendicitis, and was not able to accompany the first squad to Bradenton. But he sent his very able captain Burt Shotton in his place. Practice began with the rookie pitchers and catchers and a few veterans. Rickey soon arrived and, a few days later, Bill Sherdel and the other veterans joined him. Rickey and Shotton were well pleased with the team's hard work. On March 7, the club held a short afternoon practice and then headed by car to nearby Cortez Beach to swim in the warm Gulf water. Two days later, the Bradenton residents treated the players to a seafood dinner in Sarasota. Oddly, Sunday baseball practices and games were prohibited in the state of Florida. This worked for Rickey, who continued to uphold his promise to his parents to skip Sunday baseball.

Rickey's club started to play exhibition games on March 15. Bill Sherdel looked good. He surrendered only one run in twenty innings of work. The southpaw got the opportunity to pitch against Ty Cobb and the Detroit Tigers on April 7. He hurled a six-inning three-hit shutout. The game ended suddenly because of Cobb's well-known temper. At the end of the sixth, Cobb entered a dispute with umpire Cy Pfirman after the ump called Cobb out on an attempted steal. Cobb refused to leave the field after throwing dirt in the umpire's face. The umpire waited five minutes and then forfeited the game to Sherdel and the Cards, 9–0.[4] Cobb continued the dispute in the clubhouse after the game. Umpire Pfirman was sitting in a chair, dressing, when Cobb came up to him and hit him across the side of the head.[5]

For his part, Bill Sherdel fared well against the batter Cobb. In the first inning, Cobb hit a slow roller to Sherdel. In the fourth, he hit a grounder to Hornsby. Finally, in the sixth, Cobb singled to center and was called out stealing. It was then that the argument began.

After nearly seven weeks of training, the Cards arrived back in St. Louis for a two-game series with the Browns, having won most of their exhibition games. In the spring-series matchup, though, the Browns once again outplayed the Cardinals, 2–0. Rickey's club now headed to Cincinnati for the start of the 1923 campaign.

The Cardinals opened the season on April 17, against the Reds. The starting lineup now included Jim Bottomley at first base, Rogers Hornsby at second base, Ray Blades in left field, and "Heinie" Mueller in centerfield. Rickey's new club was a blend of veterans and youth. The Cards split the opening four-game series with the Reds. Prior to the first game, Bill Sherdel had been rumored to be the opening-day starter. But there must have been something wrong with the star pitcher, because he didn't start a game until five days later, against the Cubs. In that loss, Sherdel pitched well until the sixth when he loaded the bases and Hornsby made a three-run error. Four days later, he took the ball and pitched a complete game victory over the Reds. On April 29, he closed a victory over the Pirates, 7–5. By the end of April, the club resided in seventh place, but the season was very young.

On May 5, with the Cards' record at .500, Rickey's players headed out on a long road trip in which they visited every National League city except Chicago. Rickey's squad jumped up and down the standings, moving up from seventh to second and then finishing the month in fifth place. Injuries plagued the team and the most damaging happened to Rogers Hornsby. He hurt his leg running from first to third base on May 8. After nearly 500 straight games, including three seasons, Hornsby missed his first game the following day. During the rest of the month, he pinch-hit once and started only one other game. St. Louis missed its superstar. In one game, his replacement committed four errors at second. At one point the club lost six straight games. Rickey returned Mueller to Houston for more seasoning. Southpaw Sherdel did have one outstanding outing in the month. He twirled a strong five-hit win over the Robins.

In mid-May, Marguerite Sherdel and the two children joined Bill in St. Louis for the rest of the season. Her brother Bob Strausbaugh accompanied them on the journey. Sherdel was happy to have his family, whom he hadn't seen in more than two months, with him. His wife and children were now able to attend his home games.

The month of June was another unexciting one. Rickey's club ended the month in sixth place with the Giants again in first. Cardinal injuries continued. Blades cut his leg badly chasing a ball in the outfield. Hornsby returned on June 13 and collected three hits, but then received word that his mother was seriously ill in Texas and so left for another week.

Bill Sherdel proved to be the hero of a June 17 game against the Giants—not on the mound, but at the plate. Joseph Holland of the *St. Louis Post-Dispatch* wrote:

> John [Scott] entered the game in the last half of the eighth inning after the Giants had rallied in their half to tie the three runs the Cardinals had amassed off Jack Bentley in seven innings. Scott's huge bulk and the burning fast ball that it implied made many of the 25,000 shudder. It seemed only a matter of innings until the world's champion Giants would 'get to' Southpaw Bill Sherdel, and give him a crushing defeat for his pains.

But the Cardinal in the maze was not particularly worried. His weapon, already prepared, was a baseball bat with which he compiles a meager batting average, of no material consequence, each year.

Hy Myers, the first batter to face Scott, caught the Giant infield asleep with a perfect bunt down the first base line. It was so sudden, so unexpected that it unsteadied the tall New York hurler and he walked Ainsmith. Lavan bunted and Myers took third while [Heinie] Groh turned the Doctor's effort into a force out of Ainsmith at second with a throw to [Dave] Bancroft. That play brought the mite left-hander, Billy Sherdel, to the plate. The tall, broad-shouldered, well-knit Scott towered over our diminutive Bill. . . . Scott pitched three balls, two of them strikes, and the contest looked more uneven than ever. The next pitch was the dramatic moment and the climax of the game. It was one of those same fast balls that had fanned Babe Ruth in the world's series. But it didn't fan the Cardinal David.

Instead he swung and lined a smashing single to left that scored Myers with the run that gave the Cardinals a 4-to-3 victory and reduced the New York lead over the Rickeymen to four full games. It was the first Cardinal victory over New York this year.[6]

Bill Sherdel suffered several one-run losses during the month. Rickey continued to use him mostly in relief. By month's end, young "Heinie" Mueller, the self-described "next Ty Cobb," was back in the St. Louis outfield.

Health problems continued to plague the Cardinals in July. Early in the month, Bill Sherdel suffered from a bad cold and was forced to remain in bed under a doctor's care. That stretched the pitching staff. Young reliever Johnny Stuart hurled a double-header against the Braves on July 10, and won both games. Then Sherdel brought the club back to an even record, defeating the Braves. Eight days later, he beat the first-place Giants in a victory that was no small feat since the New York lineup included five future Hall of Famers plus a Hall-of-Fame manager. As July ended, St. Louis was in fifth place. Once again that year, the pennant race included the Giants, Pirates, and Reds—but not the Cardinals.

In early August, Judge Landis cancelled all major-league games for a day in honor of President Warren Harding, who had just died in office. It gave the Cardinals' pitching staff a badly needed rest. August proved another month of average ball, with the club still in fifth. Pennant hopes were gone for Rickey, but a great final month of September could place the Cards in third and mean additional money for the players. Meanwhile, Jess Haines was having a great year. The big right-hander picked up his seventeenth win.

With the team mired in the second division, the clubhouse could be a powder keg, just waiting for a match to spark an explosion. In early September, the Cardinals were playing a double-header against the Giants in the Polo Grounds when the match was lit. In the Cards' clubhouse between games, Rogers Hornsby told manager Rickey in no uncertain terms to remove his name from the list of players participating in Rickey's postseason barnstorming tour. Rickey said something to Hornsby and Hornsby responded with a right hook to Rickey's eye. Other players quickly separated the two, but the damage had been done. Apparently, the catalyst had been a comment Rickey made on the bench while Hornsby was standing on third base during the first game. Rickey was overheard saying that Hornsby wanted to run his team. Someone relayed Rickey's comment to Hornsby and the powder keg sparked.[7] The following day, the St. Louis newspapers speculated that Hornsby would be gone, but owner Breadon stated: "Rogers Hornsby will positively not be traded or sold to any other ball club." He characterized the event as "just one of those things that come up on every ball club after a hard game. These arguments sometimes cause ill feelings for a short while, but they are soon forgotten."[8] Rickey was unavailable for comment. He had conveniently departed on a scouting trip for several days.

As the final month of the season continued, Rickey began to think about rebuilding. The 1923 Cardinals were not going anywhere, so he started making changes. The manager gained some flexibility in his lineup because Hornsby was out for a week with a skin infection and Bottomley was sent home for several weeks with a twisted knee. Rickey released Eddie Ainsmith and brought in former California University outfielder Taylor Douthit from the Ft. Smith club and promoted infielder Les Bell, who had looked great in spring training. The real strength of the Cardinals' future was already there in Haines, Sherdel, Bottomley, Blades, and Mueller.

The clashes between Branch Rickey and his star Rogers Hornsby came to another head on September 26. Hornsby had been out since September 9 with a skin infection, but his doctor had now given him the OK to play. Rickey asked Hornsby to suit up for the game, but Hornsby claimed that he was not ready and needed some additional practice. He left the clubhouse and sat in the grandstand. Owner Breadon located Hornsby and told him he was being suspended for the remainder of the season and fined $500. Hornsby argued:

> "I had not touched a baseball since September 9. I needed a lot of work before I could step in and play the sort of ball that would be a help to the club. . . . I had no thought of attempting to ignore the manager's order, but I believed that he would agree with me that I could not step in after a layoff of seventeen days and do either myself or the club justice. . . .
>
> "I told Mr. Rickey that I did not feel well enough to play and there our discussion ended. I sat in the clubhouse for a few minutes and then went upstairs into the grandstand."[9]

Several days later, Rickey made a statement. "The club has been patient with Hornsby," he said, "but his disregard of club rules has reached the point where he had to be disciplined. . . . When I asked him to return to the game recently on the advice of the doctor that he was perfectly fit, Hornsby not only refused to play but even declined to put on a uniform and sit on the bench for pinch-hitting purposes. . . . It is impossible to control a club on which there is one player enjoying privileges that are denied to others. A showdown had to come sooner or later, and Hornsby forced the present situation."[10]

The fifth-place Cardinals finished the 1923 season in early October. Once again, John McGraw and the Giants won the title and faced the Yankees in the World Series, but this time the Yankees won in six games. Babe Ruth had another outstanding year. He batted a second-best .393 and led the American League with forty-one home runs and 130 runs-batted-in. The Browns, like their National League cousins the Cardinals, finished in fifth place.

Rogers Hornsby led the National League for the fourth consecutive year with a .384 average. He also clouted seventeen home runs and led the league in on-base percentage (.459) and slugging percentage (.627). Second-year Cardinal Jim Bottomley batted a second-best .371 with eight four-baggers.

Five other Cardinals—including Mueller (.343), rookie Les Bell (.375), and Bill Sherdel (.338)—topped the magic .300 level. In several games, Branch Rickey inserted Sherdel as a pinch-hitter. Once again, the Cards' fielding was a weakness. The club finished next to last.

The 1923 Cardinals' pitching staff was led by Jess Haines. Haines won twenty games and lost thirteen. "Wee Willie" Sherdel posted a second-best fifteen wins against thirteen losses. He took the mound for 225 innings in thirty-nine games with twenty-six starts.

Rickey needed to find another catcher, another outfielder, and more pitching help for the next season, but the Cardinals' future for 1924 really depended on what happened with Hornsby. Could Branch Rickey and Rogers Hornsby resolve their disagreements and coexist on the team?

At the end of the season, the Sherdel family returned to McSherrystown, where their new home at 315 Ridge Avenue had been completed. The Sherdels now had a permanent address with their many neighbors, friends, and fans nearby. Bill and Marguerite would remain there for the rest of their lives.

In October, Sherdel pitched one more game, this one for the McSherrystown All-Stars against the Hanover All-Stars. The Hanover club included several players from the Blue Ridge League. Now the pride of McSherrystown, Wee Willie shut out Hanover, 4–0.

CHAPTER THIRTEEN

In 1924, Ford would manufacture its ten millionth Model T automobile, King Tut's tomb would be opened, and George Gershwin's "Rhapsody in Blue" would debut at New York's Carnegie Hall. It was also the year that Thomas Watson would start the IBM Corporation and J. Edgar Hoover would be appointed head of the FBI. The comic strip "Little Orphan Annie" by Harold Gray would be published. And Edwin Hubble would announce the existence of distant galaxies.

In January, Branch Rickey made a great pickup. He signed a young player who would prove another building block for his future dynasty. Shortstop Tommy Thevenow wouldn't see much major-league action in 1924, but he would be part of the Cards' future.

All winter long there had been rumors around the burning question of Rogers Hornsby's role—if at all—in the Cards' 1924 season. Both the Cubs and Giants wanted him, badly. They both made big offers, but Rickey and Breadon turned them down. They said Hornsby would remain a St. Louis Cardinals.

Another trade rumor involved Bill Sherdel. The Cards and Braves wanted to make a trade, went the scuttlebutt. The Redbirds would send pitchers Pfeffer and Sherdel to Boston in exchange for catcher Mickey O'Neill and infielder Jack Conlon. Rickey never confirmed the rumor and Pfeffer and Sherdel remained in Cardinal uniforms.

Despite the speculation about his future, Bill Sherdel and his family enjoyed the winter in their new home. The little southpaw signed his 1924 contract for $5,300—a $200 raise. Today, that contract would be worth $73,965. Sherdel was ready to play and arrived at training camp ahead of Rickey and the other veterans on February 29. The first squad of rookies had arrived four days earlier. Unlike previous seasons, few players boarded the train in St. Louis; most traveled directly to camp. James Gould commented on Sherdel's arrival:

> "Having nothing particularly on his mind but his hair (and precious little of that) William (Slow Ball) Sherdel breezed into camp yesterday. Bill stated he was forced to an early start by the stories of Bill Doak's good condition.
>
> "'So Doak is going to win twenty games this year, eh?' queried Sherdel. 'Well, I hope he does, but that makes it almost certain that my 1924 record will have about thirty victories.'
>
> "Of course, Sherdel is not overconfident or anything like that, but his attitude is illuminating in that it shows just where the Cardinal spirit is this year. Sherdel looks well. He isn't going to run Fred Toney a race for the heavyweight championship or anything like that, but he appears to have spent a fine winter and looks to be in as good shape as he ever was. That slow ball of Bill's is a tantalizer. You're all set for it; you guess it's coming and all that, and yet you miss it. Were a slow ball contest held in the National League, it is possible that Bill's teaser would win in a canter. Add to his ability Sherdel's desire to win and you have a mighty valuable addition to the present squad."[1]

A *St. Louis Post-Dispatch* special correspondent also wrote about the pitcher. "Bill Sherdel settled down in an apartment on his arrival yesterday, and then hiked to the park carrying that slow ball of his with him. Seeing Bill throw, all the kid pitchers are trying to master the knack, and the good-natured Sherdel is helping them all he can. It is doubtful, however, if the kids will get very far in their attempts, for a slow one like Bill's is a gift, rather than an acquirement."[2]

Throughout March, Rickey's club played exhibitions with nearby clubs. The Cardinals did quite well, winning the majority. A big year was predicted for Haines, Sherdel, and Doak. A *St. Louis Star* reporter interviewed Sherdel.

> Bill Sherdel is of the opinion that his pal and 'roomie,' Bill Doak, is getting too much publicity. According to "Sherry," all this stuff about the great year Doak is sure to have will go to Bill's blond head. "You shouldn't hand that stuff to a youngster like Doak," Sherdel said the other day. "You might spoil him; kids can't stand so much favorable comment."
>
> As to Sherdel himself, count on the "Wee One" winning at least fifteen games this year with a fine chance that he will rise to the heights of twenty victories. Bill admits that he is shooting at the higher mark and points out that, not in the best of shape in 1923, he annexed fifteen games.
>
> The tiny southpaw whose slow ball has made him famous with the fans and infamous to many a good batter, doesn't hurry himself in the spring, but contents himself with just enough work to bring him around for the opening of the only season that counts.[3]

Bill pitched a great three innings against the Braves on March 21. A *St. Louis Star* reporter wrote, "Bill Sherdel's slow ball continues to be the envy of all National League pitchers and the dismay of all batters. He has added a delivery [that] has a bit more speed than his 'slowest' and this has deceived several hitters in exhibition games when said hitters were 'all set' for the slow one."[4]

Bill and Marguerite with Patricia and Junior
—*St. Louis Post-Dispatch*, March 26, 1924

By April 12, the Cardinals had returned to St. Louis for the annual spring series with the Browns. The Cards' exhibition season had gone very well. They won seventeen and lost only five. Rickey's club then split two games with the Browns. Sherdel pitched the opener and lost 4–1 before 25,000 St. Louis fans.

Bill Sherdel was certainly receiving much more print coverage this year. Writers were especially noticing his hitting skills, as described in this article:

> Bill Sherdel, beside [sic] being a great pitcher, has developed into a whale of a hitter and several times down south was used as a pinch-hitter with success crowning his swinging clouts. "Sherry" hits the same way as he pitches—from the south side—and he can and does

wield a wicked willow. The improvement of this pitcher in the past five years has been remarkable. Time was when Bill, not possessing his now-famous slow ball, depended greatly on his fast one and a crossfire. Inclined to the temperamental when he first "came up," Sherdel would, when a boot was made behind him or the umpire pulled a Blind Tom stunt, grit his teeth and shove his fast one right across the heart of the plate.

Naturally, this method of showing spleen proved rather costly as the batter would lay for the speedball and knock it out of the lot. However, it didn't take the brainy Sherdel very long to come to and realize that such fits of mental aberration would curtail his big league stay. He reformed and today is one of the sweetest southpaws in captivity.

No member of the Cardinals likes to win any more than Bill, and when victory perches on the Rickey colors because of a hit Bill has made, why, that's the end of a perfect day.[5]

The Cardinals opened the 1924 campaign at home against the Cubs on April 15. The Cards' starting lineup included Jim Bottomley at first base, Rogers Hornsby at second base, rookie Les Bell at shortstop, and "Heinie" Mueller in centerfield. The Redbirds won the inaugural game as Judge Landis watched.

Twenty-two-year-old Les Bell from Harrisburg, Pennsylvania, had been in Cardinals' camp the previous year, but needed more seasoning. This year he seemed better prepared for major-league pitching. Bell's Harrisburg was located forty miles north of Sherdel's McSherrystown. The two Pennsylvania lads would remain good friends after their playing days ended.

All the preseason optimism disappeared during April. So, too, did the improved pitching. At month-end, Rickey's club ranked only one position above the league cellar. Still, Bill Sherdel was becoming quite the hitter. In the Cardinals' first nine games, he was called upon to pinch-hit five times, and he collected four hits for his trouble. Unfortunately, Rickey had to cut short the success when Sherdel developed tonsillitis, and needed to be sent home to St. Louis.

May was a break-even month for the Redbirds, but they remained in seventh place. The club was still committing too many costly errors. To improve the defense, Rickey picked up another shortstop from Milwaukee.

To open a roster spot, he optioned Les Bell to the Brewers. No Cardinal pitcher was leading the dismal staff.

There is only one word to describe the month of June for the Redbirds: horrible. The club won only seven games while losing twenty. They had now slipped into the National League cellar. Rickey's squad lost every single series during the month. It's hard to understand when your pitchers are struggling and your staff is worn out from double-headers why you'd schedule exhibition games on idle days, but Rickey did. The Cards were so bad they even lost to AA Syracuse, 12–2, on what should have been a day of rest. Jim Bottomley, one of two legitimate Cardinals' stars, was sent home to have tonsil surgery. It took "Sunny" Jim about two weeks to return to full-time duty. Often when the pitchers provided a good game, the Cardinals failed to score enough runs. For example, Bill Sherdel pitched a five-hit game against the Cubs and lost, 1–0. The preseason forecasters had totally misjudged the Cards' prospects. They had predicted St. Louis would finish in the first division. No player could have been more frustrated and disappointed than the manager, Branch Rickey.

The saddest day for Cardinal fans came on June 15 when Branch Rickey was forced to trade former staff ace Bill Doak to Brooklyn for twenty-seven-year-old pitcher Leo Dickerman. Rickey hoped young Dickerman could help the struggling staff, but it was a poignant loss for Doak. "Spittin' Bill" had been with the Cardinals for twelve seasons. He ended his Redbirds' career with 144 wins—the fifth best in franchise history. He won twenty games in 1920 and led the league in earned run average in 1914 and 1921. In 1924, he was used sparingly in relief. With this trade, Bill Sherdel lost his good friend and roommate on the road. But Doak, like other ex-Redbirds, would come back to haunt the Cardinals.

The Cardinals had a winning record in July and advanced to sixth place. Rickey continued to make moves. He had already removed seven veterans from the club. Bill Sherdel was still making his pitching appearances in relief. At that year's Tuberculosis Day game, Jess Haines thrilled the fans with a no-hitter, the only one in the National League in 1924 and the club's first since 1876. Once again, Bottomley missed several games—this time for having run into a concrete wall and losing several teeth.

One interesting thing happened to Bill Sherdel in a July 30 game against the Phillies. A sportswriter for the *Philadelphia North American* told the story.

"Bill" Sherdel, the spare-built but competent portsider of the Cardinals, will have this fascinating story to tell a grandchild sitting on his knee sometime in years to come.

Did you ever hear of a relief pitcher going into the game with two on base and nobody out and retiring the side on one pitched ball?

This is exactly what happened in a game at the Phils' park between [Artie] Fletcher's men and St. Louis last Wednesday.

It was the second inning and the score was four to one in favor of the Phillies. The Phils' half started by [Jimmy] Wilson hitting Dickerman for two bases.

Then [Jimmy] Ring walked. Bert Shotton, who directed the Cardinals' play in the absence of manager Rickey, dismissed Dickerman and called on Sherdel to stop the attack.

Sherdel saw runners on second and first and nobody out. Manager Fletcher sent Johnny Mokan, a right-handed batter, to bat in place of [George] Harper. Obviously, Mokan had been ordered to bunt, so the St. Louis infield posted itself on the grass. Sherdel wound up to deliver his first pitch.

Without waiting, Mokan tried to tap this pitch. What he did was to raise a tiny fly that first baseman Bottomley caught halfway between first and home.

Both runners at the impact of the ball and bat bolted ahead. After the catch, Bottomley whipped the ball to [Jim] Cooney and doubled Wilson. Rogers Hornsby's head was working. He ran over to first base, called for the ball, and it reached him in time to triple Ring.

To retire the side on one pitched ball with two on base and nobody out is the pinnacle of rescue pitching, and Sherdel's feat must go in the records as one of the greatest of the year.[6]

August was another troublesome month for the Cardinals. Rickey's boys remained in sixth place. Rogers Hornsby was hitting better than ever. He collected nine straight hits—three home runs, one double, and five singles. Later in the month, Hornsby sprained the muscles on the right side of his back and was out of the lineup for a week. Rickey continued to try to improve the club, but luck seemed to be working against him. At one point, the Cardinals had four players in the hospital. One was recently acquired Dickerman, who had been pitching splendidly. He was hit by a pitched ball and broke his left wrist. He would be out for the rest of the year. Add Hornsby's back problems and the team had five key players gone from the lineup. Rickey added twenty-one-year-old outfielder Charles "Chick" Hafey, who would eventually become another building block in the Cards' dynasty and a Hall of Famer. He also picked up Charles "Flint" Rhem, a big, right-handed strikeout king from the Fort Smith club. Rickey gushed over Rhem, describing the twenty-three-year-old as "the next Mathewson" and "the greatest pitcher I ever saw in my life."[7]

There was one big Cardinal highlight during the final month. Jim Bottomley set a record on September 16 against Brooklyn when he drove in twelve of the team's seventeen runs. "Sunny" Jim collected a perfect six hits in six at-bats. He belted two home runs, a double, and three singles in an outstanding effort. This high point notwithstanding, the team was universally relieved to reach the end of the 1924 season on September 29. They had fared no better during this final month of play, and the team ended the campaign in sixth place. Once again, John McGraw led his Giants to the pennant and that year would face the Washington Senators and Walter Johnson in the Series. In an upset, the Senators defeated the Giants in seven games.

Branch Rickey did schedule two exhibition games for Bill Sherdel's benefit in late September. The Cardinals stopped in the central Pennsylvania area to play games in Harrisburg and York, close to Bill's hometown. Unfortunately, rain cancelled the Harrisburg game, but the Redbirds did play the York White Roses, a minor-league team, at Eagle Park in York, approximately twenty miles from the Hanover-McSherrystown area. Rickey had promised the York club that Sherdel would pitch and, on September 26, Sherdel took the mound for the Cards in York. To Rickey's credit, he used his regulars; even Hornsby and Bottomley played half the game. Sherdel pitched the first five innings and St. Louis won, 7–5. Many of his friends were in the stands.[8]

During September, Branch Rickey continued to search for players who could improve his club. The starting lineup at the end of the season varied greatly from the one on opening day. The ending lineup included Thevenow, shortstop; Blades, left field; Douthit, centerfield; and Mueller, right field. If there was a positive to take from the season, it was that Rickey used the team's poor record to introduce new talent that would benefit the club in years to come. Hafey, Rhem, Thevenow, Douthit, and Bell, along with Bottomley, Blades, Haines, and Sherdel would become the future stars of the Cardinals.

All the optimistic comments written in March and April about the team evaporated during the course of the 1924 season. St. Louis fans were hoping for twenty-win seasons from Doak (2–1), Haines (8–19), and Sherdel (8–9), but all had disappointing turnouts. Bill Sherdel made thirty-five appearances, but only ten starts and six complete games. It seemed Rickey still envisioned him as a reliever, much to Sherdel's dismay. There really was no staff ace, as might be expected on a losing team. Sherdel improved his earned run average to 3.42, second only to recently acquired Leo Dickerman's 2.41. One statistic told much about the pitching. The Cardinals' staff threw a low seventy-six complete games. That meant Rickey had to use relief pitching in more than half of the team's games.

A recently created pitching statistic called "the clutch-pitching index" attempted to analyze how effective a pitcher was in a game. It calculated an expected number of allowed runs based upon other pitchers' performances. Then it divided these expected allowed runs by the actual allowed runs and produced an index number that could be compared to other pitchers throughout the league. Looking at that index for 1924, Bill Sherdel ranked number one in the National League in effectiveness, despite his record. No wonder, back in Pennsylvania, the hometown boy continued to gain popularity and endorsements.

Bill Sherdel advertises a piano
—*The Evening Sun*, September 26, 1924

Bill endorses a washing machine
—*The Evening Sun*, November 19, 1925

The *Philadelphia North American* wrote a nice article about Bill Sherdel and a game he pitched in September.

Bill Sherdel, southpaw star of the St. Louis Cardinals, proved last fall that he is one of the greatest left-handers on the diamond today. His feat of stopping the New York Giants in a spectacular game in September was one of the greatest games hurled during the season.

It was the easiest thing in the world for the New Yorkers to make a base hit or even a two-bagger off Sherdel that day, but a home run was necessary to score on Sherdel.

Inning after inning, the first New York batsman would line out a screaming safe drive, and even a second batsman would hit safely with much vigor and abandon; but after this impressive demonstration it was always different. Sherdel tightened and double plays and easy outs followed the first flourish. . . .

When a pitcher is "right," he is all but invincible. There cometh a certain day in the season when, if he is a fastball pitcher, he has all of his speed and perfect control; or, if he is a curve-ball artist, his curves break perfectly and with a sharp hook. Almost every big-league pitcher has his one great day in a season. And, of course, when a pitcher is working perfectly, he is a puzzle to opposing batsmen.

But here was Sherdel on this particular day in apparently worse form than usual. He was easy to hit. He could not get his stuff on the ball and he could not get his curves to work right. But instead of wilting under fire and giving up under adverse circumstances, he arose to heights and greatness in spite of everything. He seemed to flame forth to his supreme effort under punishment. The harder they hit him, the more certain he seemed to be that they could not score. When men were on second and third with only one out, it was then that Sherdel really began to pitch.

When they called on him to surrender his sinking ship, his curve ball seemed to say that he had not yet begun to fight. . . .

To a thoughtful man who will study the baseball scores of 1924, the work of Sherdel that summer afternoon on the Polo Grounds will surely stand out above anything done by any star pitcher during the year, even though he pitched a no-hit game.[9]

Once again, Rogers Hornsby led the National League in hitting for the fifth straight year with a .424 mark. He proved why he was the greatest hitter in the National League. Young Bottomley (.316) and Blades (.311) also topped .300.

Hornsby showed why he deserved every penny he was paid. Besides his top batting average, he led the National League in hits (.227), doubles (43), total bases (373), on-base percentage (.507), slugging percentage (.696), and runs (121). He added the second-most home runs (25) and runs-batted-in (94). He accomplished all that while missing several weeks with injuries. The winter would prove worrisome to Cards' fans because Hornsby's three-year contract had expired and he wanted $100,000 for a new three-year deal. Some writers started to think that maybe Hornsby could also manage the Cardinals better than Branch Rickey. In a *St. Louis Star* article, popular sports critic Joe Vila of the *New York Sun* was referenced. "Vila declares that Rickey can find good ball tossers, but when it comes to managing the Cards, 'he has created the impression that something is lacking.'"[10] As an example, the Washington Senators selected their young second baseman "Bucky" Harris as their 1924 manager and Harris went on to win the American League title and the World Series. Perhaps Hornsby could do the same for the Cardinals. Joe Vila would prove prophetic during the next year.

In early October, the Sherdel family returned to their home in McSherrystown, where the local baseball team of St. Mary's would ask Bill to pitch for them when he was available. Little Patricia and Bill Jr. would spend time with their grandfather Strausbaugh.

During the off season, Bill Sherdel always enjoyed fishing and hunting with his many friends. Sometimes, a "hunting party" of Sherdel and his buddies would spend several days at a friend's cabin at nearby Brown's Dam. Often at the end of the camping trip, the men would entertain their wives and guests with a meal at the cabin. Their menu usually included rabbits, pheasants, and quail that the "pioneer" boys had shot, along with many side dishes. Unassuming Sherdel was the favorite as he told stories of his experiences with the Cardinals and his travels around the country. For the rest of his life, Bill Sherdel would be most comfortable in this alternate world.

CHAPTER FOURTEEN

The year 1925 would dawn with Benito Mussolini dissolving the Italian parliament and naming himself dictator. Adolf Hitler would publish his autobiography, *Mein Kampf,* in which he outlined his political ideology and plans for Germany. Also published this year was *The Great Gatsby,* by F. Scott Fitzgerald. The United States would establish a nationwide road-numbering system and a US shield marker. This was also the year that Tennessee would make it unlawful to teach the theory of evolution. John T. Scopes would be arrested and, in a jury trial, be found guilty of teaching Darwinism. The teacher would be fined $100 plus court costs.

In sports, Red Grange would play his final college game at Illinois and sign with the Chicago Bears, and Lou Gehrig would replace Yankee first baseman Wally Pipp and begin his streak of 2,130 consecutive games.

In St. Louis, ball fans breathed a collective sigh of relief when Rogers Hornsby signed a new three-year contract for $100,000. In a break from tradition, owner Sam Breadon, alone, handled the negotiations with the superstar second baseman. Both sides seemed very happy with the new deal. Perhaps deliberately, Branch Rickey was out of town when the contract was announced.[1]

The major leagues had changed their rules and expanded the World Series money to include the fourth-place teams. It was a change that would prove beneficial to the 1925 St. Louis players.

A restless Branch Rickey announced that this year's spring training would be held in Stockton, California—over 2,000 miles away. In previous years, Rickey had not been happy with the weather in Texas or Florida, so he wanted to try California. Stockton, the first California city not given a Spanish name, had been established during the Gold Rush in 1849. This port city was in the central valley along the San Joaquin River. In 1925, Stockton's population numbered above 40,000.

Bill and Marguerite Sherdel and their two children left McSherrystown on February 18, for St. Louis, where they joined a group of forty people to travel to Stockton for six weeks of training camp. That year, Rickey allowed wives and children to accompany the players. The train stopped in Kansas City and the group transferred to a "baseball special" that took the Santa Fe route past the Grand Canyon. On February 23, after a cross-country trek, the "pioneer" group arrived in Stockton. They were met at the station by a large contingent of residents who gave them a hearty welcome. The St. Louis sportswriters applauded the Stockton facilities and labeled them the best the Cardinals had visited in twenty years.[2]

Branch Rickey must have realized that it was difficult to run the Cardinals' organization and manage the team. In a meeting before the first practice, he announced that his longtime captain Burt Shotton would be given unlimited power over the squad. Rickey told his players that Shotton could hire, fire, suspend, or fine any man as he saw fit, and he could take these actions "without consulting with anybody." Rickey had confidence in Shotton, and knew that he would not abuse the power.[3]

As practice began, the weather again became an issue. Rain seemed to follow the club from Texas to Florida to California. The team was limited to one daily practice in the afternoon, because, as Hornsby expressed, "the field was so wet in the morning that the ducks came in for a bath."[4] Rickey was trying Les Bell at shortstop instead of Thevenow. At training camp, young "Junior" Sherdel became quite the favorite of "Pep" Hornsby.

Southpaw pitcher Eddie Dyer, who had served as a football coach in the fall, formed an unusual football team during baseball spring training. Sherdel, Dyer, Dickerman, Haines, and Blades were the stars. The group even created signals and ran plays for recreation.[5]

Meanwhile, back in St. Louis, the two club owners Breadon and Ball came to an agreement to remodel Sportsman's Park and add 12,000 seats. The renovation would cost an estimated $229,000. In prior years, the two clubs had absorbed the war tax that had been added to the price of each game ticket. Now they would let the patrons pay the tax and use the additional funds to finance the park addition.⁶

The Cardinals played exhibition games with minor-league and college teams in California. These gave Rickey an opportunity to develop his youngsters and observe his veterans without the view of other major-league clubs. The biggest concern in camp was the condition of Ray Blades' arm. Blades had never recovered from an arm injury the previous season.

When sportswriter Al Santore interviewed Branch Rickey about the upcoming season, Rickey would not make a prediction, but he did share his thoughts.

> "The club has hitting power. When I say this, the fans naturally picture Hornsby. But we have other good hitters besides Hornsby. On that account, I will make the prediction that you will see the Cards among the leaders in runs at the end of the season.
>
> "That naturally puts it up to the pitching and the defense in general. I just naturally dislike to discuss pitching, for it is this department that has kept the Cardinals out of a pennant for years. I . . . have another fine prospect in Rhem, a young right-hander."⁷

Rhem had an excellent spring, pitching seventeen straight scoreless innings, although not against major-league talent.

Another sportswriter, James Gould, predicted the Cardinals would finish in the first division and earn some Series money. Other reporters were less optimistic and expected a repeat of the previous year.

The Cardinals headed east and stopped first in Texas to play games. Rain had cancelled several days of games and practices in California, so Rickey wanted to play some additional games to prepare for the season. On April 10, the Cards' aggregation finally arrived back in St. Louis and began a two-game spring series with the Browns. Once again, the teams split the series. In the second game, held on a Sunday, Rickey chose Hornsby to manage the team instead of Shotton. This was perhaps Rickey's way of judging Hornsby's ability to manage the Cardinals in the future.

The team was now ready to begin the 1925 campaign. Rickey had only one injured player—Chick Hafey had suffered a broken finger. Ray Blades' arm had improved and he was ready. The Redbirds faced an eight-game road trip. There were several new faces to this year's crew, including pitcher "Wild Bill" Hallahan, who would become a future star. On April 14, the Cardinals opened in Cincinnati before 35,000 fans. The Reds defeated Haines, 4–0. Sherdel pitched a scoreless eighth.

Rickey's club didn't start this season as well as they had the previous season, and the Cardinals closed the month with a five-game losing streak. The hitting attack was anemic. Rickey's worries increased when Hornsby was hit in the head and suffered a slight concussion. He remained out of the lineup for several games. James Gould of the *St. Louis Star* described the Redbirds' play as "just plain terrible."[8]

May proved to be an even worse month than April. Losses continued to mount. Rickey was using Bill Sherdel in a relief role and he was one of few bright spots. One day, Bottomley and Sherdel were discussing Branch Rickey's decision to use the latter as a relief pitcher all year. Bottomley said, "Sherry, you won't have much chance to compile a good record this season while acting as relief hurler. You'll go in there with the bases loaded most of the time with some weak [good] hitter . . . facing you."

Sherdel answered, "I care nothing about records. I'm on this club to do what is for its best interests. If Rickey wants to use me as a relief hurler all year, that's what I'll be. And I hope to help pitch us from last place to second before July fourth."[9] It was a statement that was typical of Bill Sherdel's unselfish attitude.

Branch Rickey was always searching for opportunities to improve the lineup. On May 23, he acquired Cubs' catcher Bob O'Farrell. In 1915, O'Farrell had signed with Chicago, whose manager Roger Bresnahan had been a Hall-of-Fame catcher. Bresnahan had cultivated O'Farrell's catching skills over the years and, by 1922, O'Farrell was considered one of the best defensive catchers in the major leagues. In July 1924, O'Farrell suffered a fractured skull when a foul ball broke his catcher's mask. He was out of the lineup for most of the year, making him available for trade. O'Farrell would be another major piece of Rickey's championship construction.

Through May, the Cards' hitting seemed to be either feast or famine, and mostly the latter. As always, Rogers Hornsby continued to hit. By May 30, he was leading the league in hitting and had clouted eleven home runs. The Redbirds' pitching staff was ineffective and overworked. No starter was leading the group. Something big had to be done to change the course of the Cards' season.

On May 30, Sam Breadon announced to the world that Branch Rickey had retired as manager of the St. Louis Cardinals and that Rogers Hornsby was replacing him. Hornsby became the seventh player-manager in the major leagues, and joined a growing fraternity. The Cards were currently dwelling in the National League cellar, after just losing four straight to the Pirates.

Breadon explained that Rickey would continue in his role as vice president and add the business manager title, also. He was doing the work of two people and now his duties would be exclusively executive, supervising scouts and developing young players. Generally, the players were positive about the move and Rickey stated he was sure Hornsby would make a good manager.

James Gould interviewed Rogers Hornsby about his new responsibilities. "Of course, I'm pleased to be favored for the Cardinals' management. As manager, I will put forth my best effort to pilot the boys in a commendable manner. I also am glad to see my friend, Branch Rickey, elevated. He has been a great help to me as a player and I know I can continue to count on his support."[10] Hornsby said all the right things. He also announced he would make no immediate changes to the lineup.

Before Hornsby's first game as manager, he called the team together in the clubhouse. With some flourish, he erased Rickey's chalk marks from the board and announced, "There'll be no more of that stuff. We're playing the game with bats, balls, and gloves. You pitchers are going to finish the game you start. Don't look to me for help every time a batter gets a base hit."[11] Hornsby told a reporter, "It looked like we had a great ball club this spring, but Rickey just couldn't get the breaks and the team went from bad to worse. He's a mighty fine fellow, knows as much about baseball as any man in the game, and I'm sorry that he didn't have the Cardinals in first place instead of last. We are mighty good friends and I hope the combination of Rickey as vice president and Hornsby as manager of the Cardinals will be a winning one."[12] Once again, Hornsby had said all the right things—even if he didn't believe them.

Breadon proved to be a genius in naming Hornsby manager. By the end of June, the Cards had climbed from eighth to fourth place behind

Pittsburgh, New York, and Brooklyn. Hornsby's boys won twenty and lost only nine since he assumed control. The team was hitting. Hornsby (.421) was leading the league and Bottomley (.387) was in third. Ironically, two ex–Redbirds occupied the fourth and fifth spots. St. Louis was also leading the league in double plays. One major injury occurred on June 2, when "Heinie" Mueller broke his leg sliding into home. He would miss four to six weeks. The biggest difference Rogers Hornsby made in the new Cardinals was in the pitching staff. Hornsby established a pitching rotation that included Sherdel, Rhem, and Haines. Hornsby brought Sherdel out of the bullpen, made him a starter, and Sherdel responded. The southpaw was pitching complete games and winning.

The Redbirds' new leader proved a fighter on June 16 in a game with the Phillies. The Cards had already beaten the Phils four straight and were going for a series sweep. Early in the game, Cards' catcher Bob O'Farrell was banished for arguing balls and strikes calls. In the sixth inning, the Cardinals loaded the bases on walks and the Phils' catcher Jimmy Wilson had words with the umpire. Umpire Pfirman gave Wilson the quick exit, also. A crowd gathered around home plate and everyone was arguing and talking about the bad calls at once. Perhaps it was the heat or the four consecutive Phillie losses, but managers Fletcher and Hornsby started an unexplained argument that ended suddenly when Hornsby landed two punches on Fletcher. Fletcher responded wildly, missing Hornsby. Policemen and players jumped in between the two leaders and restored order. Both managers were ejected. Later, Hornsby was fined $100 and Fletcher $50 for their altercation. Hornsby made a point that day. His players realized that he would fight for the team.[13]

Unfortunately, the Cardinals returned to "normal" in July. A new manager didn't seem to matter, and Hornsby's club landed back in fifth place. There were, however, several bright spots to the return to darkness. Both Hafey and Mueller returned from injuries and were ready to go. Hornsby hit his twenty-fifth home run. Bill Sherdel enjoyed a seven-game-winning streak on the mound. Since Hornsby had begun starting him every fifth day, Sherdel had responded. Hornsby had also changed his pitch selection. With Rickey in charge, Sherdel had been pitching almost all slow balls in a relief role; under Hornsby, he was now throwing more fast balls mixed with his change-ups and curves and it was working. He also enjoyed the satisfaction of hitting a home run into the right-field bleachers on July 29. Pitchers always loved to brag about their power.

1925 Sherdel Exhibit baseball card
—Coulson collection

In August, Hornsby's boys almost broke even, but remained in fifth place. Hornsby continued to fight for his team. On August 3, he was ejected for arguing a third-strike call. This time, National League president John Heydler suspended Hornsby, for three days. Meanwhile, the additional responsibility of managing was not affecting Hornsby the player. By month end, he was batting .388 with thirty-four home runs. Along with Jim Bottomley's .376 average and nineteen four-baggers, and Ray Blades' .351 and ten homers, the Cardinals maintained a potent hitting attack.

St. Louis Post-Dispatch reporter Herman Wecke wrote a complimentary article about the Cards' left-handers.

That southpaw pitchers are a mighty valuable addition to a major-league club, is evidenced in the case of the Cardinals. Hornsby has four left-handers and they are the stars of the staff. The quartet is composed of Bill Sherdel, Art Reinhart, Eddie Dyer, and Walter Mails. These four men have won twenty-six games and lost thirteen for a winning percentage of .667. And this record has been made since Rogers Hornsby took over the management of the club late in May. Against the .667 winning percentage of the southpaws, the right-handers of the hurling corps have gained but thirty-one conquests against forty-nine defeats, a percentage of .387.

Little Bill Sherdel, who did not start a game until June 2, is the star of the quartet. He has won eleven games and lost three . . . and is one of the five leading flingers in the major leagues. Sherdel, since Hornsby has taken charge of the club, has pitched 121 1/3 innings and, in that time, has been scored upon fifty times, for an average of 3.71 runs a game. Prior to the time that Hornsby took charge of the club, Sherdel was used exclusively as a relief flinger. Now he is the leader on the staff. . . .

Southpaws are the crying need of all managers on the major leagues and right now the Cardinals own a quartet able to hold their own with any in the circuit. In fact, no other club in either major league owns four left-handers who can show a winning record such as that owned by Sherdel, Reinhart, Dyer, and Mails.[14]

The Sporting News also wrote glowingly about Bill Sherdel.

There has been a wide divergence of opinion as to the most effective needs to present-day pitching. Many experts are agreed that the fast ball thrower, with good control, has the better chance of getting away. They want the fellow who can side-arm them past the batters, using just enough "stuff" to tantalize the opposition.

But Wee Willie Sherdel of the St. Louis Cardinals has some ideas of his own and they seem to be sound. Bill, only last week, hung up his seventh straight victory and his eleventh win in fourteen starts, since June 2, when he shackled the ambitions of the Phils. Now, Bill is far from a speed ball pitcher.

The little southpaw throws a slow ball, then a slower one, and sometimes one which hardly comes to the plate. His 'fast' one is simply a come-on and rarity if ever, in a desirable offering. So they can have their fast ball as far as the mite southpaw is concerned.

Sherdel pitches with his noodle as well as his arm. He is just beginning to cash in on his experience of seven seasons plus gained with the Cardinals.[15]

Bill Sherdel's seven-game-winning streak came to an end on August 28. He lost to the Giants, 4–3, after ten innings of work. He was winning in the Giants' ninth when George Kelly hit a long fly ball to the outfield. Hafey and Mueller collided going for the long fly, and the ball fell for a triple.

On September 4, Sherdel lost again—this time to Pittsburgh. And while his pitching wasn't that impressive, his base-running must have been, according to James Gould. "At odd times, a remark has been made in these columns as to the speed of Bill Sherdel as a base runner. He helped the Cards out yesterday when, in the seventh, he doubled to right center. As he rounded second, he remembered the slurs cast on his fleetness of foot and, with an 'I'll show 'em' expression, lit out for third. The movies would have the hero make it, but, as a matter of fact, he was nailed by several feet."[16]

The Cardinals had an excellent last month of the season and arrived at the final game on October 4, with an even seventy-six wins and seventy-six losses. The Redbirds were in Chicago. Bill Sherdel was not scheduled to pitch that day and went into the clubhouse to get his uniform prepared for a post-season barnstorming tour. But Hornsby explained to Sherdel what it would mean if they won and finished with a winning record. So Bill volunteered to take the mound and hurled a six-hitter and the Cards won. The club finished in fourth place and, thanks to the ruling that now included fourth-finishers in the winning pot, shared in the World Series money pool. Hornsby's club had won seventeen and lost only eight in the final month, despite second baseman Hornsby missing the last four games because of a foot injury. Pittsburgh won the 1925 title. In the junior circuit, the Washington Senators, led by Walter Johnson, again grabbed the title. Pittsburgh won the Series, four games to three.

Much of the St. Louis team's success was credited to Rogers Hornsby. When he took over the reins on May 31, the club was headed to the cellar.

Hornsby had brought them back with a strong finish and they had reached fourth place.

As for Sherdel and his contribution to the 1925 Cards, *St. Louis Star* reporter summed the subject up thus: "A great deal of credit is due to the great hurling of Bill Sherdel, the ace of the Cardinal pitching staff. The diminutive left-hander led all the hurlers in the older circuit at the end of the season and was responsible to a large degree for the percentage of .503 turned in by the club at the end of the season."[17] Sherdel credited his 1925 success to Rogers Hornsby, his manager, and to Bob O'Farrell, his catcher.

Southpaw Sherdel appeared in thirty-two games and 200 innings in the 1925 season. His 15–6 record led the league with a .714 winning percentage. He also ranked fifth with the fewest walks allowed per nine innings (1.89), fifth in earned run average (3.11), and third in the clutch-pitching index (109).

On the offensive side, the Cardinals were led by Rogers Hornsby and Jim Bottomley, again. Hornsby won the National League's Most Valuable Player award and the triple crown for the top batting average (.403), home runs (39), and runs-batted-in (143). That was Hornsby's sixth straight batting title. He also finished first in total bases (381), on-base percentage (.489), and slugging average (.756). Adding a second in runs (133) and a fourth in hits (203) and doubles (41), Hornsby was the best hitter in the National League, again. His protégé Jim Bottomley, meanwhile, led the league in hits (227) and doubles (44). "Sunny" Jim also added a second in batting average (.367); a third in runs-batted-in (128), total bases (358), and slugging percentage (.578); and a fifth-best in home runs (21). Other top Cardinal hitters included Blades (.342), Mueller (.313), and Hafey (.302). The St. Louis team batting average was a robust .299, second only to pennant-winning Pittsburgh and its .307 average.

Cardinal fans were very excited about the team Rickey was building. There was youth throughout the lineup. Players Bottomley, Blades, Hafey, Bell, Mueller, and Thevenow were young and talented.

As the season ended in early October, baseball lovers in Hanover and McSherrystown began to plan a banquet to honor their favorite son, Bill Sherdel. Sherdel's winning percentage earned him the top spot of National League pitchers. There were other pitchers with more wins, but sportswriters now viewed Sherdel as one of the best. Hanover and McSherrystown baseball fans were very proud of their boy and wanted to honor the humble southpaw. The leader of the group was McSherrystown burgess Harry Pfaltzgraff. The testimonial banquet was planned for October 29, when Sherdel arrived home after a two-week barnstorming tour with the Cardinals and Indians. Sherdel surprised the community when he returned home ahead of schedule on October 12. Sherdel had pitched the first game and defeated the Cleveland Indians in Two Rivers, Wisconsin. A second game was played in Milwaukee and then snow developed and the players scattered to their homes.[18]

On October 28, the day before the scheduled banquet, burgess Pfaltzgraff suffered a stroke and passed away suddenly. Pfaltzgraff owned the New Colonnade Hall where the banquet was to be held. Banquet organizers acted quickly and cancelled the event. Later, they would reschedule the Sherdel testimonial for mid-November.

In late October, tragedy struck again, this time on an airfield in Texas. Bill Sherdel's old friend Marv Goodwin was a first lieutenant in the Army Air Service Reserve (today's air force), and had been a flying instructor during the First World War. He was piloting a biplane from the Ellington Field in Houston, Texas, and he, along with Sergeant W. H. McMath, had just taken off when the airplane fell into a tailspin, plummeted 200 feet, and crashed into the ground. It was only Goodwin's expert handling of the plane that saved their lives. Goodwin would bring the plane down on its right wing, breaking the force of the fall. An ambulance rushed both men to a Houston hospital. McMath was lucky—he sustained only cuts and bruises. Both of Goodwin's legs were broken, the left one in several places. He also suffered a brain concussion and several fractured ribs. Initially, Goodwin was hospitalized in critical condition, but the hospital staff thought that he would recover.[19] The first night, the doctors operated, believing that he was improving. After the surgery, however, his condition worsened. The next day, thirty-three-year-old Marvin Goodwin passed away.

The sad news of his old teammate's passing hit Bill Sherdel very hard. They had been friends since their days in the Blue Ridge League. Goodwin had pitched for Martinsburg while Sherdel was hurling for rival Hanover. Next, Goodwin had followed Sherdel to the Milwaukee Brewers. It was while Branch Rickey was in Milwaukee scouting Goodwin that Rickey had noticed Sherdel and then signed both pitchers. From 1919 through 1921, Goodwin and Sherdel were teammates on the Cardinals' pitching staff. Things didn't work out as well for Goodwin in St. Louis, though, and he was sent to Houston, where he later became a manager. Late in 1925, he was picked up by the Cincinnati Reds. On September 7, Sherdel was matched against his old friend in the second game of a double-header in St. Louis. It was Goodwin's first game back in the major leagues. He pitched a good game, but Sherdel hurled an even better one and so scored a four-hit victory. Goodwin was touched for runs in only two innings, but that was enough. After the game, the two old friends shook hands and wished each other well, not realizing that it would be the last time they would ever see each other. As an upbeat Goodwin left the field, he was looking forward to the 1926 season in a Reds uniform.

The Bill Sherdel testimonial banquet was held at the New Colonnade Hall in McSherrystown on November 18. One hundred and sixty admirers, including some from Philadelphia, Harrisburg, York, and Gettysburg, attended the celebration of Sherdel's success. Guests included Eddie and Ira Plank, Cliff Heathcote, and Les Bell. After a large meal, seven speakers, including friends and sportswriters, spoke highly of their hero, referencing both the man and the baseball pitcher in glowing terms. The attendees presented Sherdel with a gold watch as a token of their admiration for him. The final speaker for the evening was Sherdel himself. The attendees expected to hear him speak about baseball, and to perhaps share some funny stories about the Cardinals, but Bill Sherdel was not a man of many words. When he reached the podium, with his wife watching proudly behind him, he simply said, "Thank you."

CHAPTER FIFTEEN

Nineteen twenty-six would prove a remarkable year. Hirohito would become Emperor of Japan, gold would be discovered in South Africa, and Richard Byrd and Floyd Bennett would fly over the North Pole. Robert Goddard would launch the first liquid fuel rockets to a height of 184 feet, and Houdini would stay in a coffin underwater for an hour. The National Broadcasting Corporation (NBC) would be created.

In sports, Gene Tunney would defeat Jack Dempsey and claim the world heavyweight boxing title. Gertrude Ederle would become the first woman to swim the English Channel.

The St. Louis Cardinals' leadership triumvirate of Breadon, Rickey, and Hornsby was still not satisfied with the roster. Hornsby felt he needed better right-handed pitching and another outfielder. Giants' manager John McGraw was interviewed about his views on the 1926 National League pennant race. McGraw stated, "The Cardinals are a mighty powerful club, with a tremendous attack and good spirit. If Rogers Hornsby gets some good pitching next season, or is able to land another experienced hurler, his club will be most formidable." The Giants manager predicted a three-team race among the Giants, Pirates, and Cardinals.[1]

Over the winter, Branch Rickey got to work improving the Redbirds. He traded an extra infielder to the Chicago Cubs for right-handed pitcher Vic Keen. Like Sherdel and Goodwin, Keen was a product of the Blue Ridge League. He had spent the last five years on the Cubs' staff as an average pitcher. Hornsby wasn't worried. He believed the twenty-six-year-old Keen would win with the Cardinals' hitters behind him.[2] Rickey also purchased right-hander Sylvester Johnson from the Pacific Coast League. Johnson would become a quality hurler.

Rickey next added former Cubs manager Bill Killefer to the ranks, as a coach for Hornsby. Picking Killefer was pure Rickey genius. The thirty-eight-year-old Killefer had caught for thirteen years and managed for five in the majors. He was known for his ability to develop pitchers—precisely what the Cardinals needed. Hornsby commented, "Killefer is one of the shrewdest men in the game and his knowledge of baseball will be an invaluable asset to the team. He will have sixteen hurlers under his wing down south and I am confident he will be able to round out a capable hurling corps from the collection."[3] Bringing in potential managers as coaches would prove to be part of Rickey's strategy and one that would play out several times for the Cardinals. Rickey was doing everything possible to help Hornsby win a pennant. He would make his two biggest deals after the season began.

James Gould wrote another nice article about Bill Sherdel on January 29. He stated:

> Every fan in St. Louis knows that Bill Sherdel, the Cardinal southpaw, led the National League hurlers last season, and Bill, though a modest youth, also is aware of that fact because his home town presented him with a watch on which the record of his prowess is inscribed. But how many fans know whether or not Bill has a winning percentage since that day, a few years back, when Bill came here from Milwaukee with grit, determination, a fast one—and little else.
>
> In his eight years of service with the Cards, "Sherry" has figured on the winning or losing end of 166 games. This means he has been charged with defeat or credited with victory at least twenty times each year. And it may as well be stated right off the bat that Bill has a lifetime percentage of .515, having won eighty-three and lost eighty during his career.
>
> When you figure that, in Bill's eight years, the Cards have been as high as third only twice and finished last once and seventh once in that period, that looks like mighty sweet pitching. As a reliever, Sherdel has ranked high and, in his eight years, has participated in 305 games, or in at least thirty-three every year. . . .
>
> Sherdel today is a great pitcher. When he first came up he had one big fault. Stated simply, he used to get mad and his method then was

to wind up and try to speed his fast one past the batter, waist-high, with a sort of "I'll show you" attitude. Needless to say, the ball didn't always get past the batter.

But Bill progressed in years and wisdom. Now nothing ruffles him and he has developed one of the most amazing slow-deliveries ever seen on the diamond. The wonder to most of the fans is that Bill's sagger ever reached the plate. But it does, much to the discomfiture of many splendid batsmen. . . .

There may have been poison in those tonsils, which Bill recently left in St. Louis, but there are some teams in the National League [that] think Bill is all poison.[4]

Hornsby's star pitcher
—*St. Louis Star*, January 30, 1926

Jack Conway of *The New York Daily Mirror* provided an accurate description of Bill Sherdel for his readers:

> He is a slow ball pitcher, this Sherdel. A left-hander of slight build, dark, expressive face, soft voice, modest ways, and a tantalizing, mesmerizing slow curve ball.
>
> He has also the courage to float that ball up to the plate as large, and also as elusive, as a Halloween pumpkin carried by a witch.[5]

The Cardinals moved training camp again this year—this time to San Antonio, Texas. Manager Hornsby was very happy with the move since his home was nearby. At Union Station in St. Louis, a large crowd of well-wishers gathered to cheer the initial group of pitchers and catchers as they departed for camp. There was no question that the fans expected an outstanding season. Many players traveled directly from their homes to San Antonio.

The first practice began on February 22. Manager Hornsby did not place any harsh rules on his team. However, he only allowed pitchers to play golf, because he believed that golf was bad for hitters. Bill Sherdel was missing from camp. He was a holdout. Sherdel had received his new contract in January and had returned it unsigned. He felt he deserved more money based upon his breakout year in 1925—but Rickey had not sent another contract.

It was good that Sherdel was still in McSherrystown on February 22. His mentor and friend Eddie Plank suffered a paralyzing stroke while getting dressed that very morning. It was a great surprise. He had been fine the night before, although he'd complained for several months that he just didn't feel right. Ironically, perhaps the greatest left-handed pitcher of all time was completely paralyzed on his left side. He could not even talk. Two days later, fifty-one-year-old Plank died. The entire baseball world mourned his passing. That evening, Bill Sherdel stopped by in person to express his sympathy to Eddie's wife and ten-year-old son, Eddie Junior.

Sherdel's mentor Eddie Plank
—Coulson collection

The following day, Bill, Marguerite, Patty, and Junior headed by train to St. Louis so Bill could discuss his contract with Branch Rickey. He hoped to work out an agreement and leave from there for San Antonio. Two days later, Sherdel signed a new contract to play for the Cardinals in 1926, just in time to join Sam Breadon and the second group of players leaving that night for training camp. Branch Rickey was noticeable by his absence.

When the veterans arrived, Hornsby started his regular practices. The 1926 camp was loaded with talent. The Cardinals began playing exhibition games against Texas minor-league clubs on March 10. Many times, Hornsby split the squad. He managed the one team and Killefer the other. Hornsby felt that was the best way to judge his players. The manager made it known that he preferred using the same lineup every game, instead of platooning his players as Rickey had done. Hornsby allowed veteran Bill Sherdel to progress at his own speed. Sherdel entered his first game on March 15, and hurled an excellent five innings.

At training camp, writer James Gould wrote about manager Hornsby, "this writer has never noticed a bit of difference in Hornsby 'before and after taking' the management. Perhaps that statement should be qualified. There is a difference. Hornsby, while as quiet as ever, has become more forceful, but, while letting his men know he is the leader, he has done so in such a way that the assumption of command has seemed the most natural thing in the world."[6]

As camp progressed, some veteran pitchers found themselves headed to the minors. It seemed no matter where the club trained, every year they had to contend with rain. In every case, the residents said the foul weather was unusual. That year in San Antonio was no different. Many players, including Sherdel, Hallahan, and Bell, were suffering from colds and were unable to play for several days. Despite the bad weather, the Cardinals did play many exhibition games throughout Texas. They didn't lose a game until April 6, when Shreveport defeated them.

On April 9, Hornsby brought his club home to St. Louis for the spring series with the Browns. The Redbirds' manager was well-pleased with his club. They had just finished with a 25–1 record down south. The Cards and Browns were primed to open a brand-new Sportsman's Park. The old wooden park had been updated with beautiful, larger concrete grandstands, pavilions, and bleachers. The new park was ready for a World Series. Now all St. Louis needed was a pennant-winning team—either the Cardinals or the Browns. Both clubs had strong teams—on paper. In the two-game series that followed, the Browns proved the superior team, winning both contests. All the talk was now over. It was time for the St. Louis Cardinals to live up to their potential.

The 1926 National League season began on April 13 with the Redbirds hosting the tough World Champion Pittsburgh Pirates. Young right-hander Flint Rhem was on the mound as the Cards won in front of 17,000 partisan fans. In the end, they managed to win three of the four-game series with the World Champs. In the only loss, starter Haines was hit in the right instep by a line drive in the third inning and had to be taken to the hospital. He would be out for ten days. Maybe this year would be different.

Bill Sherdel took the mound for the first time on April 18, and won an exciting game, 3–2, which wasn't decided until the final out. In the fifth inning, Cubs' pitcher Tony Kaufmann sailed two pitches close to Sherdel's head. After the second headhunter, Sherdel let his bat fly toward the mound and then began to charge Kaufmann. Players and umpires rushed in before anything else could happen. In the ninth, Cubs' pinch-runner Cliff Heathcote was on first base with two outs. Heathcote represented the tying run. Sherdel picked him off first with a quick throw to Bottomley to end the game and preserve the Cards' victory.

By month's end, Hornsby's squad had dropped to fifth place. Player Hornsby was batting .397, but the Redbirds' bats had not yet started to win games. Manager Hornsby remained very optimistic about their chances.

The Cardinals held onto fifth place during May. The club's hitting still had not reached everyone's expectations and they weren't scoring runs. They needed Rhem, Keen, Sherdel, and one or two other starters to pitch well for the Cards to have any chance of winning the pennant.

Bill Sherdel was improving. On May 22, he threw his best game of the new season, allowing only three hits through the first seven innings. In attendance were baseball commissioner Landis and National League president Heydler. St. Louis was celebrating Rogers Hornsby Day in honor of his outstanding 1925 season. The city celebration began with a large parade of civic groups, Boy Scouts, and drum corps from the fairgrounds to Sportsman's Park, where 14,000 fans had gathered. A band played the national anthem, and then Hornsby was presented with a $1,000 cash prize and a gold medal for his 1925 Most Valuable Player award.

One day in early June, the Cards' trainer, Kirby Samuels, was working on Hornsby, who was lying on the trainer's table. Samuels said, "Something's worrying you, Mr. Rog."

Hornsby responded, "You're right, Kirby. What's wrong with this ball club?" He went on to name all the talented players on the squad. "What's wrong with us?"

"Mr. Rog, you know I usually keep my mouth shut around here," came back Samuels. "You asked for my opinion, and you're going to get it. Nothing wrong with the boys' legs and arms. They're all right. It's their stomachs."

Hornsby jumped up. "Their stomachs," he shouted. "What has a stomach to do with pitching, batting, and fielding?"

"That's my point, Mr. Rog. Our boys don't eat enough. You know, they get that $4 a day, and I see them sneaking into cheap places for their meals. Why, they must be saving $3 a day at least every day we're on the road. Now, Mr. Rog, if you could get them to eating enough food, the right food, I know we'd start winning."

Immediately, Hornsby went to Rickey to change the way the players' meals were handled. The club eliminated the per diem and started allowing the players to eat in their hotels and sign the tab, with no limits. Did Samuels' advice make a difference? Perhaps.[7]

June was a great month. Historically, the Cardinals never played as well on the road as at home, but this month was different. Hornsby's squad won fourteen and lost only eight away from St. Louis. Next, Sherdel and the Cardinals had the opportunity to play another exhibition game in York, Pennsylvania, against the minor-league York White Roses on June 6. Hornsby guaranteed the fans that he would play his regular lineup. Four thousand area fans loved the chance to see Sherdel pitch and Harrisburg native Les Bell play third. Sherdel pitched only two scoreless innings in the Cards' 6–2 win, since he was scheduled to start the next day in Philadelphia. Later that month, Sherdel had a great week. He blanked the Robins twice—twirling a five-hitter and a two-hitter.

The Cardinals made two acquisitions in June that would put the team in pennant contention. Before the season started, the club knew that they needed another good outfielder and a veteran pitcher to win a pennant. Club leadership addressed those needs by acquiring outfielder Billy Southworth and pitcher Grover Cleveland Alexander—both would become Hall of Famers.

On June 14, the Cards swapped outfielders with the Giants. St. Louis traded twenty-six-year-old "Heinie" Mueller for thirty-two-year-old veteran Southworth. John McGraw wanted youth. Rogers Hornsby wanted experience. The Cards' manager had this to say: "I have always been an admirer of Southworth's playing. He is older than Mueller and it is this greater experience that he has had that makes me believe that he will be a big help to the Cardinals. While I have always had a high regard for Mueller's playing, I think that Southworth will be of more benefit to the club. We are in the thick of the pennant fight right now and I am hopeful that Southworth will help us climb to the top."[8]

Mueller possessed all the tools. He could hit, run, and field, but his head was not always in the game. The older Southworth had played briefly with the Indians from 1913–1915, and then joined the Pirates in 1918. In the winter of 1920, Southworth was traded to the Braves, where he hit over .300 for three straight years. He became a Giant in 1923 and was hitting .328 when the Cards acquired him. The *St. Louis Post-Dispatch* wrote, "Southworth is an accomplished all-around ball player. A comparatively small man, he is a 'wrist hitter' of high caliber. . . . Billy hasn't a weakness in the field. He covers ground well and can get as many fly balls as the ordinary center-fielder. His throwing arm is good and, above all, Southworth has the reputation of being a brainy ball player."[9]

The Cardinals made their second major acquisition after they arrived home. Seeing an unbelievable opportunity, St. Louis picked up outstanding Cubs' hurler Grover Cleveland Alexander for the waiver price of $4,000. The Cards, Pirates, and Reds put in a waiver claim for the big pitcher, but at the time, the Cardinals were lower in the standings, so St. Louis was awarded Alexander. Redbirds' coach Bill Killefer had been the superstar pitcher's manager in Chicago until this year, when the Cubs hired Joe McCarthy to manage the team. McCarthy and Alexander did not get along, and Alexander was suspended for breaking training rules prior to being waived. Killefer quickly called the big right-hander to ask about his arm. Alexander told him, "I'm in condition and ready to pitch right now. I hope that I can do something to help you boys win a pennant."[10] Prior to this season, he had won 318 major-league games against 168 losses. *St. Louis Post-Dispatch* reporter J. Roy Stockton wrote, "Alexander, though he is thirty-nine years old, ought to be of great assistance to the Cardinals. He has a terrific fast ball and never has been bothered by a sore arm. Fast-ball pitchers last longer than curve-ball artists and undoubtedly the change in scenery and the chance to cut in on the World Series melon will cause Alexander to strive his hardest to be a winner for the Cardinals."[11] "Alex" was happy to be joining his old manager, catcher, and friend Killefer and his favorite Cubs' batterymate, Bob O'Farrell.

By the end of June, Hornsby's club had climbed into second place—only three-and-a-half games behind the Cincinnati Reds. Ironically, ex-Cardinal skipper Jack Hendricks was now managing the Ohio club. Flint Rhem and Vic Keen were leading the Cards' pitching staff, although Bill Sherdel, Jess

Haines, and Grover Alexander would now provide greater help. By month end, Sherdel had won three straight games and held the opponents scoreless for twenty-one straight innings. Haines was now starting again with two successive wins. Alexander got his first start on June 27, and pitched a four-hit victory in ten innings before a record crowd of 37,196 fans at Sportsman's Park. The local fans were excited to see their newest hurling ace.

There were a few negatives for the team at this juncture in time. Star outfielder Chick Hafey was suffering vision problems from an infection under an eyelid, and would eventually require glasses. On June 29, Rogers Hornsby entered St. John's Hospital in St. Louis for minor surgery. Hornsby had been playing in intense pain for several weeks because of a carbuncle on his thigh. A carbuncle was defined as a cluster of boils and was very painful. A surgeon operated to remove the growth and Hornsby was expected to miss about a week.

July provided a hint that this was going to be the closest pennant race in many years. The Cardinals dropped to third, but only two games behind the second-place Reds and four games back of the first-place Pirates. No team was pulling away from the others. Cardinals' pitching was still the problem. Keen and Rhem—the two pitchers who had carried the club through June—were struggling. Keen suffered a sore arm and didn't win again until July 27. No one was sure what was wrong with Rhem—he suddenly couldn't pitch very well. He was getting hammered. Finally, by July 18, he seemed back to form. Replacing Keen and Rhem at the top of the staff was now Haines. Both Sherdel and Alexander were up and down in July. They just hadn't hit their stride, yet.

Third baseman Les Bell had a fantastic July. He hit safely in twenty-one consecutive games—a streak that was stopped at month's end. His batting average jumped to .357. During one string of fifteen games, Bell hit .518 and drove in eighteen runs. Bottomley and Blades continued to hit well, too—as expected. Bottomley was leading the league with fifteen home runs and Blades was tops in runs scored. The club played much of July without its superstar Rogers Hornsby. At the beginning of July, he was recovering from minor surgery and at month-end he was recovering from getting hit in the right eye. Amazingly, without Hornsby, the team still held together. The next two months and perhaps the final few days would determine the pennant winner. The Cardinals were still in the hunt.

The Cardinals began August in the middle of a long eastern road trip. When they returned to the friendly confines of Sportsman's Park on August 14, they had just won twenty-two of twenty-nine games against the eastern clubs. The team had moved into second place behind only Pittsburgh. Bill Sherdel pitched and batted his way to a big victory over Brooklyn on August 4. Slugger Sherdel blasted a double, triple, and home run in four plate appearances. He ran his winning streak over the Robins to six before getting knocked out of the box in an August 17 game the Cards ultimately won.

In the second half of the month, the Redbirds won fifteen and lost only five at home. The St. Louis fans were filled with pennant hopes and responded with increasing attendance records at the ballpark. Ball and Breadon, the two St. Louis owners, proved to be very smart when they enlarged and improved Sportsman's Park before the season.

St. Louis fans were on an emotional rollercoaster in August. The Cardinals changed places in the standings seven times during the month. Most importantly, Hornsby's squad ended August at the top of the National League after a very important series' victory over the World Champion Pittsburgh Pirates. The pennant race was not over. The Reds were only a half game back, while the Pirates were one game from the top. Now leading the Cards' pitching staff were Haines (11–3), Sherdel (12–9), and Alexander (10–8). The Cardinals were hitting despite the physical ailments of Hornsby, Bottomley, and Blades. Their team batting average was third best. The Redbirds left town to spend September on the road. Their dirty home uniforms could finally be washed in time for a possible World Series.

Although the Cardinals remained confident, they lost an important series in Cincinnati early in September and that put them back in second. But when Hornsby's squad played the Pirates again, they regained the lead. Bill Sherdel defeated the Pirates, 8–0, in their final match of the year. The *St. Louis Post-Dispatch* wrote, "Bill Sherdel was in great form in handing the Buccaneers a farewell drubbing yesterday afternoon. Bill was touched for nine hits but they were all singles and he kept them so well scattered that only one Pirate advanced as far as third base and none scored. While Sherdel was baffling them with his crossfire and his curves, his slow ball and the best fast ball he has had in a month, the Cardinals were pounding Vic Aldridge for eight runs."[12]

In theory, it seemed that St. Louis would win, since they were playing ten games with the seventh- and eighth-place teams while Pittsburgh and Cincinnati were playing each other. The seventh-place Boston Braves had their own opinion, however, and defeated the Cards in three of four games, dropping St. Louis back down to second. Even worse, the Redbirds moved into Philadelphia to play six games in four days. Could the Cards' pitching staff hold up? It could, as it turned out. Hornsby's squad won five of six games. Sherdel and Haines won their games, while Rhem gained two victories; the second was his twentieth win of the season. The Cardinals were now one-and-a-half games ahead of Cincinnati.

Hornsby, catcher O'Farrell, and pitchers Alexander, Haines, Sherdel, Rhem, and Keen attended a September Red Sox-Yankees game in New York. A very smart Hornsby was scouting and preparing his pitching staff for a potential World Series matchup against the Yankees' sluggers.

As the Cardinals were nearing a title, everyone was wondering how Hornsby had succeeded in his first full season where Rickey had failed. J. Roy Stockton of the *Post-Dispatch* described his methods thus:

> Hornsby's system is easily explained. He makes the job of manager as simple as possible. He has no rules, except that the men must be fit to deliver winning baseball on the diamond. If the players can't do that, they are fired, traded, or given away.
>
> Hornsby is absolute BOSS. The players know that. When he gives one of his few orders, the player obeys quickly and absolutely. . . .
>
> Hornsby completely changed the system, the fundamentals of the clubhouse meeting. Instead of having half a dozen men express their opinion on how a pitcher should pitch to certain batters, Hornsby, when it was necessary, consulted the smart pitchers, the strategists. Then Hornsby would take the pitcher of the day aside and tell him how to pitch to each man on the opposing team that day.
>
> "Pitch that way," Hornsby would say, "and if they hit you or beat you, I'll take the blame. But pitch that way to them."
>
> Hornsby's position at second base gave him a chance through the years to study the batters. He soon learned what each opposing hitter

could hit and what he could not hit. The pitchers on the Cardinal team say it is remarkable how seldom Rogers goes wrong on the hitters.

Hornsby did away with as many signs as possible. The hit-and-run and the sacrifice sign, of course, had to be kept, but one signal would do for both. The runner on first had to advance anyhow and the batter had the option of bunting or hitting straight away. Unless ordered specifically by Hornsby to do one thing.[13]

In a second *Post-Dispatch* article, an unidentified writer added more insightful comments about Hornsby as manager:

Hornsby realized that his pitching staff needed a veteran as coach and he went out and signed Bill Killefer, former manager of the Cubs. Hornsby is absolute boss of the Cardinals and makes all decisions. But he is big enough to consult Killefer. . . . On the bench, he will say, "Bill, what had we better do here?" If he doesn't like Killefer's suggestion, he'll say so, but if he likes the idea, he'll follow the advice. There is never a question of credit on the club. But when there's any question about the blame, Hornsby takes it.

"I want to decide everything important," Hornsby says. "If we succeed, they'll naturally give me the credit, but if we fail, I'll also get the blame. And I want it, but I want to take the decisions, so I'll have the blame coming to me."[14]

Bill Sherdel earned a unique distinction on September 17. *The Evening Sun* reported it this way:

The so-called Wee Willie, who is not so wee as some sportswriters would have him appear, pulled his team back into first place for the third time this season with yesterday's victory [over Phillies, 10–1]. On August 31, he pitched his mates to a spectacular triumph over the Pirates in the first game of a double victory for the Cards [that] lifted the St. Louis club into first. Earlier in the season, he had performed the same little stunt, defeating the Chicago Cubs on April 17 in a 3–2 game and forcing the Phils out of first place. He is the only pitcher in the big leagues this season to be credited with returning his club to first place three times.[15]

On September 24, Rhem and Sherdel pitched the Cardinals to their first pennant since 1888. The Redbirds' 6–4 road victory over the Giants coupled with the Reds' loss in Philadelphia gave St. Louis the title they had wanted for so long. Owner Sam Breadon said, "Nothing could possibly have made me happier than the winning of the pennant. When I took charge of the club seven years ago, I did it with the sole hope of winning a championship for St. Louis. It has been a long, hard fight, but that ambition has finally been realized."[16] The National League race was the closest it had been since 1908.

When the fans back in St. Louis learned the Cards had won the pennant, the city went crazy. "With one great roar of whistles, bombs, horns, and other noise-makers, including the human voice," *The Evening Sun* expounded, "St. Louis late yesterday burst into its most joyous and whole-hearted celebration since Armistice day eight years ago. . . ."

> Passing motorists pounded their horns and heads bobbed from the high windows of office buildings. Sirens began to blow, ten bombs were set off at the city hall, and hundreds of pigeons nesting there swooped out over the streets.
>
> From the doors of downtown buildings, crowds poured forth. From offices came shirt-sleeved workers who had not time to think of hats or coats or bother about the thunderstorm that began just prior to the celebration.
>
> From the windows floated masses of torn paper, confetti, and ticker tape. From everywhere appeared noise-making instruments, which fans had been buying for the hour when the victory would be known.[17]

Manager Hornsby explained his club's success.

"We felt confident from the beginning. It was confidence that won for us; that's half of any battle. The boys got nervous at times, but what cost us the most in games lost was the inexperience of some of the players. [Taylor] Douthit, for instance, came right on a championship contender practically straight from college. He would be the greatest outfielder in the game next year.

"I had just one policy all year, and that was to try our best for each game as it was played. I gave our pitchers all the chance in the world in every game.

We refused to get excited, and I guess that's why we won. All I ask of the boys was their best. They gave me that, and it was enough."[18]

Hornsby's club was the youngest team to ever win a National League pennant.[19]

One day later, the New York Yankees clinched the American League pennant. Their competition in the junior circuit was not as strong. Only the Cleveland Indians challenged the Yanks. The St. Louis Browns finished in seventh place.

The pennant-winning Cardinals' staff was led by right-handers Flint Rhem (20–7) and Jess Haines (13–4). The duo finished in the league's top five. Veteran right-hander Grover Alexander (9–7) also pitched well after his June acquisition. Hornsby had this to say about "Old Pete" Alexander: "Alexander has taken good care of himself and has been an important factor in our success. He has helped our pitchers. He has volunteered to pitch out of turn. He went to the hill in Cincinnati right after the Reds had won two straight and taken the lead. Aleck beat the Reds that Sunday afternoon, working with only two days' rest."[20] Left-hander Bill Sherdel (16–12) added many quality starts.

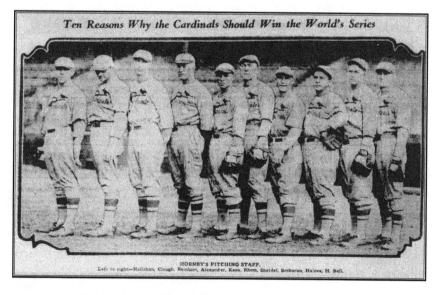

Hornsby's pitching staff.
Sherdel 4th from right
—*St. Louis Post-Dispatch*, October 2, 1926

Although Hornsby and Bottomley did not hit as well due to physical problems, other Cardinals helped. Hornsby did hit .317 with eleven home runs, still a very good year after winning the last six batting titles. Bottomley's average dropped to .299, but he led the league in doubles (40), runs-batted-in (120), and total bases (305). "Sunny Jim" also added a second-best-home-runs claim (19). Les Bell had a breakout season. He batted a fourth-best .325, while collecting 189 hits, seventeen homers, and 100 runs-batted-in. Ray Blades also had a great season, batting .305. Billy Southworth proved a great pickup, hitting .317 with eleven four-baggers in his ninety-nine St. Louis games. Hornsby's other youngsters Taylor Douthit (.308), Chick Hafey (.271), and Tommy Thevenow (.256) proved they would be future stars.

1926 National League champs.
Sherdel 2nd from right in middle row
—*St. Louis Post-Dispatch*, September 27, 1926

CHAPTER SIXTEEN

During the week leading up to the first World Series game, everyone offered an opinion of which team would win. They were divided. Ty Cobb picked the Yankees. John McGraw chose the Cards. As with all World Series, several storylines developed. Yankees manager Miller Huggins had given Cardinals manager Rogers Hornsby his first start, buying him for $600 from the Dennison, Texas, club when Huggins was piloting the Redbirds. Now the mentor and pupil would be matched against each other.

A second storyline involved Rogers Hornsby's mother, Mrs. M. D. Hornsby, of Austin, Texas. Hornsby's mother had been an invalid for eleven years, but she never missed reading about her son's games. Her son would send her clippings of each one. Hornsby stated, "After trying to make a score that will satisfy Mother, my most important daily job during the season is to see that she gets it!" Hornsby had begun playing baseball at age three and was captaining his own team by ten. His mother made him his first baseball uniform. He played three games a day and walked five miles to the baseball diamond. In high school, he was good enough to play with the adults of the meat-packing teams in Fort Worth, Texas. "There's where I got my real training," Hornsby would say. "I've never seen more serious-minded players anywhere than in those home-town teams. Those boys had to be serious minded! The bleachers were filled with second-guessers, and one of the very hardest to convince, especially when it came to my playing, was Mother!"[1] The Wednesday before the Series began, Mrs. M. D. Hornsby passed away. She had prayed that she might linger long enough to see her son win the World Series, but her wish was denied. Her dying request was that Hornsby remain with the team—and that's what he did. Personal tragedy could provide an incentive for a team to play their hardest, and that would be true for the Cardinals.

The Series was set to begin on Saturday, October 2, in Yankee Stadium. Both clubs were in New York by Monday evening. Many Cardinal regulars had remained there after their final series with the Giants and the Robins. They were well rested. The Yankees arrived back in town—oddly enough from St. Louis, and a final series with the Browns—on Monday evening. With a crowd gathered at the train station to meet the Yankees, Babe Ruth commented, "We'll beat 'em. There'll be nothing to it."[2] The Cardinals were just as confident.

The Cardinals practiced at Yankee Stadium for the first time on Tuesday. They wanted time to learn the nuances of the ballpark—how did balls carom off the outfield walls, where were the shadows during game time, etc. During the week, the weather was cold. Reporters guessed maybe Alexander or Haines would start the first game since Rhem and Sherdel were better in warmer weather. It was commonly known that the Yankee sluggers had more trouble with lefties, so maybe Sherdel would start despite the cold. Neither manager was quick to announce his starting pitcher for game one. One thing was certain—the umpires. Commissioner Landis announced that Bill Klem, Hank O'Day, Tommy Connolly, and George Hildebrand would work the Series. The first three became members of the Baseball Hall of Fame. During the week, Connolly became ill and was replaced by Bill Dineen behind the plate.

A *St. Louis Post-Dispatch* reporter asked Yankee skipper Miller Huggins his opinion of the two teams. Huggins provided very insightful comments.

> "The Yankees and Cardinals are clubs of much the same type—more alike, I think, than most clubs that meet in the annual baseball clashes.
>
> "Both clubs have a serious pitching problem. By that, I mean that their pitching may be very, very good, or very, very bad. Men like Alexander, Sherdel, and Rhem of the Cardinals and [Herb] Pennock, [Urban] Shocker, and [Dutch] Ruether of the Yankees, are capable of pitching almost perfect ball if they happen to be right. On the other hand, they may be terrible if they get away to a bad start.

"Being hitters of the free-swinging type, both clubs are weak offensively and defensively on the sacrifice and bunt plays. They can't be called upon to pull the play successfully themselves and they have a lot of difficulty stopping it when the other fellows attempt it."[3]

A *Post-Dispatch* reporter then interviewed Rogers Hornsby. The first question was not who would pitch the first game or who would win the Series, but, instead, would they pitch to Babe Ruth?

"Of course, we will pitch to Ruth. Why shouldn't we? Who is he that we should be afraid to pitch to him?

"Don't misunderstand me. I consider Ruth a great ballplayer, a dangerous hitter, a good baserunner, and an outfielder with an accurate arm. Of course, having been in the National League all my big-league life, I've had few chances to see Ruth in action. But I have seen enough, and his records speak for themselves. He is a great ballplayer. A great many persons have the idea that Ruth is just a slugger, and is carried along for that reason.

"That is far from the truth. Ruth's fielding and his throwing and his base running would make him an asset on any old ball club, even if he were not such a dangerous man at the plate. He always hustles, and that's one of his strong points.

"But Ruth is just a good ballplayer. He's no great menace that is going to cause us to pitch four balls every time he walks to the plate. Of course, if he comes up in a pinch with a man on base, we'll treat him like any other good hitter."[4]

Hornsby's big five hurlers
—*St. Louis Post-Dispatch*, September 26, 1926

Herman Wecke of the *Post-Dispatch* wrote of Bill Sherdel against the Yankees. "When Sherdel goes to the hill, the Yankees will see something new in the pitching line. Sherdel has a slow ball and then a slower one. There is no hurler in the American League who pitches just like 'Little Willie.' And that slow ball of his may have the Yankee sluggers swinging futilely at the air. If Hornsby decides not to use Alexander, Sherdel will without a doubt get the honor of starting the World Series."[5]

Babe Ruth wrote, "A lot of people have asked me what Cardinal pitchers I expected to give us the most trouble. That's a tough one. Maybe all of them will. And maybe none of them. From what I can learn, though, it looks as though Alexander and Sherdel would be the two toughest ones for us."[6]

Miller Huggins was asked the same question about the Cardinals' pitching. "Among the Cardinal pitchers, the fellow I figure to give us the most trouble is Billy Sherdel, the left-hander. Here's why. Sherdel, in addition to being a left-hander, is a slow curve-ball artist. My club is made of what we in baseball call 'swing hitters.' A swing hitter is a chap who takes his bat at the end and takes a full cut at the ball with plenty of 'follow through.' We've had more or less trouble with these slow curve boys all season and I imagine Sherdel will be just as troublesome. I pick him as the toughest man we'll have to beat."[7]

An interesting prediction was made by John Foster, a New York sportswriter. He analyzed the previous twenty-one interleague clashes and determined that, in most cases, the team with the best catcher won. That would favor the St. Louis Cardinals and Bob O'Farrell. O'Farrell had had what many considered an MVP year. The ironman caught 147 of 154 games and hit .293 with seven home runs. O'Farrell also excelled in directing the pitching staff. He was considered the best backstop in the National League. The Yankees' starter Bennie Bengough was out with a broken arm. New York had to rely on Pat Collins and Hank Severeid—neither of whom was as good all-around as O'Farrell.[8]

Comparing the opposing lineups revealed a matchup that was very close. The New York Yankees outfield of Babe Ruth (.372, 47 HRs), Bob Meusel (.315, 12), and Earle Combs (.299, 8) was probably a little better than Southworth (.320, 11), Douthit (.308, 3), and Hafey (.271, 4). Unfortunately, Ray Blades (.305, 8) missed the Series because of an injured knee. In the infield, the Cardinals earned the edge with Bottomley (.299, 19), Hornsby (.317, 11), Thevenow (.256, 2), and Bell (.325, 17), compared to Lou Gehrig (.313, 16), Tony Lazzeri (.275, 18), Mark Koenig (.271, 5), and Joe Dugan (.288, 1). Gehrig was just beginning his outstanding career, while Lazzeri and Koenig were rookies. The Cardinals were tops in catching while the Yankees pitching staff of Herb Pennock (23–11), Urban Shocker (19–11), Waite Hoyt (16–12), Bob Shawkey (8–7), and Dutch Ruether (14–9) was probably a little better. Basically, it was a very close contest. The Series might be determined by whichever team won the first game.

Hornsby selected Bill Sherdel to pitch the opener. After learning of this, Giants manager John McGraw had this to say: "Sherdel is not only a southpaw, but he is one of the best pitchers in the country. He is a student of the game."[9]

Huggins countered with his own southpaw ace, Herb Pennock. Teammate Babe Ruth spoke complimentarily of Pennock.

"To my mind, Herbie Pennock is one of the greatest pitchers who ever wore spikes. And the reason is that he is cool under fire, he knows his business, and most of all, he's out there on the mound trying to make the other fellow hit—and hit where he wants him to. . . . Herbie has the best curve ball of any left-hander in the business. He has a peach of a change of pace. . . . Herbie Pennock is a master. That's why I'm picking him right now to be one of the stars of the World Series—and one of the pitchers who will cause the Cardinals the most trouble."[10]

The opening game of the Series began at 1:30 in Yankee Stadium on Saturday, October 2. The weather was cold with threatening skies and a harsh east wind. In a battle of left-handers, World Series veteran Herb Pennock was matched against Series rookie Bill Sherdel.

Bill Sherdel showing Junior how to strike out Babe Ruth
—Sherdel family

Yankee Stadium had opened in 1923. It was called "The House That Ruth Built," because it was constructed to accommodate the large crowds that Babe Ruth's huge popularity brought into the ballpark. When it was built, it was the first stadium to have three tiers. The Yankees' owners chose to call it a "stadium," to distinguish it from the names always used in the past for accommodating baseball games: ball fields and ballparks. It was built with a short right-field line to accommodate left-handed-swinging Ruth. The right-field bleachers became known as "Ruthville."

The two managers exchanged lineups at home plate. Hornsby's lineup included: Douthit, CF; Southworth, RF; Hornsby, 2B; Bottomley, 1B; Bell, 3B; Hafey, LF; O'Farrell, C; Thevenow, SS; and Sherdel, P. Miller Huggins countered with: Combs, CF; Koenig, SS; Ruth, RF; Meusel, LF; Gehrig, 1B; Lazzeri, 2B; Dugan, 3B; Severid, C; and Pennock, P. The Yankees' lineup was gaining fame as "Murderers' Row," referencing the first six hitters in the New York order—Combs, Koenig, Ruth, Gehrig, Meusel, and Lazzeri. Four would later join the Hall of Fame.

After the national anthem, Pennock took his place on the mound. Herb Pennock had signed with Connie Mack and the Philadelphia Athletics in 1912 when he was only eighteen. He pitched sparingly for the A's and Mack questioned his desire. In 1915, he sold Pennock to the Red Sox for the waiver price of $2,500. Later, Mack would call this the biggest mistake he ever made. Pennock had a rather lackluster career with Boston, eventually settling in as the third starter. The Yankees traded for him in 1923 and he became the staff ace. In 1926, his twenty-three wins and .676 winning percentage ranked second in the American League. Pennock had pitched 266 innings, allowing only 1.45 walks per game—best in the league. Pennock was at the height of his career in 1926.

On that day, 61,658 screaming baseball fans had crowded the Yankees' home to watch the evenly matched champs from the two major leagues compete for baseball's highest honor. At the time, that was the second-largest crowd in the history of a sporting event. Interestingly, the crowd seemed impartial and cheered vociferously for both clubs.

Back in Hanover, McSherrystown, Gettysburg, and St. Louis, Bill Sherdel's many fans gathered around the radio to hear of the game's progress. Sherdel's brother-in-law and seven friends drove from McSherrystown to New York to see the first two Series games and greet the pitcher.

Douthit was the first batter. He doubled to right field. Southworth grounded out Lazzeri to Gehrig as Douthit moved to third. Hornsby grounded to the pitcher, who threw to first for the second out. Bottomley singled through the hole at shortstop, scoring Douthit with the first run of the Series. Bell flied out to Ruth for the third out. Cardinals 1, Yankees 0.

Now Bill Sherdel took the mound in front of the largest crowd he had ever seen. He must have been nervous. The Yankees' initial strategy was to wait out Sherdel's pitches and to make him work deep into the count. He walked the first batter, Combs. Koenig flied out to right-fielder Southworth. Sherdel walked Ruth, sending Combs to second. Sherdel continued to be wild and nervous as he walked Meusel and loaded the bases with only one out. Gehrig hit a ball into right field, where Southworth quickly fielded it and threw to Hornsby for a forced out at second. But Combs scored and Ruth moved to third. Lazzeri grounded to shortstop Thevenow, who threw to Bottomley to get the final out. Cardinals 1, Yankees 1.

Pennock and Sherdel settled down through the next four innings and the score remained tied. Babe Ruth provided some comic relief to the tense game in the bottom of the third inning. He singled and then slid safely into second on a bunt by Meusel. A distressed Ruth jumped up and signaled quickly for the trainer to approach. The crowd gasped, fearing that Babe had injured an ankle or a leg. No, the Great Bambino had torn his pants on his slide. The trainer was forced to sew up the embarrassed Ruth's pants while he stood on second with his hands on his hips.[11] Ruth remained in that spot until the inning ended, harmlessly.

Excitement was reignited when the teams entered the sixth. Pennock retired Douthit, Southworth, and Hornsby in order, and Sherdel took the mound again in the bottom of the inning. Now the Yankees changed their strategy and decided to go after the first pitch. Ruth led off with a single between Bell and Thevenow. Meusel placed a sacrifice bunt in front of the plate and O'Farrell threw him out at first while Ruth moved to second. Gehrig now singled to right, scoring Ruth with the go-ahead run. Lazzeri singled to left but left-fielder Hafey fielded the ball and threw out Gehrig at third, while Lazzeri traveled to second. The next batter Dugan hit to Bell, but Lester couldn't come up with the ball and Dugan was safe at first. Lazzeri was now on third base with two outs. Sherdel forced Severid to ground to

Thevenow, who got the force on Dugan at second and the inning ended. Yankees 2, Cardinals 1.

The Cardinals failed to score in the top of the seventh and the Yankees returned to bat against Sherdel. Pennock grounded out Thevenow to Bottomley. Combs hit a hard smash to the right side of the infield. Hornsby stopped the ball, but slipped on the wet grass. While off balance, he managed to bounce the throw to first in time to get the speedy runner by inches. This was the play of the game. Then Koenig flied to Hafey in left for the third out. Bill Sherdel had thrown only four pitches to get the necessary three outs. Yankees 2, Cardinals 1.

Sherdel left the game in the Cards' eighth for a pinch-hitter with Bob O'Farrell on second base and one out. The Redbirds managed to load the bases, but failed to score. Yankees 2, Cardinals 1. Vic Keen replaced Sherdel and held the Yankees scoreless in the bottom of the eighth. In the Cardinals' ninth, they again failed to score, and the game ended in favor of New York. Both Pennock and Sherdel had shackled the hitting power of the two clubs. Bottomley had collected two of the Cardinals' three hits off Pennock. Sherdel had allowed only five Yankee safeties, but his wildness in the first inning probably cost him the game.

After the game, the reporters caught up with both managers in the clubhouse. Huggins said, "What can I say but point with pride to Herb. The game was all pitching. You can't take any credit away from a pitcher who holds the Cardinals to three hits and one run. Sherdel pitched great ball, too. All in all, the pitchers were the whole game." Hornsby was not without confidence, "We didn't hit. Of course, they didn't hit much either, but they hit enough. We got some great pitching and the fielding was all right. The only note off the key was the hitting, and we'll change that in the other games.

"The boys played just like it was a regular game of the season; if anything, a little better than they did to win the pennant. Pennock pitched great ball against us, but I liked the way Sherdel worked, too. He will give the Yankees a lot of trouble before the Series is over."[12]

The second game of the Series in New York was held the next day, on Sunday, October 3. The crowd increased to 63,600 for that game. Hornsby selected his thirty-nine-year-old veteran Grover Cleveland Alexander, while Huggins picked another veteran, Urban Shocker, to follow Pennock.

The two unwanted players the Cardinals acquired in June won the second game for the Cardinals, 6–2. Alexander pitched a four hitter, striking out ten and retiring twenty-one straight after the first batter Combs singled in the third. Only one Yankee hit a ball to the outfield all day. New York struck first when Meusel, Lazzeri, and Dugan singled for two runs in the bottom of the second, but the Cards came right back with a pair of runs in the top of the third to match New York. After Southworth and Douthit singled, Bottomley doubled to score both. That's when "Alexander the Great" took over the game, holding Huggins's club hitless after Combs's single to open the Yanks' third. The game remained tied until the seventh when the other June acquisition, Billy Southworth, stepped to the plate. O'Farrell was standing on second after a double. Thevenow waited on first with a single. The Cards were down to their last out, fearful that another rally was about to end in frustration—but not this time. Southworth was known to like inside pitches. Shocker knew that, but liked to pitch to a batter's strength and make it his weakness. He threw a spitball inside to Southworth and he smacked it into the right-field seats for three runs. Thevenow added an insurance home run in the ninth, and the happy Redbirds left New York on a train labeled "The Cardinals Special" that was bound for St. Louis and the third game of the Series. With the next three games scheduled in friendly Sportsman's Park, Hornsby felt the Cards had the advantage.

The St. Louis mayor and citizens found out the Cardinals' train was scheduled to arrive at the Washington Avenue Station at 4:00 Monday afternoon. Government offices and many businesses shut down at 3:00 in anticipation. Plans were made to explode twelve bombs on the levee to signal the train's arrival. Then the city would erupt with cheers and noise-makers to welcome its heroes. Unfortunately, the Cards' train was delayed by an accident in Johnstown, Pennsylvania, and the train carrying the Yankees arrived first. Thinking that it was the Redbirds' train, the bombs were ignited prematurely, welcoming the Yankees instead. Recognizing the mistake, the Yankees grinned from the windows as they passed on the way to the other railroad station, Union Station.

When "The Cardinals Special" arrived at Washington Avenue station, the players could not believe the reception. The mayor greeted manager Hornsby, his wife, and son, and presented them with the keys to a brand-new Lincoln

Continental from the fans. The players fought through the crowd to get to twenty cars that were waiting to parade the team through St. Louis. Bill Sherdel, along with fellow Pennsylvanian Les Bell and St. Louis native Ray Blades, rode in car number nine. A pennant listing their names was attached to the car's radiator. Hornsby rode in the last car, as always placing his men before himself. Unfortunately, a brief shower had occurred before the train arrived and the convertible tops were up on the cars, limiting player visibility. The parade, led by mounted police, motorcycle riders, and a fire wagon, had great difficulty clearing the way. The crowd stretched from curb to curb. Flying paper floated everywhere from office windows. The noise was loud and endless as the fans sought to greet, thank, and offer support to the team. The crowding was so overwhelming that it took the parade hours to travel thirty-four blocks of the city's streets.[13]

The first World Series game at Sportsman's Park was scheduled for Tuesday, October 5. Hornsby tapped big right-hander Jess Haines while Huggins countered with another of his veterans, Dutch Ruether. By game time, the St. Louis crowd had set a record attendance of 37,708. Even standing room was filled to capacity. During the Cardinals' batting practice, a rain shower had developed that scattered fans for cover, but the sun was shining by the opening pitch.

Once again, Hornsby proved a smart manager. Jess Haines pitched an outstanding game. His slow balls and big curves seemed to confound the Yanks. He allowed only five Yankee hits and hurled a 4–0 shutout. No New York runner passed second base. The flawless Cardinals' defense added two double plays. The game was halted for thirty minutes in the fourth because of a downpour, and the delay probably helped Haines. The Yankees were starting to rattle the Cards' pitcher, but the break seemed to settle him down. Later, Haines even helped his own cause with a home run.

After the game, Hornsby stated, "We had an unbeatable combination. Haines pitched as good a game as was ever pitched in a World Series or any other series. The Cardinals hit when hits were needed and the team played a perfect game in the field."[14] Huggins remarked, "I take off my hat to them and particularly I take off my hat to Jess Haines, their pitcher." In pitching a shutout, Haines accomplished what only three American League pitchers could do all season against the Yankees.[15]

The Yankees were in a hitting slump—only fifteen hits in three games. Their joyful mood had soured. They grumbled as they reached the dressing room. Ruth expressed his unhappiness with these comments. "I can't see the Cardinals as a ball club no matter if they did lick us. There are at least two better clubs in the National League—Pittsburgh and Cincinnati. The Cardinals have been lucky, that's all, by getting a lot of fluky hits. We are not licked yet. When we start hitting, it will be a different story." Huggins was more careful with his words. "We have faced three of the best pitchers in the St. Louis staff. We are bound to hit better from now on. The Cardinals staff cannot hold up the standard of pitching set by Alexander, Sherdel, and Haines."[16] The most surprising point after three games was the batting averages of Hornsby and Ruth, perhaps the two greatest hitters in the major leagues. Hornsby was hitting .182 and Ruth .200.

With a 2–1 Series lead, Hornsby now chose to use his young twenty-game-winner Flint Rhem. Huggins felt he had an advantage with future Hall-of-Famer Waite Hoyt. The game conditions were much better than the previous day. The field was dry and fast. The sky was blue with a few clouds and there was a cool wind blowing into the park from the west. Batting practice indicated there might be a few home runs in this game. Ruth hit ball after ball into the stands. There was another capacity crowd of 38,825, and the stands were a solid mass of faces by game time. Before the game, the St. Louis mayor presented each of the Cardinals with an engraved watch, purchased by the fans.

Cardinals are presented with watches
—Sherdel family

The crowd roared as Rhem struck out the first two batters with his sweeping curve ball. However, the third batter, Babe Ruth, was not as easy. On the first pitch, Ruth lofted a long fly ball into the right-field stands for a home run—the first Yankee extra-base hit of the Series and the first Yankee run in seventeen innings. Was their hitting slump finally broken? As Ruth circled the bases, the St. Louis crowd gave the Babe a great ovation. He received another ovation as he returned to right field for the next inning.

The scoring wasn't over. The Cardinals tied the game in their half of the first on singles by Douthit, Southworth, and Hornsby. But the Yankees' bats came alive again in the second and they regained the lead. In the third, Ruth clouted a second first-pitch home run. The lead switched back and forth until the fifth, when the Yankees tied it and then went ahead for good. After a walk in the fifth, Ruth returned to the plate the next inning. The Mighty Babe belted a third four-bagger, this time on a full count. By the end of nine innings, the Yankees had won, 10–5, to tie the series 2–2. In the game, Ruth set nine World Series records and tied four more. Hornsby used Rhem, Herman Bell, Hallahan, Reinhart, and Keen to no avail. Combined, the St. Louis pitchers walked ten. Oddly enough, each team collected fourteen hits, but the New York club profited more. Billy Southworth was having a great Series. After four games, he had eight hits in fifteen plate appearances. The Redbirds' loss removed the opportunity to win the title in front of the hometown fans. The Series would now end in New York.

After the game, a beaming Ruth stated:

> "At last, we've come out of our hitting slump. And now we'll win the World Series. That's as sure as fate. The handwriting is on the wall.
>
> "I'm not taking anything away from the Cardinals. They have a great ball club, a fighting ball club. But I don't believe there's a club in the country can beat us when we're pounding the ball.
>
> "The cause that looked hopeless twenty-four hours ago looks entirely different now. From here on out, the burden of the job rests on the Cardinals. We've come from behind, we've shown our teeth, we've taught them to respect our hitting ability. Now it's up to them. . . .
>
> "I imagine Hornsby will pitch Sherdel and Alexander against us in the next two games. Both of them are great pitchers. They have proved it all season long and in the Series, as well. But I'm not boasting when I say, here and now, that the Yankees today don't fear a single pitcher in the world. We've started to hit. The old batting punch has come back. We're back on an even keel and ready to go."[17]

Manager Hornsby was not as impressed with the Yankees' hitting as he was unhappy with the Cardinals' pitching.

> "There's only one thing to be said about the game and that is that you can't expect to win a game that is as badly pitched as this one was. Our pitchers could not do what they wanted to do. Not once was Ruth pitched to properly and that's the story of the game. It goes to show how pitching can completely dominate the situation.
>
> "Ruth certainly is a great hitter when he hits, and he hit this afternoon. But you didn't see him do any slugging when Alexander and Haines and Sherdel were pitching. And we'll see if he can do any more

when these pitchers return to the hill. It will be Sherdel, probably, tomorrow. I guess he'll face Pennock again.

"Ruth was not the only man to whom our pitchers pitched badly. In fact, the game was poorly pitched from start to finish and because of that, we did not deserve to win."[18]

Babe Ruth's three home runs became a legend because of a sick boy named Johnny Sylvester. Earlier in the year, eleven-year-old Sylvester had been horseback riding when the horse tramped in a hole and both boy and horse fell. In trying to get up, the horse kicked Sylvester in the head. Differing newspaper reports from October 1926 claimed that Sylvester suffered from blood poisoning, a spinal infection, a sinus condition, or a condition requiring a spinal fusion. In any event, his health weakened all summer. Babe Ruth heard about the young ill Yankee fan and sent him a package from St. Louis during the Series. Inside the package was a ball autographed by his favorite team. On it, Ruth had written, "I'll knock a homer for Wednesday's game." Wednesday's game had been the fourth game of the Series, the one in which Ruth had hit his record three homers. After receiving the ball and learning of Ruth's accomplishment, the boy's health improved and he lived a long life. Thus, another Babe Ruth legend was born.

Both managers picked the first game starters to take the mound in game five. Sherdel and Pennock were rested and ready to pitch their best. With the Series tied at two games each, the fifth game was critical, especially for the Cards. To win the final two games in Yankee Stadium would be a real challenge.

In front of 39,552 fans, Bill Sherdel took the mound to start the fifth game. He was at his best. His opponent Pennock was not quite as good as the first meeting. The game was scoreless until the bottom of the fourth. Bottomley doubled and Les Bell singled to bring him home. Cardinals 1, Yankees 0.

During the fifth inning, O'Farrell struck Sherdel on his pitching hand in returning a throw, and it badly bruised his index finger. Sherdel's finger became swollen and his nail turned black and blue. The other players and the fans would not learn of this until after Sherdel had pitched another five innings and the game had ended.

In the top of the sixth, Pennock lofted a lazy fly ball to left. Young Chick Hafey, who was the age of a college sophomore, misjudged the ball, and while desperately trying to recover, he slipped and fell. The easy out fell over his head for a lead-off double. Then catcher O'Farrell, seeing Pennock with a large lead at second, gunned the ball to shortstop Thevenow for the tag. The throw was in time and the umpire signaled out, but Thevenow dropped the ball and Pennock remained. That was the Cards' second mistake of the inning. Sherdel then walked Combs to create a force situation. But the next batter Koenig singled to score Pennock and tie the game. Pennock should have been out twice before he scored the first run. At this point, Sherdel rose to greatness. He struck out Ruth and retired Meusel and Gehrig to end the inning—Cardinals 1, Yankees 1.

In the Cardinals' seventh, Bell doubled and O'Farrell singled to plate a go-ahead run, again. Cardinals 2, Yankees 1. The game remained scoreless in the eighth.

In the Yankees' ninth, leadoff batter Gehrig popped up to short left field. Both Thevenow and Hafey lost the ball in the sun and the wind seemed to carry it away from the players. Thevenow made a desperate attempt at the last second to grab it, but the ball hopped out of his glove for a double. Another Cardinals' misplay. Gehrig was now on second base. Lazzeri beat out an infield single and Gehrig moved to third. Pinch-hitter Ben Paschal next dropped a pop-up behind second base and Gehrig scored the tying run. Pennock held the Cardinals in the bottom of the inning—Cardinals 2, Yankees 2.

Now in the Yankees' tenth, Koenig led off with a single. After a wild pitch put Koenig on second, Sherdel intentionally walked both Ruth and Gehrig to load the bases for Lazzeri. Lazzeri drove in the winning run with a long fly ball to Hafey. Koenig scored. Once again, Pennock rose to the occasion and the Cardinals failed to score. Game over. Yankees 3, Cardinals 2. Poor Bill Sherdel lost a 3–2 game in ten innings that he should have won, 2–0, in nine. The record crowd of 39,000 fell suddenly silent. They had been cheering wildly only moments before. If there would be a Cardinals' title won in New York, the St. Louis fans would need to listen to their radios.

Reporter Davis Walsh wrote:

> Bill Sherdel turned loose a left-handed epic, and all he got was a pain in the collar and his second straight defeat in the Series at the hands of Herb Pennock.
>
> What the Yanks did to Bill was little, if anything. What the Cards did to him was ample, sufficient, and enough.[19]

Cardinals' catcher Bob O'Farrell had another great game. Besides handling everything behind the plate, he collected three of the team's seven hits off Pennock. O'Farrell added his thoughts:

> "It was a tough game for Bill Sherdel to lose—mighty, mighty tough. Bill pitched the kind of baseball that would have won nine out of ten ball games. His misfortune is that this was the tenth.
>
> "The great arm of Bill, his lion-hearted courage, and his fine pitching brain weren't enough to whip a Yankee ball club that seemed to be wearing nothing but four-leaf clovers."[20]

A reporter caught up with umpire Hank O'Day on the Cardinals' train and asked him about the game. O'Day replied, "It was lost by your left-fielder [Hafey]. He misjudged Pennock's easy fly and should have caught Gehrig in the ninth in his back-pocket. That is not the opinion of an umpire, but of an old ballplayer."[21]

Famous sportswriter Grantland Rice wrote about the sixth-inning matchup of Sherdel and Ruth.

> Sherdel began to envelop Ruth's great form with a volley of slow curves and these slow twisters kept him baffled all the afternoon. He grounded out in the first, he walked in the fourth, and in the sixth he came up with two men on base. It was here that Sherdel rose to the heights. With the game in danger where another base hit would have broken it up, the Cardinal left-hander sent his slow curve up to the plate and the Babe hacked the ozone apart with terrific blows that never came within a foot of the ball. He struck out at this important moment with a rally on, and once again the aroused multitude stood up and howled its tribute to the slender left-hander who had not only dared to pitch to Ruth, but in addition had struck him out.[22]

On the train speeding back to New York, the Yankees were exultant. They had beaten "Wee Willie" Sherdel, Cardinal ace, for the second time in the Series. Even Babe Ruth admitted he was glad to be rid of the diminutive lefty. "I can't hit those soft ones and Sherdel is one fellow who will not give you any kind of a good ball to work on."[23] Indeed, Sherdel struck out Ruth once, forced him to hit two little infield taps, and walked him twice. The Babe was 0 for 3 after hitting three home runs the day before.

The Cardinals' train was less jubilant, but still optimistic. Manager Hornsby called his players together for a short meeting. He pointed no fingers for the loss and focused the team on the next two games in New York. Hornsby believed without any question that they would win the Series there. The seven-car "Pennsylvania" train, carrying the Cardinals to their destiny in New York, set a new speed record for the trip from St. Louis to New York City. The boys made it in twenty-one hours and twenty-two minutes. Maybe their luck had changed.

On a cool, sunny Saturday afternoon on October 9, 48,615 fans arrived at Yankee Stadium to see the sixth game of the 1926 World Series. New York was leading the Series three games to two. Most hoped to see the Yankees clinch in this game, but a surprising number were gunning for the Cardinals forcing a seventh game. On the hill was Bob Shawkey for the home team and Old Pete Alexander for the visiting Cards. Shawkey, who had previously worked three-and-two-thirds scoreless innings as a relief pitcher in the Series, was picked by Huggins to bring the Yankees another world title. Hornsby was hoping that the wily old veteran Alexander could work his magic arm one more time.

Before the game, Hornsby called his team together. "If we don't do it today, there ain't no more Series and there's gotta be some more Series. We gotta win today and we gotta win tomorrow. Go out there and fight your heads off and don't concede a thing. Knock the ball down the pitcher's throat. Knock the ball out of the lot and if a fly ball or a grounder comes your way, go and get it."[24]

As if to quickly prove the better team, the Cardinals pounded Shawkey for three runs in their first at-bat. "Wattie" Holm, playing for the sore-armed Douthit, led off with a sharp single to right. Southworth then hit a grounder, forcing Holm out at second. Hornsby drew a walk. Bottomley hit a low liner down the third-base line that rolled to the corner for a double, scoring Southworth and sending Hornsby to third. After fouling off several pitches, Bell lined a single to left, scoring Hornsby and Bottomley. The Yankees had mistakenly thought the Cards couldn't hit fastballs. Shawkey settled down and struck out Hafey and O'Farrell, but those three runs in the top of the first turned out to be all the runs Alexander would need. Once again, "Alexander the Great" dominated the Yankees. It took another eight-and-a-half innings to prove the point, but the game had really ended before the New York team even came to bat. The final score was 10–2.

Counting his previous performance, Old Pete ran his hitless streak to twenty-four Yankee batters before Meusel singled to start the second inning. The thirty-nine-year-old Alexander's control was so good that he only threw twenty-nine balls out of 104 pitches. The mighty Ruth, who had been so boisterous in St. Louis, was now quiet in New York, going hitless in three official plate appearances. The crowd of 48,615 left the stadium surprised, but prepared for a thrilling game seven to decide the Series.

In St. Louis, fans followed the game by listening to the staccato voice of Graham McNamee of station KSD on the radio. Crowds gathered in the downtown area where scores from the radio were relayed by a self-appointed announcer using a megaphone. When the final score was determined, bits of paper floated like snow from office windows onto the streets below. Once again, every conceivable noisemaker was used to celebrate the Cards' victory and to signal a seventh game. Fans sent Hornsby close to 300 telegrams of congratulations and well wishes.[25]

With the whole country looking forward to the final game and reading the papers, reporters gathered whatever forecasts they could get from the participants. Miller Huggins said, "I'll pitch Waite Hoyt in the final game of the Series. Hoyt won his last game, and though he was hit fairly hard at times, he is the type of pitcher who goes better the second time he faces a club."

Hornsby stated, "We will have Haines to face them and if Big Jess is half as good as he was when he gave them a good trouncing in that St. Louis game, the boys at home can start shouting."

Babe Ruth remarked, "The Yankees play their best ball in the pinches. They are strongest when there's something at stake. Watch us go out and win."

Grover Cleveland Alexander added, "We're hitting now and are going into the final battle with a pitcher who shut out the American League champions in the third game of the series."[26]

The weather forecast told of overcast skies with temperatures a little warmer than Saturday. No rain was expected until Sunday night. Overcast skies seemed to favor Haines as a fastball pitcher. Game time was set for 2:00, to allow the churchgoers time to arrive. A huge crowd was expected to fill the House That Ruth Built. Oddly, a less-than-capacity crowd of 38,093 arrived for the final game.

Cardinals pose in street clothes.
Sherdel front right
—*St. Louis Post-Dispatch*, October 10, 1926

The first two-and-a-half innings were a pitchers' duel between Hoyt and Haines, as neither team could manufacture a run. In the bottom of the third, Babe Ruth hit a tremendous home run into the right-centerfield bleachers for the game's first score. It seemed Ruth was going to carry the Yankees on his shoulders to victory. The pressure now shifted to Hornsby's squad.

The Cardinals came right back in the top of the fourth. With one out, Bottomley lined a single to left. Next batter Bell hit a sharp grounder to shortstop Koenig for a sure double play. However, the rookie Yankee bobbled the ball and Bottomley and Bell were safe. Then Hafey singled to left, filling the bases with Cardinals. Hoyt was showing signs of weakness. O'Farrell flied to left center. Combs was prepared to catch the ball, but Meusel moved in front of him. Meusel had the stronger arm and wanted to make the throw to the plate after Bottomley tagged up at third. But Meusel dropped the ball and Bottomley scored. The pressure was supposed to be on St. Louis, but New York had made two errors in the inning. The score was tied, 1–1.

Tommy Thevenow then came to the plate. The Cards' shortstop singled for his fourth straight hit to score Bell and Hafey for a two-run lead. The inning ended: Cardinals 3, Yankees 1.

The score remained the same until the Yankees came to bat in the bottom of the sixth. With two outs, Dugan singled. Old catcher Hank Severid came to the plate. The veteran hit a sinking liner to left. In a huge rookie mistake, Hafey tried to make a shoestring catch but missed. The ball bounced past him for a double, scoring Dugan with the Yankees' second run of the game. With two outs and one runner on first, the smarter play would have been to let the ball drop and hold the batter to a single and the lead runner to second. Haines got the third out when Paschal, batting for Hoyt, failed to reach base. It was Cardinals 3, Yankees 2. Pennock then took the mound. He was not as effective as usual, but he somehow managed to stop Hornsby's men from any more scoring.

In the Yankees' seventh, Ruth and Company remained down one run and were running out of time. Haines continued to do his best, despite great pain from a raw and sore forefinger on his right hand—the hand he needed to grip and throw the ball. He showed great courage and determination. Combs led off with a single to left. Koenig sacrificed Combs to second. One out. Ruth was walked intentionally. Meusel hit a grounder to third baseman Bell, who threw to Hornsby to force Ruth at second. Hornsby relayed the throw to first, but Meusel beat the throw. Two outs. Gehrig came to bat. Haines pitched two quick strikes, but then threw four balls and walked him.

The bases were now loaded. Hornsby and his other infielders gathered at the mound. Haines showed them his finger, which had gotten even worse. He wanted to continue, but the manager realized that was impossible. Hornsby looked out to the bullpen and pointed for Alexander, who had been sitting against the left wall. No one, including Alexander, had been warming up. The crowd was going wild.[27]

The *St. Louis Post-Dispatch* described the moment.

> A tall, lank figure, with a gaudy red sweater coat, stalked from the bullpen toward the infield. Hornsby walked out to meet him. It was Alexander, who had pitched nine innings only the day before.
>
> "The bases are filled, Alex," Hornsby said. "But there's two out and Lazzeri's coming up. Do you feel all right?"
>
> "Sure, I feel fine," Alex replied. "Three on, eh? Well there's no place to put Lazzeri, is there, with the sacks all loaded up? I'll just have to give him nothing but a lot of hell, won't I?"
>
> Alexander had not even been warming up.
>
> "I'm not going to warm up out there," he told Hornsby before the game. "I know this old soupbone [arm] of mine and I know I can't do any good if I warm up. Don't expect to see me warming up. But if you need me, don't worry. I can go in there and pitch plenty of ball for an inning. I hope I can throw four or five of the damdest balls they ever saw. Maybe a couple of innings. But I won't warm up."
>
> Alexander did his warming up on the pitching slab. He threw five practice balls to O'Farrell and then Lazzeri took his place at the plate. The base runners took their lead.
>
> Alexander threw a curve; it was on the inside. A ball. The next, another curve on the inside, was called a strike. The next was another zipping curve, and Lazzeri fouled a hot one into the left-field seats. One more pitch to Lazzeri, a bad ball, but Lazzeri swung viciously and missed and he was out and the danger was passed.[28]

In the Cardinals' eighth, Hornsby led off with a single. Bottomley advanced him to second with a bunt, but there, the Cards' manager died as his players failed to bring him home and extend their lead. A relaxed Alexander returned to the mound with two innings and six outs in the way of a title. The old veteran hurler forced Dugan to hit a slow grounder to short where Thevenow cleanly fielded it and threw to first. Five outs to go. The next batter—Collins—popped a harmless little foul to Bottomley. Four outs remaining. The third Yankee up in the eighth was Pennock, the pitcher. The New York fans gave him a big hand as he stepped in the box. Again, "Old Pete" worked his magic and Pennock popped lightly to Hornsby to end the eighth. Three outs left.

Now, Pennock took the mound to begin the ninth. He set down Thevenow, Alexander, and Holm with little trouble. The Yankees were coming to bat for the final time and Ruth was due up third.

Considering all the pressure, Hornsby had chosen the perfect hurler for the situation. All of Alex's baseball career had prepared him for his biggest moment. The speedy Combs stepped in the box. Ball one. Now a called strike. Then Combs swung at another and missed. Now ball two. Earle fouled off the next pitch and the count remained 2–2. The Yankee lead-off batter hit a grounder to third. Bell fielded cleanly and threw to first in time. Only two outs remained. Rookie Koenig approached the plate. Ball one. Mark then fouled off two pitches before also grounding out Bell to Bottomley. One out left.

Before fans looked at their scorecards, they knew from the overwhelming crowd noise that Ruth was coming to bat. The Babe loved to be at center stage. Pressure seemed to bring out his best. With one mighty swing of his bat, the Sultan of Swat could tie the game. No one could have wanted a better matchup. Two of baseball's best, squaring off individually in a team sport. Hornsby called time and walked over to talk with his pitcher. Alex did not want to walk Ruth intentionally, but he also didn't want to give him anything too good.

Alexander's first pitch to Ruth was a perfect strike, but the Babe ignored it. Now a ball. Ruth fouled off the next pitch into catcher O'Farrell's mask. The fans were roaring and yelling. Some wanted Alexander to strike him out. Most wanted Ruth to hit a home run. Two balls followed and the fans booed. The count was full. Ruth was swaying in the batter's box, eagerly awaiting a pitch he could drill. Old Pete threw the next pitch just an inch outside and umpire Hildebrand called "Ball four!" Babe threw his bat aside and trotted down to first as the pressure mounted.

Heavy-hitting Meusel strode into the box with Gehrig on deck. The Yankee left-fielder had hit a double and a triple against Alex in game six. Old Pete threw two quick strikes to Meusel, which he swung at, mightily, trying to make up for his previous costly error. On the second whiff, unexpectedly, Ruth made a mad dash to second, trying to catch the Cards' catcher by surprise. O'Farrell threw a bullet to second baseman Hornsby for the tag and Ruth and the Yankees were out.[29] The St. Louis Cardinals had defeated the mighty New York Yankees in seven games.

As the game ended, the disbelieving Yankees departed quietly. For once, Ruth had very little to say. Hornsby and his players jumped into each other's arms, hugging and congratulating one another. They carried their celebration into the clubhouse as they prepared to head home. Baseball commissioner Landis was the first to congratulate them. Sadly, no one realized this would be the last time this group would be together as Cardinals. Breadon and Rickey were already considering roster changes for the next season.

On the train back to St. Louis, a reporter asked Alexander how he'd felt when he entered the game with the bases loaded.

"How did I feel? Go and ask Lazzeri how he felt. I felt fine. I have no nerves. The strain, naturally, was on Lazzeri. The only thing that hurt me was that Jess hadn't been able to finish it out. Say, I'd love to have seen him go through without having to have any aid from an old stiff like me.

"But there's another thing. Isn't there some way to take one of the games I won and give it to Bill Sherdel? It ain't fair for Bill to pitch the great ball he pitched and not win either game. I'd feel a whole lot happier tonight if Bill Sherdel could have one of my games.

"But I'm pretty happy. Do you know why? I'll tell you. I'm happy because I came to St. Louis and was able to do something for Rogers Hornsby. There's a great fellow, if there ever was one. Who couldn't pitch for Rog? I wish I could have done ten times as much this year as the little bit I did for him. He makes this a great ball club. I've been in baseball a long time. But I never was treated as squarely as I have been treated by Rog and the St. Louis fans. But Rog is the man."

As Alexander was finishing his story, Tommy Thevenow came walking from the dining car and sat across the aisle from him. The old hurler said, "There's the hero of the Series. There's the greatest shortstop in the world. There's the kid that won the Series."

A somewhat embarrassed Thevenow replied, "Don't hero me. If it hadn't been for Hornsby and Southworth and Bottomley and Bell and the pitchers, we'd got licked sure. Don't give me any credit."[30]

It was true. The quiet, modest Thevenow was a hero. He'd played a fantastic Series, both offensively and defensively. He'd played every inning, collecting ten hits with a double and home run in twenty-four at-bats for a .417 average. Giants' manager John McGraw wrote after the game, "Thevenow was undoubtedly the real spark plug of this Series. His fielding was simply marvelous and he hit the ball solidly. He rose to real heights in the pinches. In the infield, he got about lightly and speedily as a dancing master. This establishes him as a really great ball player."[31] Sadly, that Series would be the highlight of Thevenow's career. Injuries and an automobile accident would limit his greatness.

Alexander also singled out his catcher, Bob O'Farrell, for praise. O'Farrell had caught every inning of the Series. "He's a great catcher—one of the best that ever stood behind the plate. Not one mistake did he make in the Series."[32] O'Farrell also batted .304.

The Cardinals hit well in the Series. Thevenow, Bottomley (.345), and Southworth (.345) led the attack. Les Bell drove in the most runs—six. Hornsby batted just .250, but there was no question that the team couldn't have won the title without their skipper and second baseman. He'd had a difficult season. Hornsby had missed more games than ever because of a range of health problems. And during the Series, it was amazing that he could focus on baseball after losing his mother. The Cardinals' top three pitchers in the Series surrendered very few runs. Their earned run averages were: Haines, 1.08; Alexander, 1.33; and Sherdel, 2.12.

Chick Hafey became the goat of the Series for his defensive mistakes and poor batting average (.185). What no one knew at the time was that Hafey had serious sinus troubles and had been advised not to play. When he looked for a fly ball, he saw double. As soon as the Series ended, Hafey went to the hospital for sinus surgery. He had also been injured in an outfield collision with Taylor Douthit. Douthit did not play the rest of the Series. With Blades already out, Hafey had to continue to play.³³

The New York Murderers' Row had hit poorly, although Combs (.357), Gehrig (.348), and Dugan (.333) had had a good Series. Babe Ruth had hit a record four home runs and batted .300. The Cards' pitchers had also walked Ruth eleven times—the same number as the whole Redbirds' team. Future Hall-of-Famers Pennock (1.23) and Hoyt (1.20) pitched well in defeat.

As the "Pennsylvania" train approached the St. Louis station, all the other locomotives in the yard whistled a chorus of greeting. Many of the players had already left New York on other trains headed directly to their homes. Bill Sherdel was one of that group. Other players on the train back feared the reception at the station and exited through the railyards to waiting taxicabs. All those players had previously witnessed first-hand the enormous celebrations when they won the pennant and when they returned after the first two games of the Series. They were tired and ready for time at home with their families. They really did not need another celebration. But Hornsby and ten other Cardinals remained on the train back into Union Station.

Even though the players had experienced two previous celebrations, they could not have been prepared for this one. There were over a thousand fans at the station to greet them. Hornsby and his wife left quickly for Texas. The Cards' manager had held off his mourning for his mother until after the last out. Now he let the pain and anguish overwhelm him and headed home. The remaining players, led by Alexander, Bottomley, Southworth, and O'Farrell, worked their way to their cars and were escorted from the station to the Jefferson Hotel. Fans mobbed the players. Women tried to kiss and hug Alexander. He seemed to enjoy every minute of the adulation. It took hours to get through the city streets to the hotel. A major celebration was scheduled for that evening at Sportsman's Park, so the players wanted to get some rest before the trip to the ballpark.

The crowd overflowed that evening at Sportsman's Park. Some 30,000 fans made it into the park while thousands more were forced to remain outside. A temporary stand had been placed on the field so that the players could be seen. It was also hoped that a microphone could carry the players' speeches to the adoring fans. However, the noise was so great that no one could hear the players. A newspaper reporter stated that he was only six feet from the speakers and couldn't hear a word they were saying. After about an hour of trying to quiet the crowd, the mayor gave up and police escorted the players out of the park. The fans were not finished. They continued to celebrate all night, even though the players were gone. The crowd was totally beyond the control of the police. Such was the wild enthusiasm of the St. Louis citizens for their world champions.[34]

Later in October, Sherdel's many friends in McSherrystown and in nearby Hanover held another testimonial banquet for their hometown hero, held at the Richard McAllister Hotel in Hanover with 200 attendees. Never much of a speaker, the guest of honor was applauded to his feet. He arose, smiled, and then sat down again.

During the offseason, Sherdel received an honorable mention in the 1926 National League Most Valuable Player voting. That was fine, but he was just as happy at home with his family and hunting with his dog Jack and two pups. Sherdel also received a check for $6,254—his winning share from the World Series. In today's dollars, that check would be $84,353!

For the second straight year, a St. Louis Cardinal was named National League Most Valuable Player. The previous year, it had been Rogers Hornsby; this year, it was catcher Bob O'Farrell. O'Farrell received seventy-nine of eighty votes—a clear-cut decision. He had appeared in 147 games during the regular season and hit .293. In the Series, he caught every inning of every game, allowed only one stolen base, and batted .304. Hornsby could not have won the pennant or the Series without O'Farrell.

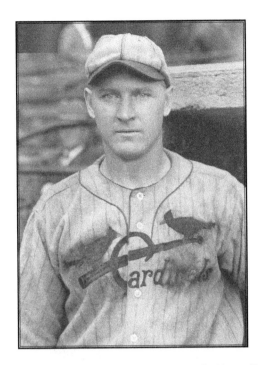

Catcher and National League MVP Bob O'Farrell
—Coulson collection

CHAPTER SEVENTEEN

Everyone remembers where they were and what they were doing when significant events happened in their lives. It could have been something only important to them or something that happened on a national or world level. In any case, the memory remains. Such a remarkable happenstance took place for the citizens of St. Louis and McSherrystown when the St. Louis Cardinals won the World Series in October 1926. And another memorable event happened less than three months later, on December 20, when the St. Louis Cardinals announced that Rogers Hornsby had been traded to the New York Giants for infielder Frankie Frisch and pitcher Jimmy Ring.

Cardinals' owner Sam Breadon reported that it had been an unsurmountable salary dispute with Hornsby that had triggered the trade. Breadon told reporters:

> "I realize that this is a sensational trade, but it had to come. I did my best to reach a contract settlement with Hornsby, but I learned at the conference with Hornsby today that a settlement was impossible. I offered what I considered a very fair contract. Hornsby still had a year to run on his old contract, which was at $30,000 a year in 1925 and 1926. I desired to combine this contract with new terms to cover the season of 1927 and to increase Hornsby's salary [by] $20,000, from $30,000 to $50,000.
>
> "Hornsby turned down this offer. He still insisted on a three-year contract, and he asked for $150,000 for three years. He said he would stand pat on the demand and I realized then that I would be unable to sign Hornsby to a manager's contract and that, to protect the Cardinals' interest, I would be compelled to trade Hornsby.

"I am very sorry that I could not come to terms with Hornsby, but there was no further use in dickering and I felt that the best thing I could do was to make the best trade I could get for him.

"I believe it to be a good trade. We get a star second baseman to replace Hornsby and we get a first-string pitcher to fill a first-string pitching gap that has been in our club.

"Right now, I do not know who will be the next Cardinal manager. Before I sign another manager, I will give the matter much thought. I do not intend to rush into the matter hurriedly, as I realize the importance of signing the right man."

There are always two sides to every story and Hornsby had this to say to the writers:

"I always wanted to play in St. Louis. My friends and my family are here, and my home is here. I cannot forget the great reception and support given me and the Cardinals when we won the pennant and the Series, and I still feel I would prefer to play in St. Louis.

"However, I do not think that a one-year contract is a fair contract to offer a man who has done what I have done, and that is why I have declined to accept it. Mr. Breadon said he was sorry we could not reach an agreement, and I am sorry, also."

Hornsby had received only his player's salary of $30,000 for the previous two years, even though he had also managed the team. He had signed a three-year deal before he became manager in 1925.[1]

When Bill Sherdel learned of the trade, he was dumbfounded. "I was playing pinochle here with several friends last evening at about 10:30," he said, "when I got a telephone call from the Associated Press in York stating that they thought I might be interested to know that Hornsby was figured in a trade. The news got me so that I couldn't play any longer. 'Pep' [Hornsby] was liked by every man on the team and by all the fans. I never played for a team with a man who was as well liked as 'Pep,' and since he's to go to New York, I don't care if they trade me for the Giants' bat boy."

Sherdel didn't criticize the owner, but he couldn't understand why Hornsby would be traded after he won the world championship. Sherdel and Horsnby had grown close over the previous nine years with the Cards.

It was Hornsby who had given Sherdel the opportunity to become a regular starter. Unfortunately for Sherdel, he had already signed his 1927 Cardinals' contract and mailed it in to St. Louis headquarters.[2]

It would take years to determine if Sam Breadon had made a good trade. Frisch was two years younger than Hornsby. He'd been in the majors for eight seasons and had a .321 batting average. He had played in 1,000 games. Hornsby was a twelve-year veteran who had led the league in hitting for six straight seasons and had won a world's championship. His average had "dropped" to .317 because of many injuries. Frisch had batted .314 with the Giants in 1926. Both players had their difficulties with their clubs' ownership. Late the previous season, Frisch had had a fallout with John McGraw and had left the team without permission. He was destined to go somewhere else. Rickey had wanted Frisch for many years. Right-handed pitcher Jimmy Ring, meanwhile, was a ten-year veteran who had labored most of his career with second-division clubs—the Reds and Phillies. He was nearing the end of his career.

On December 27, Breadon announced that Bob O'Farrell would manage the Cardinals in 1927. He would follow Hornsby as a player-manager. James Gould wrote:

> O'Farrell would seem to have the ideal temperament for a manager. In the first place, he will have the goodwill and, more, the affection of his men. There are many types of ball players in the big leagues, but in years of travel and acquaintances with all sorts and conditions, this observer never heard a voice against the new Cardinal leader. . . .
>
> The players, liking him and having confidence in his baseball judgment, will, once signed, work their heads off for him and there is no derogation of Hornsby in saying that President Breadon appears to have come as close as possible to the right move, things being as they are.[3]

Maybe as a back-up plan, Breadon signed former Pirates' manager Bill McKechnie as a general assistant to O'Farrell. McKechnie had won the pennant and world's championship with the Pirates in 1925, before his dismissal at the end of the previous season. To make room for him and remove any connection to Hornsby, the club released Bill Killefer.

Sportswriter Ray Gillespie interviewed Breadon. The Cardinals' owner said, "O'Farrell is acquainted with the team in all its departments and it will be up to him to make whatever changes he believes necessary. He knows where the Cardinals may be weak and where we might need patching. So I will depend on Bob to make suggestions. In my estimation, he is going to make a great manager. With the assistance of such an able man as McKechnie, O'Farrell is bound to make good."[4]

CHAPTER EIGHTEEN

In 1927, the Ford Motor Company would manufacture its fifteen-millionth Model T "Tin Lizzy." Soon after, Ford would replace it with the Model A, a cutting-edge new automobile that would sell for $385. Louis B. Mayer would form the Academy of Motion Picture Arts and Sciences and launch the Academy Awards. Philo Farnsworth would demonstrate the first use of television in San Francisco and the Columbia Broadcasting System (CBS) would begin as a radio network. In Nashville, the Grand Ole Opry would produce its first radio broadcast. In China, the giant panda would be discovered.

In sports, the Harlem Globetrotters would play their first game. Johnny Weismuller, who would become a movie Tarzan, would set new swimming records in the 100- and 200-meter freestyle. And Babe Ruth would become the highest-paid baseball player, earning $70,000 per year.

In a move to distance the Cardinals from Rogers Hornsby, Sam Breadon relocated the 1927 training camp from Texas to Avon Park, Florida. Avon Park was in the middle of the state's citrus groves. The population here was very low in 1927—by 1930, there were only 3,400 residents. There was one outstanding hotel in Avon Park, Hotel Jacaranda, built in 1926. It would become the Cardinals' headquarters while in Florida. The town would have a new state-of-the-art concrete baseball park finished within ninety days of the Cards' arrival. The park's center-field wall would be located 525 feet from home plate—a long distance for a home run.

Training camp was scheduled to begin with pitchers and catchers on February 19 and the rest of the team a week later. Most players traveled directly from their homes. It was a forty-hour train ride from St. Louis to Avon Park. There were some late arrivals. Bill Sherdel and Jess Haines had business transactions to complete, and so received permission to arrive later. The pitching duo had spent the most years in Cardinal uniforms. Sherdel had arrived in 1917 and Haines in 1918. Manager O'Farrell scheduled two practices per day to get the players in shape.

Sherdel arrived at spring training on February 23 twenty-one pounds heavier. He wasted no time working to shed the extra weight. It was reported that, on the second day of training, he jogged around the park three or four times, chased drives in the outfield, played in pepper games, and ran around the bases after hitting against the rookie pitchers. By the end of the day, he had lost two pounds.

While the Cards were getting settled in their new camp, Rogers Hornsby upset his former teammates with a comment in a New York paper. He stated that the Giants would finish first, the Pirates second, the Reds third, and the Cards fourth. Bob O'Farrell responded, "So Hornsby thinks the Cardinals will barely finish in first division this year? Well, such a statement just tends to make the job easier for me. But I'll say this for my Cardinals: They're world champions now, and I can see no reason why they shouldn't make Hornsby mighty disagreeably surprised this year when they repeat."[1] Soon after, Hornsby stirred the emotions of the Cards again when he boasted, "The Cardinals are a one-year club."[2]

The players rested on Sunday before the remainder of the team arrived the following day. Bill Sherdel and Jess Haines went fishing. Between them, they caught a string of fish weighing thirty-five pounds.

Fishermen Sherdel and Haines with their catch
—Sherdel family

This year's exhibition schedule was very different from other years. In the past, the Cardinals had played mostly minor-league clubs with an occasional major-league game thrown in. This time, St. Louis played only major-league squads. They finished with "The Little World Series" of eight games with the Yankees as the two clubs moved north. Finally arriving in St. Louis, the Cardinals played their customary spring games with the Browns.

The early highlight of training camp was a game against Hornsby and the Giants on March 17. O'Farrell saved Alexander and Sherdel for the grudge match. The Cardinals shut out the Giants. Hornsby went hitless. Alexander pitched the first five innings and allowed only three hits, with Sherdel hurling the final four and surrendering a harmless four more. With this, the Cardinals enjoyed some payback.

In the *New York World,* Bozeman Bulger wrote of the matchup between Sherdel and Hornsby.

The appearance of Sherdel on the mound when Hornsby was playing for an opposing team was looked forward to by many of Bill's friends with great interest, most of them wondering just what would happen, as these two had been, and still are, the best of friends. It was Hornsby who gave Sherdel his chance in regular games for the Cardinals, and it was Sherdel who felt Hornsby's loss to the Cardinals more than any other individual member of the club.

But all is fair in love and baseball, and Sherdel set down to the task of doing the one thing that 'gets' a batsman who knows his own ability to hit. He threw four wide balls in the eighth inning of a sizzling ball game, with men on third and second and only one out, while Hornsby pawed up the dirt and the crowd puckered its face in cat-calls and hisses.

Bill Sherdel grinned in his own little way, and put Hornsby on first to fill the bases. Then he proceeded to knock over the next two men. The inning was over. Hornsby and two others were stranded on the bases and the Giants fumed over "Little Bill," the goat-getter.[3]

The next day, shortstop Tommy Thevenow signed a one-year contract, but he wouldn't report for another three days. In all, he would miss a valuable three weeks of training and, more importantly, three weeks of working with his new infield partner Frisch.

Flint Rhem remained the last holdout. The twenty-game winner had been paid $5,000 the year before. Late in the season, he learned that Reds' pitcher Eppa Rixey had made $20,000. Rhem wanted $15,000 for 1927, but the club only offered $7,500. In response, Rhem remained in South Carolina.

The long-awaited series with the Yankees began on March 27. O'Farrell selected Bill Sherdel to start the first game. Sherdel pitched five innings. He held Babe Ruth hitless and won the game, 13–2. Forty-year-old Alexander took the mound in the third game, after two quick Cardinal victories. "Alex" looked in mid-season form until he was hit in his pitching hand by a batted ball, eventually losing, 3–2. Old Pete's hand remained sore for several days but, luckily, no bones were broken.

Alexander's sore hand seemed to be part of an extensive list of Cardinal injuries that threatened the team's run at another pennant. Despite sinus surgery, Hafey was still having vision problems in his left eye and was told by his doctor that he should not play every day. Blades was yet several weeks away from full strength in his left knee. O'Farrell's arm hurt. Bell sprained his wrist when he did a handspring after a ground ball. Even Bill Sherdel was suffering from a strained back.

Finally, with the exhibition season almost over, Rhem signed a one-year contract. He reported seventeen pounds overweight, and needed two more weeks to prepare to pitch. Rhem admitted he was fat and had not picked up a ball since the Series. The 1927 team was now complete, but not healthy.

Bill Sherdel took the mound versus the Yankees' Murderers' Row again in the series' sixth game. Despite an ailing back, he pitched ten innings, and lost 5–4. Only a four-run fourth inning prevented Sherdel from a victory. He did hold Ruth to one hit in five at-bats. Something happened in that game that would repeat itself later. Writer Ray Gillespie described the events.

> Sherdel shot a strike past Ruth and then followed up with a slow one, which Ruth watched and [umpire] Moran called [another strike]. The Bambino growled and grumbled and finally appeased himself by scattering the dust around the plate with his heavy bludgeon. While this was going on, Sherdel tried to sneak over a fast one, but Moran refused to call it and players on both teams appeared ready to resort to fisticuffs.
>
> When play was resumed, Sherdel tossed a slow one high in the air and Ruth, with his bat ready, raced up a few feet from the plate, met the ball as it came out of the clouds, and sent it on a line to center for a single.[4]

The Cardinals' exhibition series with the Yankees ended with each club winning four games. Just like the 1926 World Series, it proved how close these teams were in ability. As an end to spring training, the Cards and Browns split two games in St. Louis. The local fans were ready for the start of the new baseball season. It was time to begin.

The Cardinals opened the 1927 campaign on April 12, in Chicago. O'Farrell delayed naming his starting pitcher Alexander or Sherdel until almost game time. Old "Alex" wanted badly to face his former team, but he had been experiencing problems with his right elbow. Apparently, Alexander thought he could pitch, so the manager handed him the ball. "Alex" went four innings, allowing six runs, and the world champs lost, 10–1, in front of 42,000 baseball crazy fans—the largest opening crowd ever in Chicago. Alexander was booed and cheered on every pitch. Jess Haines pitched the Cards to a 5–0 victory in the second game.

In the third Chicago game, Bill Sherdel earned his first start of the new season. In it, he suffered another heartbreaking loss, 1–0. Sherdel surrendered only two isolated hits, but one was a Hack Wilson home run and that was enough.

After two dominating victories over the Reds, the Cardinals returned for their home opener. O'Farrell picked Sherdel to pitch. The day started with a parade and the ceremonial hoisting of the National League pennant. Then Sherdel took the mound against the visiting Cubs. Sherdel won, 4–2, with a five-hitter, and did not disappoint the home crowd. The following day, Rhem got his first start of the season and added a 7–0 triumph, allowing only two hits. The Cardinals' starting staff of Alexander, Haines, Sherdel, and Rhem looked unstoppable.

After a good start, the Cardinals ended April in second place, one-and-a-half games behind John McGraw, Hornsby, and the Giants. O'Farrell had missed half of April because of a sore arm. Alexander was also ailing.

May was just an average month for the world champs. The Redbirds remained in second place behind the Pirates. Haines continued to win while the other members of "the Big Four"—Alexander, Sherdel, and Rhem—struggled from time to time. Bill Sherdel had some rough stretches in which he pitched great ball for several innings but then weakened. He did twirl a nice five-hitter against the Reds on May 29.

In May, Frank Frisch was leading the club with a .361 average, followed by Hafey's .350 and Southworth's .318. Manager O'Farrell commented on his new second baseman: "Frisch has been playing a wonderful second base. His fielding has been better than that of any pivot man I have seen in action this season and we have opposed every club in the league. He makes hard chances look easy and he has been a wonder on double plays. Not only that, he has been hitting better than Hornsby last year and he's running the bases in great style. He has been a mighty valuable addition to our ball club."[5]

An unusual event occurred during a Cardinals' game in Philadelphia on Saturday, May 14. Suddenly, in the seventh inning with the Cards at bat, hundreds of panicked fans started running onto the field. Bill Sherdel was in the dugout. He said he heard what he thought was a rumble of thunder, and did not realize anything was wrong until the spectators started to jump on top of the Cardinals' dugout. Then he ran to the playing field and saw what had happened. Part of the lower right-field grandstand had collapsed. Many fans were injured, but none seriously; however, one fan did die—from a heart attack. The game was stopped at that point to be continued later. Sherdel, Frankie Frisch, Jim Bottomley, Chick Hafey, and Billy Southworth motored to McSherrystown to spend the night at the Sherdel home.[6]

With an open date the next day, the Cardinals scheduled an exhibition game in York, Pennsylvania, against the White Roses. Bill Sherdel and his four future Hall-of-Fame teammates joined the team in York for the game. O'Farrell gave Sherdel the opportunity to pitch in front of his local fans. He pitched the first two innings masterfully, retiring the minimum six batters. All the Cards' starters played as the major-league club won, 4–1.

Injuries continued to plague the champs. In the last week of May, Ray Blades finally returned from his off-season left knee surgery, but he lasted only a few days before pulling a tendon in his right leg. O'Farrell missed the last ten days of the month. He continued to struggle with a sore arm.

In the American League, the New York Yankees were again leading the league. Babe Ruth hit his sixteenth home run at month-end. He was now ahead of his record-breaking 1921 pace. Everyone had expected Ruth to better his record, since the Yankees had played in the Polo Grounds in 1921 and now called right-field-friendly Yankee Stadium home.

In another record-breaking event on May 20, Charles A. Lindbergh departed from Long Island, New York, in his "Spirit of St. Louis" plane on a solo trans-Atlantic flight to Paris. Lindbergh landed safely and instantly became a national hero. The famous aviator and Bill Sherdel would later meet in St. Louis.

The Cardinals won their fifth straight game on Bob O'Farrell Day at Sportsman's Park on June 4. The National League and the St. Louis fans presented the Cardinals' manager with his 1926 Most Valuable Player Award of a medallion and a $1,000 check. Bob was the second Redbird to win the award, following Rogers Hornsby in 1925.

While the Cards were celebrating O'Farrell Day in St. Louis, at 4:30 in the afternoon that Saturday, a light went out in Bill Sherdel's world. His mother Margaret passed away suddenly from a cerebral hemorrhage. She had been suffering from heart disease. A long-time resident of Long Island, New York, Mrs. Sherdel had been visiting with her daughter Ruth in Gettysburg for the previous week. She had been seated in her daughter's kitchen preparing strawberries when her head nodded at the table and she was gone. Margaret Sherdel was sixty-five years old. Bill was playing in St. Louis when he heard the news. He left immediately and arrived home on Monday. That was one of three deaths that would hit the Cardinals' pitching staff within a week in that early June stretch.

And the bad luck continued, so much so that the 1927 Cardinals might have felt that Hornsby had put a curse on the team when he left. Bob O'Farrell's arm remained sore, limiting his playing. The Cards added young John Schulte from their Syracuse farm team as a backup catcher. But before the game on June 8, Schulte had just finished batting practice and was headed to the dugout when he was struck on the back of the head by a bat that slipped from the hands of another player. Schulte dropped unconsciously to the ground, with blood streaming down his face. The players hurried over to comfort him while they awaited an ambulance. It was suspected that Schulte had suffered a fractured skull. Later, a doctor determined that he had a concussion but, thankfully, no fracture. He was sent home for several weeks to recuperate. Luckily, he would rejoin the club later in the month.

In the middle of June, the Giants arrived in St. Louis for a three-game series with the Cards. The world champs used the series to honor Hornsby. Before the first game, the St. Louis fans presented their former manager with an engraved watch in appreciation for his 1926 title.

The day of the third game was also planned as a St. Louis celebration to honor Charles Lindbergh's accomplishments. Two St. Louis businessman had helped finance his flight, and he had named his plane the "Spirit of St. Louis," so the city had adopted Lindbergh as its favored son. The day began with Lindbergh's arrival in the mound city and a parade through the downtown. He attended a luncheon and then traveled to the ballpark. Before the game, he assisted Bob O'Farrell and Rogers Hornsby in raising the world championship flag. Next, he greeted the Cardinals and presented each player with his world championship ring. National League president Heydler gave the twenty-five-year-old flyer a gold admission medal that would grant him free entrance to any National League ballpark for life. The 37,000 excited fans, including Lindbergh, then cheered as Alexander and the Cards defeated the Giants, 6–4.

Lindbergh, at the Cardinals' baseball game, meets Alexander and O'Farrell. —By Post-Dispatch staff photographer.

Charles Lindbergh greets O'Farrell and Alexander at the ballpark
—*St. Louis Post-Dispatch*, June 19, 1927

1926 World Series ring
—Sherdel family

The Cardinals' pennants flying over Sportsman's Park
—*St. Louis Post-Dispatch*, June 19, 1927

Bad luck struck again on June 22, when World Series hero Tommy Thevenow fractured his ankle while sliding into second base during Alexander's defeat of the Cubs. Thevenow would miss the rest of the season. Of all the Cardinals' injuries, that was perhaps the greatest loss.

The Redbirds had spent June at home. Despite the injuries to the championship team, the Cardinals were still only a half-game behind the first-place Pittsburgh Pirates by the end of the month. Sam Breadon was thrilled, as Frankie Frisch (.384) was leading Rogers Hornsby (.373) in the batting race. Jess Haines was having a super year. Alexander and Rhem were winning. Bill

Sherdel pitched an eleven-inning six-hit victory over the Reds on June 24 to show "the Big Four" were ready for a pennant race.

In the American League, there was a different kind of race. Babe Ruth and Lou Gehrig were battling for the home-run crown. By month-end, the two Yankee stars were tied, with twenty-five home runs each.

The world champions began July with a six-game-losing streak. Bill Sherdel stopped the losses when he hurled a five-hit-win over the Braves. But it was a difficult month for the Cardinals. They just couldn't gain ground on the league leader. O'Farrell's crew dropped to third place on July 2 and remained there through month's end. The Pirates continued to lead, with the Cubs now in second ahead of the Cards. The only consolation was that Hornsby and the Giants were in fourth.

It was amazing that the team could continue to do that well, as injuries continued to plague them. In early July, Chick Hafey's knee worsened and he was out indefinitely. Blades had returned, but he still favored his injured leg. O'Farrell remained out with arm troubles. Les Bell twisted his knee and missed most of the month. Southworth dislocated a rib from swinging the bat. Bottomley suffered ptomaine poisoning and missed a game.

In an unfortunate incident, the previous year's twenty-game winner and this year's holdout, Flint Rhem, was "fined" $2,000 for breaking training rules. The pitcher had imbibed in alcohol while the team was playing in Philadelphia, and that was not allowed. Indeed, Breadon had placed a $2,500 bonus clause in Rhem's one-year contract if he refrained from drinking. Since the season was partly over, Rhem had earned $500, but with this transgression, the other $2,000 was cancelled. Rhem objected vehemently and stated:

> "I will not play ball in St. Louis again unless the Cardinal management reinstates the bonus clause in my contract.
>
> "While we were in Boston, I'll admit I did drink. But, there were others...." "I appear to have been picked out for punishment. Because of this treatment, which I consider unjust, I will not play for the Cardinals."[7]

Owner Breadon was unmoved and replied:

"So far as the penalty inflicted on Rhem goes, the case is settled. We had overlooked many infractions of the drinking clause in Rhem's contract and it became necessary to take drastic steps. Here is one of the younger players on the team arrogating to himself the right to act as he pleased. . . .

"I cannot see any chance to compromise. Rhem's future with the Cardinals is distinctly up to him."[8]

After a few days, Rhem changed his mind and returned to the club. Breadon had placed the non-drinking clause in Rhem's contract for good reason. Rhem enjoyed alcohol way too much and drinking would eventually ruin his career, prematurely.

By the end of July, Lou Gehrig led teammate Babe Ruth with thirty-five home runs to thirty-four.

August was a good month for the Cardinals, but they still couldn't gain much ground on the Cubs and Pirates. To make matters worse, the Giants were closing fast. They had won twelve of their last fourteen games. A frustrated John McGraw had left the New York club on a scouting trip and Hornsby was now leading that team. In St. Louis, Breadon gave Branch Rickey a new five-year contract as the Cards' president and business manager.

There continued to be more Cardinal injuries: Bill Sherdel's back was still bothering him, Hafey returned only to leave again—this time with infected gums, Southworth was still nursing sore ribs. By the end of the month, O'Farrell's club was getting healthier, but pitching remained a problem for the final pennant run. Haines and Alexander were at the top of their game. In fact, the duo led all major-league pairs in combined wins and complete games. On August 29, Haines won his twenty-first game. The Cardinals needed more from the remaining staff. Bill Sherdel added several key wins during the month. He also contributed with his bat, going four for ten with a home run in two starts. Recalcitrant Flint Rhem added a four-hit victory at the end of August. He had previously lost seven games in a row. It appeared the Cards might be able to duplicate their 1926 success if they could just play well in the final month. It was going to be a four-team race to October.

John Wray wrote an interesting column in the *St. Louis Post-Dispatch* in which he opined that:

"The year has proved one thing—that no individual means everything to a ball club, either as a player, or manager, or both. The Cardinals have done wonderful work without Hornsby. Neither his playing nor his leadership was found to be a necessity. O'Farrell and his associates have really done more under far worse conditions with this club, than did Hornsby.

"Last year, Hornsby had little or no bad luck. Rogers had Rhem pitching worthwhile ball for him. Sherdel was better. . . . O'Farrell was in there for all but a few games of the entire season. So was Tommy Thevenow. Accidents to Blades and Hafey came late.

"Hornsby's way was much smoother than O'Farrell's has been; but the Cards are right there with the leaders today.

"It might have been a very different matter, however, had not Frankie Frisch been available to step in there with his marvelous playing and his fine spirit that lent inspiration and strength both to the club."[9]

From the beginning of September—which arrived with continued excitement over the home-run race in the American League, where Ruth (43) was now two ahead of fellow Yankee Gehrig (41)—through the season's end in early October, the Cardinals continued to chase the Pirates and the pennant. On September 26, John Wray, in a column entitled, "Those Amazing Cards," described the year.

> Still in the hunt for the pennant, our astounding Cardinals continue to amaze us. They still had an outside chance to win this morning, although the odds were rather heavily against them.
>
> No matter what happens now, it can be said with full truth that the Cardinals have run the greatest pennant race of any team in either league, handicaps considered.
>
> Their difficulties have been detailed before. Everyone knows that every department of play that represented the team in the World's Series, went on the rocks. . . . The entire outfield was mangled—and still is far below par. Only two places on the infield have been sound throughout the year. The catching staff lost the ace who carried on

almost throughout the entire 1927 season, and the pitching was weaker by at least two of its first-string hurlers of last year.

Minor leaguers were dragged in—are still in the lineup—but the old machine, shaking in every joint, is still steaming on the heels of the Pirates.

The mighty leadership of a Hornsby no longer explains it. Whatever spirit animates the team it certainly has sufficed to lift it above the most extraordinary series of discouragements that probably every afflicted a world's title winner.[10]

The Redbirds finished strong, but not strong enough to catch the red-hot Pirates. O'Farrell's club spent much of the time in third place, fighting against the Giants. In the end, Frisch and the Cards finished second, a game-and-a-half away from another pennant, but a half-game ahead of Hornsby and the Giants. Oddly, St. Louis finished seventh in batting and fielding, but second in the standings. With two Cardinals having won the MVP voting in the previous two years, this year, Frisch finished second and Hornsby third to the Pirates' Paul Waner in 1927. Finally, Breadon and Rickey felt vindicated for their preseason trade.

The Cards' management tried to do everything possible to bring another pennant to St. Louis. Early in September, Rickey purchased shortstop insurance in veteran Walter "Rabbit" Maranville from Rochester. He also promoted several youngsters from Syracuse who would prove valuable the following year. Maranville had come to fame in 1914 with the miracle Boston Braves. He also played in Pittsburgh, Chicago, and Brooklyn before spending time in Rochester. He would later be elected to the Hall of Fame.

Still, the Cards' injuries continued. Poor Bob O'Farrell, who'd spent most of the season recovering from one injury after another, dislocated his thumb and splintered the bone in late September. (Fortunately, Chick Hafey was able to finally show what a healthy Hafey could have done all season at this point—the last week of September, he homered in four successive games). Still, the team's performance was truly amazing. Even with all the injuries, the Cardinals' mark (92–61) topped their (89–65) championship season of 1926. There were so many places to find another two victories that would have meant a pennant. It was easy to start identifying what might have been with a look at 1926 twenty-game-winner Flint Rhem. He missed training camp and then pitched with a sore arm through most of the season. After an amazing .325 batting average and a seventeen-home-run 1926 season, Les Bell hit .259, with nine homers. Bob O'Farrell played in only sixty-one games. World Series hero Tommy Thevenow was limited to fifty-nine, hitting .194 before he broke his ankle. Chick Hafey was in the lineup 103 times, but did hit .329 with eighteen four-baggers. Ray Blades played in only sixty-one games and hit .317.

Only two key players—Frisch and Bottomley—avoided major injuries. Frisch, who played in every game, batted .337, hit ten homers, scored 112 runs, and stole a league-leading forty-eight bases. Frisch did have one scare. In a mid-September home game against the Giants, he was hit in the head while batting in the first inning. He lost consciousness for several minutes, but stayed in the contest. He was awarded first base and then proceeded to steal home. This incident represented how tough Frisch was. Bottomley, for his part, played in all but one game, hitting .303, with nineteen homers, fifteen triples, and 124 runs-batted-in. In a July 15 game, "Sunny Jim" hit for the cycle, collecting two singles, a double, a triple, and a home run.

The 1927 staff was led by Jess Haines (24–10) and Grover Alexander (21–10). Bill Sherdel added a (17–12) record with a league-leading six saves in 232 innings and a club-high thirty-nine appearances. He was listed as the twelfth-best National League hurler in wins and losses. Considering he'd lost a two-hitter and a three-hitter, he could have possibly won twenty games with a little luck. Within the National League, Jess Haines was first in complete games and shutouts, and second in wins, winning percentage, and innings pitched.

Throughout, Bill Sherdel was cultivating popular recognition for his work on the mound as a starter and reliever. James Gould wrote:

> Bill Sherdel, the Cardinals' southpaw, once was a relief pitcher. Then he became a regular starter. Now he is both, for when Bill isn't in there winning them on his own book, he is saving them for some other curver. . . .
>
> When the 1927 Cardinal season is writ into history, Bill Sherdel's name will deserve a decorative page all to itself. To save a game these days is just as valuable as to win one.[11]

Each Cardinal earned an extra $1,033 from the club's second-place finish in the pennant race. Today that amount would be $14,091.

Apparently, the 1927 Cardinals team was not just a team of good players. Like most clubs, there were always some "characters." Those characters kept the whole team loose, but sometimes caused peripheral damage while having a good time. In 1955, Roy Stockton talked with Cards' trainer Dr. Harrison Weaver on the anniversary of his twenty-ninth year with the club. Weaver recalled how Branch Rickey had invited him to temporarily serve as trainer for the 1927 season. The doctor spoke about the players' tricks.

"They almost drove me crazy the first two years. Chick Hafey and Tommy Thevenow were the worst. Oh, that Thevenow! You'd never think it to look at his baby face. And he was so quiet. But they really gave me the works! When the day finally was over and I retired for some sleep, I never knew when my bed would fall down with me. After it collapsed several times as I climbed between the sheets, I got to inspecting everything before I used it—chairs, beds, talcum powder.

"The worst times were on the trains. The boys went crazy. We were on our way to an exhibition game one night and it was all your life was worth to stick your head out of your berth. They were playing snowball fight with wads of soaked paper for snow. I got popped a couple of times. Then I went to the washroom for rest and safety. But they had taken my medicine bag and had taken everything out of it and arrayed the articles on a shelf and there were big signs proclaiming that this was 'Dr. Weaver's Drug Store.'

"I got so mad I braved the storm of paper snowballs, got my bag, and when the train stopped or almost stopped at a little station in Indiana, I stepped off. I fell and tore my trousers' knees. I was a sight. I went in to buy a ticket back to St. Louis and found I was almost broke. I had to give the ticket man a book of stamps to make up the price of my ticket back to St. Louis. And when I got to Union Station I didn't have a dime in my pocket. I took a taxicab and borrowed cab fare from the clerk at the Fairgrounds Hotel.

"I got a break. The game was called off and so the boys didn't need a trainer. You'd think that might have made them ease up a bit, but it didn't. Oh, that Hafey and that Thevenow were terrible."[12]

The Pittsburgh Pirates met the New York Yankees in the 1927 World Series. The Pirates' lineup included Hall-of-Famers Paul and Lloyd Waner, Pie Traynor, Kiki Cuyler, and Joe Cronin. Once again, the Yankees' Murderers' Row was led by Ruth and Gehrig. Their exciting home-run competition produced Ruth's record sixty home runs and Gehrig's forty-seven. The Yankees won an amazing 110 games, with a .324 team batting average. In the Series, the Yankees won four straight games, adding to their reputation as the greatest team ever.

Back in McSherrystown in mid-October, local idol Bill Sherdel organized a baseball game to benefit hospitals in Hanover and Gettysburg. He pitched for McSherrystown with Les Bell and Cliff Heathcote on his squad. Their opponent, Hanover, included Hack Wilson and stars from the Raiders' minor-league club. Sherdel's club won, 5–1. The highlight was the matchup of Sherdel and Wilson. Sherdel fanned the future Hall of Famer the first two times at bat, and then induced him to pop up in his third plate appearance. The charity event collected $3,000 for the hospitals.

On October 21 in Baltimore, Sherdel pitched for Merwyn Jacobson's all-star team against the Baltimore Black Sox. Hack Wilson was his teammate this time. The Black Sox club, led by the great Oscar Charleston and Ben Taylor, proved the better club, winning 8–7.

Rumors that the Cardinals would make a management change began to circulate during October. It was hard to understand how Bob O'Farrell could be replaced after the outstanding job he did winning more games than the previous year with constant injuries. Finally, on November 7, Sam Breadon announced that forty-year-old veteran skipper Bill McKechnie would manage the club in 1928. McKechnie had led the Pirates for five years, winning the pennant and the World Series in 1925 before joining the Cards' coaching staff in 1927.

Breadon explained his reasoning:

> "I do not want to spoil a good catcher by keeping on his shoulders the responsibilities of management. Perhaps the managerial worries had something to do with O'Farrell's having an unfortunate year. It certainly is true that he was not injured at all during 1926 when he did not have to worry about who was to play the outfield or who was to

pitch the next game. But when he was manager, it was just one accident after another. The same was true of Hornsby. His worst batting year in the last seven was the year he managed the Cardinals. Perhaps the worries of management had something to do with that . . . I think the world of Bob. I don't think there is a finer man in baseball and I would not part with him for money."[13]

Breadon gave O'Farrell a $20,000 contract just to catch in 1928. That made O'Farrell the highest-priced catcher in the major leagues. Breadon also announced that Billy Southworth would leave the team to manage the Cards' Syracuse club in 1928. Southworth had been a hero in 1926, but due to injuries, he'd played in only ninety-two games in the past season, though he did bat .301. Listing his physical problems documented the jinx that followed the 1927 club. First, the outfielder suffered an abscessed ear on the way north from training camp. Next, he received a charley horse in his leg, followed by a foot injury. Then came a badly sprained thumb and, after that, a dislocated rib. Mercifully for him, the season ended.

CHAPTER NINETEEN

The 3M Company would invent Scotch tape in 1928 and Mickey Mouse would make his first appearance in film—"Steamboat Willie"—in the same year. George Eastman would show the first color motion pictures, the first color television broadcast would occur in London, and the first tennis match would be televised. The Boston Garden would open for hockey games.

For the second straight winter, fans were surprised by the trading of Rogers Hornsby. This year, the Giants traded Hornsby to the Boston Braves for two mediocre players. But why? Hornsby continued to be an outstanding player, having managed New York very successfully in John McGraw's absence over the past season. In fact, McGraw had intimated that Hornsby would take over the team when McGraw retired after the 1928 season. So why was the trade made? The answer would be revealed several days later, when a newspaper story reported that eight New York players had signed a petition saying they could not play another year with Hornsby. Either he had to go, or they would leave the team.

In Cardinal news over the winter, Bob O'Farrell had surgery to regain the movement in his dislocated thumb, and it appeared to be successful. Unlike the previous year, Tommy Thevenow quickly signed his 1928 contract and asked permission to report with the pitchers and catchers. Chick Hafey also had surgery to improve his eyesight and was now wearing glasses. The Cardinals' owner announced that, once again, Flint Rhem would be a holdout.

Bill Brandt of the *Philadelphia Public Ledger* wrote a February column about Sherdel's off-season training program. "Bill's son, known in McSherrystown as 'Junior,' has a Shetland pony. So 'Junior,' as jockey for the pony, goes along with Sherdel when papa does his roadwork. Monday, Wee Willie gave the pony five yards' start and beat him to the 100 yards. That was the day Sherdel wrote to the St. Louis president for more money."[1]

Bill Sherdel's family—Junior, Marguerite, Patricia
—Sherdel family

The Sherdel family left by train from Baltimore to Florida for the start of training camp on February 22. The Cardinals returned to Avon Park. Sherdel arrived the night before the first practice. He and fellow veteran hurler Grover Alexander were the first to race around the field. The first workouts were light, but the players were sweated as they entered the locker room.

Ray Gillespie wrote, "Bill Sherdel took possession of a uniform for the first time yesterday and was one of the first to grace the field. The little southpaw worked harder than any one on the squad throughout the day. He pitched, played with the medicine ball, chased fungo drives . . . and participated in bunting games on the sidelines until big beads of perspiration dripped from his brow."[2]

New manager McKechnie gathered the early arrivals for his first talk. Besides the pitchers and catchers, Blades, Thevenow, and Les Bell were there to test their bodies and get some advance work. The manager told them:

"Do not do as I say, but do as I do. Drinking is strictly forbidden. Not even the consumption of a glass of beer will be allowed. I have the backing of president Breadon in this and will enforce this measure to the limit. I will give you my word that I will not touch a drop as long as I am connected with this club. . . .

"Gambling is forbidden. Stud poker and dice must not be played. Golf is permissible only on days on which we have an open date."[3]

The first week of March, after discussion with Sam Breadon, Flint Rhem signed his contract and reported to camp. Rhem delivered this message to the Cardinals' fans: "I am going to give them my very best this year, will not take a drink of liquor, and will be on my absolute good behavior. With my proper spring training this year, I should be able to win twenty or twenty-five ball games. I want vindication from the fans. There is absolute harmony between myself and president Breadon."[4]

The Cardinals scheduled spring training games against a variety of teams from the National, American, International, South Atlantic, and Triple-I Leagues. McKechnie's pitching aces—Alexander, Haines, Sherdel, and Rhem—looked good.

In late March, Breadon and Rickey made another deal. They traded third baseman Les Bell to the Braves for third baseman Andy High and $20,000. Thirty-year-old High had arrived in the majors in 1922 and split time between Brooklyn and Boston. Bell had had a great 1926 season, but his production had dropped off significantly in the last year. Ironically, Bell had come to camp early this year and had four hits in an exhibition game the day he was traded. Hornsby, now a Brave, was instrumental in Boston's acquisition of Bell. The two had been good friends in St. Louis.

The Cardinals and Browns returned to St. Louis for their spring series before opening day. In Florida, Bottomley and Frisch had led the Redbirds' hitters to a great record. The biggest health concerns continued to be Blades, Hafey, and Thevenow. The two St. Louis teams split the series and were optimistic about their chances in the regular season. Most sportswriters thought the Cards or Cubs would win the National League pennant, while the Yankees seemed a lock for the American League title.

As the Cardinals practiced at Sportsman's Park the day before the opener with the Pirates, Ray Gillespie wrote about Bill Sherdel:

> Sherdel, always a glutton for work, has not changed his policy this spring and voluntarily finds various duties to perform while the rest of his mates are running through their workouts. Only yesterday, even though he had hurled three rather strenuous innings the day previous, "Sherry" sauntered out to a spot in front of the home dugout and asked Coach [Jack] Onslow to catch him in a long warmup.
>
> "Why, you only pitched yesterday," Onslow told him.
>
> "What's the difference?" Sherdel asked. "My arm feels better today than it did when I was hard at work against the Browns. I want to keep it in shape."[5]

The 1928 season began on April 11. All fans were optimistic. All teams were even. Jess Haines took the mound against the world champion Pittsburgh Pirates in St. Louis. One of the new players on the 1928 Cardinals was John "Pepper" Martin. He would get some limited playing time that year, but his best years would be later, when he would be a member of the famous mid-1930s Cardinals' Gashouse Gang. That team would be known for its shabby and smelly appearance and its rough play. They would win the 1934 World Series. Martin was certainly an odd character. In an article entitled, "Prepare for Pepper," Roy Stockton wrote, "Martin played with Houston, batted over .350, stole a flock of bases, and distinguished himself in the field. In polite language, he is said to be a bit eccentric. A product of Arkansas [Oklahoma], he does not believe in wearing socks, and they had to tie him to put on his first pair of shoes. He travels light, never bothering with a suitcase and figuring that, in summer, a shirt and a pair of trousers constitutes enough raiment for any person."[6]

The home team Cards won the first game, defeating the Pirates, 14–7, in a slugfest. Haines pitched all nine innings for his first victory. Forty-one-year-old Grover Alexander won the second contest, allowing seven hits and only one runner to third base. Haines and Alexander continued their rivalry for the Cards' top pitching spot.

There was a different feeling in the dugout this year. Ray Gillespie wrote, "Instead of figuring his victories by the series or half-dozens, McKechnie is concentrating his efforts on each game individually and lets the morrow take care of itself. In fact, he has instilled this spirit into the 1928 Cardinals, who have adopted as their motto: Win the first hundred games and be satisfied with an even break in the rest."[7]

The Cardinals ended April in fourth place behind Brooklyn, New York, and Cincinnati. It was still too early to determine how the club would finish. On the mound as expected, Haines and Alexander were leading the staff.

In Bill Sherdel's first start on April 16, he pitched a six-hitter against the Cubs and added a home run to win, 4–3. Three days later, Sherdel saved a victory when the Cards scored ten runs in just two innings. He then lost his next two starts.

In Sherdel's second loss to Cincinnati, Chick Hafey ran into a concrete wall in right field and was knocked out. Although tests showed he did not fracture his skull, he endured dizziness and severe headaches for several days. The doctor would keep Hafey out of action for a week. Joining Hafey in St. John's Hospital at month-end was Bill Sherdel, who had been hit on the ankle by a batted ball. The ankle became badly swollen, his foot became infected, and Sherdel developed a temperature of 104. Besides those injuries, Bob O'Farrell's thumb had become badly swollen and he was on the bench, also. Two rookies were now doing the catching.

May was a better month for the St. Louis club. The Cardinals won despite some health issues with the pitching staff. Alexander developed a sore arm and Haines was weak from a bout of the flu. Rhem, Sherdel, and the relievers were carrying the load. Rhem appeared to be back to his 1926 form, and Sherdel pitched several excellent games. By month-end, Hafey had returned to the lineup.

Breadon and Rickey made two big deals during May. In the first, they traded away their 1927 MVP manager and high-priced catcher Bob O'Farrell to the Giants for left-handed slugging outfielder George Harper. So much for Breadon's commitment to keep O'Farrell. The Cards' owner had said he wouldn't sell O'Farrell, but he didn't say anything about a trade. Fans were scratching their heads about that deal. The Cards needed a strong left-handed bat in the lineup, but now they had only two inexperienced backstops. Breadon answered his critics the following day when he acquired catcher Jimmy Wilson from the Phillies for two "minor" talents. The trade would turn out to be a steal for the Cardinals.

Twenty-seven-year-old catcher Jimmy Wilson had spent his whole career in Philadelphia. He began with the Phillies in 1923 and had a career .291 batting average. Wilson was batting .300 when the trade was made.

Again, the Cardinals had ignored any loyalties and done what they felt was in the best interest of a pennant run. At present, the Reds, Giants, and Cubs were ahead of the Cards in the standings. Centerfielder Taylor Douthit (.370) was leading Bottomley (.355) and the rest of the Cards in hitting. As a team, the Cards were batting .293 with twenty-eight home runs. Rabbit Maranville had now replaced the weak-hitting and fragile Thevenow at short.

Speaking of hitting, Robert Paul wrote an article in the *Daily News* of Philadelphia when the Cardinals arrived to play the Phillies on June 1.

> Bill Sherdel, here with the St. Louis Cardinals, does have an ambition, though he is a pitcher and probably will see action against the Phillies Monday or Tuesday. Bill wants to climb into the Select Five Hitters while here in Philadelphia and hopes to gain such recognition before departing for New York.
>
> The Cardinals' star southpaw can't understand why he isn't listed in the Select Five. He claims he's hitting at a better clip than the great Rogers Hornsby. . . .
>
> Sherdel says he's had at least thirteen hits this season and his average must be above .400. "Why," he tells his roommate, Jess Haines, every day, "I've even had a home run. I should be included in the Select Five."
>
> There is nothing exceptional about his hitting this season, according to the southpaw. He always could swing the bat, which is the first requisite for hitting success in Sherdel's opinion.

"No," declared Sherdel last night while awaiting a bridge game at the Hotel Adelphia, "there is no mystery to my success as a hitter. I swing as I always have—only this year, the pitchers seem to be pitching where I'm swinging."

If the Phillies' hurling staff continues to bounce hits off the other players' bats it wouldn't surprise us if Sherdel even made a homer at Baker Bowl. All he needs is pitching to where he happens to be swinging, and that's what some of Shotton's hurlers do best.[8]

Although the story was humorous, Bill Sherdel was hitting .409 with nine hits including one home run in twenty-two plate appearances in ten games.

Perhaps June was the month the Cardinals won the 1928 pennant. They won twenty games and lost only six and moved from a lowly fifth place to first in the standings. Maybe it was the long road trip that began in late May and included almost all of June. The Cards won twenty-one of twenty-seven games in other parks. Regardless, McKechnie's club played outstanding baseball during June. The month began with Alexander and Haines struggling because of nagging injuries. Bill Sherdel became the pitching staff's ace, winning six straight games while saving several others. Rhem was pitching better ball. Syl Johnson added three victories. By month-end, Alexander and Haines had returned to their 1927 form.

The most surprising hurler was left-handed spitball artist Clarence Mitchell. Breadon signed the thirty-seven-year-old veteran on June 4. He had been pitching for the Phillies, but was released when manager Shotton decided to go with youth. Several clubs wanted Mitchell, but he chose St. Louis because of his friendship with former Phillies' catcher Jimmy Wilson. Interestingly, Mitchell was a good hitter, and he now provided a backup for Jim Bottomley at first base in addition to his mound duties. Mitchell immediately stepped in as a reliever and also pitched several complete game victories during the month.

The Cardinals were hitting very well. Defensively, they were just as strong, going forty-seven innings without an error. On the negative side, Frankie Frisch had been struggling with a wrenched back. Instead of resting, he continued to play, but his batting average suffered. If only Hafey could remain healthy. He had been terrorizing opposing pitchers since returning from his concussion, and now had six homers. But by month-end, Hafey was out again—this time with an injured left thumb.

McKechnie's squad spent most of July at home. They had another good month in first place, and St. Louis was now comfortably ahead of Cincinnati and New York. Nobody, however, was printing World Series tickets—yet.

Frankie Frisch continued to experience health issues. He spent time in the hospital to rest and recover from a bruised thumb and various leg bruises. Frisch was a hard-nosed competitor. Locking him up in the hospital was the only way the Cardinals could keep him off the field.

Breadon and Rickey made another great acquisition on July 13. Veteran catcher Earl Smith was released by the Pirates. McKechnie remembered Smith from his days as Pittsburgh's manager and brought him to St. Louis to join another former Pirate, Rabbit Maranville. Smith was a veteran of four World Series—two with the Giants and two with the Pirates.

Cardinals' hitting continued to win many games. At the end of July, the club was hitting an incredible .300. The mighty swinging Sherdel's average was still a respectable .291—the second-best pitcher's average behind Alexander's .298.

As for the pitching itself, Bill Sherdel continued to lead the staff. Alexander's arm had improved, and he won his twelfth game in July. Haines and Rhem were still inconsistent. Even Mitchell was starting to look human, and was shelled in several starts. For the Cards to maintain their lead, the "Big Three" of Sherdel, Alexander, and Haines had to win.

Bill Sherdel's son was a popular attraction in the Cardinals' dugout before games. "Junior" even had his own Cardinals' uniform, as this photo from the *St. Louis Star* indicates. He was pictured under the newspaper heading "Cardinals' Unsung Heroes of the Pennant Parade."

LITTLE WILLIE SHERDEL turns out in uniform when his dad pitches against the enemy. Little Willie likes baseball games and he is quite a hitter himself. Here he is, all ready to take a cut at one of Pop Sherdel's slow ones.

Little Bill in his Cards' uniform
—*St. Louis Star*, July 16, 1928

If June was the month the Cardinals may have won the pennant, August was the month the St. Louis club almost lost the pennant. The Cards went through a rough period where they lost ten of fourteen games. They dropped into second place behind the Giants, after having a six-and-a-half-game lead. Roy Stockton interviewed Bill McKechnie. The Cards' manager said:

> "We realize that our situation is serious and we are not going to sit still and moan over our misfortunes. We are going to do everything in our power to check this slump.

"Sentiment gets you nowhere in baseball. It will be tough to cut players off the list, but the big thing is to protect our lead and win the pennant and sentiment will have no place in our operations."

Branch Rickey added, "It is plain to the layman that something will have to be done. Slumps are inevitable in baseball. They are as sure as the tide. If they persist, pennants can be lost by them and it is our job to try to check the slump. If we can't work from the inside to stop it, perhaps it will be necessary to operate outside and put new blood into the Cardinals. . . ."[9]

By the end of August, the Cardinals had recovered and were back in first with a five-and-a-half-game lead. Much of the credit went to the "Big Three." Bill Sherdel had seventeen victories—fifteen were complete games. Alexander won his fourteenth and looked like his old self. Haines hurled a five-hitter on August 24. It was Haines's first complete game in over a month. Bottomley was batting .338 with twenty-seven four-baggers. The Cubs were now in second, the Giants in third.

September was an exciting month for baseball fans. The pennant races were the closest they'd been in twenty years. In the American League, the Philadelphia A's were thirteen games behind the Yankees on July 4. By September 23, the Athletics had closed the gap to two games. Babe Ruth and the Yankees would eventually win the pennant, but not without some serious worries about seeing that through.

In the National circuit, the Cardinals took the lead in mid-June, had a great July, struggled in August, and then came on strong during an eastern road trip in September. They did not clinch the pennant until the next-to-last day of the season when Bill Sherdel won his twenty-first victory, 3–1, over the Braves. Once the Cards had gained first, they only surrendered the top spot for five days in August. The Redbirds were really in a four-team race with New York, Chicago, and Cincinnati throughout 1928. The Giants were down three times during the season, and came back each time to challenge the Cardinals. At one point, the Giants won four double-headers in four days. Ironically, three former Giants—George Harper, Earl Smith, and Frankie Frisch—helped to win the pennant for St. Louis.

Bill Sherdel was now recognized as one of the outstanding left-handed pitchers in the majors. He continued to get endorsement opportunities. In this one, he and Junior did a sweater ad.

Bill and Junior advertise sweaters
—Sherdel family

It was a veteran Cardinals' club that won the 1928 National League crown, with ninety-five wins. Key acquisitions of older, experienced players had made the difference. Thirty-six-year-old outfielder George Harper provided a strong left-handed bat in the lineup. Thirty-five-year-old Rabbit Maranville fielded sensationally at shortstop while Thevenow continued his recovery. The summer heat wore Maranville down offensively, but then Thevenow was ready to return. Thirty-one-year-old Earl Smith provided backup behind the plate, although Jimmy Wilson was an ironman and caught most games. Maranville and Smith also brought World Series experience to the Cards.

Offensively, Jim Bottomley had a tremendous year. "Sunny Jim" led the league in triples, runs-batted-in, and total bases, while tying Hack Wilson for the most home runs (31). Bottomley scored the second-most runs and hit .325 in 149 games. A less-than-healthy Chick Hafey also had an outstanding year at the plate. Hafey batted .337 in 138 games. He finished in the top five in many offensive categories—doubles, home runs, total bases, and runs-batted-in. Frankie Frisch suffered physically through much of the season. The "Fordham Flash" did manage to hit .300, steal twenty-nine bases, and hit ten homers.

The team's pitching was critical down the stretch. In late September, with only four games remaining, McKechnie's club was a mere half-game ahead. Then his veteran pitchers took over. Haines beat the Braves to increase the Cards' lead to a game. Next, Alexander defeated the Braves to clinch a tie for the title. Finally, Sherdel whipped the Braves, 3–1, to win the pennant, as he had done in 1926. Ironically, Sherdel had a bad cold and was supposed to remain in New York and not make the train trip to Boston. He could not let his team down, so he went along to pitch and won the title contest.

A key addition to the Cards' pitching staff was veteran Clarence Mitchell, one of the few remaining spitball pitchers. The left-handed Mitchell earned his salary when he defeated the Giants three times in critical games. Sherdel and fellow Cardinal Hal Haid tied for the most saves (5) in the league. Former twenty-game winner Flint Rhem pitched well at times, but lost his spot in the starting rotation. He suffered most of the season with tonsillitis and a sore throat.

McKechnie's "Big Four" of thirty-two-year-old Bill Sherdel (21–10), thirty-five-year-old Jess Haines (20–8), forty-one-year-old Grover Alexander (16–9), and thirty-seven-year-old Clarence Mitchell (8–9) would now determine the Cardinals' success against the New York Yankees in the World Series.

CHAPTER TWENTY

The New York Yankees had won the American League pennant by two-and-a-half games over Connie Mack's Athletics. The Bronx Bombers had blown a thirteen-game lead, dropped to second, regained the lead, and then barely held on to win. Miller Huggins' Murderers' Row of Ruth, Gehrig, Lazzeri, Combs, Meusel, and Koenig won 101 games and lost only fifty-three. Babe Ruth had another monster year with fifty-four home runs, 142 runs-batted-in, and a .323 batting average. Lou Gehrig added twenty-seven four-baggers, 142 runs-batted-in, and a .374 mark. Both superstars played in every game. Lazzeri (.332), Koenig (.319), Combs (.310), and Meusel (.297) hit for high averages, as well. New York's pitching staff was led by George Pipgras (24–13), Waite Hoyt (23–7), and Herb Pennock (17–6). Late-season pick-up Tom Zachary (3–3) provided badly needed help down the stretch.

On paper, the Yankees looked like they would repeat as world champs. But the Yankees at the end of September were not a healthy group. Ruth was limping badly. Gehrig had a knot on his head. Lazzeri's arm was so bad he could not complete a double play. Combs was out with a bad wrist. Dugan had a trick knee. Koenig had tonsillitis. Top left-handed pitcher Herb Pennock and starter Wilcy Moore were at home resting their arms. This was a badly crippled ball club.

The Yankees' opponents, the Cardinals, on the other hand, were in great shape. Finally, everyone was healthy enough to be playing on the St. Louis team, and the newspapers were predicting a St. Louis World Series win. Cards' owner Sam Breadon said, "I am confident the Cardinals could defeat the best team New York could put in the field. The team [Cardinals] this year is a better one than that which won the 1926 Series."[1]

"Old Pete" Alexander also wrote of a Cardinals' victory.

The Cardinals are going into the Series with the belief that we are going to win easily from the Yankees. We have beaten them before and we can beat them again and I personally do not expect it to take us seven games.

We felt right along that the Yankees would be the easier team to beat and the fact that they are going to be our opponents adds to our confidence. Not that we are going into the Series overconfident. Not at all. When I say we ought to win easily, I do not mean that the Yankees are a pushover.

I would not be surprised to see the Series end in five games and if Hoyt does not stop us we may make a clean sweep as these same Yankees did in 1927 over the Pirates.

You can put one thing down and bet on it and that is if the Series is a four-game or a five-game affair, we will be the one to do the winning. And I really believe the Yankees will be doing very well if they manage to win as many as two games.[2]

Veteran shortstop Rabbit Maranville also expressed his optimism.

"I have played on many ball teams in my time and I consider this year's St. Louis Cardinals by far the best of them all. I think we have much better all-around strength than the Yankees; therefore, I believe we will win the World Series. My guess is that we will win four out of five games. I base this prediction on the fact that Hoyt is the only pitcher the Yanks have who figures to last nine innings against us. . . .

"In predicting that we will take four out of five from the Yanks, I don't want the fans to think I believe we have an easy Series ahead of us. I don't. The games will undoubtedly be hard fought. The Yanks are fighters and are past masters in the art of coming from behind to win.

"But I believe we have the best team. I hope the Series will prove it."[3]

Always-confident Babe Ruth was also asked about who would win this year's Series.

"As I see it, the defeat or victory of the Yankees in the Series will be strictly up to ourselves.

"If we can come out of our slump and play the sort of baseball we're capable of playing, then I believe we will be a little bit stronger than the Cardinals. If we don't shake out of it, we're likely to take it on the chin. The Yankee club of May and June was an unbeatable club. The Yankee club of September wasn't so hot.

"A lot of people think that we will stagger through the World Series like we did the last half of the season. Personally, I don't believe we will. I've got a hunch we'll do the same thing in the World Series as we did against the Athletics. Players like Lazzeri, Combs, Meusel, [Bennie] Bengough, and the rest are at their best when the going is toughest. One thing you don't need to worry about is the Yankee spirit of fight."[4]

The Yankees were the underdogs because of their crippled lineup, though how any team with Ruth and Gehrig could be considered longshots is hard to imagine. Probably the best analysis was provided by *St. Louis Star* sportswriter James Gould: "[The statistics] are actually worth little in a Series of seven games except as a guide to the probabilities. In short clashes, the weak become strong and the strong suddenly fade away into powerlessness."[5]

In 1928, the first two Series games were scheduled for Yankee Stadium, with the next three in Sportsman's Park, followed by a return to New York, if needed. The St. Louis club was staying at the Alamac Hotel on upper Broadway. Hundreds of writers and important baseball figures could be seen roaming the lobby. Both the Cardinals and Yankees showed signs of nervousness during their workouts at Yankee Stadium. Cards' manager Bill McKechnie was seen pacing the hotel hallways early in the morning.

McKechnie delayed naming his World Series pitchers until the day before the first game. The St. Louis skipper announced he would use the same rotation as in the 1926 Series. Top winner Bill Sherdel drew the opening assignment, followed by "Pete" Alexander in the second game, and Jess Haines in the third. By hurling the first game, Sherdel was almost certain to pitch a second game in the Series, like he had in 1926. Without Pennock, Yankee manager Miller Huggins chose Waite Hoyt, George Pipgras, and Tom Zachary as his starters.

Philadelphia Public Ledger reporter Billy Duncan asked Sherdel about pitching in the World Series. "Pitchers are divided into two classes: those who have nerve and those who haven't. If you haven't plenty of nerve, stay out of a World Series. Followers of baseball know that I don't have the variety of natural stuff possessed by Lefty Grove, Dazzy Vance, and other speed kings.

I depend on a slow ball, control, knowledge of batters, and nerve to win my games in the National League. All of them are indispensable to a man who wants to be considered a money pitcher."[6]

That year's Series was going to be heard by millions of listeners around the country. Veteran broadcaster Graham McNamee was once again chosen to provide the play-by-play through KSD in St. Louis and forty other broadcasting stations of the NBC network. People in homes, farms, apartments, and offices would gather to listen to the games' progress. Hundreds of newspaper reporters were given access to watch the games and write about them. Even two sports correspondents from Japan would be writing for newspapers with a circulation of 1.37 million readers in the Far East.

The major leagues announced the four umpires for the Series. The National League selected Charles "Cy" Rigler and Charles "Cy" Pfirman, while the American League added Clarence "Brick" Owens and future Hall-of-Famer Bill McGowan.

First game starters Hoyt and Sherdel
—Sherdel family

The 1928 World Series opened in warm weather in Yankee Stadium on October 4. McKechnie and Huggins exchanged their lineups at home plate before the national anthem was played and the umpire announced, "Play ball!" The visiting Cardinals' lineup included: Douthit, CF; High, 3B; Frisch, 2B; Bottomley, 1B; Hafey, LF; Harper, RF; Wilson, C; Maranville, SS; and Sherdel, P. The home Yankees featured: Paschal, CF; Koenig, SS; Ruth, LF; Gehrig, 1B; Meusel, RF; Lazzeri, 2B; Dugan, 3B; Bengough, C; and Hoyt, P. Ben Paschal replaced the injured Earle Combs in center.

Waite Hoyt began the game by easily retiring Douthit, High, and Frisch, in order. Next, Bill Sherdel stepped to the mound in front of 61,425 fans in Yankee Stadium, while residents in McSherrystown and millions throughout the world listened by radio. Paschal started the Yankees' first by flying to Hafey in left. Then Koenig followed with another fly to Hafey. Two outs. That brought Babe Ruth to the plate for the first time against his buddy, "Wee Willie." Ruth had always performed best when the world was his stage. Sherdel led off with a strike and a ball, before Babe smashed the third pitch to right center. Douthit hurried to stop the ball after one bounce, but Ruth rounded first and immediately headed to second, beating the throw for a double. Next came Lou Gehrig with two outs and Ruth on second. Sherdel worked the count to two balls and two strikes. Gehrig then lined a pitch that hit the bleachers' screen in right on one bounce. Ruth scored the first Series' run and the "underdogs" took the early lead. The home crowd stood and wildly applauded their local heroes. Sherdel then settled down and forced Meusel to loft a pop fly to short right. Frisch drifted back and hauled down the popup for the third out—Yankees 1, Cardinals 0.

Both Hoyt and Sherdel matched each other with no-run, no-hit innings until the Yankees came to bat in the bottom of the fourth, and Sherdel took the ball to face the heart of the New York order for the second time. J. Roy Stockton of the *St. Louis Post-Dispatch* described what happened next.

> Then up came the big siege gun. Ruth didn't waste any time. Sherdel offered him a slow ball and the Babe, taking a step forward and timing carefully, shot a fly to left center. Douthit was far over on the other side of center, and when Hafey was unable to reach the ball, Babe turned it into his second double. The Bambino was limping painfully when he reached second, but he took the extra base without hesitation.

Sherdel got rid of Gehrig this time without trouble, taking his tap to the box and throwing him out after bluffing Ruth back to second base.

Bob Meusel, however, refused to live up to his World Series reputation. Big Bob has been the goat of many a World Series. Even last year, when the Pirates were being beaten in four straight, Meusel failed to get his share of hits.

But today he delivered. He picked on a fast one and blasted a home run into the right-field seats. Ruth scored ahead of Bob and the Yankees were three runs to the good. That was all for the inning, as Lazzeri fouled to Wilson and Dugan popped to Maranville.[7]

In the Cards' fifth, George Harper lined a single to left-center with one out for the first hit off Hoyt. Harper died on first as Waite retired the next two batters. Sherdel retired the Yankees in order to end the inning—Yankees 3, Cardinals 0.

Hoyt dominated the Cards' bats in the top of the sixth, allowing no hits. The St. Louis southpaw Sherdel returned to center stage. Stockton wrote:

> Koenig, leading off in the sixth, could not resist the temptation when Sherdel floated a slow ball over the plate. Mark tried to pull his bat back, but the ball hit the end of the club as Sherdel, diving for the ball, knocked it down and retrieved it in time to throw out Koenig at first.
>
> Sherdel finally stopped the Bambino. He gave him nothing but slow stuff until the call was two balls and two strikes. Then Bill thought he had cut the corner with another slow one, but umpire Owens called a ball. That made it three and two, and the Babe ignored the next one, a sweeping curve on the outside corner, and was out when Owens called it a strike.[8]

Gehrig then hit a weak grounder to Frisch for the third out.

To start the seventh inning, Huggins replaced the ailing Tony Lazzeri with young Leo Durocher. Apparently, that had been the New York manager's strategy during the season, to replace Lazzeri with Durocher when he felt the game was won. The Cardinals, however, did not yet believe the game was over. With one out, Jim Bottomley hammered a home run deep into the right-field bleachers for the Cards' second hit and first run. Ruth, in right field, never moved. He knew it was a homer when it left the bat of "Sunny Jim." Hafey tried to repeat Bottomley's feat to left, but Meusel raced back to the wall to haul it in and the Cards' chances ended when Harper fouled to Dugan—Yankees 3, Cardinals 1.

Bill Sherdel retired the Yankees without much effort in the seventh and, in the Cards' eighth, McKechnie replaced Sherdel with a pinch-hitter. The Cards failed again to score. The St. Louis manager then did a double-substitution, putting Syl Johnson on the mound and Tommy Thevenow at shortstop.

Johnson surrendered one final Yankee run in the eighth. Koenig, Ruth, and Gehrig hit successive singles to score Koenig with the Yanks' last run. That was Ruth's third hit of the game—Yankees 4, Cardinals 1.

Hoyt started the St. Louis ninth by striking out High for the second time. Frisch then hit a grounder for the second out. Bottomley returned to the plate again and collected his second hit of the game, and the third and final hit off Hoyt. Hafey then flied to Ruth to end the contest.

Waite Hoyt had pitched a masterful complete game, allowing only three scattered hits. Except for Bottomley's four-bagger, no other Cardinal advanced past first base. Bill Sherdel had also pitched a great game. He'd surrendered only four hits in his seven innings—but every hit was an extra-base hit. He'd also displayed excellent control, not walking a single Yankee. If the Cards could have provided any more offense, Sherdel could have won a four-hitter. Once again, however, the hard-luck Sherdel lost a World Series game, despite great pitching. Hoyt was just better with his dazzling fast ball and curve. The "underdogs" now had a 1–0 Series lead.

Bill Sherdel took his third Series loss gracefully. He stated, "One bad pitch to Meusel did it. I pitched low to him all day, but the one he hit out of the park was intended for a high curve, but it did not break an inch."[9]

Despite losing the first game, the Cardinals and their fans were not concerned. Sherdel had lost the first game in 1926, but then Alexander had evened the Series with his mastery of the Yankees in the second game. "Alex" was going to start the second game again this year. Even better, he was matched against twenty-eight-year-old George Pipgras. Pipgras had started with the Yankees in 1923 but had not accomplished much until this year. The Cardinals did not expect to have any trouble winning that game.

Miller Huggins made two changes to his lineup. He replaced Paschal in center with Cedric Durst and Dugan at third with Gene Robertson. McKechnie made no changes.

The Yankees made it two in a row with a decisive 9–3 victory. Pipgras handcuffed the Cards' hitters the entire game except for one inning. At the beginning, he was wild because his curve was breaking too sharply, but he settled down and became invincible.

The Redbirds only scored in the second inning. After Harper walked, Wilson doubled to score him. Maranville followed with a single. Lazzeri's error on a throw to first scored Wilson for the second run. Then Maranville scored on a double play and that was it for the Cardinals. Later, Frisch added two singles to end the St. Louis hit total at four.

The Yankees scored all the runs they needed in the first two innings with three in the first and one in the second, but they added another four in the third for insurance. The game was essentially over at that point. A beaten Alexander was removed for Clarence Mitchell. Mitchell held Huggins' club to two hits over the final five-and-two-thirds innings—but it was too late.

After the game, "Alex" said, "Everything I threw up to the plate was batted. Then my control was bad and you know when I am without control, I have a tough time of it. . . . I walked four batters in less than three innings. . . . And every one of those base on balls was turned into a run, which did not help our cause a bit."[10] But, the Cardinals just weren't hitting—as their .115 batting average proved. Bottomley struck out three straight times against Pipgras. In two games, they had managed only seven hits. The Cards' other big gun, Hafey, had yet to get a hit. The players hoped to change their luck as they traveled to St. Louis for game three. Certainly the pressure was on. If the Cardinals were to win the title, they would need to win four of the next five games.

On the train, square-jawed Bill Sherdel said, "I guess I'll have to shut 'em out without any hits the next time. I'm going to try that. And you sissies see if you can't get me one run in nine innings. If you do, I'll square this Series for you. Jess will win his game, and then, maybe, we can go back to New York one to the good."[11]

Roy Stockton described it this way, "It was tragic, the sight of old Alexander knocked out, but more impressive still has been the utter helplessness of the Cardinal batters. And unless they find the range, unless they go up to the plate with a little more determination and turn that determination into base hits, all the Haines, all the Sherdels, and all the Mitchells won't do them any good, unless, as Sherdel suggests, the St. Louis pitchers hurl nothing but no-hit games."[12]

Walter Johnson, one of the greatest pitchers of all time, added, "So far, St. Louis has played bad baseball. The Cards have put out on the diamond just what was expected from the Yankee cripples."[13]

An interesting theory to explain the poor Cardinal hitting in New York was advanced by one of the players. Because of the large crowds, white-shirted fans were sitting in the centerfield bleachers where normally a green canvas background would exist. Hoyt and Pipgras were throwing high fast balls that were harder for the hitters to follow. The pitches seemed to be coming from the white shirts of the fans and it was hard to judge depth. Sherdel, Mitchell, and Alexander were throwing slower pitches, which created fewer problems for the Yankee batters. The player said, "You could not judge those high fast balls. You could see them, but there was no depth to the ball. You could not tell how far the ball had traveled. It was just a white spot out there and, before we could time it, the thing was on us, past us, and in Bengough's glove. Our timing was terrible."[14]

In St. Louis, the fans had prepared a homecoming parade to honor their pennant-winning heroes. On October 5 at four o'clock in the afternoon, the club arrived by train at Union Station. The players and other personnel moved into eighteen waiting cars. A brass band playing "Hail, Hail, the Gang's All Here" led the automobile parade through the downtown streets for forty-five blocks, as a large crowd of fans cheered and applauded. Bill Sherdel rode in the seventh car. The parade finished on Jefferson Avenue, where the players then left for their homes.

World championship fever ran high. All the hotels were filled with both Cards' and Yankees' fans. Late arrivals were forced to travel to Illinois to find accommodations. The Cardinals' organization had to return 28,000 ticket requests, totaling over a million dollars.

After the first two games, the Redbirds were now considered the underdogs. Big Jess Haines was McKechnie's choice to pitch the third game and change the momentum. For his part, Miller Huggins selected crafty thirty-two-year-old veteran Tom Zachary to continue the Yankees' dominance. Zachary had begun in the majors with the 1918 Phillies, but his greatest success had been in a Senators' uniform. He had won ninety-six games in Washington. He had also spent 1926 and part of 1927 with the Browns. Zachary had returned to the Senators for the end of 1927 and the first part of this year before the Yankees acquired him on waivers. Interestingly, he had surrendered Babe Ruth's sixtieth home run in 1927, and now a year later was joining Ruth and the Yankees. Huggins' choice of the left-handed slow-ball artist to start game three was a gamble. Zachary had pitched in only seven Yankee games and had a 3–3 record.

Before game three, the Cardinals received gifts from the fans. Each player was given a diamond stick pin with a gold enamel cardinal over a bat resting his feet on a diamond. A local manufacturer also presented each player with a new hat as he entered the ballpark.

McKechnie made only one change to his lineup for the next game. He replaced left-handed George Harper with right-handed Wattie Holm in right field. Huggins repeated his lineup from the second game.

Jess Haines took the mound at 1:30 on October 7, in front of 39,602 fans in Sportsman's Park. The big Cardinal hurler with the great fast ball and baffling knuckleball was serious and focused on changing the direction of the Series. He put the Yankees down in order in the top of the first. In their half of the initial inning, the Cards quickly took the early lead when Durst misplayed Bottomley's hit into a triple, scoring two runs—Cardinals 2, Yankees 0. But in the top of the second, Haines gave Lou Gehrig a shoulder-high fast ball and Gehrig deposited it into the stands for a home run—his second of the Series—Cardinals 2, Yankees 1. Haines continued to tame the Yankees until Douthit's misplay in the fourth. With Ruth on base after a single, Gehrig hit a sinking line drive to shallow center. Douthit could have stopped the ball and awarded Gehrig a single. Instead, he tried for a shoe-string catch and missed. The ball rolled the whole way to the flagpole, and Gehrig circled the bases with the hobbling Ruth ahead of him. It was the first major Cardinal mistake. Yankees 3, Cardinals 2. The Cards fought back to tie the game in the bottom of the fifth at 3 each.

The Yankee sixth inning decided the game and probably the Series. Two plays—Ruth's slide at home and a double steal—sealed the Cardinals' fate. Koenig began the inning with a single to left. Ruth then forced Koenig at second. Gehrig walked. Meusel hit a grounder to High, who threw to Frisch to start a double play. As Frisch turned to make the relay throw to first, Gehrig hit him and the throw to Bottomley was wide of the bag. Ruth rounded third and headed home. Bottomley threw to Wilson in time to tag Ruth, but the Babe hit Wilson, knocking him over and kicking the ball loose. Wilson then recovered and saw Meusel headed to second. The Cards' catcher grabbed the ball and threw to second, but no one was there. The ball flew into center and Meusel scampered to third. Haines now walked Lazzeri. Huggins gave the double-steal sign. Lazzeri broke for second and Wilson threw late. Meusel scored from third. Next, Robertson singled and Lazzeri crossed the plate. Yankees 6, Cardinals 3.

McKechnie replaced Haines with Syl Johnson and the Yankees scored once more in the seventh and that was it. The Yankees won game three, 7–3. Zachary had pitched a complete game victory, allowing nine hits to the Cards' seven.

After Haines was removed, the frustration was visible on his face. He threw his glove into the corner of the dugout, picked up his jacket, and headed to the clubhouse. Reporter Harry Brundidge shadowed him. "A minute later, this writer followed Jess to the club house and found him sitting on a bench in front of his locker, gazing at his raw and bleeding knuckles; hurling a knuckle ball as Jess had been hurling it for six innings tears away the skin. The big pitcher looked up, and there were tears in his eyes, as he said: 'Well, we ought to challenge the Clayton High School team for a series; maybe we could beat the kids with the kind of ball we played today—maybe, but I doubt it.'"[15]

After the game, Wilson talked about the play on Ruth at the plate. "[Ruth] kicked the side of my head first, then struck my chest protector here and I went over. You are bound to spread when a 225-pound guy falls on top of you."[16] Had Wilson held onto the ball and made the tag, the inning would have ended with the Yankees scoreless. Instead, they scored three and the game was over. That was a third straight complete-game victory for a Yankee pitcher.

Associated Press reporter Charles Dunkley wrote of the St. Louis locker room. "The Cardinals, their jaws tightly set, were fighting mad when they reached their dressing room. Inwardly, they pledged themselves to turn the tide tomorrow. There was no hilarity, no backslapping. Those willing to talk were making excuses for defeat. The place resembled a morgue, with the mourners talking things over."[17]

The fate of the Cardinals now rested on the left arm of Bill Sherdel. McKechnie said, "Bill Sherdel, gamest of the game, and recognized as one of the best 'money-pitchers' in baseball, will do our pitching. Of those hurlers who have worked for us in this Series, he has given the best account, holding the Yanks to four hits in seven innings of the first game in New York."[18]

It seemed the St. Louis fans recognized that the Cardinals' situation was hopeless. Unlike the first game at Sportsman's Park, there was no lineup for tickets this time. Four hours before game time, fans could walk up to the ticket window and gain admission. Apathy had set in and it was visible in the prices the scalpers were trying to collect for tickets. During practice, the autograph seekers headed for Babe Ruth. The Great Bambino signed everything except scorecards. New wrist watches were presented to the Cardinals' players before the game.

Bill Sherdel took the mound in front of 37,331 fans on a clear, sunny day. There was a slight wind from the west, favoring the left-handed sluggers Ruth, Gehrig, and Bottomley. The fourth game had been scheduled for the previous day, but Mother Nature had had other plans and rain had caused a delay. On this day, the field was dry. McKechnie made three lineup changes. Ernie Orsatti replaced Douthit in center, Earl Smith was behind the plate, and Harper returned to right. The crowd seemed to approve. Huggins again started Waite Hoyt and put Paschal back in center.

Sherdel's first pitch was a strike and the crowd roared, thinking that a good omen. Paschal fouled to catcher Smith for the first out. Koenig then singled to left, bringing up the Babe. Sherdel got Ruth to ground to Bottomley at first, who touched the base and then threw to Maranville at second to tag the runner for the third out. The partial Cards' fans stood up and cheered loudly for Sherdel and his handling of Ruth. The Cards failed to score in the bottom of the first and Sherdel again returned to the hill. He pitched carefully to Gehrig and walked him. No damage occurred as Sherdel succeeded in retiring the next three batters.

Both teams continued to put zeroes on the scoreboard until the Cardinals came to the plate in the bottom of the third. Orsatti led off with a double to center. Andy High then bunted, safely advancing Orsatti to third. Next, Frisch hit a sacrifice fly to center, scoring Orsatti with a lead run. No more runs scored. Cardinals 1, Yankees 0.

The Yankees were not to be denied. In the fourth, Sherdel made the mistake of offering Ruth an inside fastball over the plate, which the Babe promptly hit over the right-field pavilion for his first home run of the Series. No more runs scored. Cardinals 1, Yankees 1.

St. Louis came right back in the bottom of the fourth. Earl Smith singled for the second time in the game. Maranville then grounded to Lazzeri at short, who threw to second for the force on Smith. In an attempt for a double play, Koenig threw wild to first and Maranville advanced to second. Next, Rabbit got a good lead off second and Hoyt tried to pick him off, but Hoyt's throw went into centerfield and Maranville scored the Cards' second run. Cardinals 2, Yankees 1.

Sherdel stopped a New York rally in the top of the fifth. After two singles and a pop-out, Ruth grounded out weakly to Bottomley. Next, Sherdel intentionally walked Gehrig to load the bases. Meusel then hit a hard grounder to Maranville, who made a backhand stop and flipped to Frisch for the third out. The Cardinals maintained a one-run advantage. Tensions mounted as both Hoyt and Sherdel pitched well until the Yankee seventh.

The seventh inning began innocently enough for the Cardinals' southpaw. Koenig popped to Maranville for the first out. That brought Ruth to the plate. Sherdel gained two quick strikes on the Babe. Then he tried to throw a third strike past Ruth. This time, the pitch was disallowed. Umpire Pfirman claimed he had called time-out, even though Ruth was in the batter's box. All four umpires, the Cardinals' infield, and Ruth gathered around the mound as tempers flared. The quick pitch had been legal during the National League season, but not in the American League. It had been decided before the Series began that the pitch could not be used. Bill Sherdel knew this, and didn't believe it was a quick pitch. He was highly upset that he hadn't gotten the strikeout—so much so that it affected his next deliveries to the plate. He threw two balls and then the Babe smashed his second home run of the day over the right-field pavilion. Two pitches later, Gehrig followed with his own homer on top of the right-field pavilion. That was Gehrig's fourth home run of the Series, tying Ruth's four in 1926. It also gave Gehrig a new record for driving in nine runs in a Series. Next, Meusel hit a single past the mound and McKechnie replaced Sherdel with Alexander. As Sherdel walked slowly from the mound to the dugout, the entire Cardinals' side of the ballpark stood up and applauded his efforts. Reporter William Allen of the *St. Louis Post-Dispatch* reported, "No St. Louis pitcher ever received a better demonstration than Sherdel when he left the game in the seventh inning."[19]

The Big Show 269

Most of the St. Louis players take part in the argument with the umpires over Sherdel's "quick return" pitch to Ruth in the seventh inning. Ruth, in the foreground, seems to be the least concerned.

Argument about Sherdel's controversial quick pitch
—*St. Louis Post-Dispatch*, October 10, 1928

After the game, Cards' owner Sam Breadon would comment on Pfirman's call. "That unfair decision by umpire Pfirman nullified a smart and nervy play. It was a legal delivery. Ruth was in the box and Sherdel took his windup and pitched a ball right over the plate. That [call] was enough to rattle Sherdel. He put one over a little too good and Ruth tied the score. Sherdel is one of the smartest pitchers in the game and Pfirman's mistake was in thinking that Sherdel didn't know what he was doing."[20] Later that night, Ruth would say, "Did you hear Sherdel moan when I hit that one?"[21]

Now, Alex pitched to Lazzeri, who lofted a ball to centerfielder Orsatti, who dropped the ball. Robertson then grounded to Frisch, and Meusel beat the throw to the plate. The Yankees had scored four runs to put them ahead for good—Yankees 5, Cardinals 2.

In the Yankees' eighth, they added two insurance runs off Alexander. Durst hit a homer into the right-field pavilion and then Ruth clouted his third four-bagger of the day into the same area, tying his 1926 record—Yankees 7, Cardinals 2.

Hoyt surrendered one harmless run in the bottom of the ninth. Smith collected his third hit of the game and McKechnie put in Pepper Martin to run. Martin stole second and third with no play on him. Holm batted for Alexander and grounded to Koenig with Pepper scoring the Redbirds' final run—Yankees 7, Cardinals 3. That was it. The St. Louis club that thought it might sweep the Series was swept instead. The New York Yankees were champions of the world. They had now swept two World Series in a row. Ruth and Gehrig were the reason the Yankees had won. Babe Ruth had hit .625—the highest average ever in a Series—and Lou Gehrig had batted .545. The team's batting average, meanwhile, was a mediocre .267.

Later, reporter Harry Brundidge asked Babe Ruth what he and Bill Sherdel had talked about during the argument about the quick pitch.

Ruth told Sherdel, "The National is a helluva league."

Sherdel replied, "It sure is."

Then Ruth said, "Put one right here, and I'll knock it out of the park for you."

Brundidge asked Ruth what happened next. He replied, "He did and I did."[22]

To understand why the Cardinals lost, you need only look at the Series' batting averages of their heavy hitters—Frisch .231, Bottomley .214, Hafey .200, Harper .111, and Douthit .091. As a team, the Cards had hit a meager .206. Only Maranville (.308) and High (.294) had batted well.

Babe Ruth wrote about his friend Bill Sherdel. "The tough-luck champion of the Series is Willie Sherdel. Unless I had seen with my own eyes, I wouldn't have believed it possible for any pitcher to pitch four such games as he has pitched against the Yankees and lose them all."[23]

Grover Alexander added these comments about his teammate: "I'm sorry that Sherdel couldn't have won his game. He surely deserved better luck. He has pitched great ball in four World Series games and all he has to show for it is four defeats in the book. But he's a great pitcher despite those bad breaks, and if we played the Yankees in another Series starting tomorrow, he'd be my pick as the best bet to beat them."[24]

Even though the Cardinals lost, Bill Sherdel and his teammates each received $4,181—a new record for a losing team. In today's money, that would be $58,353 for each player.

On October 10, Bill and Marguerite Sherdel headed east from St. Louis on the "Spirit of St. Louis" train. They arrived at their Pennsylvania home a day later. Bill was looking forward to a relaxing off-season filled with hunting and family time. His local fans had other ideas. The residents of McSherrystown and Hanover honored their favorite southpaw with a third testimonial dinner in Hanover's Hotel Richard McAllister on October 30. Over 100 supporters attended the event. J. Vincent Jamison, Jr., president of the Blue Ridge League, served as master of ceremonies. Former teammate Cliff Heathcote was one of the speakers.

After the World Series, Breadon stated that there would be changes to the Redbirds' lineup for 1929. He would not be specific, but within a few days, Tommy Thevenow was no longer a Cardinal. In a move that was not unexpected, Breadon had traded 1926 World Series hero Thevenow to Philadelphia.

Manager Bill McKechnie had indicated before the Series that he was not anxious to remain in baseball much longer. He'd said, "I wouldn't go through another race like the National League race of the past season for a million dollars."²⁵ That led to speculation that McKechnie would resign over the winter.

On November 21, Breadon removed that speculation and announced that former Redbirds' outfielder Billy Southworth would replace Bill McKechnie as the Cards' manager. McKechnie agreed to stay with the organization as manager of the Rochester club in the International League. Southworth had played for St. Louis in 1926 and 1927 before moving to manage this same Rochester team in 1928. Southworth was a playing manager—hitting .350 and leading Rochester to the International League championship—and he hoped to be a playing manager in St. Louis also. Southworth was known as a strict disciplinarian, and at thirty-four years old, would be the youngest manager in the National League. He would now become the fifth St. Louis manager in five years.

1929 Cards' manager Billy Southworth
—Coulson collection

For the third time in four years, a Cardinal was named the National League Most Valuable Player. First baseman Jim Bottomley won the honor in 1928, with a .325 batting average, thirty-one home runs, twenty triples, and forty-two doubles. Bill Sherdel was among the Cards' named for honorable mention.

Later, the Cardinals acquired promising shortstop Charley Gelbert from their affiliate in Rochester. Breadon gave up outfielder Ray Blades, an unnamed pitcher, and cash to get Gelbert. Experts thought Gelbert would be a superstar and might have been worth $150,000 to any other major-league club.[26]

In a surprising move in early December, the Cardinals sold shortstop Rabbit Maranville and outfielder George Harper to the Boston Braves. Both veteran players had been instrumental in the Cards' 1928 pennant chase. Maranville had sparked the team's comeback in August with his great play at shortstop, but his age had shown and he had become tired as the season grew longer. Harper had added a badly needed left-handed bat to the lineup.

In other moves, the Cardinals sent Flint Rhem and Pepper Martin to their Houston affiliate. Breadon added new coaches Earle "Greasy" Neale and Charles "Gabby" Street to assist manager Southworth. It seemed to be a St. Louis pattern to bring in coaches who were qualified to manage the club if needed. Neale had played for the Reds but would be recognized later in the Pro Football Hall of Fame. Street had many years' experience as a catcher in Washington and then as a successful minor-league manager.

It seemed Breadon had been true to his prediction. The St. Louis owner was making many changes. Only time would tell if they would bring another pennant to the Missouri city.

CHAPTER TWENTY-ONE

The Roaring Twenties would come to an end in October 1929, sparked by the stock market crash on Black Thursday when the Dow Jones Industrial Average dropped by more than 12%. And the losses would continue the following Monday with another 13% decline. Then Black Tuesday would signal more losses and the start of the Great Depression. It would be many years before the country would recover.

In other news that year, Herbert Hoover would become the thirty-first president and Admiral Richard Byrd would make his first flight to the South Pole. The first telephone would be installed in the White House and the Atlantic City Convention Center would open. Louie Marx would introduce the world to the wonders of the yo-yo. The first US roller coaster would be built. Edwin Lowe would introduce the game of Bingo. Buck Rogers, Tarzan, and Popeye would make their first appearances in the funny papers.

In mid-January, special correspondent for the *St. Louis Post-Dispatch* Davis Walsh was asked to make his predictions for the new baseball season. He picked the Cubs and Giants to fight for the championship, with the Pirates in third. Walsh predicted that the Cardinals would finish a distant fourth in the National League. He added this about the Cards: "They have torn up half their infield and thrown it away. This Gelbert may be all they say he is, but the chances are he isn't quite that good and, anyhow, at least one infield position must suffer no matter how you figure it. The pitching has helped considerably in carrying this outfit a long way, and it is about due to call the pitching a career. Psychologically, their showing in the World Series will encourage the Cards almost not at all. I think they are shot."[1]

The Cards announced that they would be taking only twenty-seven players to training camp at Avon Park that year. That was the smallest group of players ever in the St. Louis camp. Branch Rickey said that he didn't want to spend any time on recruits. He wanted as much focus as possible on the ten pitchers and seventeen position players who would make up much of the new club.

Interestingly, National League president John Heydler proposed that the National League teams use ten players in the lineup for 1929 games. An extra hitter would bat for the pitcher. That idea was shot down by the owners and it would be another forty-four years before the American League would decide to adopt a designated hitter in 1973. To this day, the National League has not.[2]

The first group of Cardinals arrived in Avon Park and began their initial workout on February 27. Manager Southworth proved to be a tough taskmaster. A typical workout lasted four hours. Bill Sherdel joined the club for the second day of training and, by March 3, he was pitching to batters.

Southworth scheduled fewer exhibition games. He felt there was more value in practice than in games. The Cardinals played nineteen games against major-league clubs. Their most important opponent was the Yankees. St. Louis looked good, and they defeated the Yanks. Alexander and Sherdel gained some revenge for the World Series loss by combining to defeat the Yankees, 10–2, in a five-hitter.

In mid-March, Bill Sherdel was slightly injured when he was riding in a car driven by pitcher Syl Johnson. Luckily, there were no serious injuries, although Johnson's car was demolished. Branch Rickey must have thought about the serious accident in 1919 that destroyed his pitching staff and probably cost the Cardinals a chase for the pennant. Bill Sherdel was in that accident, also.

When the Cards broke camp, they played exhibition games against minor-league clubs as they headed to St. Louis to face the Browns in their annual spring series. In the first game with their city rivals, Southworth pitched his Big Three—Alexander, Sherdel, and Haines—for three innings each and they won, 2–1, surrendering only six hits. They were ready for the opener.

Almost every sportswriter predicted the club would finish in fourth place. Breadon, Rickey, and Southworth felt differently. They believed the club was stronger than the team that had won the pennant the previous year. Gone from that year's championship squad was Rhem, Maranville, Harper, Blades, and Martin. Of the new hopefuls, only Charley Gelbert would make an impact. Now it was time to see who would be correct about the Cardinals' season.

Opening day was April 16 in Cincinnati. Southworth picked forty-two-year-old Alexander to start the campaign. "Old Pete" delivered a 5–2 victory, allowing only five hits. He appeared to be a young forty-year-old. Hafey hit a home run and added a single. Gelbert collected two singles and played outstanding defense.

Bill Sherdel was handed the ball for the second game with Jimmy Wilson behind the plate. It was a rough outing for Sherdel. He allowed twelve hits and seven runs in six innings and the Cards lost. Then the Cards won the next two games of the opening series and the new St. Louis squad suddenly looked like it could challenge for another pennant.

The team moved on to Chicago to meet Rogers Hornsby and the Cubs. After losing the first two games, Bill Sherdel pitched the Cards to a 9–6 victory in the final game of the series. Proudly, he also collected a triple and two singles in four plate appearances.

The Cardinals returned home for the St. Louis opener on April 26, a game that had been delayed several days because of rain. St. Louis celebrated its 1928 National League championship with a parade to centerfield where the pennant was raised. Then Jess Haines pitched the Cards to another win over the Reds to complete the happy day.

Southworth's club played well through the rest of April and May, moving up and down the standings. As May ended, the Cardinals were riding high in first place ahead of the Pirates and the Cubs. The Cards' pitching staff was led by Jess Haines, who ran his regular-season winning streak to fourteen games. Syl Johnson added a strong arm to the starting staff of Alexander, Sherdel, and Mitchell. Johnson ran off a string of twenty-six scoreless innings.

Jim Bottomley received his Most Valuable Player medal and $1,000 in cash during a celebration before a Phillies game on June 8. He was the third Cardinal in four years to win the award.

In June, the Cardinals dropped to the fourth spot in the league. They had been winning early in the season because they'd been playing the weaker clubs. The Cards were still hitting, but the pitching was the problem. Alexander was ailing with "lumbago," or lower back pain. He was missing starts and, for those games he did start, he had to be removed after a few innings. Reporters were being kind in describing Alex's problems as non-alcoholic. The loss of Alexander was extremely damaging to the rotation. Haines and Sherdel were getting pounded. Mitchell was now the staff ace. To make matters worse, Branch Rickey's farm system was not producing any quality pitchers. Top new hurler Johnson had come from another club. The only good homegrown player added to the roster that year was Gelbert.

John Wray wrote in his *St. Louis Post-Dispatch* column on July 1, "The Cardinals' situation is now more than acute. It hurts. In fact, it appears that the entire machine is letting down, due to the weakening of that universal joint—the pitching defense. There is little doubt, on the record of the club for the past two or three weeks, that its pitching is in its second childhood. And without pitching, there is nothing to be done but weep. . . . The Cardinal farms do not appear to have any replacements."[3]

Reporter James Gould asked Branch Rickey what they might do about their situation. "What CAN we do? We will go ahead and do our best with what we have. I really think the team will recover soon. Alexander will rejoin the club shortly in a much-improved condition. We have at this time nine pitchers who are physically able to take their turn, and I can't conceive that they will all continue to do badly."[4]

The major leagues were concerned about the number of home runs. On July 18, National League president John Heydler ordered the umpires to rub down all balls with soil before putting them into play. It was thought that would reduce the home runs and give the pitchers a better chance to compete with the lively baseball.

The Cardinals' situation only worsened in July. By July 23, St. Louis was still in fourth place. They'd now lost more games than they'd won. The club returned home after a disastrous eastern road trip whose failure was widely ascribed to the pitching aces. Bill Sherdel had been pounded for over eight runs per nine innings. Even worse, Haines had surrendered ten runs per game. Not much better, Mitchell had given up six. Alexander was still missing.

It was now that Sam Breadon announced that he'd made a mistake the previous winter when he'd removed Bill McKechnie as manager. The Cards' owner returned Billy Southworth to Rochester and brought McKechnie back to manage the Redbirds. Breadon stated:

> "McKechnie's record shows that he had been a success wherever he served. He won a pennant with the Pittsburgh Pirates before we obtained him as an assistant to Bob O'Farrell during the 1927 season. Then in 1928 he won a pennant for us and this year he had the Rochester 'farm' in first place in the International League race.
>
> "You can't get away from that record and now I realize that I took the World Series last fall too much to heart. I still believe that we have the best ball club in the National League and I think that under McKechnie we will get back into the pennant race."[5]

Until McKechnie arrived, coach Gabby Street took over the club. Breadon also sent coach Greasy Neale to Rochester to assist Southworth. The players had complained that all Neale wanted to talk about was football.

With McKechnie back, the Cards ended the month still in fourth place. Realistically, it would be very hard for St. Louis to challenge for the lead. Although if the pitching could just improve, anything was possible. Certainly, the hitting was great with an incredible team batting average of .298. Eight players were hitting over .300.

Bill Sherdel's young son, Bill, Jr., had surgery during July and the Cardinals allowed the pitcher to remain with him until he recovered. When Bill returned to the lineup in August, he continued to struggle. He worked hard to regain his form, shagging flies every day and hitting to the outfield to get into better condition.

On August 14, reporter Roy Stockton chatted with Bill McKechnie about the club's problems. The Cards' manager said:

> "I would not undertake to determine what caused Haines and Sherdel to crack the way they have done, but the failure of the pitching staff, of course, is the big reason why the team slipped to fourth place. Mysteriously enough, Haines and Sherdel both have lost their control.

You know what that means to a pitcher. People make the mistake of remarking that Haines and Sherdel haven't their usual stuff. That's all wrong. Their curves are as good as ever and both have shown me their normal speed. But they can't put the ball where they want it. That's the cause of their trouble. . . .

"I can only guess what caused Haines and Sherdel to go wrong. Probably they pitched a couple of games when they were not in their best form. Or perhaps a few batters happened to lambast well-pitched balls. The result was defeat and loss of confidence. Haines and Sherdel began to try harder and soon they were trying too hard. They go out there on the hill and worry about their control and strive hard to get the ball exactly where they want it and they're all keyed up so that they can't control their muscles.

"I expect both pitchers to improve steadily and to be at their top form before the end of this road campaign. . . .

"And don't let anybody tell you that our pitching staff is through. Haines and Sherdel have many years of great pitching ahead of them and they'll both start winning consistently again as soon as they regain their confidence in themselves and pitch with the free motion and poise they showed in 1928."[6]

In late August, manager McKechnie sent Alexander home in disgrace for repeatedly breaking training rules. Alexander had been warned in Philadelphia on the eastern road trip, but he continued his activities in New York and McKechnie felt it was time to get tough with this team. It was a sad situation. Earlier in the month, Alexander had joyously celebrated winning his three-hundred-and-seventy-third game.

To make matters even worse, "Old Pete" had never saved any money. Alexander was one of the four greatest pitchers in the game. The other three—Mathewson, Young, and Johnson—had become wealthy and successful. But not Grover Alexander. Forlornly, "Alex" stated as he left the club, "Well, I came out of Nebraska without a dime and it looks like I am going back there the same way."

Owner Sam Breadon felt badly for the pitcher who had led the Cardinals to the 1926 World Series championship and the 1928 National League pennant. He announced, "Alexander has done too much for this club and for the City of St. Louis, to be shuffled out into the cold. I am sending him home for the remainder of the season on full pay. He is not even under suspension. The winter will take care of the situation satisfactorily in some way, I am sure. In the meantime, he can rest and build up. Alexander has been a great pitcher and a likeable fellow and I feel that he still can be of service to us."[7]

August ended with St. Louis still holding tight to fourth place. McKechnie's club continued to hit with a .296 team batting average. Syl Johnson was now leading the staff.

In the final month of the season, McKechnie replaced his "Big Three" starters with young hurlers Syl Johnson, "Wild Bill" Hallahan, and Fred Frankhouse. The Cards needed to give them experience and decide if these new pitchers could be the foundation for the 1930 club. Alexander had gone to Nebraska while Sherdel and Haines were pitching mostly in relief.

On September 25, New York Yankees' manager Miller Huggins passed away at age fifty-one. Huggins was still managing the Yankees at the time and had checked into a hospital about a week earlier with a bacterial skin infection. The infection spread quickly throughout his body and he died. The Yankees organization and all the baseball world were shocked by his death.

Babe Ruth stated:

> "The finest little fellow in the world has left us. It seems hard to believe that Huggins is dead and that he'll not be around to guide our footsteps on the ball field.
>
> "We were all shocked when we heard the news at the ballpark. Yes, I even noticed tears in a few eyes. A couple crept down my face.
>
> "He was a wonderful fellow and one of the smartest little managers in the country."[8]

The 1929 season turned out to be the year of the Chicago Cubs. When the club added Rogers Hornsby to the roster, they determined their fate. The Cubs finished first, followed by the Pirates and the Giants. Just as many had predicted, the Cardinals finished in fourth place, a distant twenty games back.

As expected, the Cardinals' pitchers did not have great statistics. Johnson (13–7) and Haines (13–10) led the staff, followed by Sherdel (10–15) and

Alexander (9–8). Bill Sherdel appeared in thirty-three games, started twenty-two, and surrendered a high 5.93 runs allowed per nine innings.

The failure of the Cards' top hurlers brought to memory a prophetic article by John Wray that had been published a year earlier in the *St. Louis Post-Dispatch*.

> Pitchers can carry on only so far. There are not warning signs to indicate that the splendid aggregation of veteran Cardinal pitching arms will shortly be just a collection of useless soupbones.
>
> The fact that all of the Cardinal pitchers of 1928 were very slow to attain form is an indication that the time is near when the club management must look for younger arms. If the Big Four [Alexander, Haines, Sherdel, Mitchell] collapsed simultaneously, the club today would drop like a broken elevator.
>
> Sherdel should be good for a number of years. The others may or may not be. The chances are against their continuance as aces.
>
> And the Cardinals have not as yet shown adequate replacements, despite the numerous and productive baseball farms.[9]

The St. Louis batters had hit for a .295 team batting average. Seven players had batted over the magic .300 line. Bottomley and Hafey had tied for the St. Louis home run lead with twenty-nine each. Highly rated rookie shortstop Charley Gelbert had batted .262 and the home-run-hitting pitcher Bill Sherdel had claimed a modest .229 average.

Right after the Cardinals' season ended in early October, Breadon granted Bill McKechnie permission to seek a long-term managing position with another team. The Cards' owner had offered him a one-year contract with a substantial salary increase to lead the 1930 Cardinals, but McKechnie wanted a longer commitment. It didn't take long for him to accept a four-year deal with the Boston Braves. St. Louis would now seek its seventh manager in six years.

The Chicago Cubs met the Philadelphia Athletics in the 1929 World Series. It was Joe McCarthy, Rogers Hornsby, and Hack Wilson against Connie Mack, Lefty Grove, and Jimmie Foxx. The A's won the World Series in five games.

In the voting for the Most Valuable Player award, Rogers Hornsby was selected for the second time. It was interesting to think what the Cardinals could have accomplished if Hornsby had remained in St. Louis. He was truly an outstanding hitter, but difficult to deal with. Hornsby had now played with four different clubs in four seasons.

Owner Breadon wasted little time in interviewing and selecting the next Cardinals' manager. On October 31, Breadon introduced Charles "Gabby" Street as the new St. Louis skipper. Street had a long history in baseball. He had caught Walter Johnson for four years with Washington. Then he had managed for nine years in the minors before joining the 1929 Cards as a coach. Once again, Breadon signed his manager to a one-year deal. He had this to say about his new leader: "Street is just the type of man we have needed. He is a man who knows the game from his long experience as a player and minor-league manager. He is a hustler and one who will have the respect of his men. He showed me in 1929 that he would not stand for any foolishness. He is well liked by the players and should get the Cardinals back where they belong—in the thick of the pennant fight. I am very well pleased to have such a man as Street as manager and I know he is tickled with the appointment."[10] Street was probably most famous for catching a baseball dropped from the Washington Monument in 1908.

The new manager was interviewed at his home. "I'm not going to be tough, but I've been through the mill and I know the importance of discipline and I'm going to be foreman on my ball club, make no mistake about that. I'll be the boss and I'll run the club. We don't need much help in the way of players, and I believe I have a great chance to win a pennant in my first year as a big-league manager."[11]

New Cards' manager Gabby Street
—Coulson collection

Meanwhile, a year-end column by Roy Stockton described Bill Sherdel's situation.

> Sherdel's trouble probably was due to lack of condition and to the fact that he was worked out of turn and thrown off his stride.
>
> Wee William realized his trouble before the campaign ended and, by hard work, managed to regain approximately his old winning form. He undoubtedly will work earnestly at training camp and probably will be an ace again.[12]

On a sad note, the St. Louis Cardinals sent Grover Cleveland Alexander to the Phillies for several minor players on December 11. Breadon thought that Alexander might overcome his problems better in the city where he had gained so much fame years earlier. So began the dismantling of the Cards' pitching staff that had led the Redbirds to two pennants, one close second, and one world title.

CHAPTER TWENTY-TWO

In 1930, the "Lone Ranger" and "Death Valley Days" would debut on the radio. "Happy Days Are Here Again" by Benny Mereoff would hit number one on the music charts, an ironic choice given the stock market crash. Clarence Birdseye would develop a method to quick-freeze foods, the first red and green traffic lights would be installed in New York City, and a bakery executive would invent an enduring food favorite called a Hostess Twinkie. "Blondie" would debut in the comic strips.

In sports, Gallant Fox would win horse racing's triple crown. German Max Schmeling would defeat Jack Sharkey to win the heavyweight boxing title.

Sam Breadon announced that the Cardinals would be leaving Avon Park for spring training. He had asked city leaders for certain guarantees around that training ground that the city could not deliver, and so the club was returning to Bradenton. For several years, the Bradenton field had already been considered one of the best in Florida, but the people wanted to make it even better for the return of the Cardinals. They imported rich, black soil for the baseball infield.[1]

Over the winter, McSherrystown residents had the opportunity to see Cardinals' personnel at the Sherdel home on Ridge Avenue. Shortstop Charley Gelbert, a Pennsylvania resident, stopped to visit and probably go hunting with his pal Sherdel. Later, in February, Branch Rickey, Sam Breadon, and their wives, along with Gabby Street, spent several days with the Sherdels before the group left for spring training. Too bad there was no record of what that group may have discussed with their host. The Sherdels were scheduled to leave for Florida two weeks later.

The Redbirds invited fifty-one players to camp that year. That was the largest group ever in Cards' spring training. The previous year, the St. Louis club had had the smallest squad, but that didn't seem to work out. The team scheduled seventeen exhibition games—fifteen with major-league clubs.

The players began arriving in Bradenton in the beginning of March. Bill Sherdel landed there on March 2. Roy Stockton wrote:

> Bill Sherdel motored from his home in Pennsylvania and appeared to be in unusually good condition. . . .
> "How many left-handers in camp?" he asked, and when told that five southpaws would be seeking jobs, he said he guessed it was up to him to work hard if he wanted to stay on the payroll.
> "And I already have started to get in shape," he added."[2]

The Cardinals began to play exhibition games by early March. They played the world champion Athletics and beat them three of four games. One of the bright spots in camp was infielder Earl "Sparky" Adams. Adams had played with the Redbirds earlier in his career before being traded to the Pirates. Rickey now claimed him back on waivers. Street hoped to play Adams—whom catcher Jimmy Wilson described as a sure fielder and dangerous little batter—on second and move Frisch to third base.

In spring training, Stockton commented about manager Street and his players. "The writer might add that he has never seen a manager who stood higher in the regard of his players than does old Gabby. They respect him but they do more than that. It could be called affection and if the Cardinals don't win it won't be his fault."[3]

Street admitted to the press that he needed one or two more starting pitchers in addition to Haines, Sherdel, Mitchell, and Johnson. Flint Rhem was back in camp and looking good. Bill Hallahan was getting a lot of work. His nickname was "Wild Bill" for a reason. Notoriously wild on the mound, Hallahan had great pitches but had trouble finding the plate. Branch Rickey stated that he must be pitched to gain control, so that's what the Cardinals were doing.

Sherdel, meanwhile, was having some challenges of his own. He had come to camp in better shape than ever, but he was getting hit hard when on the mound. The Cardinals were worried about him. Stockton wrote about it in the *Post-Dispatch*.

Bill Sherdel's failure to show his best pitching skill has been one of few disappointments of the Cardinal spring training trip. Nobody can say that Wee William hasn't been working. He came to camp in unusually good physical condition minus the watermelon that he has been carrying to Florida of recent years. He has shagged flies and run around the park and engaged in pepper games and he has pitched and pitched and pitched.

But Sherdel has not regained his mastery of the curve, fast ball, slow ball, and cross fire. It may be that he has reached the class of the veterans who require the full training period and a week or two of the regular campaign to reach his best pitching form. That is the hopeful way Gabby Street and his Cardinals are looking at the situation. But it is a fact that Bill's showing in exhibition games thus far has not been encouraging....

Sherdel is a courageous athlete. He won't give up. He'll be out at the park early today and he'll toil through the two workouts. And perhaps he'll find what is causing his trouble. The batters are clubbing his slow ball to all fields and they are warming the fences with his fast one.[4]

Several days later, manager Street announced to the press that he had remedied Sherdel's weakness. "Sherdel has had some trouble, but I believe we found out his fault in our last workout. He was not going through with his pitch. He was releasing his grip on the ball before he had gone through with his delivery and the result was he was outside the strike zone most of the time. I noticed what he was doing while warming him up Saturday afternoon, and after he changed and followed through, he pitched thirteen straight strikes."[5]

Babe Ruth made his annual prediction for the National League. The Sultan of Swat picked the Cubs to repeat with the Pirates, Reds, and Giants behind Chicago in the first division. Ruth slotted the 1930 Cardinals in fifth place.[6] Most sportswriters picked St. Louis to finish in fourth, again.

In April, rumors circulated that the Cardinals wanted pitcher Burleigh Grimes. Grimes had spent the previous season with the Pirates, but had failed to sign a 1930 contract. He wanted more money. Pittsburgh had traded Grimes to the Braves and now Breadon was discussing a trade with Boston manager McKechnie.

With spring training over, manager Street analyzed his pitching staff. He listed Haines, Johnson, Rhem, and Hallahan as dependable starters. Sherdel and Mitchell were listed as doubtful. Apparently, Street had not solved Sherdel's problem and the pitcher was still struggling to find his 1928 form.[7]

On April 15, the Cardinals opened their 1930 campaign against the National League pennant-winning Cubs in Chicago. Both teams were optimistic about their chances. Street tapped Rhem for the opener. The Cubs prevailed, as the Cards used five pitchers. Bill Sherdel pitched the ninth inning, retiring the Cubs in order with no hits and no runs.

Sherdel got his first start of the year on April 19 against the Pirates. He surrendered three early runs, and then pitched scoreless ball into the tenth inning. In the extra stanza, he gave up a lead-off triple and then Street brought in Johnson. Sherdel wanted to stay in the game, but Gabby thought he had pitched enough. The Cards lost, 5–4.

Street handed Sherdel the ball again on April 25 against the Pirates. He was hit hard for six innings and St. Louis lost. Hallahan and Johnson were now the aces of the staff. Clarence Mitchell got hurt sliding into second and would be out for two weeks. By the end of April, the Cards were in fifth place.

As May began, the Redbirds lost four straight to Brooklyn. By May 7, the club was in the National League cellar. Then they started an unbelievable winning streak that placed the St. Louis squad in first place fifteen days later. Street's team won seventeen of eighteen games before losing a series to Chicago at month-end. Pitching had greatly improved. Hallahan, Johnson, Haines, and Grabowski were in the starting rotation. Street was also getting outstanding relief work from Sherdel and several others. Breadon traded Clarence Mitchell to the Giants.

Bill Sherdel looked like his old self when he relieved in a game against the Braves on May 9. Johnson had started the game, but was driven from the mound in the fourth inning after surrendering seven hits. Sherdel entered with one out in the fourth and allowed only three hits over the next five-and-two-thirds innings, while striking out five and walking only one. On May

20, Sherdel injured his side while sliding into second. He was ordered to rest for several days, but six days later, he picked up his second straight victory, although he had to be removed after five innings. He was still ailing.

The pitching in this revised 1930 scene was much better now, but the hitting was outstanding. Street's team was batting an incredible .325 with eleven players over .300.

In other news, former Cardinals' star Rogers Hornsby broke his left ankle in a game against St. Louis. The Cubs' star would be lost until mid-August and the Cubs' hopes of another pennant would also disappear.

The first half of June was very difficult for the Missouri team. Frisch had been out for an extended time. A runner had slid into the bag and spiked him while he was covering the base. He had a badly wounded right ankle. Gelbert had pulled a tendon and had been missing since the end of May. The worst loss of all was once again Chick Hafey. Hafey's eyes had gotten worse and he was hospitalized with terrible sinus problems. The club's leading home-run hitter—with ten home runs and a .326 batting average—was out indefinitely. The Cardinals had now slumped and were in danger of dropping out of the first division. Something had to be done to save the season.

Normally, the major leagues set June 15 as the trade deadline. No team could trade a player beyond that date unless the player passed through waivers. Waivers allowed other clubs to claim the player for a specific nominal price. In 1930, June 15 was a Sunday, so the deadline was extended until midnight on June 16. It took until that final hour for Sam Breadon and Boston Braves' owner Emil Fuchs to hammer out an important trade. For several months, the Cardinals had been letting the world know that they wanted spitball veteran Burleigh Grimes. Many different player combinations were rumored during that time. Fuchs wanted to unload Grimes because of his high salary. Finally, Breadon announced that St. Louis had acquired Grimes in exchange for pitchers Fred Frankhouse and Bill Sherdel.

Grimes, like Hornsby, seemed to wear out his welcome wherever he played. He had begun his major-league career with the Pirates in 1916. Since then, the nearly thirty-seven-year-old Grimes had hurled for Brooklyn, New York, Pittsburgh again, and now Boston. Grimes had won 227 games and lost 174, for a winning percentage of .554. The grizzled old veteran had won more than twenty games in five different seasons. He was one of the last pitchers allowed to throw a spitball.

Manager Gabby Street announced, "I believe we have made a deal that will make us a more dangerous pennant contender. Grimes is a great pitcher. He can work every four days and win his share of games and he always is ready and eager to serve in the relief role. I believe Grimes will win a dozen games and save a half a dozen more for us and that he will do more for us than Sherdel and Frankhouse could have done."

Roy Stockton interviewed Bill Sherdel. "So, I am leaving St. Louis. I don't know how to act. I've pitched for St. Louis for thirteen years. And now I'm with Boston. Well, I guess I will get the Boston viewpoint, but I believe I'll be pulling for the Cardinals, except when I pitch against them, and I hope I draw Grimes for my opponent the first time I hit the old home town."

Fred Frankhouse told Stockton, "I was hoping we'd land Grimes, but I didn't even think that I might be sent away. I've always thought of baseball in terms of St. Louis and I suppose it will be difficult to get the alien slant on affairs. Sam Breadon always has been mighty fair to me and I hate to leave the old town. I hope the Cardinals win the pennant. But maybe I'll get a chance to work more regularly in Boston."

Sam Breadon commented, "I have been eager to see Grimes on the Cardinal roster, but it is with real regret that I see Sherdel leave the Cardinals. He always has been a loyal worker. He didn't have a very good record in 1929, but he worked hard to regain physical condition and this spring indicated that he was ready to be one of the game's greatest pitchers again. I hope that he does well with the Braves and that he enjoys many good seasons in the league."[8]

Massachusetts newspapers had a different opinion about the trade. The *Fitchburg Sentinel* wrote, "Grimes was traded by the Braves to the St. Louis Cardinals for pitchers Frankhouse and Bill Sherdel. That is a trade in which it seems the Braves got the better of the deal. Grimes had been of no value to the Boston team since it took over his Pittsburgh contract. He may be better at St. Louis, but was not effective in a Boston uniform. Sherdel is one of the veterans who should be able to help the Braves while Frankhouse may develop into a comer."[9]

Braves' manager Bill McKechnie said, "Sherdel, who is thirty-five, has been twelve years in the heat of St. Louis and surely will profit by a change. He is a crafty left-hander, usually with great control and a famous slow ball."[10]

The Cardinals ended a disastrous road trip in this stretch, losing fifteen of twenty games, but they remained hopeful. With the addition of Grimes and the return of its injured stars—Frisch, Gelbert, and Hafey—St. Louis still had time to turn its season around. But it would attempt to do so for the first time without "Wee Willie."

CHAPTER TWENTY-THREE

The Boston Braves had been a perennial losing franchise. They had managed only one winning season from 1900 to 1913, and many years had lost more than 100 games. Finally, in 1914, the Braves put together a memorable year. On July 4, 1914, Boston was in last place. But from July 6 through September 5, the club won forty-one games and lost only twelve. The miracle Braves won the National League pennant and were the only team ever to be in last place on July 4 and win a championship. Bill Sherdel's teammate Rabbit Maranville had been a member of that club. Since Sherdel had joined the Cardinals in 1918, the Boston Braves had finished in the first division only once, in 1921.

The Braves played their home games at Braves Field on the corner of Commonwealth Avenue and Babcock Street. When it was built in 1915, it was the largest concrete stadium of that era. Braves Field held a capacity of 40,000 fans and boasted the special feature of a trolley system leading to the park.

The current Braves' owner was Judge Emil Fuchs. He had purchased the team in 1923 and had placed Christy Mathewson in charge. Unfortunately, Mathewson had died a few years later and Fuchs had to run the club. He tried his best to place a winning club on the field, but he didn't have the finances to obtain and keep top players.

In 1930, Fuchs hired a winning manager—Bill McKechnie. McKechnie was willing to listen to trade proposals for any of his Braves. He wanted to build a winner. Future Hall-of-Famers George Sisler and Rabbit Maranville were there. McKechnie had a promising power-hitting outfielder named Wally Berger obtained from Los Angeles of the Pacific Coast League. The rest of the roster was a bunch of no-names. Of the hurlers, only Tom Zachary had been a star, with the Browns and Yankees.

Boston manager Bill McKechnie
—Coulson collection

At the time of the trade with the Cardinals, the Braves were two positions below fourth-place St. Louis in the standings. The day after the trade, Frankhouse and Sherdel joined their new club. Frankhouse entered the Braves' game with the Reds in the sixth inning, where he surrendered only two hits in three-and-a-third innings and gained a win.

Bill Sherdel got his wish to pitch against his former teammates on June 23, in St. Louis. He was hit hard and removed from the game for a pinch-hitter after the third inning. Later, the Braves won the game, 12–9. By the end of June, the Braves were only two games below .500 and had moved into fifth place.

During July, the Braves dropped back to sixth place. The team was batting .282, with Sisler (.326), Maranville (.307), and Berger (.304) leading the attack. Bill Sherdel got revenge against Flint Rhem and the Cardinals with a 5–4 complete-game victory on July 25. Four days later, Sherdel defeated league-leading Brooklyn and star hurler Dazzy Vance, 4–3, in ten innings.

On July 26, Boston held a Rabbit Maranville Day before a game with the Cardinals. Both teams showed appreciation for the wily veteran. Maranville received an automobile, a silver set, a humidor, and two rabbits, along with other gifts from the fans of both cities.

Babe Ruth hit his thirty-eighth home run of the season on August 1. He was twelve games and two weeks ahead of his 1927 pace when he hit a record-breaking sixty homers.

In early August, the Braves won five straight games from the lowly Phillies. Sherdel pitched two complete game victories in the series. The sixth-place Braves still trailed the fourth-place Cards. In St. Louis, there was little happiness. Jim Bottomley announced he wanted to be traded to Boston or Cincinnati. Several days later, he changed his mind.

Bill Sherdel in a Braves uniform
—Sherdel family

After losing 4–2 to his old Cardinal teammates on August 12, Bill Sherdel talked candidly about the St. Louis club.

> "When I was in a St. Louis uniform, I was prejudiced in the club's favor. But now I'm in a Boston uniform, and I look at all the clubs in the same way. And there's no question about it. The Cardinals ought to be six or seven games out in front with their pitching and their punch. I've pitched against all the clubs and now I've pitched several games against St. Louis. And there's no tougher batting order to face than the Cardinals'. Usually, there's a few men in the lineup that you don't have to worry about so much. But there's not a cripple among the St. Louis hitters, and a pitcher facing them has to bear down on every batter, with the exception of the pitcher, of course."[1]

By the end of August, the Braves were still mired in sixth place. Meanwhile, the Cardinals had started to move up the standings. Finally, Street's club advanced to third place and were only four-and-a-half games off the lead.

On the evening of September 2, Sherdel's old team, the Cardinals, played their first night game. Baseball had begun trying night baseball in the minor leagues that year and now the major leagues were testing it in exhibition games. The Cards took the field under the floodlights in Indianapolis against the class AA club. St. Louis won, 7–5. Cardinal players did not like the new experience. Jim Bottomley said, "I wouldn't like it if it was good. In two months, everybody would have rheumatism playing night baseball." Taylor Douthit commented, "Fly balls looked about like they do in the daytime, but I didn't have any low line drives hit at me either in the game or in practice. But they tell me night baseball makes your eyes bloodshot, and that's bad."[2]

Although Bill Sherdel was now pitching for the Braves, the real story in September was the winning streak of his old club in St. Louis. The Redbirds took over first place on September 13, capping an amazing run. Gabby Street's club had still been in fourth place and twelve games behind the leading Cubs on August 9. But after that, his squad won thirty-three games and lost only eight. They clinched the National League title on September 26. The difference for the Cards was the pitching of Bill Hallahan, Flint Rhem, and Burleigh Grimes during the previous two months.

Flint Rhem was an enigma. He had tremendous talent, but with that talent came problems. His problems showed up again on September 16 in New York. Rhem disappeared from the team for several hours. When he returned, he was inebriated. He told the story that he had been kidnapped by several men and forced to drink while his kidnappers threatened him with pistols. They warned him not to pitch against Brooklyn. In response, Rhem was placed under the watchful eyes of the trainer. He had won six straight games and was needed by Street for the stretch drive.[3]

Over the next winter, Rhem would be the subject of a skit staged by the New York chapter of the Baseball Writers' Association of America's annual dinner. The nonsensical skit was entitled "Kidnapped," and depicted what might have happened to Rhem when he disappeared the night before an important game with the Robins. It showed the pitcher held up in a hotel room and ended with Rhem drinking all his captors under the table.[4]

Bill McKechnie's Braves finished the 1930 season in sixth place, the highest finish for the Braves since their fifth position in 1925. With three more years on his contract, McKechnie was hopeful for the future. His pitching staff was led by Socks Seibold (15–16) and Tom Zachary (11–5). Sherdel (9–7) and Frankhouse (9–9) split their seasons with two clubs. Seibold was among the league leaders in complete games and innings pitched.

Outfielder Wally Berger looked like a future star with a .310 average and thirty-eight home runs. George Sisler hit .309 in his final year.

Babe Ruth did not continue his 1927 home-run pace. He finished with forty-nine and was runner-up to Hack Wilson of the Cubs with fifty-six.

The St. Louis Cardinals won the National League pennant for the third time in five years—each time with a different manager. Their opponents in the 1930 World Series were Connie Mack and his Philadelphia Athletics. For the second straight year, the Athletics won the championship—this time in six games. Bill and Marguerite Sherdel traveled to Philadelphia to see the first two games of the Series. He still supported the Cardinals.

It was at about this time that Bill Sherdel decided to capitalize on his popularity and to go into business for himself. In November, he opened Bill Sherdel's Café in the Colonnade Hotel Building on Main Street in McSherrystown. Residents patronized the café to spend time with their local hero and to see other visiting major leaguers such as Les Bell and Cliff

Heathcote of the Cubs and Charley Gelbert of the Cards. Sherdel's café adjoined Sure Putt, an indoor miniature golf course that was also a popular location. Plans were for Marguerite to run the café while Bill was playing ball.

Bill, Marguerite, and the children also spent a week in New York City with Bill's family during mid-December. After they returned home, Bill continued to run his café. The Sherdels entertained Mr. and Mrs. Les Bell and Mrs. Joseph McCarthy, wife of the New York Yankees' new manager, at the café on New Year's Eve.

CHAPTER TWENTY-FOUR

In 1931, the "Star-Spangled Banner" officially would become the American national anthem. The Empire State Building would open in New York City, Nevada would legalize gambling, and Alka-Seltzer would be introduced. Gangster Al Capone would be sentenced to eleven years in prison for tax evasion. Dupont would produce the first synthetic rubber. "Little Orphan Annie" would be broadcast on the radio and the "Dick Tracy" comic strip by Chester Gould would debut. Donald Duck would make his first appearance in a cartoon.

On October 20 in Spavinaw, Oklahoma, Mickey Charles Mantle would be born. Mantle, who would debut in major-league baseball in 1951, would become one of the most popular and greatest New York Yankees of all time. Considered the best switch-hitter ever, he would win baseball's triple crown in 1956, and become a member of the Hall of Fame and the All-Century Team.

During January of 1931, trade rumors reached Bill Sherdel in McSherrystown. Apparently, Brooklyn Manager Wilbert Robinson and his Robins were trying to acquire him. In one rumored deal, they offered an infielder and an outfielder. But Boston owner Emil Fuchs nixed the deal because he believed the National League's decision to use a baseball with a heavier cover and a new style of stitching—a change undertaken that year to allow the pitchers a better grip—would help pitchers, especially Bill Sherdel.

By early February, Sherdel trade rumors surfaced again with different Brooklyn players involved. Fuchs, though, would still not trade his veteran left-hander. A trade to the Robins would have been a blessing for the McSherrystown resident. Robinson had fielded a good team in 1930 and had spent much of the early season in first place. The Brooklyn manager felt he just needed one or two more quality players to win it all in 1931.

Emil Fuchs and Bill McKechnie did make some minor changes to strengthen the Braves for the new season. McKechnie revamped his outfield to improve the club's hitting. He acquired Red Worthington from Rochester to play right field and he moved hard-hitting Wally Berger to center. The Braves had been last in batting in 1930 and McKechnie felt that hitting was where the most help was needed. McKechnie said:

> "We want to hit fifteen or twenty points higher as a team than we did last year and that added thump will win games for us. Our pitching ought to be better than it was a year ago. Men like . . . Sherdel, Frankhouse, and Zachary, who were only with us part of last season, will start with us this year and should be able to deliver their best at the very outset. Practically all of these pitchers are good curve-ball artists.
>
> "It is vital to a team in the spring of the year to have its curve-ball chuckers in condition. The opposing teams have not properly attuned their batting eyes for twisters until the Fourth of July. Socks Seibold, for instance, is a great spring pitcher because his curve ball gets going rapidly. Of course, Socks is good all the year round, for that matter. I simply want to stress the idea that a curve-ball pitching corps gets the jump on the other fellows in the spring of the year, and we intend and expect to have a curve-ball pitching staff this year."[1]

In late February, the Sherdel family journeyed to St. Petersburg, Florida, for spring training. St. Petersburg was founded in 1888 and became a city in 1903. It was located on the west coast of Florida, bounded by three bodies of water known collectively as Tampa Bay. The city had experienced major growth through tourism in the 1920s, but the tourists had disappeared by the 1930s because of the Great Depression. It became known as the "Sunshine City" due to an average of 361 days of sunshine per year. By 1930, the population was 40,000.

When Sherdel arrived there, many of the players were already working out. As a veteran pitcher, Sherdel could train at his own pace, but by the second week, he was ready for action. Asked about the new baseball, Sherdel said: "I can't say much about it until I see the ball. The raised stitches should help the curve-ball pitcher though." He didn't think it would help his floater ball that much since he already threw it with a loose grip and could make it do what he wanted. Sherdel did think it might cut down on some of the long home runs.[2]

The Braves began an exhibition schedule the second week of March. McKechnie's squad played games against other major-league teams. Bill Sherdel got his first mound work against the Yankees on March 11. The little southpaw pitched four innings, allowing only two hits, but the Braves later lost.

The spring weather was not particularly good that year. By March 20, many of the Boston players were suffering from bad colds. Sherdel was in the worst shape of all, and was confined to bed for several days. The team was in such bad health that manager McKechnie would not let his Braves play golf in their free time. He was worried that the healthy players would get sick.

One of the pleasant surprises in St. Petersburg was outfielder Red Worthington. He looked like a future star. Fuchs and McKechnie had acquired the young red-headed outfielder from Rochester, a Cardinals' farm club, in a rare mistake made by Branch Rickey. Almost immediately, the Cardinals regretted the move and started working to get Worthington back. After a game against Boston, Brooklyn manager Robinson commented that Worthington was the best hitter in the Braves' lineup.

St. Louis reporter Roy Stockton wrote a March 31 article about the Braves.

> Bill McKechnie hasn't decided on the lineup of his Braves for the 1931 pennant campaign, but it is not too early to say that the Cardinals and other pennant contenders in the National League race will be making a grave mistake if they expect their series with the Boston club to be soft spots or breathing spells.
>
> McKechnie still needs pitching. That always is the department that is the most difficult to build up. Good pitchers are hard to find, but Bill has polished up his infield and outfield and the Braves of 1931 will be troublesome. . . .
>
> Worthington is so good that the Cardinals have been trying to buy him back. . . . He can play any place in the outfield, and since Breadon and Rickey have been considering trading Douthit and Hafey, it is

understood, the Braves have been asked if they would like to make a quick profit on Worthington. . . .

Tom Zachary, Bill Sherdel, and Socks Seibold are the big three of the Boston staff . . . and McKechnie must find two more to join them if the Braves are to do any serious climbing.

McKechnie added, "My club looks better. It is improving slowly. I can't tell where it will go in the race. It's like most other teams in the league. It will be as strong as the pitching staff and you never can tell about that."[3]

Meanwhile, in the St. Louis camp, Breadon and Rickey had their hands full. Chick Hafey's three-year contract had expired, and he wanted considerably more money. Breadon offered him a sizeable increase, but it was not good enough for Hafey, and he decided to hold out. Salary negotiations reached an impasse and it appeared the Cardinals would trade their future Hall-of-Fame outfielder. Breadon and Rickey were also having trouble with a young pitcher named Dean who had been called up from the Houston club. Dean had incredible talent, but he was very hard to handle. Depending on the day, he was either in the Cards' camp or on his way home. It would take all the management skills Gabby Street could muster to develop this ball player into a top-notch starter. The goofy pitcher quickly acquired the nickname "Dizzy."

Before the official 1931 campaign began, the Braves played two exhibition games with their cross-town rivals, the Red Sox. That series was like the ones in St. Louis between the Cards and Browns. The Red Sox earned the bragging rights that year by winning both games.

On the eve of the opener, Gabby Street complimented the Braves' manager. "Bill McKechnie is one of the greatest managers in the game. He can get the most out of a team and he has plenty of good material this year. They may even finish above the .500 mark."[4] Street's own club was expected to repeat with competition from the Pirates, Cubs, and Giants.

The Braves opened their 1931 schedule at home against the Brooklyn Robins on April 13. The Boston bunch jumped into first place with a 7–4 victory over Brooklyn. Bill Sherdel pitched the final four innings, walking one, striking out two, and allowing three harmless hits. He also added a double and single with his bat. Fuchs must have been happy that he had not traded Sherdel to the Robins.

The Braves got off to a great start and jumped into second place behind the Cardinals. The rapid ascent made the Boston club national news. The *Associated Press* caught up with manager McKechnie for an interview in New York.

> "You know I'm a pessimist. I can't see how some of these fellows got the idea that we'll beat out such clubs as Pittsburgh. But my boys are going mighty good. We're liable to give them a race, at that.
>
> "Did you notice how my pitchers are going? Say, that Ed Brandt and Socks Seibold have each pitched a couple of the finest games I ever saw. Brandt has as much against the Giants as any pitcher in the game. And my two other old-timers, Sherdel and Zachary, have been doing fine work. . . .
>
> "We've got a team that can go out and get some runs this year. It's changed the whole spirit of the team. My pitchers feel that if they can hold the opposition to two or three runs, they are pretty likely to win. They don't feel like they have to bear down on every throw. The same with my infield. It's playing further back and getting balls that went for hits last year when it had to stay in close and try to cut off every run.
>
> "Red Worthington and Earl Sheely have added a lot of punch to the lineup. I like both of them. They're betting around Boston that Berger won't hit .300 with the new ball, but they're wrong."[5]

On April 27, the Braves flirted with first place, but two losses to end the month quickly dropped McKechnie's club into fourth. Bill Sherdel pitched two complete games, but lost both.

Over in St. Louis, Breadon solved one of his problems when Chick Hafey finally accepted the Cardinals' terms and signed a new contract. It would take until mid-May for him to rejoin the league leaders. The Cards' owner addressed Dean, his other problem, by sending him back to Houston. Dean had set a possible record by getting into debt to the Cards for $400 more than his annual salary before the season even started.[6]

The Boston Braves continued to surprise the league in May. McKechnie's club spent most of the month in third place. Rumors continued to circulate about the Braves' pitchers. One rumor had Tom Zachary going to the Cardinals for centerfielder Taylor Douthit. And another swirled about Bill Sherdel heading to the Robins—this time for five players. But neither deal occurred because McKechnie needed his pitching. In fact, the Braves even purchased another hurler from Brooklyn. The biggest surprise was the development of Ed Brandt. The big left-hander had finished 1930 with a 4–11 record. By the end of May, Brandt had won eight games without a loss. Zachary and Seibold were also pitching well, but Bill Sherdel had disappeared from the box scores. His last mound appearance in May was a four-hit loss to the Phillies on May 6. The Boston club finally hit a snag the end of the month when the Giants defeated them four out of six games.

In June, the Braves continued to surprise the National League, but the club had dropped into fifth place behind the front-running Cardinals, Giants, Cubs, and Robins. Unbelievably, the Braves won six of ten games with the high-flying Redbirds. Bill Sherdel started to pitch better ball. He tossed a complete-game victory over Rogers Hornsby's Cubs and provided credible relief work against the Cardinals. The big question remained: Could the Braves continue to compete with the first-division clubs?

Bill Sherdel was happy that Marguerite and the children joined him in Boston for a few weeks during the summer after school ended for Patricia and Junior.

The first-place Cardinals made a deal before the trade deadline. Chick Hafey's return and the development of Pepper Martin into an outstanding outfielder had made Taylor Douthit expendable. Douthit had been a premier centerfielder for several years, but he was expensive and suffering from a hip injury that season. Breadon sent Douthit to Cincinnati.

McKechnie's club continued to hold its own in July. The Braves remained in the fifth spot, while McKechnie's old team the Cardinals were running away from the competition. Rickey's farm system was producing homegrown talent that would keep the St. Louis team in the pennant race for years. Manager Street had players like Dizzy Dean, Pepper Martin, Paul Derringer, Tex Carleton, and Rip Collins prepared to become the next Cardinal stars.

Owner Breadon bragged that the Cards' farm system was also suppling other major-league teams with quality players.

Boston remained competitive because of the outstanding performance of its pitching aces—Zachary, Brandt, and Seibold. Bill McKechnie was also blessed to have three left-handed starters—Zachary, Brandt, and Sherdel. Top left-handers were still hard to find. Unfortunately, Sherdel continued to struggle and was getting few starts. Fans were wondering if the thirty-four-year-old southpaw was reaching the end of his outstanding career.

The Braves' biggest weakness was their hitting—last in the National League. The pitching kept them competitive, but the Braves needed a few more top-notch hitters. In the last two months, the Boston club had lost twelve games by one run.

The Tribe faded in August. McKechnie had predicted that curve-ball pitchers would have an advantage until July, and he was right. His club won only twelve and lost twenty-one in August and remained in fifth. At that point, St. Louis looked unstoppable. Ed Brandt won his sixteenth game, making him one of the top left-handers in the league. Sherdel, meanwhile, was pitching a bit better. He started and won three games, lost a close contest, and left another in the eighth inning with the score tied. Sherdel had one bad outing against the Cards.

All the high hopes for a better 1931 season for the Braves disappeared quickly in the final month of the season. McKechnie's squad ended the season in seventh place. Not even Brandt could change the club's direction. He finished at 18–11 and led the staff. Although he weakened in the last month, Brandt's twenty-three complete games were second in the league. Zachary (11–15) and Seibold (10–18) were the only two other staffers with double-digit wins. The McSherrystown southpaw (6–10) appeared in twenty-seven games with a 4.25 earned run average. Sherdel's pitching ability had declined rapidly over the previous three years, or so it seemed. He dejectedly returned to his home on September 29.

Despite Bill McKechnie's hopes for a better hitting club, the Braves' team average was a league-low .258. As expected, Wally Berger's .323 average and nineteen home runs led the club.

Even with the new baseball, Babe Ruth and Lou Gehrig battled all season for the home-run title. Ironically, they tied for first with forty-six each; in the National circuit, the Phillies' Chuck Klein led with thirty-one. The baseball did make a difference in batting averages. In the National League, the aggregate team batting average dropped from .303 to .277.

The Cardinals of Breadon, Rickey, and Street led the National League. They finished thirteen games ahead of the second-place Giants. The Cards were only out of first place for three days during the entire season. They were headed to the World Series for the second year in a row. Once again, their opponents were Connie Mack's Philadelphia Athletics. The A's had had an even more impressive season than the previous year, finishing thirteen-and-a-half games better than Ruth, Gehrig, and the Yankees. The Series was expected to be closer than the previous one. Once again, Bill and Marguerite Sherdel traveled to Philadelphia to see the World Series games there. The Cardinals prevailed in seven games and became world champions for the second time. Sadly, Alexander and Sherdel were gone and Haines hurt his arm and missed the Series.

During the off-season, the Sherdels managed their café where all their friends gathered to discuss baseball and other issues of the day. In November, the loving couple celebrated their twelfth wedding anniversary in the usual way, with music and card-playing with their many friends.

CHAPTER TWENTY-FIVE

In 1932, Amelia Earhart would become the first woman pilot to fly solo across the Atlantic and to perform a solo transcontinental flight. Twenty-month-old Charles Lindbergh, Junior, would be kidnapped and then murdered in New Jersey. Ford would unveil the V-8 engine, and Pearl S. Buck would win the Pulitzer Prize for *The Good Earth*. Gandhi would begin his hunger strike against the horrible treatment of India's untouchable class in this year. Radio City Music Hall would open and Groucho Marx would first appear on radio.

In sports, Lake Placid, New York, would host the third winter Olympic games. Sonja Henie would win her sixth straight world women's figure skating title. Jack Sharkey would reclaim the heavyweight boxing title from Max Schmeling.

In early February, a reporter interviewed Bill McKechnie about the 1932 Braves. The Boston manager described his plans. He must rebuild the infield and his batters must hit harder and more consistently. The great Maranville was still at short. McKechnie said, "He's been one of the greatest and you can take it from me he's got many a good ball game in him yet. If his legs hold out, he'll be there, and how!" About his outfield, he added, "Berger has learned to keep away from bad balls and should hit harder than ever. Of course, he'll hold down one outfield post."

As far as Boston hurlers, McKechnie figured his veterans Brandt, Seibold, Zachary, Sherdel, and Frankhouse would be hard to replace.[1]

Even the world champion Cardinals worked to rebuild their roster after two consecutive pennants. Breadon and Rickey sent Burleigh Grimes to the Cubs. Other veteran players were also sent packing. Gabby Street would need to develop his youngsters. Were Breadon and Rickey being clever with this approach? Only time would tell.

Over the winter, there were indications that Bill Sherdel's father, William Martin, was in declining health. Bill's sister, Ruth Butt, traveled to Valley Stream, Long Island, New York, to spend a week with their father in February. The elder William Martin Sherdel was living with his other daughter, Theresa Kerwin, and her family. His older son Fred and family also lived in Valley Stream. William Martin's health had been in decline since the loss of his wife in 1925.

At the beginning of March, the Boston Braves headed back to St. Petersburg for spring training. Almost everyone except Bill Sherdel was in camp by March 2. Sherdel left for Florida the following day. He had received permission to arrive later due to his father's illness.

Bill McKechnie ran double sessions each day of camp. When the weather was bad, the Boston manager had his squad run sixty-yard dashes. Berger and Sherdel were in camp but unsigned. Fuchs wanted Sherdel to take a cut in pay based upon his poor 1931 record. By late March, Fuchs had both players signed for another season.

Bill Sherdel's spring was not very impressive. On March 20, he pitched two-and-two-third innings against the Yankees, surrendering twelve hits and three walks before leaving. Six days later, he and two other hurlers lost to Brooklyn. Finally, Sherdel started an exhibition with the Orioles in Baltimore on April 6. Many of his hometown friends made the hour-long trip to see him pitch. Sherdel hurled the first four innings, allowing eight hits and three runs. It was taking longer each year for him to work into shape on the mound.

In the St. Louis camp, 1931 batting champion Hafey was missing again. It seemed every year that the Cards' star outfielder was a holdout. This time, a frustrated Breadon traded him to the Reds, where he would join Taylor Douthit in the outfield.

As spring training ended, the Braves headed north. A consensus of baseball writers picked the Cardinals to repeat again and the Braves to finish in last.

In 1932, McKechnie's club opened in Brooklyn against the Robins. Marguerite Sherdel had traveled to New York to join her husband. McKechnie had fulfilled his promise to rebuild his infield and they defeated the Robins. Now only 153 more games remained.

Who could have imagined the standings at the end of April? McKechnie's Braves were only a half-game behind the first-place Cubs. Meanwhile, the Cards were in seventh place. Veterans Brandt, Zachary, and Seibold were starting and winning. Bill Sherdel remained on the bench with arm troubles.

The Braves continued to play well in May. The Boston club was in second place when it announced the release of thirty-seven-year-old Bill Sherdel on May 16. Ironically, the Braves were playing in St. Louis when the announcement was made. It was not unexpected. Sherdel had appeared in only one game for one-and-two-third innings. In it, he'd allowed three hits and one walk. McKechnie was still starting Brandt, Zachary, and Seibold. Young hurlers had taken Sherdel's place.

An unidentified *St. Louis Star* reporter found Sherdel sitting in the lobby of the Hotel Kings-Way the morning after his release. He was staring straight ahead with an opened newspaper next to him. Sherdel didn't notice the reporter until he spoke.

Sherdel responded: "Huh! Oh, hello. Sit down. No, I don't know what I am going to do. I haven't been able to make any plans. I've just been thinking that when the papers published my release, any team that wanted me might get in touch with me. McKechnie told me I was through last Friday. Maybe I should have got on the wires right away. I don't know."

Sherdel shook his head and then added, "I never had this happen to me before. I don't know how to go about looking for a job."

The reporter then asked Sherdel if he still thought he could pitch.

"Yes, I do. And I'll tell you why. I sprained my thumb on my left hand a year ago and couldn't use it pitching all last summer. Doc Hyland here in St. Louis took some pictures of it last June and said there was something wrong with it, and that, apparently, the muscles in my arm had been strained from the way I was trying to pitch.

"When McKechnie told me about my release I asked him if I could come along to St. Louis to see Doc Hyland. Now Hyland tells me the thumb's all right again, just stiff. He's giving me treatments to take the soreness out.

"In a few days, my arm will be OK again, and I'm sure I can still win in this league. You see, I never had much stuff at my best. I was a spot pitcher. I know the batters in this league. I think I'd be a better pitcher here, with what I know, than in the International League, where I don't know any of 'em."

The *Star* reporter also asked Sherdel if he would consider the minors. He replied that he would, but only if there was no alternative.

Finally, the writer asked the long-time pitcher how he was fixed financially.

"Well, I haven't got enough, but I am not broke. I've got a little restaurant back home in Hanover [McSherrystown], PA. That'd give me a living.

"But, Lord, how I hate to quit! I love this game. Why, I even like to pitch in batting practice and hit fungoes. I couldn't make any magnates believe me, but I'd love to do all the work like that for some club. After fifteen years in this league, eighteen in the game—gee, it's tough to quit."[2]

The little southpaw did not have much time to consider his next move. Cards' owner Sam Breadon offered Sherdel a contract two days later and he signed immediately. With this development, Sherdel merely moved to the other side of Sportsman's Park and changed uniforms. Did Breadon offer him a contract so that he could retire as a Cardinal? The wee left-hander had been one of the most popular members of the team. Perhaps Breadon thought Sherdel could still help the Redbirds, who were struggling in fourth place. Rickey had told the press that he needed a fifth starter. Regardless of the reason, Sherdel was very excited to join his beloved Cardinals again.

Bill joins Cards again
—*St. Louis Post-Dispatch*, May 18, 1932

Billy Duncan, sportswriter for the *Philadelphia Evening Public Ledger* and lifelong friend of Sherdel, talked to the pitcher about re-signing with St. Louis.

"I don't think I'm through yet. This season will tell the tale. You [Duncan] and Ned Crowder [Raider teammate] and everyone else thought I'd last two or three years, but I've stayed fifteen because I've made a study of how to pitch.

"Lefty Grove doesn't have to worry about learning how to pitch because he has natural stuff. I haven't been gifted with 'stuff' like Grove or Vance. I realized that early and started a study of all the hitters in the league, learned their weaknesses, and pitched to those weaknesses.

"This is nothing new, of course, as many pitchers have done it before me and after me, but none of them worked harder on it than I did.

"I have always had a good curve, but my fast one wasn't fast enough to get me by. So I perfected a slow ball that made my fast one look faster and worked and worked on that change of pace. Without my slow ball, I would never have lasted."

Sherdel also talked about bad breaks. "So far as bad breaks go, it was tough to leave the Cards in 1930 and to miss the World Series games of '30 and '31. My bad fortune was Burleigh Grimes's good fortune, however, and all of us can't get the breaks. I was glad to be on two pennant winners. A lot of fine pitchers never got in any World Series games."

Lastly, Duncan asked Sherdel about his hopes. "All I ask is that my arm gets right and that I can help the Cards win another pennant. It sure is great to be back with the club and Mr. Breadon and Mr. Rickey again."[3]

The St. Louis team Bill Sherdel joined in 1932 was very different from the one he'd left in 1930. Jim Bottomley was still there, but Rip Collins was now the future first baseman. Frisch, Gelbert, and Adams remained in the infield. Blades was back in right field with Pepper Martin in center and Ernie Orsatti in left. Gus Mancuso now handled the backstop. Hallahan was the new ace of the pitching staff with Johnson, Rhem, and Haines remaining. Promoted farm hands Paul Derringer, Tex Carleton, and Dizzy Dean were promising future stars. Sadly, only Bottomley and Haines had remained constantly with the club since the Cards won the world championship in 1926.

Sherdel's first day back, the Cards lost to the Braves. His old friend Jess Haines took the loss. The Cardinals had struggled through April and May in fourth place, while Boston continued to fight for first.

On May 22, Sherdel took the mound again in a Cards' uniform. It was in the first game of a double-header with the Pirates. Dean started and was getting pounded. Street called time and brought in Sherdel. Walter Smith of the *St. Louis Star* wrote, "The fans greeted Sherdel with a nice hand. And his performance indicated that the Cards made a good move when they signed him after Boston had cut him loose. Coming in with two men on base and one out, he retired two batters on infield balls. . . . In the next inning, he allowed one harmless hit and then was taken out for a pinch-batter."[4]

Bill Sherdel got his next opportunity to toe the rubber in the second game of a Memorial Day double-header in Chicago. Tex Carleton had started and pitched the first six innings, allowing four runs. Sherdel took the mound in the seventh. He pitched two innings, allowing four hits and two runs.

St. Louis ended May in sixth place. Chicago was leading the amazing Boston Braves by two-and-a-half games. McKechnie was proving to be a great manager—so far. Poor Bill Sherdel had left the high-flying Braves and returned to the Redbirds just as Boston was trying to escape the second division.

The little left-hander from McSherrystown next entered a game on June 11 in Brooklyn. He relieved in the sixth with the Cards down, 11–1, and retired the Robins in order on two grounders and an infield pop-up. In the seventh, he walked the first batter. Two singles later, the Robins scored their twelfth run. Sherdel then set down the next three hitters in order. He was removed to start the eighth. He had hurled two innings, allowing two hits and one run. At bat, the mighty Sherdel hit a seventh-inning double then scored the Cards' second run on two fly balls. It was only the second St. Louis hit of the day. The final score was Robins 12, Cardinals 3.

Dean and Martin were the most unusual characters on the club. On the evening of June 15, Dizzy Dean once again quit the team and headed for home. He was unhappy with his salary and the club's need to budget his money. Although the Cards paid him $7,000 for the 1932 season, he only received $3,000 because the club used the other $4,000 to pay off his debts. Dean had a habit of buying anything that he happened to see in a store window, from silk shirts to motorboats.[5] He returned to the club three days later. Pepper Martin was a real outdoorsman from Oklahoma. He never wore underwear, slept outside, and sometimes went several days without a bath. But he could hit and run. Branch Rickey once said, "He [Martin] was so fast, when he went rabbit hunting, he'd outrun the rabbit, overtake it, reach down, and feel how plump it was before deciding whether to put it in his sack or not."[6]

Walter Smith of the *Star* discussed the Cards' lack of trades and commented on Sherdel in his June 16 article. "Sherdel (may the gods love his courageous old heart and weep for the arm which simply isn't there anymore)."[7] Smith's words were a foretelling of what was to come.

On June 23, Bill Sherdel's career with the St. Louis Cardinals and with major-league baseball came to an end. Manager Street needed help for his floundering club. His team had dropped into seventh place. Breadon bought back an infielder from Minneapolis and someone had to go. It was Bill Sherdel. He was given his unconditional release. The Cardinals' AA farm team, the Rochester Red Wings, immediately signed Sherdel to pitch for them. The Rochester manager, George "Specs" Torporcer, had played with Sherdel on the Cards for several years.

Sherdel managed to pitch in eight games for Rochester that summer. In twenty-six innings, he allowed twenty-nine hits and eight walks. His record was one win and two losses. On July 22, Bill, Marguerite, and the children were with the Rochester club in Toronto when Bill learned of the death of his father in Valley Stream, Long Island, New York. The elder Sherdel, age sixty-nine, had been ill for six months and was living with the Kerwins—his daughter and son-in-law. The body of William Martin Sherdel was brought back to Hanover, where he was buried with his wife in Mt. Olivet Cemetery. After the funeral, Bill returned to Rochester for the rest of the baseball season.

Rogers Hornsby and the Cubs finished the 1932 season in first place. The Braves dropped to fifth, still an improvement over the previous year, while the Cardinals disappointed their fans with a sixth-place finish, eighteen games behind frontrunner Chicago. In the American League, the New York Yankees returned to first after three years behind the A's. In the 1932 World Series, the Yankees defeated the Cubs in four straight games to become world champions, again.

Now gone from the Cardinals, Bill Sherdel continued to be well-known. No stranger to newspaper columns, the famous ballplayer made appearances still, including this one, in Charles Regan's column, "On the Sport Trail": "Honorable Franklin Rudolph Reidelberger, former chief justice of the Supreme Court of Venice, IL, was right up to date. 'Hornsby's pitchers ain't so hot,' he advised. 'Give Rog a couple more flingers like Willie Sherdel and them Athletics [should be Yankees] would quit in a jiffy.'"[8]

POST SEASONS

CHAPTER TWENTY-SIX

In 1933, German president Paul von Hindenburg would appoint Adolf Hitler chancellor. Two days later, Hitler would dissolve the parliament. Later, the German Reichstag would grant Hitler dictatorial powers. The Nazis would burn books, ban trade unions and opposing political parties, and begin their drive for world domination that would eventually lead to World War II.

In other news, Franklin Roosevelt would become the thirty-second president and take on the task of providing jobs and an economic recovery. Congress would pass the first minimum wage law of thirty-three cents per hour. Mount Rushmore would be dedicated and the game of Monopoly would be introduced. Newsweek would debut on the newsstand and the movie "King Kong" would premiere at Radio City Music Hall. Albert Einstein would flee Germany and arrive in the United States.

After Bill Sherdel's release from the Cardinals, he sent a letter to Branch Rickey requesting a job in the St. Louis organization. In January, Rickey replied, "At the present time, we simply have no place open for anybody. We are going along with less employees at every point, and have reduced not only our office help, but player limits on all clubs have been decreased."[1] The Great Depression had begun, and it was affecting major-league baseball organizations.

When the spring of 1933 arrived, no teams came looking for the little southpaw from McSherrystown and Bill Sherdel realized his baseball springs and summers had passed. It was now time for someone else to take his place and live his dreams. There was a sadness in Sherdel in the knowledge that he now had to think about the rest of his life. With his parents gone, his children, Patsy (13) and Junior (11), were becoming the focus of his new world, and Bill and Marguerite were enjoying every activity. There were parties for all occasions—birthdays, anniversaries, Halloween, Christmas, and just playing cards. Sherdel was even selected as a judge of the town's Halloween competition. The family was very much at home in McSherrystown.

The demise of his professional occupation notwithstanding, baseball and other sports were still very much a part of Sherdel's life. He played right field for the Hanover Eagles and then later for the McSherrystown team, but did not pitch the first year. He gave his old, weary arm a rest.

One unfortunate incident happened on the evening of December 6 near St. Joseph's Academy in McSherrystown. Junior, Ernest Eckenrode, and Dennis Becker were playing with a rifle when one of the boys pulled the trigger to determine if the gun worked. The gun fired, and a pellet struck ten-year-old Eckenrode in the upper leg. Luckily, the wound was just a flesh wound and was not considered serious. Young Ernest spent several days in the hospital before returning home.

Later in December, Bill Sherdel closed his café in the Colonnade and opened Sherdel's Beer Garden in his home on Ridge Avenue. This move allowed him to reduce his expenses and still capitalize on his fame. Sherdel would change the restaurant's name several times, to The Home Plate, The Outside Inn, and Sherdell's Restaurant. The restaurant, located in the front-right section of his house, seated fifty patrons and advertised home cooking, short orders, beer, Italian spaghetti, a soda fountain, and dinners by appointment. It was difficult to count how many children became St. Louis Cardinal fans at Sherdel's restaurant. The neighborhood children would stop after school and Sherdel would give them candy or ice cream if they declared the Cards their favorite team.

Outside Sherdell's Restaurant. Note the different spelling
—Sherdel family

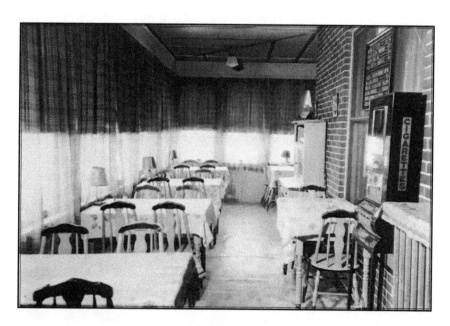

Inside of the restaurant
—Sherdel family

By the following year, Sherdel was coaching and pitching for McSherrystown. The team competed in the York-Adams League, named for York and Adams Counties. His summers in the 1930s and 1940s continued to include baseball.

Bill Sherdel was gone from the Cardinals, but not forgotten. He continued to be recognized for his accomplishments on the mound. In 1936, the National League celebrated its sixtieth year. Noted sportswriter Hugh Fullerton developed his all-star, all-time teams for each major-league city. His picks were listed in *The Sporting News*. Fullerton combined the Cardinals and Browns for his St. Louis team. He selected four pitchers—Dizzy Dean, Bobby Carruthers, Bill Doak, and Bill Sherdel. In describing his pitching selection, Fullerton offered, "Cy Young was not there long enough to become a St. Louis institution. . . . A score of other fine pitchers fail to meet the test as deserving all-time honors."[2]

As part of the 1936 National League celebration, the Cardinals decided to honor the tenth anniversary of the 1926 world championship team. An exhibition game was planned between the 1926 and 1936 clubs. Nineteen of the twenty-five players returned. Bill Sherdel, however, was not among them. He was held back because of his business interests.

Back in St. Louis in early June of 1936, Branch Rickey traded away another of his star pitchers, Bill Hallahan. Sid Keener of the *St. Louis Star* took the opportunity to sit down with the Cardinals' vice president. Rickey was reminiscing about the past Cardinals. Keener wrote:

> Baseball fans following the fortunes of a ball club are unfamiliar with the deep sentiment that often exists between players and club officials. Rickey was very fond of Hallahan.
>
> "This isn't the first time I've had a heartache after releasing a player," remarked Branch. "You see I become so attached to some of the boys that I hate to see them leave me. . . .
>
> "There was Bill Sherdel, another fine boy. Bill had given us everything he had. He helped us with that first pennant in 1926. He pitched the game that clinched the 1928 flag for the Cardinals. He was an ideal player on a ball club—a thorough team man.

"Then, in 1930, we saw that we needed better pitching if we expected to win. And, we sacrificed Bill Sherdel by trading him to the Boston Braves for Burleigh Grimes. It was a great deal for us, all right, but it was another heartache for me—trading Sherry."[3]

Also in 1936, the major leagues provided Bill Sherdel with a silver lifetime pass to all National and American League parks. Baseball awarded these passes to all long-term players, past and present. Sherdel was overjoyed. He attended at least one Cardinal game in Philadelphia every year.

In 1939, Bill Sherdel sold his equipment and discontinued his restaurant business. He became the Adams County salesman for Helb's Keystone Brewery in York, Pennsylvania. By July, he had decided to run as a Republican candidate for Adams County Sheriff. He said that he worked as hard for political office as he ever did on the baseball fields. Campaigning for office must have been difficult for Sherdel, because he'd always been reluctant to speak in public. Unfortunately, Sherdel lost in the primary election in September. Despite the disappointment, he still had baseball. He continued managing the McSherrystown team and now he enjoyed having his son on the roster.

Bill Sherdel runs for sheriff
—Sherdel family

By the late 1930s, Junior, young William J. Sherdel, had grown into a teenager and was involved in high school sports at Central Catholic. He was an outstanding athlete, distinguishing himself on the football field, the basketball court, and the baseball diamond. Patricia was not an athlete, but did very well in school and graduated from St. Joseph's Academy in 1938. She began work in the office of the Beaudoin Shoe Company.

Young Bill Sherdel had a great junior year on the basketball court. The 1940 Central Catholic Crusaders were in the fight for the league championship, and Junior was leading the team. One game highlighted the ability that Junior possessed. This passage was taken from *The Evening Sun* article the next day:

> Fans, who a few years back were singing the praises of Wee Willie Sherdel, "king of the National League and pride of McSherrystown," were today whooping it up for his son, little Bill Sherdel, who last night tossed the Central Catholic High School Crusaders to the Adams County Scholastic Basketball championship.
>
> With a coolness that rivaled that of Sherdel, the older, in the days when he matched slants with Herb Pennock before the World Series crowds in the House that Ruth Built, Sherdel, the younger, a bundle of nerves with speed to burn and an uncanny eye for the basket, came through like a veteran last night in a situation as trying as any ever faced by the Rover Boys in College. . . .
>
> The score was 27–27. The final whistle was twenty-five seconds away. The crowd, numbering approximately 500, of whom more than 300 were from McSherrystown, was behaving like jitter bugs with St. Vitas dance.
>
> Up to the foul line walked Bill Sherdel. . . . On the one charity toss awarded him hung the success or failure of a remarkable campaign. . . . Through the cords it swished.
>
> But this title-winning toss was only fifty percent of the story. . . . Arendtsville's Apple Pickers were out in front by two points, had the ball in their possession, and were doing a grand job of freezing it.
>
> Then up cropped this same Bill Sherdel. Stealing the ball near the equator, he dribbled down the middle with two rivals on his heels. Kane caught up with him just as he shot and made an honest effort

to spoil the toss. The ball dropped through to deadlock the score as referees Dayhoff and Morgan teamed up on a whistle duet to acclaim the fact that Kane had fouled the Crusader. The goal counted. What Sherdel did with the foul has already been written.[4]

Young Bill ended his junior season as the third-leading scorer in the league. He then spent the summer at second base on Hanover's American Legion baseball team.

In Europe, war had once again begun. Germany had invaded Poland in September 1939, and Great Britain and France had then declared war on Germany. In the Pacific, Japan and China were also at war. The Americans didn't want to be involved in another war like World War I, and so were trying to remain neutral—but it was proving very difficult, again.

In the fall of 1940, Junior was a high school senior. On the football team, he was a star halfback and kicker. Near the end of the season, he fractured his ankle in a game against Harrisburg Catholic and was on crutches for several weeks. He returned just in time for the final football game of his high school career.

Young Bill played basketball again his senior year. The school and team, now named Delone Catholic, finished an average season, winning just slightly more than it lost. Junior was again a star, making his dad very proud.

As the winter weakened and the older Bill's thoughts turned again to baseball, he received another visit from one of his old teammates. Rabbit Maranville and his wife stopped to visit with the Sherdels while on their way to South Carolina for training camp. The Rabbit was now the manager of the Springfield (Massachusetts) club. Sherdel continued to manage the 1941 McSherrystown baseball team with Junior as a utility player, capable of playing infield or outfield.

On June 21, 1941, the Sherdels celebrated the wedding of twenty-year-old Patsy to James Lawrence of Midway at St. Mary's Catholic Church in McSherrystown. Patsy's brother, Bill Junior, was the best man. It was a very happy day for Bill and Marguerite and the rest of the family. Twenty-one-year-old Lawrence was also a good athlete, having played football and tennis at Hanover's Eichelberger Senior High School.

After graduation, Junior and many of his high school teammates continued to play basketball with the St. Mary's Catholic Club team in an open league. Young Bill was usually one of the high scorers. In early November, Junior and other alumni took on the Delone high school team in a football game. The Old Grads won, 14–0, with Bill Sherdel scoring both touchdowns. Showing that he was still a star, young Sherdel ran back kickoffs, threw passes, and ran the football. Less than two weeks later, Junior and several of his friends enlisted in the Naval Reserves and left for the Great Lakes Naval Training Station in North Chicago, Illinois.

War seemed a certainty. It was just a matter of time before the United States was involved. That time came on December 7, 1941, when the Japanese bombed our Pacific fleet at Pearl Harbor. President Roosevelt led the United States into war with Japan and then Japan's ally Germany declared war on the United States. Young American boys like Junior would now join the armed forces and travel to unknown places in the world. Many would die on foreign soil. Families would be torn apart.

On March 3, 1942, Patsy (Sherdel) Lawrence was transported by ambulance to Johns Hopkins Hospital in Baltimore, Maryland. The family learned that she had inherited Bright's disease from her mother's family. Marguerite's brother and sister had already died from the dreaded kidney disease and now the young Patsy was stricken. She returned home but continued to suffer from chronic nephritis (kidney disease). At one point, she lost her sight temporarily. Patsy loved to knit and her husband, Jim, would read the directions to her.

On January 4, 1943, Patsy was once again transported by ambulance to the hospital—this time, Hanover General. Four days later, twenty-two-year-old Patricia Kathryn Lawrence passed away. Her death was listed as lobar pneumonia, but she had been in failing health from Bright's disease for some time.

One of the greatest tragedies for any parent is to bury a son or daughter. Bill and Marguerite were heartbroken. Patsy had been a wonderful daughter full of fun. She was outgoing and loved by all. Her young husband, Jim, now faced life without his lovely wife after only eighteen months of marriage. His pain was unimaginable. In the small town of McSherrystown, residents were very close. They had celebrated Patsy's wedding with the Sherdel family and now they also felt the terrible loss.

Patricia Sherdel Lawrence
—Sherdel family

The senior Bill Sherdel took the mound again after a few years away on August 15 in West York. The County Old Timers played the City Old Timers in an exhibition game to sell war bonds. A crowd of several thousand saw "Wee Willie" pitch the first inning for the County. He struck out one, walked one, gave up one hit and allowed no runs. Old Brooklyn hurler Norman Plitt opposed Sherdel on the mound. The County team won, 9–6, and the fans pledged $48,000 in war bond purchases.

Another death in the family occurred on October 21, 1943. Marguerite Sherdel's father, James Peter Strausbaugh, passed away. The seventy-nine-year-old former cigar maker had been bedfast for more than two years.

World War II impacted the Sherdel family in several ways. Young Bill was serving in the US Navy. He had spent time in South America after his enlistment and now he was stationed in the Armored Guard Center in Brooklyn, New York, and was sailing the seas. So far, he had survived seven trips across the Atlantic. He was at risk every trip. Junior would come home to McSherrystown several times during the year. In late November, he married Amy Moore of New Oxford in Valley Stream, Long Island, New York. Both Bill Junior and Amy were 1941 graduates of Delone Catholic High School. Amy was now working in the draft board office in New Oxford. After a short honeymoon, the young Navy man headed back into action.

The married couple, William James (Junior) & Amy Sherdel
—Sherdel family

The Sherdel family suffered another loss when Corporal John Kerwin, who was serving with General Patton's headquarters staff, was killed in the invasion of Sicily. Kerwin's mother, Teresa, was Bill Sherdel's sister and the corporal was a nephew of the former Cardinal southpaw. And the bad news continued. On April 14, 1945, Bill lost his older brother, Fred. The fifty-four-year-old Valley Stream resident had been ill for several months. Fred and his wife had five sons—Fred, William, Robert, Kenneth, and John—all of whom were serving in the armed forces. Luckily, Bill had been able to spend time with his brother in January.

And then at last, some good news! William James Sherdel (Junior) was honorably discharged from the US Navy on July 18, 1945. Young Bill had crossed the Atlantic ten times. Bill, Marguerite, and now Amy were very thankful and happy to have Junior back again. Not long after William James' release, the family celebrated the birth of Patricia Louise, the elder Sherdel's first grandchild.

CHAPTER TWENTY-SEVEN

Like most new veterans, Bill Junior tried to return to a normal life after the war. He was now a husband and father, but he continued to play sports—all sports. In baseball, he played shortstop and eventually became an outstanding pitcher for the McSherrystown team in the Adams County League and the Penn-Maryland League. In basketball, he played for the McSherrystown Knights of Columbus team and was a leading scorer. In football, he played halfback for the York White Roses semi-pro team in the Pennsylvania State League and was a star.

Marguerite Sherdel lost another sister, Mary Fuhrman, on November 7, 1948. The forty-four-year-old Mrs. Fuhrman had been in Johns Hopkins Hospital for several weeks following an operation. It seemed the Strausbaugh women did not enjoy long lives.

One day, the 1949 Cardinals' manager Eddie Dyer was reminiscing about Bill Sherdel's slow ball. Dyer had played with Sherdel back in the 1920s. He said, "Sherdel could make it good or bad, a strike or a ball, at will. And he was so effective with his change-up, we learned after a trade with the Giants that McGraw finally had issued orders that none of his players should swing at it unless they had two strikes. They either had to take the slow one or bunt it."[1]

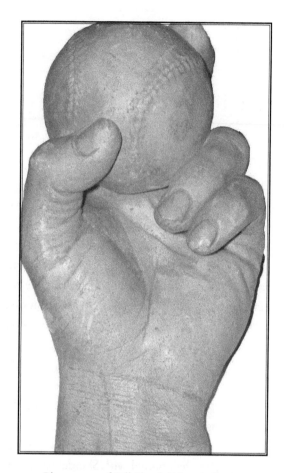

Plaster cast of Bill Sherdel's baseball grip
—Sherdel family

In late September 1949, Bill Sherdel and his son traveled back to Martinsburg, West Virginia, for the dedication of a monument at the grave site of the great Hack Wilson. Bill Sherdel and Wilson had been close friends. The Sherdels were joined by Joe McCarthy, Kiki Cuyler, Nick Altrock, and other former teammates and friends at the cemetery. Wilson had been a star with several clubs in the National League. Back in 1930 with the Cubs, he had hit fifty-six home runs and driven in 190 runs—both National League records at the time. McCarthy had been his manager with Chicago and was now managing the Red Sox.

Wilson had passed away the previous November in Baltimore. He had been sick and almost penniless. In his last summer, he had worked as a guard at one of the municipal swimming pools. His friends and some baseball organizations had paid for his funeral. Wilson had broken into professional baseball with Martinsburg in the Blue Ridge League and had always considered the West Virginia city his home. Bill Sherdel posed for pictures with McCarthy, who delivered the dedication.

McCarthy said, "To me, along with the sorrow I experience in thinking of Hack, comes the pleasant memory of happy days with him.

"This monument we unveil to his memory recalls great accomplishments in baseball. His record speaks for itself and will long be remembered by millions of youngsters and the men he played with."[2]

Joe McCarthy and Bill at the Hack Wilson memorial dedication
—Sherdel family

On November 4, 1950, Bill Sherdel's old friend and teammate Grover Cleveland Alexander passed away at age sixty-three in his home state of Nebraska. In an interview with Harrisburg sportswriter Izzy Katzman, Sherdel recalled his time with the man in the bullpen during the seventh game of the 1926 World Series. Haines had loaded the bases with two outs in the seventh inning and left the mound because of a bad blister on his finger.

"Alex, who had pitched the full game the day before, didn't throw a ball in the bullpen. I remember it very well because I, as a matter of fact, had started from the bullpen when the phone rang and they said they wanted Alexander.

"Alex was talking to one of the Yankee pitchers when the call came. The bullpen for both clubs was in left field then. He took off his sweater, threw it to Ernie Vick, who was the bullpen catcher, told him to bring it in after the game, and started toward the mound.

"He was very nonchalant as he left the bullpen. In fact, I never saw him excited in my life.

"Alexander intentionally took his time walking to the mound. The sly old veteran wanted the young batter Tony Lazzeri to remain nervous. Grover went on to strike out Lazzeri to end the Yankee seventh and then put the New York club down without a problem in the eighth and ninth to win the Series.

"I went up to the Cardinals in 1918, so I never saw [Christy] Mathewson and I didn't see [Walter] Johnson because he was in the other league. But of all the right-handers I have ever seen, Alexander was the greatest."[3]

In a later interview, Sherdel credited Alexander with teaching him that control was the most important thing for a pitcher—more important than speed.

One of the great baseball joys of Bill Sherdel's later life was a return to St. Louis in June of 1951 to celebrate the silver anniversary of the 1926 world championship team. There was a weekend planned with a Friday luncheon and then the introduction of the team before a Cards-Braves game on Saturday. Unfortunately, seven members of that club had died, but most of the others were expected to return. Notable among those who could not attend were Rogers Hornsby, who was managing in the minor leagues, and Branch Rickey, who was stranded in New Orleans. Bill Sherdel and Les Bell traveled together by plane to the Missouri city.

On Friday, the luncheon was held at Stan Musial and Biggie's Steak House with 125 people in attendance. Current Cards' president Fred Saigh presented each of the players with a gold tie-clasp with the Redbird insignia.

Sherdel, now forty pounds heavier, enjoyed the chance to talk with his former teammates and the press.

Part of the pleasure of the gathering was all the reminiscing and storytelling in which the former team members engaged. Sherdel told this story about Jim Bottomley:

> "When Bottomley came up, rookies weren't permitted to take batting practice unless given permission. Finally, he looked so good around first base that Rickey said to me, 'William don't you think we ought to see what this young man can do at bat?'
>
> "Bottomley went down the bat rack, timidly passing up favorite clubs of regulars he had met. At the end of the line he noticed a thin bat. Sunny Jim, a green pea then, stopped, and said, 'Say, I haven't met this fella yet—Mr. Fungo.'"[4]

1926 World Champions' reunion.
Sherdel 4th from right in front row.
—*St. Louis Post-Dispatch*, June 24, 1951

The next day, the team gathered in the St. Louis Browns' dressing room to talk again and try to squeeze their paunches into 1951 Cardinal uniforms. Someone yelled, "We'll let Sherdel hit—if somebody pitches a grapefruit." Jess Haines said the reunion represented "the happiest two days of my career."

Redbirds prepare to fly again.
Sherdel 3rd from left.
—*St. Louis Post-Dispatch,* June 25, 1951

When they went out on the field, Bill Sherdel was so excited he couldn't hold a pencil to sign an autograph. Cardinals' announcer Harry Caray made the introductions. Sherdel rubbed the top of his hairless head as he walked onto the infield to be introduced by Caray. The old-timers took their positions one last time—Haines to the mound, Bottomley to first, Flowers in place of Hornsby to second, Bell to third, Thevenow to short. The outfielders Hafey, Douthit, and Blades, plus the other players, were announced one by one amid a standing ovation and cheers from the appreciative fans.[5] It was a wonderful weekend for Sherdel, back in his adopted second home of St. Louis.

In 1952, Ronald Reagan and Doris Day starred in a movie, "The Winning Team," about the life of pitcher Grover Cleveland Alexander. Actor and former baseball player Johnny Beradino portrayed Bill Sherdel in the film. In one scene, Sherdel and Alexander are sitting talking in the bullpen awaiting a phone call in the seventh inning of game seven of the 1926 World Series. The handsome Beradino would go on to play a doctor in a daytime soap opera for many years.

The accolades for and remembrances of Sherdel continued. He was the guest of honor at the Philadelphia Sports Writers' Association Baseball Forum in September 1952. He shared the dais with Stan Musial, Enos Slaughter, and other sports celebrities. Sherdel also received votes for the Baseball Hall of Fame in 1953.

"Wee Willie" enjoyed his later years and worked at the Hanover Moose as a steward. He hunted and raised black turkeys in his backyard. He also loved to go with his friends to the horse races in Charles Town, West Virginia. He was not a big gambler, but he enjoyed the races with small bets.

Bill and Marguerite were joined within their home by their son, daughter-in-law, and seven grandchildren: Pat, Elaine, Larry, Bob, John, Judy, and Teresa. The grandchildren brought much joy and excitement to Bill and Marguerite and their home.

Grandson John told how his grandfather would sit on a chair inside the front door next to the stairway. His grandfather would pretend to be asleep, but when one of the children would attempt to sneak up the steps, Grandpa Bill would quickly reach out and grab them by surprise. John remembered that his grandfather still had a very strong grip.

Granddaughter Pat recalled that her grandfather always had a large garden of tomatoes, peppers, etc., in the backyard. He used organic gardening before it became popular. Sherdel would pay his oldest granddaughters, Pat and Elaine, a nickel to pick all the beetles from the plants.

Sherdel always remained just an ordinary man. He would stop by to visit friends on his way home from the Moose in the evenings, and bring them a beverage and enthusiasm for an animated discussion of the topic of the day.

Throughout the years, Sherdel remained a baseball celebrity. Many times, former teammates and opponents would stop to see him. Bill's family and local residents remembered that even Babe Ruth, while headed to Philadelphia, had stopped to visit Bill and attended church with him. Sherdel was always very humble and hesitant to talk about his many baseball accomplishments unless asked. He never collected any autographs because he considered baseball players to be ordinary people. When he received autograph requests through the mail, he usually sent the autograph back with a letter and a thank-you to the fan.

On a cold, wintery Friday morning, November 25, 1955, Bill Sherdel lost his best friend, his life's partner, his better half: his wife, Marguerite. She had been ill for three months, suffering from the Strausbaugh curse that had taken her mother, her two sisters, her brother, and, worst of all, her daughter—Bright's disease and its complications. Dear Marguerite—nicknamed "Babe"—was fifty-eight. She left behind her adoring husband and son and his family. Bill was heartbroken. Residents remembered "Babe" as a classy woman who had been a great dresser, very sociable, and well-liked by everyone.

Bill and Marguerite—the loving couple
—Sherdel family

Later, Bill Sherdel would be stricken with a nervous breakdown and a circulatory disorder that would cost him his left leg in 1961. His situation would worsen because of huge doctor bills and a paltry baseball player's pension of $100 per month. He had stopped working as a steward at the Hanover Moose. Sherdel was grateful to have his family close. A longtime St. Louis sports fan, L.X. Douglas, had corresponded with the left-hander and learned of his financial woes. Douglas solicited funds in St. Louis to help with the purchase of an artificial leg while J. G. Taylor Spink, publisher of *The Sporting News*, appealed to the Professional Ball Players' Association, whose members aided old-timers with additional financial assistance.

CHAPTER TWENTY-EIGHT

There were still some happy times ahead for the old left-hander. In 1962, Sherdel was notified that he had been chosen to receive the Brian P. Burnes Nostalgia Award at the St. Louis baseball writers' dinner in The Sheraton-Jefferson Hotel in St. Louis, on January 31. Burnes had been a commercial artist and long-time baseball fan who had, for many years, bemoaned the lack of recognition of past stars. The night after the 1959 dinner, Burnes was robbed and knocked unconscious. He died the next day. So now each year, the Brian P. Burnes Nostalgia Award was given to an old-timer who had made baseball history in St. Louis. Bill Sherdel accepted the invitation and flew to St. Louis with his son. He said, "I need someone to carry my toothbrush and rub the good old left arm so I can throw the s-l-o-w ball."

In announcing that Bill Sherdel would attend the event, Bob Broeg wrote in his column about a letter L.X. Douglas had received from Bill Sherdel. Sherdel liked to talk about his hitting.

> He commented about Jess Haines. . . . "Jesse and I were roommates for years. What a man he was, but I was a better hitter." He was, too. All pitchers like to pull up about professed proficiency at the plate, but Haines was dangerous—he hit a home run in a World Series game—and Sherdel was even more so. Bill had hit nine home runs in his major-league career.
>
> We have the impression of the little left-handed hitter going up to the plate one day as a pinch-batter. Forgetting to remove his glove from his hip pocket, he belted a triple. The glove flopped from the pocket all the way on Sherdel's trip to third base.

Sherdel also talked about the spitball. "I have to laugh, because I pitched the spitter the very next year after it was barred (1921), but only the catcher knew it. I think the pitch still should be allowed."

Sherdel is proudest, he said, of having won more games in a season than any left-handed pitcher the Cardinals ever had.

He has distinctions other than the dubious one of having been born too soon. His top pay, Bill said recently, was $12,000.

He has more pleasant memories. He won the pennant-clinching game in the Cardinals' first championship season, 1926, relieving Flint Rhem at New York. Two years later, after going 15 innings to win at Brooklyn, 4–3, Sherdel again clinched the pennant in late September, 3–1, this time at Boston.[1]

The night of the award ceremony was a great one for Bill Sherdel. Other award winners included Warren Spahn (Rawlings 300 Wins Trophy), Elston Howard (St. Louis Baseball Man of the Year), Lee Thomas (Rookie of the Year), Larry Jackson (Comeback Award), Red Schoendienst and Bill DeWitt (Meritorious Service to Sports Awards). Joe Garagiola served as the master of ceremonies. The 1,000 attendees included Stan Musial, Joe Medwick, Minnie Minoso, and many other sports celebrities. Sherdel, choked with emotion, wept on his crutches as he accepted his award before a standing ovation of St. Louis admirers. There were no dry eyes.

In his column, "The Bench Warmer," Robert Burnes, son of Brian P., and sports editor for the *Globe Democrat,* described Bill Sherdel accepting the Nostalgia Award.

> At five o'clock Wednesday afternoon, Bill Sherdel knew he was going to blow his line.
>
> The great little Cardinal southpaw of the twenties, still unbelieving that anyone was interested in his name or his career, was the great hit of the baseball writers' dinner Wednesday night, even though he barely blurted out one sentence amid a flood of tears.
>
> And when Warren Spahn, Joe Garagiola, Leroy Thomas, and Frank Slocum put their arms around Sherdel's shoulders and gently escorted him back to his seat after his tearful acceptance, an ingredient had

been inserted into the ceremonies that could not have been planned or bought.

After the dinner was over, Bill Sherdel was the center of attraction.

Stan Musial and Joe Medwick, a couple of great ballplayers who have known many tributes in their time, hurried up out of the audience after the dinner was over to converse with Sherdel. They knew what something like this had to mean to the Cardinal hurling star of the twenties.

One man in the audience admitted that he had sent in for tickets, had driven 150 miles to the dinner, just to see once more a pitcher he idolized as a youth.

Warren Spahn, perhaps the greatest left-handed pitcher of all times . . . was visibly impressed by Sherdel's reaction and by the crowd's reception of Bill Sherdel.

"This is what makes this game of baseball great," he said, simply and earnestly. "If Sherdel had made a speech, the impact couldn't have been as great. The fact that he was overwhelmed was what made it so tremendous. If you needed a demonstration of the hold baseball has on the American public, this was it."

None of the fans in the room had seen Sherdel pitch a baseball in thirty years. At least half and probably more had never seen him pitch at all. But they knew his reputation. And they came to pay homage.

It was not easy for Sherdel to be there. Long illness finally resulted two years ago in the amputation of his leg. He even demurred at the thought of coming here, although it was obvious that he wanted to if he felt he could make it.

So, in the company of his son, he came here from Pennsylvania. From the moment they arrived, both were overwhelmed.

"I have never made a speech in my life," he confessed shortly after his arrival. "Do I have to now?" It was suggested that if he would just stand up and say hello, it would be enough.

"I would like to tell the people," he said, "that my days with the Cardinals were the happiest of my life—and I would also like to say that this is the most wonderful day of my life to be back here. But I'm afraid I won't be able to do it."

Son Bill Jr. was just as overwhelmed. Despite the urging of the people at the table in the audience with him, he couldn't eat a bit of his dinner. "I couldn't," he said. "I know how much this means to Dad. He hasn't thought or talked of anything else in weeks."

He waited for the introduction by Bob Broeg and, when it was done, Sherdel was up on his feet quickly and heading bravely for the rostrum. It was a total distance of six feet and he had half of it done when he faltered. Bob Hyland, whose dad knew Sherdel well, was the first on his feet to give the pitcher the standing ovation he merited, and that was what shook him.

At the rostrum, he stood with head down and wept unashamedly.

Maybe the audience present and those listening on radio didn't hear his acceptance—but he made it and his mission and ours was accomplished.

It made the whole evening worthwhile.

"It makes everything we do in baseball worthwhile," Spahn said.[2]

Although he was unable to make a speech, he did sit and talk calmly with sportswriter Broeg after the event.

> Sherry chuckled, "I just asked Stan Musial if he thought I was in shape when I went fifteen innings in the rain to beat Brooklyn just before we clinched the 1928 pennant and he laughed,' the old pitcher said. 'Stan knew the answer to that one was obvious."

The vital extra-inning victory wasn't the greatest moment during Sherdel's playing career.

"I remember most a defeat," he said, "because, as Buck Wheat (Zach) told me, you'll never match the thrill of playing in a World Series.

"I remember opening the 1926 Series and losing to Pennock, 2–1, when Hornsby, ordinarily great on making the double-play pivot, threw low. Rog hardly could have had his heart in his work because he'd just learned his mother had died in Texas."

Sherdel recalled another he said he'd lost because Hornsby, weak on going back for pop flies, had retreated for a high fly with two out in the ninth, three on, the Cardinals leading, 3–1. The Rajah tripped himself and all three runners scored.

"If only Rog could have gone out for pop flies like Frisch, a fourth outfielder," Sherdel said, "but, oh, how that Hornsby could hit. He won many a game for me."

Wee Willie said he had hurt the late Jimmy Wilson's feelings once by saying that Bob O'Farrell was the best catcher to whom he ever had pitched.

"I didn't like to hurt Jim, but I just couldn't help it," Sherdel said. "We'd have won for Bob when he was manager in 1927 except for injuries, I guess, but I'll tell you—and the difficulty teams have repeating as champions will bear me out—that a ball club often just doesn't bear down hard enough the year after it has won.

"Not, that is, until it's too late. Then the club already has paid the penalty of self-satisfaction."[3]

In March of 1963, Bill Duncan returned to the area to speak at a banquet for Littlestown High School athletes. Duncan, a Gettysburg native, had graduated from Gettysburg College and had covered the Blue Ridge League for the local papers. That's where he and Bill Sherdel first became friends. Their friendship had lasted through the years, even though Duncan moved on to Philadelphia and a larger audience. He wrote for several Philly newspapers and later hosted a television show titled, "Grandstand Manager." He knew all the major sports celebrities through the years, including Jack Dempsey, Ty Cobb, Babe Ruth, and many more, but he always considered Bill Sherdel his closest friend. In his speech, Duncan complimented Sherdel, who was at the event as a special guest. The sportscaster said, "One of the most important attributes in sports and in life is courage. If you have the courage to get the most out of your ability, you will have done your best and will be a success." Duncan lauded Sherdel, "who through his courage made more out of his natural talent than any other he'd seen in fifty-four years of observing sports."[4]

The March 5, 1966, issue of *The Sporting News* included a feature article entitled "Willie Sherdel—Afterglow of Greatness," also written by his friend Bill Duncan. Excerpts follow.

Wee Willie Sherdel, sitting in his living room, said:
"Be sure and tell them the happiest days of my life were the ones I spent pitching for the Cardinals."

He was holding his three-month-old great granddaughter, Sharon, who was wearing a bright red outfit.

"See, she's a Cardinal rooter wearing our red uniform," he explained.

As you walk into the Sherdel home, the first picture to greet you is one of the 1926 World Championship Cardinal team. In the adjoining room, a framed St. Louis Nostalgia Award hangs on the wall. The inscription says:

"Brian P. Burnes Nostalgia Award to Bill Sherdel, St. Louis BBWAA, January 31, 1962."

"That was the greatest day and night for me since I quit pitching," Sherdel recalled.

"In the afternoon, I went out to the old ballpark and just looked and looked at the pitching mound. There were a hundred memories, believe me. Old Pete and all the rest of that great team.

"I received the award at a banquet that night and now, four years later, I thank everyone again for their kindness to me. . . ."

Sherdel calls Hornsby not only the greatest manager but the finest right-handed hitter he ever saw. One of Sherdel's career high points was when he faced the mighty Rajah in a game and fanned him twice by "pitching curves in on his fists." Bill added, "I'll have to admit the wind was behind me."

He has a yarn about Branch Rickey.

"When Rickey was managing the Cardinals, he depended on me heavily as a relief pitcher.

"He never called me Bill or Sherry but always William. He'd say, 'Warm up, William.'

"In one game, he told me to warm up early and I pitched three innings. I took a shower and dressed and sat at the end of the bench. In the ninth inning, we were in trouble. He never even looked at me sitting there in my street clothes, but just said by force of habit: 'Warm up, William.' I won't tell you what I said."

Bill closed our interview by saying he felt the most satisfying reward for an ex-big leaguer is the esteem in which he is held by kids.

"Some kids write from St. Louis and ask me for my autograph," said Sherdel. "If an ex-big leaguer knows he is appreciated by Young

America, thirty-five years after he quit, then he can feel he's been a lifetime winner."

In an accompanying article, Sherdel offered advice to young Cardinal pitchers. He said, "All afternoon, I tried to hit the plate low and on the outside corner. Learn that and you're bound to last."[5]

Bill Sherdel holding his great-granddaughter Sharon
while Junior and Patricia look on
—Sherdel family

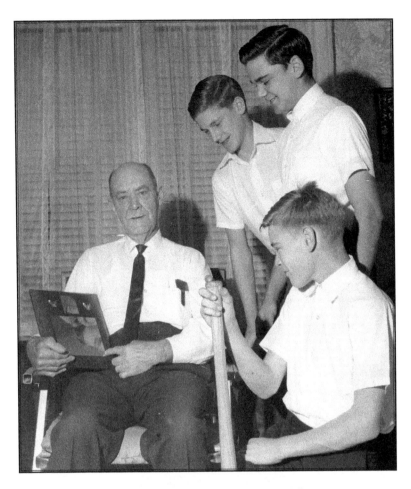

Bill with his grandsons. From top middle,
clockwise: Bob, Larry, and John
—Sherdel family

Bill with his granddaughters. From lower left, clockwise: Judy, Patricia, Elaine, and Teresa
—Sherdel family

Locally, Sherdel continued to be recognized within the baseball community. He was asked to select the most valuable player in little league tournaments. He was honored by the local American Legion and attended their father-son baseball banquets. And, in a spectacularly humbling development, McSherrystown named its little league baseball complex in Sherdel's honor.

The old left-hander lost his dear friend Bill Duncan in April 1967. Duncan had written many tributes to the McSherrystown southpaw, but perhaps his best was *The Sporting News* piece he'd penned the previous year. Maybe Bill Duncan had known his time was getting short and he wanted to provide his friend with his last great national story. Sherdel attended Duncan's funeral and burial in Pennsauken, New Jersey.

Bill Sherdel was blessed with another lifelong friend, Guy Goodfellow, of Hanover, who traveled with Sherdel to St. Louis to attend three Cardinal home games against the Boston Red Sox in the 1967 World Series. Sherdel, a forever fan, enjoyed the Busch Stadium games and the opportunity to see many of his old friends and admirers. Maybe he knew that this would be his last trip to the Mound City—his second home.

Sherdel's beloved Cardinals were again in the World Series in 1968. This time, they played the Detroit Tigers. Unfortunately, Sherdel was no longer well enough to travel to Busch Stadium, but he did watch the games on television.

On the early morning of November 14, 1968, quiet, courageous Bill Sherdel passed away in his sleep at his McSherrystown home. The seventy-two-year-old Cardinal favorite had been in poor health for several years. He had lost his left leg to a circulatory ailment back in 1961. In September and then again late October of 1968, he'd fallen seriously ill and had entered the local hospital. Sherdel returned home for the last time on November 6. At the time of his death, he was survived by his son and daughter-in-law, seven grandchildren, three great-grandchildren, and two sisters. Burial was in the cemetery of Annunciation Church in McSherrystown. He now finally had the opportunity in death to be with his dear wife, Marguerite, his lovely daughter, Patsy, and all his other relatives and friends who had waited patiently for him to join them.

Sherdel grave site
—Coulson collection

In early December of 1968, Assemblyman Francis Worley introduced a resolution in the Pennsylvania House of Representatives asking the House "to pause to mourn the loss of a fine Pennsylvanian, William H. 'Wee Willie' Sherdel, the former pitching great of the St. Louis Cardinals whose courageous spirit and warm personality were an inspiration to all who knew him; and to extend to his son, his grandchildren, and his sisters, this expression of sympathy on their loss."[6]

The accolades continued for Sherdel, even after his death. In November 1977, the little southpaw was inducted into the Pennsylvania Sports Hall of Fame at Williamsport. In 1992, Bob Broeg, contributing sports editor of the *St. Louis Post-Dispatch* and a member of the Baseball Hall of Fame's board of directors and veterans committee, undertook the arduous task of selecting the top 100 Cardinals who had had the most impact in the franchise's first hundred years. The top ten picks were Stan Musial, Rogers Hornsby, Bob Gibson, Lou Brock, Frankie Frisch, Dizzy Dean, Jim Bottomley, Chick Hafey, Pepper Martin, and Jess Haines—all but Martin are in the Hall of Fame. Bill Sherdel was ranked a prestigious number thirty-two out of more than 1,400 players.[7]

Time moved on. On June 19, 1989, William Sherdel Lauck died. Lauck had been born in St. Louis in 1926, when the Cardinals won their first National League pennant, and named by his parents after the pitcher who would start the first World Series game. He carried the name and memory of William Sherdel until his death.

Sadly, on March 17, 1993, Junior, William J. Sherdel, passed away in the Carlisle Hospital from a lengthy illness. Once again, it was the kidneys that were a weakness. Junior was seventy years old. Now it was up to the Sherdel grandchildren and great-grandchildren to continue the memory of Wee Willie and to create their own pathways through life. The next generations continued to root passionately for the St. Louis Cardinals.

Willie's grandson John Sherdel and his family—starting clockwise from the back middle: John, son John, wife Mary, grandson Jacob, granddaughter Jillian, son John's wife Jennifer, grandson Joshua, and son David. Missing is son Kenneth
—Sherdel family

Noted authors Bill James and Rob Neyer wrote a book called *The Neyer/James Guide to Pitchers,* in 2004. The book was a comprehensive study of pitching, pitchers, and pitches. For each type of pitch, the authors chose the all-time top-ten pitchers who had thrown it. On the list for the ten greatest change-ups, Bill Sherdel's pitch was ranked number nine.

In 2006, when the Cardinals opened the new Busch Stadium, they placed personalized red-brick pavers into the walkway around the ballpark. The Sherdel family memorialized "Wee Willie" on the corner of Poplar Street and Broadway, outside of Gate 1. The paver would remind all who visited the stadium of the outstanding accomplishments of the little left-hander.

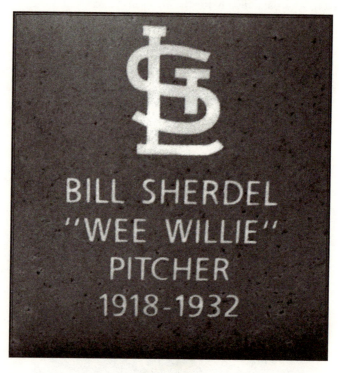

Sherdel paver in Busch Stadium walkway
—Sherdel family

ACKNOWLEDGMENTS

I wish to thank Wee Willie Sherdel's grandson John for his support in this project. John has become the champion of his grandfather's legacy. He has provided invaluable photos and mementoes that have added greatly to the telling of this story. John has become my good friend.

My thanks to my editor Laura Pratt and my publisher FriesenPress, and the individuals who have helped me take a raw manuscript and craft a professionally-looking book and an interesting life's story. Especially, I appreciate the assistance of my publishing specialist Judith Hewlett, my book designer Teresita Hernandez-Quesada, my marketing specialist James Stewart and my FriesenPress editor, Janine. They have made the long publishing journey enjoyable and fulfilling.

This project could not have been possible without digital access to the newspapers in St. Louis, Hanover, and Gettysburg. It was wonderful to read and gain an understanding of the times through the many articles and photos that helped develop this story. I doubt the people of Midway, Hanover, and McSherrystown recognized that their local unassuming hero had been a national celebrity. My thanks to the *St. Louis Post-Dispatch*, *St. Louis Star*, *Evening Sun*, and *Gettysburg Times* for digitally sharing their history with the public.

Special thanks to Dennis Pajot for his excellent history of the 1916 and 1917 Milwaukee Brewers and his willingness to share his hard-earned information for this book. His 2012 work was available through a PDF download on the SABR website. Dennis credits *Milwaukee Journal* and *Milwaukee Sentinel* publication dates for his sources but does not include page numbers. Anyone interested can review his material to locate exact references.

Local historians John McGrew, Wendy Bish-McGrew, and Ben Eline have also been helpful in my research and I thank them.

The most important heartfelt thank you is to my wife, family and friends for their never-ending support as this dream became a reality.

—John G. Coulson

NOTES

The newspaper articles referenced in this section were located through online research into the papers' digital archives. In some cases, online access provided a different digital page number than the original paper's page number. I've chosen to use the digital page numbers since most research now is done online.

Introduction
1. "Bob Shantz Compared with Wee Willie Sherdel," *The Evening Sun* (Hanover, Pennsylvania), July 31, 1952, 18.

Chapter One
1. "Fans in 9-Hour Rampage Give Vent to Noisy Joy Over Cardinals' Victory," *St. Louis Post-Dispatch,* October 11, 1926, 3.
2. Associated Press, "St. Louis Greets Cardinal Players," *The Evening Sun*, October 12, 1926, 3.
3. "Wee Willie Sherdel Wins Pennant for St. Louis Cards; Homecoming Being Planned," *Gettysburg Times,* September 25, 1926, 1.
4. Associated Press, "St. Louis Gives Rousing Welcome to Her Heroes," *The Evening Sun,* October 5, 1926, 3.
5. "Sid Keener's Column," *St. Louis Star,* May 17, 1932, 16.
6. "Hornsby Praises Sherdel's Game," *Gettysburg Times,* October 8, 1926, 1.
7. "Bill Sherdel and Family Home After World's Series," *The Evening Sun,* October 12, 1926, 1.
8. "Praises Work of Sherdel in Games," *The Hanover Record Herald,* October 13, 1926, 3.
9. "Tributes Paid to Sherdel by Speakers at Banquet," *The Evening Sun,* October 20, 1926, 3.
10. "Cullen Cain Reiterates Praise of Bill Sherdel," *Gettysburg Times,* October 26, 1926, 3.

11. "Boy Born Sept. 22 Named After Pitcher Sherdel," *St. Louis Post-Dispatch,* October 9, 1926, 1.
12. "Wee Willie Sherdel Shunned by Lady Luck in '26 Series," *The Evening Sun,* September 16, 1947, 8.
13. "Heard About Sherdel in Great Open Spaces," *The Hanover Record Herald,* November 3, 1926, 3.

Chapter Two
1. "Wee Willie Was Just Green Youth When He Broke Into Baseball," *St. Louis Star,* May 31, 1929, 3.
2. Ibid.
3. Ibid.
4. "Drowned in a Quarry," *New Oxford Item,* June 25, 1908.
5. "Wee Willie Was Just Green Youth When He Broke Into Baseball," *St. Louis Star,* May 31, 1929, 3.
6. "Willie Sherdel Paid Quarter to Pitch Ball Game," *The Hanover Record Herald,* October 25, 1926, 3.
7. "Industrial League," *Record Herald* (Hanover, Pennsylvania), May 6, 1912, 4.
8. "Loyal Fans Pay Sherdel Tribute," *Gettysburg Times,* November 19, 1925, 3.
9. "Wee Willie Was Just Green Youth When He Broke Into Baseball," *St. Louis Star,* May 31, 1929, 3.
10. "Sherdel Pitched First Ball Game for One Dollar," *The Hanover Record Herald,* October 16, 1926, 3.
11. "Diamond Dope," *Record Herald,* May 1, 1914, 4.
12. "Wee Willie Was Just Green Youth When He Broke Into Baseball," *St. Louis Star,* May 31, 1929, 3.
13. "About 'Eddie' Plank," *Record Herald,* July 20, 1916, 3.
14. "Plank Has Golden Asset of Pitcher," *Record Herald,* July 26, 1916, 3.
15. "Plank's Way Amuses Fans," *The Record Herald,* April 28, 1917, 3.
16. "Ira Plank Starts Eighteenth Year of Bright Baseball Career," *Gettysburg Times,* March 12, 1929, 2.

Chapter Three

1. John G. Coulson, "Hanover Raiders: Minor League Baseball in Hanover, Pennsylvania," *The Sheridan Press*, Hanover, 2008, 26.
2. "The League Schedule," *Record Herald*, May 20, 1915, 1.
3. "Billy Starr Elected as Player Manager," *Hanover Independent*, April 21, 1915, 1.
4. "Starr Captures Two Big Ones," *The Evening Sun*, May 3, 1915, 3.
5. "We Win Two Out of Three," *Record Herald*, June 1, 1915, 4.
6. "Bill Scherdel [sic] Puts Hanover in Second Place," *The Evening Sun*, June 12, 1915, 4.
7. "Public Opinion," *The Evening Sun*, May 19, 1917, 5.
8. "About Kid Scherdel [sic]," *Record Herald*, July 2, 1915, 4.
9. "A One-Inning Victory," *Record Herald*, July 2, 1915, 4.
10. "Kid Scherdel [sic] Hit by Officer," *The Evening Sun*, July 15, 1915, 1.
11. "Emmons Arrested," *Gettysburg Times*, July 16, 1915, 1.
12. "Birthday Party," *The Evening Sun*, August 20, 1915, 2.
13. "Blue Ridge League and Other Baseball Dope," *Record Herald*, May 11, 1916, 3.
14. "Kid Scherdel [sic] Star of Blue Ridge League," *Record Herald*, January 24, 1916, 1.
15. "Birthday Party," *The Evening Sun*, August 20, 1915, 2.

Chapter Four

1. "Pick-Ups," *Record Herald*, May 5, 1916, 3.
2. "Blue Ridge League and Other Baseball Dope," *Record Herald*, May 10, 1916, 3.
3. "Blue Ridge League and Other Baseball Dope," *Record Herald*, May 29, 1916, 3.
4. "Hanover Two-Steps Into 1st Place Via 2nd Double Bill," *The Evening Sun*, June 19, 1916, 3.
5. "Starrmen Get Revenge: Take Last of Series From Gettysburg 8–1," *The Evening Sun*, June 30, 1916, 3.
6. "Gettysburg Fans Unfair," *The Evening Sun*, June 23, 1916, 3.
7. "Blue Ridge League and Other Baseball Dope," *Record Herald*, July 12, 1916, 3.
8. "Juicy Jottings," *The Evening Sun*, July 13, 1916, 3.

9. Mark Zeigler, "Player Changes and Roster Loopholes," *Boys of the Blue Ridge*, 2017, www.blueridgeleague.org.
10. "Starrmen Drive Sherman From Mound and Beat Plank's Ponies; Score 4–2," *The Evening Sun*, July 24, 1916, 3.
11. "Around the Circuit," *The Evening Sun*, July 25, 1916, 3.
12. "Scherdel [sic] a Jinx to Other Teams," *Record Herald*, July 27, 1916, 3.
13. "The Mountaineers Win," *Record Herald*, August 12, 1916, 3.
14. "Scherdel [sic] Sold to Milwaukee," *Record Herald*, August 16, 1916, 3.
15. "Scherdel [sic] Sold to Milwaukee," *The Evening Sun*, August 16, 1916, 3.
16. "Blue Ridge League and Other Baseball Dope," *Record Herald*, August 18, 1916, 3.
17. "Blue Ridge League and Other Baseball Dope," *Record Herald*, August 22, 1916, 3.
18. "Hanover Pitcher Sold to Milwaukee Club," *The Star & Sentinel* (Gettysburg, PA), August 19, 1916, 8.

Chapter Five
1. "Bill Sherdel Credits His Success to Study of Game," *The Evening Sun*, May 26, 1932, 8.
2. "Scherdel's [sic] Fast Company," *The Evening Sun*, August 18, 1916, 3.
3. "'Wee Willie' Was Just Green Youth When He Broke Into Baseball," *St. Louis Star*, May 31, 1929, 3.
4. "Scherdel's [sic] Fast Company," *The Evening Sun*, August 18, 1916, 3.
5. Dennis Pajot, "The 1916 Milwaukee Brewers a Cellar Dwelling Year," *1902-1919 Milwaukee Brewers Research Files*, 2012, 7.
6. Ron Flatter, "Thorpe Preceded Deion, Bo," ESPN.com/sportscentury/features/00016499.html.
7. "Scherdel's [sic] First Game," *Record Herald*, August 24, 1916, 3.
8. "'Bill' Scherdel [sic]," *The Evening Sun*, August 26, 1916, 3.
9. Pajot, "The 1916 Milwaukee Brewers," 56.
10. "Scherdel [sic] Makes Good Showing in 4–1 Game," *The Evening Sun*, August 31, 1916, 6.
11. "Word From 'Kid' Scherdel [sic]," *The Evening Sun*, August 31, 1916, 3.
12. "Pleased With Scherdel [sic]," *Record Herald*, September 5, 1916, 3.

13. "Scherdel [sic] Wins Hearts of Fans in Milwaukee," *The Evening Sun,* September 30, 1916, 1.
14. Paul Purman, "Thorpe's Greatest Ambition May be Realized by His Transfer to Cincinnati," *The Evening Sun,* April 30, 1917, 3.
15. Dennis Pajot, "The 1917 Milwaukee Brewers Four Managers, One Murder, World War One," *1902-1919 Milwaukee Brewers Research Files,* 2014, 6.
16. Ibid., 8–9.

Chapter Six
1. "Blue Ridge League & Other Baseball Dope," *The Record Herald,* February 23, 1917, 3.
2. Pajot, "1917 Milwaukee Brewers," 16.
3. Ibid., 17–18.
4. Ibid., 20.
5. Ibid., 23.
6. Ibid., 28.
7. Ibid., 18–19.
8. Ibid., 19–20.
9. "Scherdel [sic] Had Some Stuff," *The Record Herald,* April 12, 1917, 3.
10. Pajot, "1917 Milwaukee Brewers," 22.
11. Ibid., 31.
12. Ibid., 24.
13. Ibid., 29–30, 34.
14. Ibid., 35–36.
15. Ibid., 36.
16. Ibid., 41.
17. Ibid., 39–42.
18. Ibid., 59
19. Ibid., 55.
20. Ibid., 56.
21. Ibid., 56–57.
22. Ibid., 57–58.
23. Ibid., 62–63.
24. Ibid., 63.
25. "Saw Scherdel [sic] Pitch," *The Record Herald,* July 23, 1917, 3.

26. "Sherdel, Howard and May Almost Certain Fixtures with Cards," *St. Louis Star*, March 27, 1918, 15.
27. Pajot, "1917 Milwaukee Brewers," 78.
28. Ibid., 68.
29. Ibid., 69–72.
30. Ibid., 74.
31. Ibid., 76–77.
32. "Blue Ridge League & Other Baseball Dope," *The Record Herald*, July 16, 1917, 3.
33. "Scherdel [sic] Goes in Cash Trade," *The Record Herald*, July 28, 1917, 3.
34. "Two Homers for Scherdel [sic]," *The Record Herald*, August 11, 1917, 3.
35. Pajot, "1917 Milwaukee Brewers," 86.
36. Ibid., 86–87.
37. Ibid., 88–89.
38. "Hendricks Looks for Sherdell [sic] to Aid Him," *St. Louis Star*, January 12, 1918, 8.
39. "How Scherdel [sic] was Bought," *The Star & Sentinel*, June 1, 1918, 5.
40. Pajot, "1917 Milwaukee Brewers," 89.
41. Ibid., 42–53.

Chapter Seven
1. Peter Golenbock, *The Spirit of St. Louis*, Avon Books, New York, 2000, 6.
2. Ibid., 13.
3. Ibid., 17.
4. Ibid., 12.
5. Ibid., 15–16.
6. Ibid., 26.
7. Ibid., 55.
8. Ibid., 14.
9. John Heidenry, "The Gashouse Gang," *Public Affairs*, New York, 2007, 1.
10. Ibid., 3.
11. Ibid., 4–11.

12. Golenbock, 70.
13. Heidenry, 12–13.
14. Golenbock, 82.
15. Heidenry, 14.
16. Ibid., 15.
17. Golenbock, 83.
18. "Jack Hendricks Signed by Rickey to Manage Cards," *St. Louis Post-Dispatch,* December 31, 1917, 12.
19. "Hendricks Lifted Club from Eighth to Second Place First Year as Manager," *St. Louis Post-Dispatch,* December 31, 1917, 12.
20. Clarence Lloyd, "The Star Presents Hendricks' View on Second Base Problem," *St. Louis Star,* January 28, 1918, 12.
21. Clarence Lloyd, "Six New Pitchers Seek Places with Cardinal Outfit," *St. Louis Star,* February 5, 1918, 11.
22. Clarence Lloyd, "Penned Contract of Bill Sherdell (sic) is Received Here," *St. Louis Star,* March 2, 1918, 9.
23. "Cardinals Sign Cliff Heathcote, Penn State Star," *St. Louis Star,* January 28, 1918, 12.
24. "Hendricks Plans Grueling Course at Training Camp," *St. Louis Post-Dispatch,* March 6, 1918, 16.
25. Golenbock, 84.
26. Clarence Lloyd, "Sherdel, Howard and May Almost Certain Fixtures with Cards," *St. Louis Star,* March 27, 1918, 15.
27. "Greets Scherdel [sic] in Houston," *New Oxford Item,* April 4, 1918, 1.
28. Clarence Lloyd, "Hendricks' System of Handling Men is Well Liked by His Players," *St. Louis Star,* March 25, 1918, 8.
29. Jack Hendricks, "Hendricks Predicts First Division: Browns Improved Club, Says Jones," *St. Louis Post-Dispatch,* April 6, 1918, 10.
30. Irvin Howe, "Famous Statistician Names Cardinals to Finish in 4th Place," *St. Louis Star,* April 15, 1918, 15.
31. Clarence Lloyd, "Great Work of Young Collegian is Bright Spot of Second Game," *St. Louis Star,* April 13, 1918, 11.
32. Clarence Lloyd, "Alexander the Great to Pitch What May be Final Game Here," *St. Louis Star,* April 16, 1918, 15.

33. "Mighty Alexander Pounded to All Corners, in Opening Game; Cards' Inaugural Draws 8000," *St. Louis Post-Dispatch,* April 17, 1918, 22.
34. Tom Swope, "Showing of Sherdel Proves Youngster is a Master on Mound," *St. Louis Star,* April 29, 1918, 17.
35. "Reds Pull Triple Play, but Cards Take First Game," *St. Louis Post-Dispatch,* April 29, 1918, 18.
36. "85 Per Cent of Men Engaged in Majors are Liable to Draft," *St. Louis Star,* May 24, 1918, 17.
37. Clarence Lloyd, "Young Texan Denies He is Dissatisfied with His Job Here," *St. Louis Star,* May 21, 1918, 9.
38. "Doak's Pitching Gives Hendricks' Men Even Break," *St. Louis Post-Dispatch,* June 9, 1918, 32.
39. Mike Lynch, "The Promising Life and Tragic Death of Austin McHenry," *seamheads,* November 30, 2008, seamheads.com/blog/2008/11/30/the-promising-life-and-tragic-death-of-austin-mchenry.
40. "Lack of Pitchers Costs Cards Dear in Chicago Battle," *St. Louis Star,* June 26, 1918, 13.
41. "Sherdell [sic] Asked to be Replaced, but was Refused," *St. Louis Post-Dispatch,* June 26, 1918, 20.
42. "Plea for $60,000 to Pay Off Cards' Debts Nets $2,000," *St. Louis Post-Dispatch,* June 30, 1918, 30.
43. "Hendricks Cites Many Reasons for Failure of Cards," *St. Louis Post-Dispatch,* July 2, 1918, 22.
44. "Cardinal Stockholders Raise $61,000 to Wipe Off Present Obligations," *St. Louis Post-Dispatch,* July 21, 1918, 31.
45. Clarence Lloyd, "Bomb Proof Jobs are Much Sought by Some Players," *St. Louis Star,* July 19, 1918, 11.
46. "Sherdel's Great Pitching Results in Close Victory," *St. Louis Post-Dispatch,* August 3, 1918, 12.
47. "Cardinal Players Pay High Tribute to Jack Hendricks," *St. Louis Star,* September 4, 1918, 11.
48. Heidenry, 20.

Chapter Eight
1. Golenbock, 84.
2. "Only Cloud on Horizon, as Cards Start Home Training, is Shortage of Hurlers," *St. Louis Post-Dispatch,* March 23, 1919, 46.
3. James Gould, "Pepper is Principal Ingredient of Cards' First Labor Session," *St. Louis Star,* March 25, 1919, 15.
4. James Gould, "Harmony Prevails in Cardinal Cohorts as Training Progresses," *St. Louis Star,* March 27, 1919, 17.
5. Heidenry, 22.
6. "Cardinal Chat," *St. Louis Star,* April 4, 1919, 17.
7. "Five Cardinal Pitchers Hurt in Automobile Smash," *St. Louis Post-Dispatch,* April 16, 1919, 30.
8. "Sid Keener's Column," *St. Louis Star,* February 16, 1943, 14.
9. "Scherdel [sic] in Smash-Up," *The Record Herald,* April 17, 1919, 1, 4.
10. John Wray, "Cards Transformed From a Last Place Team to 'Best Young Club in Big Leagues,'" *St. Louis Post-Dispatch,* September 10, 1919, 24.
11. James Gould, "Lavan Due Here for Conference; Jack Miller Keen to Get in Game," *St. Louis Star,* April 22, 1919, 15.
12. "Cards Lack Pitching," *St. Louis Post-Dispatch,* May 1, 1919, 30.
13. "Rickey Worried About Present Pitching; Club Will be O K in 6 Weeks," *St. Louis Post-Dispatch,* May 1, 1919, 30.
14. James Gould, "Faulty Pitching and Loose Fielding Give Game to Pirates, 5–2," *St. Louis Star,* May 6, 1919, 15.
15. "Coming of Lavan Compels Change in Cards' Infield," *St. Louis Post-Dispatch,* May 15, 1919, 30.
16. Golenbock, 85–87.
17. James Gould, "Pirates Only Get Fourteen Runs Off Five Card Hurlers," *St. Louis Star,* July 8, 1919, 14.
18. James Gould, "Cardinals Leave on Eastern Trip; Lose Sunday, 5–1," *St. Louis Star,* August 11, 1919, 14.
19. James Gould, "Cards' Play in Final Month of 1919 Was in Hoped-for 1920 Style," *St. Louis Star,* December 26, 1919, 15.

20. John Wray, "Cards Transformed From a Last Place Team to 'Best Young Club in Big Leagues,'" *St. Louis Post-Dispatch,* September 10, 1919, 24.

Chapter Nine

1. Golenbock, 88-91.
2. James Gould, "Purchase of Pitcher Haines Puts Cards in 1920 Pennant Class," *St. Louis Star,* February 13, 1920, 20.
3. "Sporting Column," *Gettysburg Times,* February 18, 1920, 4.
4. James Gould, "'Crabs' on Cardinals' Club Have Own Table at Brownsville Camp," *St. Louis Star,* March 3, 1920, 18.
5. "Cardinals Defeat Pittsburg [sic], 5 to 4, in Morning Game," *St. Louis Post-Dispatch,* May 31, 1920, 15.
6. James Gould, "Buccaneers Drive Sherdel Off Slab in Eighth Stanza," *St. Louis Star,* May 31, 1920, 16.
7. "Cardinals Spot Cubs Six Runs, Then Put on Rally And Win by 11 to 6 Score," *St. Louis Post-Dispatch,* June 6, 1920, 6.
8. James Gould, "Hornsby Hurt, When Lavan's Peg Fells '$200,000 Beauty,'" *St. Louis Star,* June 15, 1920, 18.
9. "Rickeymen Make a Clean Sweep of Redland Games," *St. Louis Star,* June 26, 1920, 10.
10. "Sherdel's Double Leads to Victory in Twelfth Inning," *St. Louis Post-Dispatch,* July 20, 1920, 18.
11. "Sherdel Had Been Sick," *The Record-Herald,* August 23, 1920, 3.
12. "Chapman Suffers Fractured Skull When Hit by Ball," *St. Louis Star,* August 16, 1920, 14.
13. "Fatality to Chapman May Cost Cleveland a Baseball Pennant," *St. Louis Star,* August 17, 1920, 16.
14. "Officials Pay High Tribute to Dead Cleveland Player," *St. Louis Star,* August 17, 1920, 16.
15. James Gould, "Control Shown by Southpaw Sherdel is Nearly Perfect," *St. Louis Star,* December 6, 1920, 17.
16. "Sporting Column," *Gettysburg Times,* January 29, 1921, 4.

Chapter Ten
1. James Gould, "Cardinals Give Three Players in Trade for Pitcher Bill Pertica," *St. Louis Star,* January 4, 1921, 17.
2. James Gould, "Bill Sherdel is Latest Cardinal Regular to Sign," *St. Louis Star,* February 18, 1921, 17.
3. "Rickey Satisfied Orange Camp Will be Greatest Ever," *St. Louis Star,* January 14, 1921, 19.
4. Robert Maxwell, "'Everything Depends Upon Slab Artists,' Says Branch Rickey," *St. Louis Star,* March 15, 1921, 17.
5. James Gould, "Hornsby and Ruth Clash as Yankees and Cards Battle," *St. Louis Star,* March 16, 1921, 15.
6. James Gould, "Playing of Torporcer is Greatest Feature of Scrap With Yanks," *St. Louis Star,* March 17, 1921, 19.
7. "Sherdel Believes St. Louis Cards Will be up Among Leaders," *The Evening Sun,* April 4, 1921, 3.
8. Golenbock, 87.
9. "Sherdel's Record in Sports Paper," *The Evening Sun,* April 15, 1921, 1.
10. Harry Pierce, "Tuberculosis Day Frolics Draw Big Turnout of Fans," *St. Louis Star,* July 27, 1921, 13.
11. Harry Pierce, "Police Called to Stop a Near Riot at Sportsman's," *St. Louis Star,* August 4, 1921, 17.
12. "Pfeffer Routed in First Inning by Boston Team," *St. Louis Post-Dispatch,* August 6, 1921, 6.
13. "Cardinals Take Pair From Pittsburgh and Climb to Third Place," *St. Louis Star,* September 2, 1921, 17.

Chapter Eleven
1. "Dillhoefer Now in St. John's Hospital," *St. Louis Star,* January 26, 1922, 17.
2. Harry Pierce, "Rickey Plans to Use Sherdel as Regular on Mound This Year," *St. Louis Star,* January 21, 1922, 9.
3. "Cliff Heathcote Will Join First Squad at Orange," *St. Louis Star,* February 16, 1922, 15.
4. "'Pickels' Dillhoefer, Cardinal Catcher, Dies," *St. Louis Post-Dispatch,* February 23, 1922, 1.

5. "Rickey Says Cardinals Will Have Hard Time Replacing Dillhoefer," *St. Louis Star,* February 23, 1922, 17.
6. Henry Farrell, "Rogers Hornsby Greatest Player, Says J. J. M'Graw," *St. Louis Star,* April 4, 1922, 21.
7. Harry Pierce, "Rally in Ninth Sends Winning Tally Across for Fohl's Brownies." *St. Louis Star,* April 9, 1922, 29.
8. Mike Lynch, "The Promising Life and Tragic Death of Austin McHenry," *seamheads*, November 30, 2008, seamheads.com/blog/2008/11/30/the-promising-life-and-tragic-death-of-austin-mchenry.
9. "Austin McHenry Cardinals' Star Outfielder, Dies," *St. Louis Post-Dispatch,* November 27, 1922, 23.
10. Mike Lynch, "The Promising Life and Tragic Death of Austin McHenry," *seamheads*, November 30, 008, seamheads.com/blog/2008/11/30/the-promising-life-and-tragic-death-of-austin-mchenry.
11. "Eddie Ainsmith is Real Sensation as Cardinal Receiver," *St. Louis Star,* July 14, 1922, 15.
12. "Slow Ball Wins for Bill Sherdel," *The Evening Sun,* August 8, 1922, 3.
13. Golenbock, 87.
14. Ibid., 93.
15. James Gould, "Loss of M'Henry Has Hurt Cards' Chances in Race for Pennant," *St. Louis Star,* August 21, 1922, 17.
16. "'Bill' Sherdel Has Young Son," *The Evening Sun,* August 30, 1922, 1.
17. "McHenry Operated On for Tumor," *St. Louis Post-Dispatch,* October 19, 1922, 29.
18. "Austin McHenry Cardinals' Star Outfielder, Dies," *St. Louis Post-Dispatch,* November 27, 1922, 23.
19. James Gould, "Austin M'Henry Left Baseball as He Did Life—Battling to the Last," *St. Louis Star,* January 9, 1923, 17.

Chapter Twelve
1. Herman Wecke, "St. Louis Club Leader Highest Paid in League With Single Exception," *St. Louis Post-Dispatch,* February 4, 1923, 3.
2. Herman Wecke, "Unusual Shortage of Southpaws Handicaps Big League Managers," *St. Louis Post-Dispatch,* February 7, 1923, 21.

3. James Gould, "Bill Sherdel Is Only Small 'Package,' but He Is Always 'There,'" *St. Louis Star*, February 13, 1923, 17.
4. "Cobb Tosses Dirt at Umpire Pfirman and Then Forfeits Game," *St. Louis Star*, April 7, 1923, 8.
5. "Ty Cobb Assaults Arbitrator After Game With Cards," *St. Louis Star*, April 8, 1923, 31.
6. Joseph Holland, "Sherdel's Hit Wins First Game of Giant Series," *St. Louis Post-Dispatch*, June 18, 1923, 20.
7. Harry Pierce, "Rogers Hornsby May Be Traded by Rickey in Shakeup of Team," *St. Louis Star*, September 10, 1923, 1.
8. Harry Pierce, "Breadon Declares Hornsby Will Not Be Traded or Sold," *St. Louis Star*, September 11, 1923, 1.
9. Joseph Holland, "Hornsby, Suspended and Fined $500, Will Not Be Sold or Traded, Owner of Cardinals Declares," *St. Louis Post-Dispatch*, September 27, 1923, 29.
10. John Wray, "Hornsby Disciplined Because Morale of the Club Was Being Hurt, Rickey Statement Says," *St. Louis Post-Dispatch*, September 30, 1923, 10.

Chapter Thirteen
1. James Gould, "Florida Returns to Form and Cardinals Get Chance to Work," *St. Louis Star*, March 1, 1924, 10.
2. "Rickey's One Good Catcher Has Bad Knee," *St. Louis Post-Dispatch*, March 2, 1924, 11.
3. "Southpaw Pitchers Worth Fancy Prices," *St. Louis Star*, March 25, 1924, 16.
4. "Sherdel Displays Splendid Hurling in Braves' Battle," *St. Louis Star*, March 21, 1924, 18.
5. "Bill Sherdel is One Hurler Who Can Larrup Pill," *St. Louis Star*, April 9, 1924, 21.
6. "Sherdel Stars on Pitched Ball," *The Gettysburg Times*, August 4, 1924, 5.
7. "Rickey Returns From Long Trip," *St. Louis Post-Dispatch*, August 25, 1924, 19.
8. "Bill Sherdel Pitched," *The Record-Herald*, September 27, 1924, 3.

9. "Home-Run Clout Only Hit of 13 To Score Run In Game," *The Record-Herald*, February 9, 1925, 3.
10. "New York Critic Claims Hornsby Should be Pilot," *St. Louis Star*, September 30, 1924, 17.

Chapter Fourteen
1. "Hornsby Signs 3-Year Contract With Cardinals," *St. Louis Star*, February 7, 1925, 13.
2. James Gould, "Cards, In Camp, Get Ready For First Workout," *St. Louis Star*, February 24, 1925, 14.
3. James Gould, "Cardinals Have Two Workouts at California Training Camp," *St. Louis Star*, February 25, 1925, 16.
4. James Gould, "Cards To Engage In First Practice Game Tomorrow," *St. Louis Star*, February 27, 1925, 20.
5. James Gould, "Torporcer Signs And Will Report To Camp Friday," *St. Louis Star*, March 3, 1925, 12.
6. "Sportsman's Park Will Be Improved By Baseball Clubs," *St. Louis Star*, March 5, 1925, 19.
7. Al Santore, "Rickey Says He Has Good Offensive Club, Hopes to Upset Dope," *St. Louis Star*, March 23, 1925, 19.
8. James Gould, "Cardinals to Open Series With Cubs Tomorrow Afternoon," *St. Louis Star*, April 28, 1925, 19.
9. William Duncan, "Dope From Dunc," *The Gettysburg Times*, May 26, 1925, 3.
10. James Gould, "Decision Made By Breadon," *St. Louis Star*, May 30, 1925, 15.
11. Sid Keener, "When Rog Hornsby Called Pennant Shots for Cards," *St. Louis Star*, February 14, 1950, 22.
12. "Hornsby Asks Players to Give Him Their Best at All Times," *St. Louis Post-Dispatch*, May 31, 1925, 13.
13. James Gould, "Cards Win Fifth in Row From Phils by Splendid Rally," *St. Louis Star*, June 17, 1925, 21.
14. Herman Wecke, "Cardinals Have Best Staff of Southpaws in Major Leagues," *St. Louis Post-Dispatch*, August 23, 1925, 10.
15. "He Doesn't Need a Fast One," *The Sporting News*, August 27, 1925, 1.

16. James Gould, "Corsairs Tighten Grip on Lead by Drubbing Knot Holers 5 to 2," *St. Louis Star,* September 4, 1925, 20.
17. "Rogers Hornsby Responsible For Cardinal Success," *St. Louis Star,* October 5, 1925, 16.
18. "Arrangements Made For Dinner To Be Tendered 'Bill' Sherdel," *The Evening Sun,* October 13, 1925, 1.
19. "Former Baseball Pitcher Injured In Plane Crash," *Taylor Daily Press,* October 20, 1925, 1.

Chapter Fifteen
1. Henry Farrell, "John McGraw Says Cardinals and Pirates Are Clubs New York Will Have to Defeat for 1926 Pennant," *St. Louis Star,* December 30, 1925, 12.
2. "Cards Send Cooney to Cubs in Exchange for Hurler Vic Keen," *St. Louis Star,* December 11, 1925, 24.
3. Ralph Leon, "Redbird Pilot Looks for Improvement in General Team Play," *St. Louis Star,* February 5, 1926, 20.
4. James Gould, "Hurler Has Winning Average Past Eight Seasons With Cards," *St. Louis Star,* January 29, 1926, 19.
5. Jack Conway, "Expect Sherdel To Have a Banner Season in 1926," *The Hanover Record-Herald,* March 2, 1926, 3.
6. James Gould, "Hornsby Seems 'Sartain' Sure' to Become Really Great Pilot," *St. Louis Star,* March 16, 1926, 16.
7. "Sid Keener's Column," *St. Louis Star,* August 31, 1943, 20.
8. "What Hornsby Says About Acquisition of Bill Southworth," *St. Louis Star,* June 15, 1926, 17.
9. "Southworth's Steadier Fielding Will Stabilize Outfield, Hornsby Says," *St. Louis Post-Dispatch,* June 15, 1926, 26.
10. J. Roy Stockton, "Alexander Tells Killefer He Is Ready to Pitch," *St. Louis Post-Dispatch,* June 23, 1926, 26.
11. J. Roy Stockton, "Hurler Comes To Club For Waiver Price," *St. Louis Post-Dispatch,* June 23, 1926, 26.
12. "Haines To Pitch Two Games in Boston Series, Rogers States," *St. Louis Post-Dispatch,* September 8, 1926, 19.
13. J. Roy Stockton, "Fans Pursue Him as If He Were Another Babe Ruth or Dempsey," *St. Louis Post-Dispatch,* September 10, 1926, 40.

14. "Hornsby Reduces Signs to Minimum; Makes All Decisions and Is Real Boss," *St. Louis Post-Dispatch,* September 10, 1926, 40.
15. "Sherdel Pitches Cardinal Victory," *The Evening Sun,* September 18, 1926, 3.
16. "'Nothing Could Have Made Me Happier'-Breadon," *St. Louis Post-Dispatch,* September 25, 1926, 4.
17. "Fans of St. Louis Are Wild With Joy," *The Evening Sun,* September 25, 1926, 3.
18. Associated Press, "Confidence Enabled Cards To Win National League Pennant, Hornsby Asserts," *St. Louis Post-Dispatch,* September 26, 1926, 19.
19. Herman Wecke, "Righthanders Are Stars Of Quintet," *St. Louis Post-Dispatch,* September 26, 1926, 20.
20. Rogers Hornsby, "Hornsby Tells How He Happened To Get Alexander and Southworth," *St. Louis Post-Dispatch,* September 28, 1926, 24.

Chapter Sixteen
1. Alma Reed, "Hornsby Played Baseball When He Was Three," *St. Louis Star,* March 25, 1925, 19.
2. Associated Press, "Cards Practice For First Time At Yank Stadium," *St. Louis Post-Dispatch,* September 28, 1926, 24.
3. Miller Huggins, "'Cards and Yanks Are Weak Bunters and Have Trouble Breaking Up Play'-Miller Huggins," *St. Louis Post-Dispatch,* September 28, 1926, 25.
4. Rogers Hornsby, "We'll Pitch to Ruth as to Any Other Hard Hitter, Says Hornsby," *St. Louis Post-Dispatch,* September 29, 1926, 33.
5. Herman Wecke, "Righthanders Are Stars Of Quintet," *St. Louis Post-Dispatch,* September 26, 1926, 20.
6. Babe Ruth, "Cardinals a Great Club, But We'll Win If We're Playing Up to Form, Says Babe Ruth," *St. Louis Post-Dispatch,* September 26, 1926, 20.
7. Miller Huggins, "Huggins Expects Sherdel to Give Batters of Yanks Most Trouble in World's Series," *St. Louis Post-Dispatch,* September 29, 1926, 33.
8. John Foster, "Club With Best Catcher Usually Captures Series," *St. Louis Post-Dispatch,* September 30, 1926, 29.

9. John McGraw, "Giants' Manager Hopes Hornsby Will Decide How To Pitch to the Batters," *St. Louis Post-Dispatch,* October 2, 1926, 14.
10. Babe Ruth, "Ruth Predicts Yank Staff Will Stop the Cards," *St. Louis Post-Dispatch,* October 2, 1926, 13.
11. "New York Cheers Both Teams Alike, No Real Rooting," *St. Louis Post-Dispatch,* October 3, 1926, 2.
12. Associated Press, "Clubhouse Chatter Gives Full Credit to Pennock," *St. Louis Post-Dispatch,* October 3, 1926, 18.
13. "Thousands Pack Streets To Cheer Victorious Team," *St. Louis Post-Dispatch,* October 5, 1926, 2.
14. Rogers Hornsby, "Miller Huggins Thinks Hoyt's Fast Ball Will Tame Cardinals Today," *St. Louis Post-Dispatch,* October 6, 1926, 24.
15. Miller Huggins, "Miller Huggins Thinks Hoyt's Fast Ball Will Tame Cardinals Today," *St Louis Post-Dispatch,* October 6, 1926, 24.
16. Charles Dunkley, Associated Press, "Two N. L. Clubs Are Better Than Card's Says Ruth," *St. Louis Post-Dispatch,* October 6, 1926, 24.
17. Babe Ruth, "Ruth Proud of Homers, Praises Hitting of Mates," *St. Louis Post-Dispatch,* October 7, 1926, 25.
18. Rogers Hornsby, "Pitching Wrong For Ruth Cost Game, Hornsby Says," *St. Louis Post-Dispatch,* October 7, 1926, 25.
19. Davis Walsh, International News Service, "Hornsby to Match His Two Winners Against Yanks' Pair of Losers," *St. Louis Star,* October 8, 1926, 18.
20. Bob O'Farrell, "O'Farrell Sure Cards Will Take Baseball Classic," *St. Louis Star,* October 8, 1926, 18.
21. "Umpire O'Day Says Hafey Lost Yesterday's Game For Cardinals," *St. Louis Star,* October 8, 1926, 18.
22. "Sherdel Praised Though Defeated by Sport Scribes," *The Evening Sun,* October 8, 1926, 3.
23. Henry Farrell, United Press, "Gotham Players Admit They Were Lucky to Triumph," *St. Louis Star,* October 8, 1926, 18.
24. J. Roy Stockton, "Cardinals Even Up Series By Beating Yankees, 10–2," *St. Louis Post-Dispatch,* October 10, 1926, 1.
25. "St. Louis Renews Celebration Over Its Third Triumph," *St. Louis Post-Dispatch,* October 10, 1926, 2.

26. "Forecast For Today," *St. Louis Post-Dispatch,* October 10, 1926, 1.
27. J. Roy Stockton, "'Old Pete' Saves Day After Haines Pitches Skin Off His Finger," *St. Louis Post-Dispatch,* October 11, 1926, 19.
28. "'Bases Filled, Eh? Well, There's No Place to Put Lazzeri,' Says Alex," *St. Louis Post-Dispatch,* October 11, 1926, 19.
29. "Grover Alexander Turns Back Lazzeri to Save Final Game," *St. Louis Star,* October 11, 1926, 18.
30. "'Bases Filled, Eh? Well, There's No Place to Put Lazzeri,' Says Alex," *St. Louis Post-Dispatch,* October 11, 1926, 19.
31. John McGraw, "Error Gave One Run, Paved Way for Three; Thevenow the Hero," *St. Louis Post-Dispatch,* October 11, 1926, 20.
32. Grover Cleveland Alexander, "'Thevenow's Hitting and Fielding Won Series For Us,' Alex the Great Says," *St. Louis Post-Dispatch,* October 11, 1926, 20.
33. "In the Wake of the Big Series," *St. Louis Post-Dispatch,* October 18, 1926, 24.
34. "Crowd of 30,000 Makes Bedlam of Cards' Welcome," *St. Louis Post-Dispatch,* October 12, 1926, 3.

Chapter Seventeen
1. "Hornsby Traded To Giants For Frisch And Jimmy Ring," *The Evening Sun,* December 21, 1926, 3.
2. "Loss of Hornsby To Cards Greatly Affects Sherdel," *The Evening Sun,* December 21, 1926,1, 3.
3. James Gould, "Bob O'Farrell Seems Best Possible Choice for Hornsby's Place," *St. Louis Star,* December 28, 1926, 12.
4. Ray Gillespie, "Breadon Says New Leader Was Only Man Offered Post Vacated by Rogers Hornsby Last Monday," *St. Louis Star,* December 28, 1926, 12.

Chapter Eighteen
1. Ray Gillespie, "O'Farrell Thinks Cards' Chances Good to Repeat," *St. Louis Star,* February 26, 1927, 8.
2. Henry Farrell, United Press, "Cards a One Year Best, Giants Best, Rog Hornsby Says," *St. Louis Star,* March 16, 1927, 15.

3. "Bill Sherdel Gets Hornsby's Goat When He Walks Slugger," *The Evening Sun,* March 24, 1927, 3.
4. Ray Gillespie, "Knot-Holers Must Win Final to Even Little World Series," *St. Louis Star,* April 7, 1927, 16.
5. Herman Wecke, "Frisch Leads Card Hitters with .361," *St. Louis Post-Dispatch,* May 20, 1927, 24.
6. "Sherdel and Four Teammates Visitors at Southpaw's Home," *The Evening Sun,* May 17, 1927, 1.
7. James Gould, "Bonus Clause Disputed," *St. Louis Star,* July 27, 1927, 17.
8. "Breadon Sees No Possible Chance for Compromise With Flint Rhem," *St. Louis Star,* July 28, 1927, 17.
9. John Wray, "Wray's Column: Not All Hornsby," *St. Louis Post-Dispatch,* August 30, 1927, 33.
10. John Wray, "Wray's Column: Those Amazing Cards," *St. Louis Post-Dispatch,* September 26, 1927, 16.
11. James Gould, "Cards Idle Today, Will Play Robins Twice Wednesday," *St. Louis Star,* July 18, 1927, 15.
12. J. Roy Stockton, "Extra Innings," *St. Louis Post-Dispatch,* March 2, 1955, 33.
13. J. Roy Stockton, "Off-Season Baseball Notes," *St. Louis Post-Dispatch,* November 3, 1927, 29.

Chapter Nineteen
1. "Sherdel Wins Race with Shetland Pony," *The Evening Sun,* February 17, 1928, 3.
2. Ray Gillespie, "Blades Says His Leg Will Be In Shape This Year," *St. Louis Star,* February 23, 1928, 16.
3. Ray Gillespie, "Only Flint Rhem Missing Now at Cardinals' Camp," *St. Louis Star,* February 22, 1928, 14.
4. Ray Gillespie, "Big Pitcher Wants to Vindicate Self for 1927 Showing," *St. Louis Star,* March 5, 1928, 20.
5. Ray Gillespie, "McKechnie Undecided on Starting Blades at Left Field Post," *St. Louis Star,* April 10, 1928, 20.
6. J. Roy Stockton, "May Recommend Several Deals to Club Owner," *St. Louis Post-Dispatch,* November 8, 1927, 29.

7. Ray Gillespie, "Fred Frankhouse to Twirl as Cards Seek Third Straight Win," *St. Louis Star,* April 14, 1928, 10.
8. "Sherdel Learns How to be Hitter," *The Evening Sun,* June 6, 1928, 3.
9. J. Roy Stockton, "Pitchers Hallahan and Barnes, Infielder Gelbert to be Summoned Soon," *St. Louis Post-Dispatch,* August 13, 1928, 13.

Chapter Twenty

1. "Cards Will Send Back $1,000,000 to 28,000 Fans," *St. Louis Star,* October 1, 1928, 21.
2. Grover Alexander, "Hoyt is Likely to Give Cardinals Most Trouble, In Opinion of Alexander," *St. Louis Post-Dispatch,* October 2, 1928, 15.
3. Walter "Rabbit" Maranville, "Maranville Expects Cardinals to Win World Series in Five Games," *St. Louis Star,* October 3, 1928, 23.
4. Babe Ruth, "Ruth Expects Yanks to Come Out of Slump," *St. Louis Post-Dispatch,* October 2, 1928, 16.
5. James Gould, "Absence of Combs, Pennock and Moore Certain to Hurt Yanks," *St. Louis Star,* October 1, 1928, 21.
6. "Bill Sherdel Tells of Baseball Nerve," *The Evening Sun,* October 3, 1928, 3.
7. J. Roy Stockton, "Four Blows Off Sherdel in 7 Innings All Go for Extra Bases," *St. Louis Post-Dispatch,* October 4, 1928, 18.
8. Ibid., 18.
9. Herman Wecke, "60,714 Crowd at 2nd Game; Receipts Come to $222,533," *St. Louis Post-Dispatch,* October 5, 1928, 25.
10. Grover Alexander, "Lack of Control Beat Him, Says the Old Master," *St. Louis Post-Dispatch,* October 5, 1928, 25.
11. J. Roy Stockton, "Tom Zachary Likely to Oppose Red Birds in the Third Contest," *St. Louis Post-Dispatch,* October 6, 1928, 11.
12. Ibid., 11.
13. Walter Johnson, "Cardinals Have Played Badly, Says 'Big Train,'" *St. Louis Post-Dispatch,* October 6, 1928, 13.
14. "Inability to Judge Fast, High Balls Against Background Hurt Cardinals' Hitting," *St. Louis Post-Dispatch,* October 7, 1928, 19.
15. Harry Brundidge, "Haines Wasn't Taken Out, He Quit in Disgust," *St. Louis Star,* October 8, 1928, 1.

16. Associated Press, Charles Dunkley, "Ruth Kicked the Ball Out of My Hand, Says Jim Wilson," *St. Louis Post-Dispatch,* October 8, 1928, 13.
17. Dunkley, "Ruth Kicked the Ball Out of My Hand," 13.
18. William McKechnie, "We Presented Yanks With 6 of 7 Runs, Says McKechnie," *St. Louis Post-Dispatch,* October 8, 1928, 13.
19. William Allen, "Plenty of Seats for Early Crowd at Series Game," *St. Louis Post-Dispatch,* October 9, 1928, 2.
20. "'Umpire Pfirman Spoiled a Nervy Play'—Breadon," *St. Louis Post-Dispatch,* October 10, 1928, 22.
21. Frank Graham, "Down Memory Lane with Babe Ruth," *St. Louis Star,* August 20, 1948, 31.
22. Harry Brundidge, "Babe Ruth Wants to Forget 'Bad Boy' Days as He Keeps Right on Swatting Home Runs After 16 Years in Game," *The Sporting News,* January 8, 1931, 7.
23. Babe Ruth, "We Say It With Base Hits; That's All—Babe Ruth," *St. Louis Post-Dispatch,* October 10, 1928, 22.
24. Grover Cleveland Alexander, "Slump in Series Cards' Worst in 1928, Says Alex," *St. Louis Post-Dispatch,* October 11, 1928, 29.
25. "Breadon Announces Gelbert Will Play Short for Red Birds," *St. Louis Star,* October 10, 1928, 16.
26. J. Roy Stockton, "Billy Southworth Chosen Manager of Cards For '29," *St. Louis Post-Dispatch,* November 21, 1928, 1.

Chapter Twenty-One
1. Davis Walsh, "Says Hurlers Are 'Shot' and Infield Will be an Experiment," *St. Louis Post-Dispatch,* January 16, 1929, 23.
2. J. Roy Stockton, "Maximum of Batting Practice is Cards' Spring Training Plan," *St. Louis Post-Dispatch,* January 13, 1929, 17.
3. John Wray, "Wray's Column: Time to Take Stock," *St. Louis Post-Dispatch,* July 1, 1929, 20.
4. James Gould, "Cards to Carry on as They are, Rickey Says," *St. Louis Star,* July 9, 1929, 13.
5. Herman Wecke, "McKechnie Recalled by Breadon to Take Over Managing Cardinals," *St. Louis Post-Dispatch,* July 23, 1929, 13.
6. J. Roy Stockton, "Cards' Manager Expects Stars to Return to Winning Stride," *St. Louis Post-Dispatch,* August 14, 1929, 18.

7. James Gould, "Cards Send Alexander Home on Full Pay to Build Up for Next Year," *St. Louis Star,* August 21, 1929, 17.
8. "Huggins was Finest Fellow in World, Babe Ruth Asserts," *St. Louis Post-Dispatch,* September 26, 1929, 22.
9. John Wray, "Wray's Column: Next Year? That's Different.," *St. Louis Post-Dispatch,* September 14, 1928, 24.
10. Herman Wecke, "Man Who Served as Coach During 1929 Signs One-Year Contract; Is Seventh Change in Six Years," *St. Louis Post-Dispatch,* October 31, 1929, 34.
11. J. Roy Stockton, "Street, New Cardinal Pilot, is a Popular, Plain Man and a Fountain of Wit and Wisdom," *St. Louis Post-Dispatch,* November 1, 1929, 46.
12. J. Roy Stockton, "Extra Innings: May Be Sweet William," *St. Louis Post-Dispatch,* December 28, 1929, 35.

Chapter Twenty-Two
1. J. Roy Stockton, "Extra Innings: A Diamond in the Muck," *St. Louis Post-Dispatch,* January 2, 1930, 21.
2. J. Roy Stockton, "Manager Street Cuts Opening Day's Workout 24 are in Camp," *St. Louis Post-Dispatch,* March 3, 1930, 22.
3. J. Roy Stockton, "Gabby Not Sure About Coaching at Third; Will Direct Attack and Shift Men Himself," *St. Louis Post-Dispatch,* March 31, 1930, 18.
4. J. Roy Stockton, "Left Hander Has Faltered in Exhibitions; Red Wings Have Field Day and Drub Red Birds," *St. Louis Post-Dispatch,* March 27, 1930, 26.
5. J. Roy Stockton, "Looks to Frankhouse and Rhem for Pitching Help; Expects Players to Make Suggestions," *St. Louis Post-Dispatch,* March 31, 1930, 18.
6. Babe Ruth, "Babe Ruth Picks Cardinals to Finish in Fifth Place; Looks for Cubs to Repeat," *St. Louis Post-Dispatch,* April 2, 1930, 22.
7. "Gabby Street Expects Johnson and Haines to Prove Consistent Winners," *St. Louis Post-Dispatch,* April 10, 1930, 24.
8. J. Roy Stockton, "Veteran Spitball Pitcher is Traded to the Redbirds for Sherdel and Frankhouse," *St. Louis Post-Dispatch,* June 17, 1930, 16.

9. *Fitchburg Sentinel,* June 17, 1930, 8.
10. "Grimes Traded to Cardinals," *Pittsburgh Post Gazette,* June 17, 1930, 15.

Chapter Twenty-Three
1. J. Roy Stockton, "Rain Gives Two Stars a Chance in Doubleheader Tomorrow, With Both Due Again Sunday," *St. Louis Post-Dispatch,* August 13, 1930, 14.
2. J. Roy Stockton, "Syl Johnson to Pitch; Redbirds Have Taste of Night Baseball," *St. Louis Post-Dispatch,* September 3, 1930, 14.
3. J. Roy Stockton, "No Punishment for Rhem, Back After Day's Absence," *St. Louis Post-Dispatch,* September 17, 1930, 20.
4. "Scribes Burlesque Rhem's Kidnapping," *The Sporting News,* February 12, 1931, 3.

Chapter Twenty-Four
1. Burt Whitman, "McKechnie to Start Rookies in Outfield," *The Sporting News,* January 15, 1931, 1.
2. "Sherdel to Leave Soon for Florida," *The Evening Sun,* February 25, 1931, 8.
3. J. Roy Stockton, "McKechnie Will Show Improved Club for 1931 Pennant Chase," *St. Louis Post-Dispatch,* March 31, 1931, 20.
4. "Gabby Street Gives McKechnie and His Braves a Boost," *St. Louis Post-Dispatch,* April 6, 1931, 26.
5. Associated Press, "Cardinals Need Hafey to Gain Another Flag, McKechnie Says," *St. Louis Post-Dispatch,* April 23, 1931, 16.
6. "Cardinals Send 'Dizzy' Dean to Houston Club," *St. Louis Post-Dispatch,* May 2, 1931, 11.

Chapter Twenty-Five
1. "McKechnie Plans Infield Changes," *The Evening Sun,* February 4, 1932, 8.
2. "'Wee Willie' Sherdel, 35, Sure He Can Still Pitch in Majors," *St. Louis Star,* May 17, 1932, 16.
3. "Bill Sherdel Credits His Success to Study of Game," *The Evening Sun,* May 26, 1932, 8.

4. Walter Smith, "Fans Show They Want Dizzy, Be He Good or Bad," *St. Louis Star*, May 23, 1932, 14.
5. "Dizzy Dean Quits the Cardinals, 'Through for Good,' He Declares," *St. Louis Post-Dispatch*, June 15, 1932, 17–18.
6. Golenbock, 160.
7. Walter Smith, "Cards' Hopes for Flag Sag as Club Fails to Trade," *St. Louis Star*, June 16, 1932, 20.
8. Charles Regan, "On the Sport Trail," *St. Louis Star*, October 1, 1932, 6.

Chapter Twenty-Six
1. Branch Rickey letter sent to Bill Sherdel, January 10, 1933, 2.
2. "Cabbage and Kings," *The Evening Sun*, January 14, 1936, 8.
3. "Sid Keener's Column," *St. Louis Star*, June 3, 1936, 22.
4. "Sherdel's Goal and Foul in Last 25 Seconds Turn Tide," *The Evening Sun*, March 13, 1940, 8.

Chapter Twenty-Seven
1. Bob Broeg, "Southpaw with Slow Stuff is Candidate for All-Star Starter," *St. Louis Post-Dispatch*, June 29, 1949, 18.
2. "Diamond Old Timers Honor Memory of Hack Wilson," *The Evening Sun*, September 28, 1949, 14.
3. "Bill Sherdel Recalls How Alexander Stopped Yankees," *The Evening Sun*, November 6, 1950, 12.
4. Bob Broeg, "Redbird Champs of '26 in Uniform Again Today," *St. Louis Post-Dispatch*, June 24, 1951, 59.
5. "Ghosts of the Past Parade," *St. Louis Post-Dispatch*, June 25, 1951, 16.

Chapter Twenty-Eight
1. Bob Broeg, "Sports Comment," *St. Louis Post-Dispatch*, January 23, 1962, 14.
2. Robert Burnes, "The Bench Warmer," *St. Louis Globe Democrat*, January 31, 1962.
3. Bob Broeg, "Sports Comment," *St. Louis Post-Dispatch*, February 2, 1962, 20, 22.

4. "Duncan Tells Athletes to Have Courage," *Gettysburg Times*, March 18, 1963, 5.
5. "Willie Sherdel Staunch Rooter," *The Sporting News*, March 5, 1966, 5–6.
6. "Note Sherdel Death," *Gettysburg Times*, December 3, 1968, 1.
7. "A Century Marked," *St. Louis Post-Dispatch*, April 12, 1992, 63.

Sherdel's 15 Hall of Fame Teammates (Alphabetical)

Grover Cleveland Alexander
Jim Bottomley
Dizzy Dean
Frankie Frisch
Chick Hafey
Jesse Haines
Rogers Hornsby
Rabbit Maranville
Bill McKechnie (Coach, Manager)
Greasy Neale (Coach, Football HOF)
Branch Rickey (Club President, General Manager, Manager)
George Sisler
Billy Southworth (Player, Manager)
Jim Thorpe (Football HOF)
Bobby Wallace

Sherdel's 5 Hall of Fame Umpires/Commissioner (Alphabetical)

Tommy Connolly (Umpire)
Bill Klem (Umpire)
Judge Kenesaw Landis (Commissioner)
Bill McGowan (Umpire)
Hank O'Day (Umpire)

Sherdel's 85 Hall of Fame Opponents (Alphabetical)

Grover Cleveland Alexander
Dave Bancroft (Player, Manager)
Jim Bottomley
Roger Bresnahan (Manager)
Mordecai Brown
Max Carey (Player, Manager)
Oscar Charleston
Ty Cobb (Player, Manager)
Mickey Cochrane
Eddie Collins (Manager, Player)
Earle Combs
Stan Coveleski
Joe Cronin
Kiki Cuyler
Bill Dickey
Leo Durocher
Johnny Evers (Manager, Coach)
Red Faber
Jimmie Foxx
Frank Frisch
Lou Gehrig
Charley Gehringer
Lefty Gomez
Goose Goslin
Burleigh Grimes
Lefty Grove
Chick Hafey
Jesse Haines
Bucky Harris (Player, Manager)
Gabby Hartnett
Harry Heilmann
Billy Herman
Harry Hooper
Rogers Hornsby (Player, Manager)

Waite Hoyt
Carl Hubbell
Miller Huggins (Manager)
Travis Jackson
Hughie Jennings
Walter Johnson (Manager)
George Kelly
Chuck Klein
Tony Lazzeri
Fred Lindstrom
Ernie Lombardi
Al Lopez
Ted Lyons
Connie Mack (Manager)
Heinie Manush
Rabbit Maranville
Rube Marquard
Christy Mathewson (Manager, Coach)
Joe McCarthy (Player, Manager)
John McGraw (Manager)
Bill McKechnie (Player, Manager)
Greasy Neale (Player, Football HOF)
Ernie Nevers (Player, Football HOF)
Mel Ott
Herb Pennock
Sam Rice
Eppa Rixey
Wilbert Robinson (Manager)
Edd Roush
Red Ruffing
Babe Ruth
Ray Schalk
Joe Sewell
Al Simmons
George Sisler

Billy Southworth
Tris Speaker (Player, Manager)
Casey Stengel
Ben Taylor
Bill Terry
Jim Thorpe (Player, Football HOF)
Joe Tinker (Manager)
Pie Traynor
Dazzy Vance
Arky Vaughan
Ed Walsh (Coach)
Lloyd Waner
Paul Waner
Zack Wheat
Hack Wilson
Ross Youngs

INDEX

Adams, Earl "Sparky", 285, 310
Ainsmith, Eddie, 134, 135, 147, 148
Alexander, Grover Cleveland, 7, 79,
    80, 111, 112, 117, 120, 122,
    183-187, 190, 193, 195, 200,
    201, 203, 205, 209-211, 213-
    217, 226-229, 234, 236, 239,
    244, 245, 247, 249, 250, 252,
    254-256, 258, 262-264, 268, 270,
    271, 275-281, 283, 304, 329,
    330, 332, 333, 341
Altrock, Nick, 328
Ames, Leon "Red", 76, 79, 84, 92, 94,
    95, 97, 98
Athletic Park, 53, 61
Austin, Jimmy, 130
Avon Park, Florida, 224, 244, 275, 284

Baker, Frank "Home Run", 121
Ball, Philip, 70, 71, 106, 165, 186
Bancroft, Dave, 147
Barbeau, Bill "Jap", 51
Barnhart, Clyde, 35
Barrow, Ed, 104
Bell, Herman, 205
Bell, Les, 148, 150, 155, 156, 159,
    165, 173, 175, 181, 183, 185,
    191, 196, 198, 199, 202, 206,
    207, 210, 212, 214, 216, 228,
    235, 239, 241, 245, 295, 296,
    330, 332
Bengough, Bennie, 196, 258, 260, 264
Bentley, Jack, 146
Beradino, Johnny, 333
Berger, Wally, 291, 292, 295, 298, 301,
    303, 305, 306
Bill Sherdel's Café, 295
Blades, Ray, 100, 135, 136, 138, 145,
    146, 148, 159, 162, 165, 166,
    170, 173, 185, 186, 191, 196,
    202, 217, 228, 230, 235, 237,
    239, 245, 246, 273, 276, 310, 332
Blue Ridge League, 19, 20, 24, 25,
    30-35, 38, 42, 43, 47, 74, 137,
    150, 174, 176, 271, 329, 340
Borchert Field. See Athletic Park
Bottomley, Jim, 100, 135-138, 145,
    148, 149, 155-159, 162, 167,
    169, 170, 173, 182, 185, 186,
    191, 196, 198-201, 206, 210,
    212-214, 216, 217, 230, 235,
    239, 246, 248, 249, 252, 254,
    260-263, 265-267, 271, 272, 276,
    281, 293, 294, 310, 311, 331,
    332, 346
Boyer, Charles H., 18
Bradenton, Florida, 144, 284, 285
Brandt, Ed, 301-303, 305, 307

Breadon, Samuel, 105, 106, 143, 144, 148, 149, 151, 164, 165, 168, 176, 180, 186, 189, 215, 220-224, 234-236, 238, 241, 242, 245, 247-250, 256, 270-273, 276, 278, 279, 281-284, 287-289, 299-301, 303-306, 308, 310
Bresnahan, Roger, 167
Brian P. Burnes Nostalgia Award, 336, 341
Britton, Mrs. Helen, 70, 71, 84-86
Brock, Lou, 346
Brownsville, Texas, 107, 109
Busch Stadium, 345, 348
Butt, Ruth, 9, 100, 104, 231, 306

Cain, Cullen, 7
Carey, Max, 131
Carleton, Tex, 302, 310, 311
Carruthers, Bobby, 319
Cathro, Captain T. T., 53
Chapman, Ray, 114
Charleston, Oscar, 241
Chesbro, Jack, 69
Cicotte, Eddie, 118
Clemons, Verne, 91, 93, 103, 108, 129
Cobb, Ty, 89, 121, 135, 145, 147, 192, 340
Collins, Pat, 196, 214
Collins, Rip, 302, 310
Combs, Earle, 196, 198-201, 207, 212, 214, 217, 256, 258, 260
Connolly, Tommy, 193
Cooney, Jim, 157
Cronin, Joe, 241

Cruise, Walton, 85
Cuyler, Kiki, 241, 328

Day, Doris, 332
Deadball Era, 35
Dean, Dizzy, 300-302, 310-312, 319, 346
Delgado, Eleanor. See Sherdel, Eleanor
Derringer, Paul, 302, 310
DeWitt, Bill, 337
Dickerman, Leo, 156, 158, 159, 165
Dillhoefer, William "Pickles", 41, 42, 44, 47, 90, 91, 103, 108, 123, 127-129
Dineen, Bill, 193
Doak, Bill, 76, 77, 79, 94-99, 102, 104, 107, 110-116, 122, 125, 127, 134, 138, 143, 152, 153, 156, 159, 319
Douthit, Taylor, 148, 159, 189, 191, 196, 198, 199, 201, 204, 209, 217, 248, 260, 265, 267, 271, 294, 299, 302, 306, 332
Doyle, William "Billy", 34, 52, 55, 56, 83, 139
Dugan, Joe, 196, 198-201, 212, 214, 217, 256, 260, 261, 263
Duncan, William "Billy", 7, 37, 258, 310, 340, 344, 345
Durocher, Leo, 261
Durst, Cedric, 263, 265, 270
Dyer, Eddie, 165, 171, 327

Eicholtz, Burgess J. W., 24
Emmons, Wallace, 24, 25

Euel, Clarence, 55, 63
Felsh, Happy, 118
Flack, Max, 84, 132
Fletcher, Artie, 157, 169
Foxx, Jimmie, 281
Frankhouse, Fred, 280, 288, 289, 292, 295, 298, 305
Friel, William "Bill", 56, 57, 59
Frisch, Frank, 99, 100, 220, 222, 227, 229, 230, 234, 237-239, 246, 249, 250, 252, 254, 260-263, 266, 268, 270, 271, 285, 288, 290, 310, 340, 346
Fuchs, Emil, 288, 291, 297-299, 301, 306
Fuhrman, Mary, 327

Gandil, Chick, 118
Garagiola, Joe, 337
Gehrig, Lou, 3, 6, 164, 196, 198, 199, 207, 208, 212, 215, 217, 235-237, 241, 256, 258, 260-262, 265-268, 270, 304
Gelbert, Charley, 273, 274, 276, 277, 281, 284, 288, 290, 296, 310
Gettysburg, Pennsylvania, 9, 14, 19, 24, 25, 30, 31, 100, 104, 107, 117, 121, 141, 175, 198, 231, 241, 340
Gibson, Bob, 346
Gonzales, Mike, 75, 91, 98, 103
Goodwin, Marvin, 33-35, 47, 48, 50, 53, 54, 56-62, 74, 91-93, 95-99, 101, 102, 104, 110, 116, 122, 123, 126, 138, 174-176

Great Bambino. See Ruth, Babe
Griffith, Clark, 33, 47, 69
Grimes, Burleigh, 81, 82, 286-290, 294, 305, 310, 320
Grimm, Charlie, 85
Groh, Heinie, 147
Grove, Lefty, 19, 258, 281, 310

Hafey, Charles "Chick", 6, 158, 159, 166, 169, 172, 173, 185, 191, 196, 198-200, 207, 208, 210, 212, 216, 217, 227, 229, 230, 235-240, 243, 246, 247, 249, 250, 254, 260, 262, 263, 271, 276, 281, 288, 290, 299-302, 306, 332, 346
Haid, Hal, 254
Haines, Jesse, 107, 108, 110-113, 116, 117, 120, 121, 124, 125, 127, 130, 134, 137, 138, 148, 150, 153, 156, 159, 165, 167, 169, 181, 185-187, 190, 193, 202, 203, 205, 210-213, 216, 224-226, 229, 234, 236, 239, 245-250, 252, 255, 258, 264-266, 275-281, 285, 287, 304, 310, 311, 329, 331, 332, 346
Hallahan, Bill, 167, 181, 205, 280, 285, 287, 294, 310, 319
Hanover Hornets, 19-25
Hanover Raiders, 28-35, 37, 45, 137, 174
Hanover, Pennsylvania, 7, 9-11, 13, 14, 18, 19, 27, 29-31, 33-35, 37-39, 42, 43, 45, 49, 57, 60, 74,

75, 77, 86, 87, 89, 100, 103, 104, 141, 150, 158, 173, 174, 198, 218, 241, 271, 308, 312, 322, 345
Harper, George, 157, 248, 252, 254, 260-263, 265, 267, 271, 273, 276
Harris, Bucky, 163
Heathcote, Cliff, 74, 75, 79, 80, 83, 85, 96, 98, 100, 102, 109, 113, 122, 123, 128, 130, 132, 175, 182, 241, 271, 296
Helb's Keystone Brewery, 320
Hendricks, Jack, 55, 72-78, 80, 82-88, 184
Heydler, John, 170, 182, 232, 275, 277
High, Andy, 245, 260, 262, 266, 267, 271
Hildebrand, George, 193, 214
Holm, Wattie, 209, 210, 214, 265, 270
Home Plate, 317
Hopkins Wagon Works, 11, 14
Hornsby, Rogers, 76, 80, 82, 85, 92, 96-100, 102, 103, 106, 110-113, 115, 116, 120-125, 130, 132, 134, 138, 143, 145, 146, 148-151, 155, 157, 158, 162-173, 176, 177, 179-183, 185-192, 194, 196, 198-202, 204, 205, 209, 210, 212-218, 220-222, 224-227, 229, 231, 232, 234, 236-238, 242, 243, 245, 248, 276, 280-282, 288, 302, 312, 313, 330, 332, 339-341, 346
Horstman, Oscar, 85, 92, 94, 95, 97
Howard, Earl, 74, 75, 77, 80

Howard, Elston, 337
Hoyt, Waite, 196, 203, 210-212, 217, 256-262, 264, 267, 268, 270
Huggins, Miller, 59, 62, 71, 72, 78, 192, 193, 196-198, 200-203, 209, 210, 256, 258, 260, 261, 263-267, 280

Jackson, Joe, 118
Jackson, Larry, 337
Jacobson, Bill "Baby Doll", 130
Johnson, Syl, 176, 249, 262, 266, 275, 276, 280, 285, 287, 310
Johnson, Walter, 134, 158, 172, 264, 279, 282, 330
Jones, Fielder, 15

Keen, Vic, 176, 182, 184, 185, 187, 200, 205
Kelchner, Charles "Pop", 31, 34, 60
Kelly, George, 172
Kerr, Dickie, 53, 54, 56, 57, 60, 62
Kerwin, Corporal John, 325
Kerwin, Theresa, 9, 104, 306, 312, 325
Killefer, Bill, 84, 177, 180, 184, 188, 222
Klein, Chuck, 304
Klem, Bill, 112, 193
Knot-Hole Gang, 71, 72, 79, 136, 140
Koenig, Mark, 196, 198-200, 207, 212, 214, 256, 260-262, 265, 267, 268, 270

Landis, Judge Kenesaw Mountain, 118, 121, 147, 155, 182, 193, 215

Larrupin Legion, 110, 113, 115
Lauck, Keith Sherdel, 8
Lauck, Mr. and Mrs. James, 8
Lauck, William Henry Sherdel, 8, 347
Lavan, Dr. Johnny, 98, 101, 103, 108, 110, 111, 130, 147
Lawrence, James, 322, 323
Lawrence, Patricia. See Sherdel, Patricia Kathryn
Lazzeri, Tony, 196, 198, 199, 201, 207, 213, 215, 256, 258, 260, 261, 263, 266, 268, 270, 330
Lindbergh, Charles, 230-232
Livingston, Patrick "Paddy", 59, 61-63
Luque, Dolf, 112

Mack, Connie, 14, 15, 59, 99, 107, 109, 119, 120, 198, 256, 281, 295, 304
Mails, Walter, 171
Mancuso, Gus, 310
Mantle, Mickey, 297
Maranville, Walter "Rabbit", 101, 131, 238, 248, 250, 254, 257, 260, 261, 263, 267, 268, 271, 273, 276, 291-293, 305, 322
Marquard, Rube, 88
Martin, Jack, 40, 42, 44
Martin, John "Pepper", 246, 270, 273, 276, 302, 310-312, 346
Mathewson, Christy, 33, 45, 89, 123, 158, 279, 291, 330
May, Frank "Jakie", 77, 79, 92, 95, 97
Mays, Carl, 114
McAllister Field, 13, 19, 34, 42

McCarthy, Joe, 184, 281, 296, 328, 329
McGowan, Bill, 259
McGraw, John, 40, 41, 46, 61, 99, 100, 123, 130, 137, 143, 144, 149, 158, 176, 183, 192, 196, 216, 222, 229, 236, 243, 327
McHenry, Austin, 42, 44, 47, 54, 57, 61, 62, 83, 92, 100, 102, 113, 116, 122-125, 132, 134, 135, 137-141
McKechnie, Bill, 222, 223, 241, 245, 247, 249-251, 254, 258, 260, 262-268, 270-272, 278-281, 287, 290-292, 295, 298-303, 305-307, 311
McMullin, Fred, 118
McNamee, Graham, 210, 259
McSherrystown, Pennsylvania, 6-9, 11, 24, 27, 45, 104, 117, 126, 139, 141-144, 150, 155, 158, 163, 165, 173-175, 179, 198, 218, 220, 230, 241, 243, 260, 271, 284, 295, 297, 303, 308, 311, 316, 317, 319-323, 325, 327, 344, 345
Meadows, Lee, 76, 79, 85, 91, 92, 94, 95, 97
Medwick, Joe, 337, 338
Meusel, Bob, 196, 198, 199, 201, 207, 210, 212, 215, 256, 258, 260-262, 266, 268, 270
Midway, Pennsylvania, 9-11, 132, 322

Milwaukee Brewers, 34, 37- 40, 42-48, 50, 52-57, 59, 60-62, 68, 74, 80, 83, 91, 92, 155, 174, 177
Milwaukee, Wisconsin, 28, 35, 37-1, 42, 49, 52, 53, 56, 68, 174
Minoso, Minnie, 337
Mitchell, Clarence, 249, 250, 254, 255, 263, 264, 276-278, 281, 285, 287
Mitchell, Fred, 124
Mokan, Johnny, 157
Moore, Amy. See Sherdel, Amy
Moore, Wilcy, 256
Mueller, Clarence "Heinie", 100, 121, 125, 136, 145-148, 150, 155, 159, 169, 172, 173, 183, 184
Musial, Stan, 105, 330, 333, 337-339, 346
Myers, Hi, 147

Neale, Earle "Greasy", 96, 273, 278
New Oxford, Pennsylvania, 10, 325

O'Farrell, Bob, 167, 169, 173, 184, 187, 196, 198-201, 206-208, 210, 212-219, 222, 223, 225-232, 235-239, 241-243, 247, 248, 278, 340
O'Day, Hank, 193, 208
Orange, Texas, 119, 121, 127, 128, 130
Orsatti, Ernie, 267, 270, 310
Outside Inn, 317
Owens, Clarence "Brick", 259, 261

Packard, Gene, 76, 79, 84

Paschal, Ben, 207, 212, 260, 263, 267
Paulette, Gene, 85, 94, 118
Pennock, Herb, 5-7, 193, 196-200, 206-208, 212, 214, 217, 256, 258, 321, 339
Pennsylvania Sports Hall of Fame, 346
Pfeffer, Jeff, 124, 138, 143, 151
Pfirman, Charles "Cy", 145, 169, 259, 268, 270
Pipgras, George, 256, 258, 262-264
Plank, Eddie, 14-17, 19, 33, 121, 143, 175, 179, 180
Plank, Ira, 16, 19, 21, 121, 175
Plitt, Norman, 324

Reagan, Ronald, 332
Reinhart, Art, 171, 205
Rhem, Charles "Flint", 158, 159, 166, 169, 181, 182, 184, 185, 187, 189, 190, 193, 203-205, 227, 228, 234-238, 243, 245, 247, 249, 250, 254, 273, 276, 285, 287, 292, 294, 295, 310, 337
Rice, Grantland, 7, 208
Richard McAllister Hotel, 7, 218, 271
Rickey, Branch, 57, 60, 69-75, 79, 82-84, 86, 88-103, 105-115, 118-121, 123-132, 134-138, 140, 143-146, 148-156, 158, 159, 163-168, 173, 174, 176, 177, 179, 180, 183, 187, 215, 222, 236, 238, 240, 245, 247, 250, 252, 275-277, 284, 285, 299, 300, 304-306, 308, 310, 312, 316, 319, 330, 331, 341

Rigler, Charles "Cy", 259
Ring, Jimmy, 157, 220, 222
Risberg, Swede, 118
Rixey, Eppa, 227
Robertson, Gene, 263, 266, 270
Robinson, Wilbert, 130, 297, 299
Ruether, Dutch, 193, 196, 202
Ruth, Babe, 3, 4, 6, 7, 104, 113-115, 120, 121, 123, 125, 130, 147, 149, 193-199, 203-212, 214, 215, 217, 224, 227, 228, 230, 235-237, 241, 252, 256-258, 260-262, 265-271, 280, 286, 293, 295, 304, 321, 333, 340

Saigh, Fred, 330
Samuels, Kirby, 182, 183
San Antonio, Texas, 75, 77, 179-181
Scherdel, Wilhelm Martin. See Sherdel, William Martin
Schoendienst, Red, 337
Schulz, Joe, 102, 122, 123, 136
Schupp, Ferdie, 108
Seibold, Socks, 295, 298, 300, 301, 303, 305, 307
Severeid, Hank, 196, 198, 199, 212
Shawkey, Bob, 196, 209, 210
Shay, Danny, 46-48, 50-55, 63
Sherdel, Amy, 325
Sherdel, Eleanor 12
Sherdel, Fred, 9-12, 104, 306, 326
Sherdel, Margaret, 9, 231,
Sherdel, Marguerite, 27, 89, 104, 107, 114, 115, 117, 126, 137, 141-143, 146, 150, 154, 165, 180,
197, 244, 271, 295, 296, 302, 304, 306, 312, 317, 322-324, 326, 327, 333, 334, 345
Sherdel, Patricia Kathryn, 114, 115, 117, 126, 154, 163, 180, 244, 302, 316, 321-324, 345
Sherdel, Patricia Louise, 326, 342, 344
Sherdel, Ruth. See Butt, Ruth
Sherdel, Theresa. See Kerwin, Theresa
Sherdel, William James, 137, 154, 163, 180, 197, 243, 244, 250-252, 278, 302, 316, 317, 321-328, 338, 339, 342, 347
Sherdel, William Martin, 9, 11, 24, 306, 312
Sherdel's Beer Garden, 317
Sherdell's Restaurant, 317, 318
Shocker, Urban, 193, 196, 200, 201
Shotton, Burt, 93, 102, 136, 144, 157, 165, 166, 249
Sisler, George, 70, 89, 112, 114, 115, 134, 138, 291, 292, 295
Slaughter, Enos, 333
Smith, Earl, 250, 252, 254, 267, 268, 270
Smith, Jack, 85, 102, 136, 143
Snyder, Frank "Pancho", 75, 77, 85, 91, 103, 123
Southworth, Billy, 183, 184, 191, 196, 198, 199, 201, 204, 205, 209, 210, 216, 217, 229, 230, 236, 242, 272, 273, 275, 276, 278
Spahn, Warren, 337-339
Speaker, Tris, 122
Spink, J. G. Taylor, 335

Sportsman's Park, 5, 106, 123, 131, 132, 165, 181, 182, 185, 186, 201, 202, 217, 230, 234, 246, 258, 265, 267, 308
St. Petersburg, Florida, 298, 299, 306
Starr, Billy, 19, 21, 28-30
Stertzer, Margaretha. See Sherdel, Margaret
Stock, Milt, 103, 129, 140
Stockton, California, 164, 165
Stoneham, Charles, 99
Strausbaugh, Bob, 146
Strausbaugh, Charles, 142
Strausbaugh, James, 117, 126, 142, 163, 324
Strausbaugh, Marguerite. See Sherdel, Marguerite,
Street, Charles "Gabby", 273, 278, 282, 284-289, 294, 295, 300, 304, 305, 312
Stroh, George, 22, 29, 31
Stuart, Johnny,
Sugden, Joe, 32, 75, 77, 92, 93
Sultan of Swat. See Ruth, Babe
Sylvester, Johnny, 206

Taylor, Ben, 241
Thevenow, Tommy, 7, 151, 158, 159, 165, 173, 191, 196, 198-201, 207, 212, 214, 216, 227, 234, 237, 239, 240, 243, 245, 246, 248, 254, 262, 271, 332
Thomas, Lee, 337
Thorpe, Jim, 40-42, 44, 45

Timme, A. F. "Al", 45, 46, 51, 53, 55-57, 59, 60
Toney, Fred, 143, 152
Torporcer, George "Specs", 121, 312
Traynor, Pie, 131, 241
Tuero, Oscar, 98

Valley Stream, Long Island, 12, 306, 312, 325, 326
Vance, Dazzy, 258, 293, 310
von der Ahe, Chris, 67, 68

Wagner, Charles "Heinie", 31
Waidley, Sergeant John, 52, 53
Waner, Lloyd, 241
Waner, Paul, 238, 241
Weaver, Buck, 118
Weaver, Dr. Harrison, 240
Weeden, Bert, 32, 137
Wheat, Zach, 107, 113, 339
Wichita Falls, Texas, 50, 51
Williams, Lefty, 118
Wilson, Hack, 19, 229, 241, 254, 281, 295, 328, 329
Wilson, Jimmy, 157, 169, 248, 249, 254, 260, 261, 263, 266, 276, 285, 340
Winning Team, 332
Winslow, "Wick", 32
Worley, Assemblyman Francis, 346
Worthington, Red, 298-301

Yankee Stadium, 4, 8, 118, 193, 197, 198, 206, 209, 230, 258, 260
York White Roses, 158, 183, 230, 327

Young, Cy, 279, 319

Zachary, Tom, 256, 258, 265, 266, 291, 295, 298, 300-303, 305, 307

CPSIA information can be obtained
at www.ICGtesting.com
Printed in the USA
BVHW03s0214090718
521151BV00001B/78/P